Anglo-Castilian trade in the later Middle Ages

Map 1   Iberia in the fifteenth century

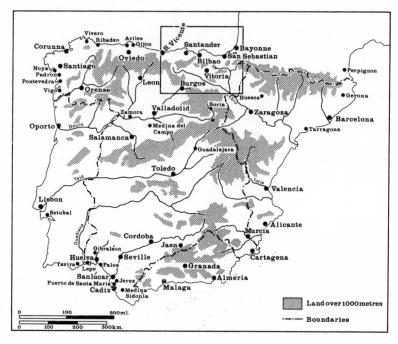

WENDY R. CHILDS

Lecturer in Medieval History, University of Leeds

Anglo-Castilian trade in the later Middle Ages

Manchester University Press

Rowman and Littlefield

First published 1978
by Manchester University Press
Oxford Road, Manchester M13 9PL

British Library cataloguing in publication data

Childs, Wendy R.
  Anglo-Castilian trade in the later Middle Ages.
  1. England – Commerce – Spain – Castile –
  History   2. Castile – Commerce – England –
  History
  I. Title
  382'.0942'0463   HF3518.C/

  ISBN 0–7190–0691–0

USA
Rowman and Littlefield
Totowa, N.J. 07512
ISBN 0–8476–6071–0

Printed in Great Britain
by the Pitman Press, Bath

Phototypeset in V.I.P. Melior
by Western Printing Services Ltd, Bristol

CONTENTS

TABLES AND MAPS

ABBREVIATIONS

A.G.N.   Archivo General de Navarra
A.G.S.   Archivo General de Simancas
A.M. Bilbao   Archivo Municipal de Bilbao
A.M. Burgos   Archivo Municipal de Burgos
B.I.H.R.   *Bulletin of the Institute of Historical Research*
B.L.   British Library
Cal. Cor. Rolls   Calendar of the Coroners Rolls of the City of London
C.Ch.R.   *Calendar of Charter Rolls*
C.Ch.R.V.   *Calendar of Chancery Rolls, Various*
C.Ch.Warr.   *Calendar of Chancery Warrants*
C.C.R.   *Calendar of Close Rolls*
C.F.R.   *Calendar of Fine Rolls*
C.L.R.   *Calendar of Liberate Rolls*
C.M.I.   *Calendar of Miscellaneous Inquisitions*
C.P.R.   *Calendar of Patent Rolls*
C.R.   *Close Rolls*
C.S.P. Spanish   *Calendar of State Papers, Spanish*
E.E.T.S.   Early English Text Society
E.H.R.   *English Historical Review*
Ec.H.R.   *Economic History Review*
H.G.B.   *Hansische Geschichtsblaetter*
J. Ec. Hist.   *Journal of Economic History*
Letter Book   Calendar of Letter Books . . . of London
Ms. S.P.B.   Manuscript Southampton Port Book (at Southampton Civic Centre)
P.R.O.   Public Record Office
R.B.P.H.   *Revue Belge de Philologie et d'Histoire*
R.G.S.   Registro General de Sello
R.H.S.   Royal Historical Society
R.L.C.   *Rotuli Litterarum Clausarum*
R.L.P.   *Rotuli Litterarum Patentium*
Rot. Parl.   *Rotuli Parliamentorum*
S.P.B.   Southampton Port Book
T.R.H.S.   *Transactions of the Royal Historical Society*
V.C.H.   *Victoria County History*
V.S.W.G.   *Vierteljahrschrift für Sozial- und Wirtschaftsgeschichte*

ACKNOWLEDGEMENTS

Most of the research for this book was originally done for a Cambridge Ph.D. dissertation accepted in 1970, and at that time and in preparing a revised version for publication I have incurred many debts.

My warmest thanks go to Professor C. R. Cheney, Dr G. V. Scammell, and Dr A. A. Ruddock for all their help and guidance while I was a post-graduate student, and to Dr Scammell and Dr Ruddock for their advice and encouragement since. I would particularly like to thank Dr Scammell for the time he always found for discussion of trade and for his patience in reading sections of the manuscript more than once.

A major debt of any researcher is to those who have previously worked in allied fields and without their studies of medieval political and economic life this survey of Anglo-Castilian trade would have taken years longer; my debts to them will be apparent in the footnotes and the bibliography. I would also like to thank the staff of libraries and archives in which I worked, particularly those at the Public Record Office, the London Records Office and the Exeter City Library. My thanks are also due to Professor D. C. Coleman for reading and commenting on the final manuscript.

With such help I have been saved from many errors, but those which may remain are my own responsibility.

Not least my thanks go to my husband without whose constant optimism and support this book would have been much longer in the making.

I wish also to acknowledge a grant made by the University of Leeds towards the cost of publication.

August 1976

INTRODUCTION

Despite the many references to Anglo-Castilian trade by modern writers on medieval trade, the many traces it has left in contemporary records, and the known importance of Spanish wool, oil and iron to the English economy in the later period, there has been no study of the early trade for itself. Yet it is interesting, persistent and important enough to both countries to deserve one and this book attempts to fill part of the gap with a general survey of the fortunes of the trade from the thirteenth to the fifteenth centuries, followed by a more detailed survey of the commodities exchanged and the organisation of shipping and mercantile activity. Future monographs on particular ports or commodities, especially from the Spanish side, will add to the accuracy of the picture but already the general outlines are clear.

Among previous works perhaps Professor Carus-Wilson's studies on Bristol have done most to highlight the important of the trade for England, but Dr Ruddock's work on Southampton and Dr Williams' study of early London have also pointed to the presence of Spaniards there. Much of the writing on Channel routes and ports, from the older works of MM. Finot and van Severen on trade between Spain and Flanders to the modern works of MM. Mollat, Touchard, Wolff, Trocmé, Delafosse and Caster which illuminate Franco-Spanish trade, also passingly but constantly refers to Anglo-Spanish contacts. Dr Connell-Smith at last devoted a full-length study to it and showed how strongly it flourished under the early Tudors before coming under pressure and breaking down in the face of military and religious hostilities, but the enormous importance of the Spanish market was not then new and had a long and vigorous history.

It is not wholly surprising that a specific study of Anglo-Castilian medieval trade should be a relative latecomer. A far greater mass of documentary evidence was left behind by Italian traders who were also exceptionally interesting for their sophisticated techniques and their importance in English Crown finance and the wool trade. The Hanseatic trade too left well-defined traces through English records because of its vigorous co-operative organisation, and its near-monopoly of the important trade with the north-east in naval supplies, grain and furs. The Gascon trade with its one major commodity and good series of specialist records found its very able historian in Dr James, and the trade with the Low Countries, although more diffuse, concerned every writer on English trade because of its age, proximity and importance for the wool trade.

The Spanish trade lacks any such concentration of commodity, area, organisation or documentation, but references to it are richly scattered through a multiplicity of sources, and while it is usually difficult and often impossible to provide tabular information for long periods, a fairly complete pattern of trade can be constructed and quantified conclusions can be sometimes drawn. The result shows a trade arguably as important and certainly as old as many others in England's economy, and one which formed a constant underlying contact between the people of the two countries, above which the better-studied military and political turbulence eddied.

In the present state of economic studies, any work on Anglo-Spanish trade is perhaps more important from the Spanish side than the English. In 1940 M. Verlinden wrote of the need for a study of Spanish overseas trade in the Middle Ages. The enormous flowering of Spanish overseas activity and importance in its Golden Age was apparent to all: Spanish silver, shipping, wool, colonies and Spain's presence in Flanders all underline its immense wealth and ubiquity of interest, but far less emphasised were the previous developments which made this possible and the long-standing nature of the economic strengths (and weaknesses), which were so much in evidence then only because they were at last backed by political unity, strength and ambition. Since 1940 more Spanish historians have turned to detailed studies of Spanish economic and commercial history, but medieval overseas trade is still badly served, largely because Spanish sources, compared with the riches of English or Flemish archives, are undeniably poor for this; Sr Vicens Vives' published studies relied on work from foreign archives for surveys of overseas trade, and the detailed study of fifteenth century Biscay by Sr García de Cortázar, published as late as 1966, had to rely on them still for overseas commerce despite exhaustive work in Spanish archives. Regional studies of the trade of Flanders, La Rochelle, Normandy, Brittany and Genoa have helped Spanish studies, and work in English archives can further illuminate the picture.

In this study *Spain* is taken to have its medieval significance, referring to territories acquired by the Kings of Castile and Leon, which covered the greatest area and contained the greatest population of the Iberian Peninsula and which was by far the most important of the four kingdoms commercially to the English merchant. Navarre with a population of perhaps a hundred thousand is too small to justify a separate study but is considered here from time to time as some of its trade passed through Spanish Basque ports. Aragon was usually insignificant in England's general trade: although some of her goods were brought in by Castilian and Italian merchants and a few of her carracks sailed into English harbours in the fourteenth and fifteenth centuries, her commercial interests, like her military and political ones, lay largely in the Mediterranean world. Portugal was of more constant interest and supplied olive oil and kermes dye for the cloth industry as well as wine, fruit and salt, but here ability to absorb large quantities of English cloth was limited by her size—her population was perhaps one-seventh of Castile's. Moreover part of the importance of the Portuguese trade was dependent on the Castilian, since shipping plying between England and Andalusia, for which Andalusia was the main destination, could make additional attractive landfalls at Oporto or Lisbon. However, although some of the earlier work on Anglo-Portuguese trade may need updating, that is no part of this study, which is concerned with the larger but much worse known Castilian trade.

The period taken is the two and a half centuries from the mid thirteenth to the late fifteenth century. The boundaries are partly set by the limits of the sources and previous works but it is also possible to see the period as one with its own particular characteristics.

The thirteenth century saw a major change in the potential and character of Castile's trade when her kings drove through to Andalusia and Murcia. Until then Castile had been small and could offer only the hides and wines of northern areas, and the iron of the Basque Provinces, as yet only imperfectly under her influence; after the Reconquest she could offer also the products of the warmer south, so attractive to northern markets—wines, including sweeter ones, dried fruits, olive oils, kermes dye, some salt, mercury and (for the rest of Europe if not England) wool from sheep grazed in Estremadura. Not until the sixteenth century was there any further change, when the fast developing Atlantic trade brought new products, new markets and new rivalries to Europe.

The thirteenth century also saw the foundation of the problem which prevented the trade fulfilling its potential, and the late fifteenth century saw its removal. The three western monarchies were all concerned with expanding their 'national' territories and making effective their control within them; and while Castile's expansion was relatively easy and brought no conflict with other Christian kingdoms, France's brought her into direct conflict with English kings striving to maintain their Angevin inheritance. The newly extended monarchy of Castile was dragged into this conflict as it looked so strong and large, a military power to reckon with, and one with a permanent royal naval squadron to boot. Each side sought its favour and, after a period of close alliance with England in the thirteenth century, Castile's eventual alliance with France led to several upheavals of varying intensity which checked the development of Anglo-Castilian trade. Not until the petering out of the Anglo-French wars in the later fifteenth century and the renewal of Anglo-Castilian friendship were the traders offered the peace which they needed. Even so trade throve for little more than two generations before new and far more disruptive factors appeared in the sixteenth century. By that time Anglo-Castilian conflict was no longer indirect and largely a consequence of French activities, but direct: the opening of the New World, the religious differences, the political hegemony of a united Spain and particularly her dominance in the Low Countries bred a suspicious rivalry which soon became enmity riddled with fear, bitterness and hatred which over-whelmed for a time the many mutual interests which still remained.

Other thirteenth-century developments had importance for Anglo-Spanish trade. It was certainly stimulated by and part of the high intensity of European commerce which, increasing since the eleventh century, reached such a peak by the late thirteenth and early fourteenth that it has been described as a boom. As well as benefiting from larger market demands the trade was also stimulated by the opening of regular direct shipping routes from the Mediterranean to the north by the Genoese. They finally found that the volume and value of their trade was enough to justify the equipping of small fleets for the north; these ships called at southern Spanish ports, which the Genoese were helping to exploit, and at South-ampton and London, and without a doubt they made the route familiar and showed its profitability to those willing to see. The regular use of this route tied English and Castilian trade even more closely to the European economy, and marks a period of two centuries when the Mediterranean and northern economies were more closely integrated than ever before.

The previous isolation of England and Iberia must not of course be overemphasised, but from the thirteenth century they were much more closely linked to European trading routes. Spanish and Basque ships were soon familiar with most western Mediterranean ports and sailed to some eastern ones and their ports were also firmly linked to the central and eastern Mediterranean by Italian enterprise. By the fifteenth century English ships long familiar with the Atlantic Iberian ports had also begun to venture into the Mediterranean and were joining the Spaniards in competing with the Portuguese on the routes to West Africa and the Atlantic Islands. In the Channel the Spaniards and Englishmen joined many other nationalities—Italians, Portuguese, Frenchmen, Flemings and Hansards—whose shipping passed and re-passed carrying all kinds of goods from many ports. The Spaniards had well-established trading con-tacts with La Rochelle, Nantes, Dieppe and Rouen, the English very good ones with Gascony, and both with Bruges, which was important to the English as an international entrepot, if less so to other nations. The cargoes each carried could thus be of foreign origin and other nations could easily act as middlemen too. Anglo-Castilian trade was far from an isolated exchange between two countries on the outskirts of medieval Europe, but was part and parcel of a bustling and complex continental trading net-work.

The increase of centralised and more effective royal administration in the major western European monarchies at this time also affected the general framework in which the merchants worked. The stages of development differed of course: Castile found that the enormous dif-ferences in background of her relatively easily won lands limited the amount of control and uniformity possible; France was still struggling for most of the period to regain full control of her territories, but when won they were more homogeneous; England had the advantage of smaller size, more easily controlled by royal officials, and consequently her military and economic strength was better organised—which allowed her to confront the larger powers on more equal terms: but despite such differences economic organisation showed considerable similarity of aim and means. All the rulers were aware of their responsibility to promote their subjects' prosperity, and also of the benefit they might gain in revenue from a large volume of well-conducted trade; so from the thirteenth century onwards came an increasing amount of legislation for the proper regulation of fairs, markets, ports, transport, prices, contracts and credit throughout their territories. Laws, practices and customs varied in detail from time to time and place to place, but they clearly had much in common as responses to common problems and to the needs of merchants long familiar with each other's countries and usages. A merchant may at times have felt himself more oppressed as royal officials breathed down his neck, but he was also now far better protected within a stable and enforceable framework of law and custom then he had been before.

The first two chapters provide a chronological framework for the trade and trace its development and the determined efforts of the merchant communities to protect their prosperity against a background of the political actions of the English and Castilian monarchs. Governmental activity was of vital interest to the merchants: much of the governments' commercial legislation benefited them and they were further helped by special royal licences, letters of protection, privileges and customs concessions, but the monarchs gave military, political and dynastic motives precedence over economic ones. Although they generally wanted a prosperous economy, they were far more likely to use an economic lever such as a trade embargo to promote political interests than vice versa, should political and economic interests conflict the political were sure to win; and at such times merchants were caught willy-nilly in the violence of open warfare and had to protect their business as best they could. The immediate responses of the merchants to the battle of Les-Espagnols-Sur-Mer in 1350 and to the French-backed Trastamaran usurpation in 1369, for examples, were to begin negotiations for special commercial treaties, successful in the first instance but not the second.

Throughout the period there was a clear response of trade to changes in the political relations of England and Castile, and for much of the time this depended on the relations of each with France. England's interest in France was strictly territorial as she struggled to keep Gascony against mounting French pressure, but Castile's interest in France was simply as a rich and powerful neighbour who might intervene in Castile's internal troubles or her quarrels with Aragon, and Castile's short common border with Gascony could never make distant England the potential help or menace that France was. Castile's interest would be best served by keeping clear of war and remaining friendly to each, or by allying with France but doing little to fulfil obligations which might injure England—an example set by Alfonso XI. England and France sought Castilian alliance because she was rich, close and militarily successful, as Pero Tafur the Castilian traveller described her in 1437.[1] But her permanent squadron of ships and galleys was the real crux of negotiations during the Hundred Years War—England wanted it to be neutral, but France wanted the right to use it.

The early friendship and healthy trading conditions between England and Castile ran into trouble in 1293 and Sancho IV's alliance with France during her quarrel with Edward I over Gascony foreshadowed the troubles of the Hundred Years War. But trade disruption was in fact shortlived then, and for the next seventy years trade veered only between the modest and the good according to the state of the Anglo-Franco-Castilian diplomacy and wars, with trade reaching peaks in the 1320s and 1330s and again after the Black Death. Then England repeated her mistake of inadequately supporting the legitimate ruler in a Spanish civil war and found herself confronted after 1369 with a king owing his throne to France and having every reason to fear England, which gave asylum to the legitimate court in exile. Direct trade was severed for no more than a decade, and indirect trade hardly at all, but it took nearly eighty years to flourish again as it had in the heyday of Edward I's reign, since the Franco-Castilian alliance, although weakened, continued until 1466 and the trade was still subject to short outbreaks of open hostility. Moreover this was a time of contracting economic activity in Europe which made it relatively more difficult for a badly disrupted trade to recover, although Anglo-Castilian exchanges suffered less than some others from stagnation or recession: the English cloth trade on which Anglo-Castilian trade so much depended was one of the brighter spots in the fifteenth-century economy, and Spain's production of wool, iron, oil and wine seems to have been steadily thriving.

Despite all obstacles to the free development of the trade, its attraction, value and traditions were enough to persuade hard-headed merchants that it was well worth persistence, and when the general European economic expansion coincided at last with a period of political peace the trade expanded rapidly.

To understand the attractions of the trade and the rapid increase in the fifteenth century the commodities exchanged by England and Castile must be examined in detail. Chapters 3 and 4 emphasise the sound economic reasons for the trade, which if left to itself could not but have prospered since so many of the goods were complementary: Spain supplied wool-oil and dyes for the cloth industry and also iron and supplementary foods and wine which England could not provide herself. She took in return cloth. It needs to be emphasised here that when England's cloth industry grew and her merchants needed to look for new markets, while they found them in the Baltic and Iceland, in Spain and Portugal and in the Mediterranean, only in Spain and Portugal did they find a permanent outlet not only for their cloth but also for their own activity and shipping; elsewhere they were resoundingly rebuffed by Hansards and Italians determined to keep the carrying trade to themselves. Spain was therefore particularly attractive to those eager to be active abroad themselves.

The examination of cloth carried to Spain is important, not only because it shows clearly the great variety in types and qualities of cloths produced by England for export from the fourteenth century but also because it demonstrates another characteristic of the medieval cloth trade which is still often underestimated, namely the skill of the English dyers and the range of shades they could offer. Contemporary criticisms of the English dyeing industry in the sixteenth century have tended to obscure the competence which it clearly had in the fifteenth; and that the Spanish market in the sixteenth century, one of the richest in Western Europe, and one with easy access to cloth dyed and finished in Antwerp, continued to import cloths dyed and finished in England suggests that the increasing export of undyed and unfinished cloth from London was due less to the alleged lack of skill of English dyers than to the deliberate protective measures of Antwerp industrialists abetted by the Merchant Adventurers.[2]

In this exchange of goods there was little danger of rivalry and every expectation of satisfaction on both sides. Of course, for Spain England had the disadvantage of not wanting her increasing wool exports, and so would remain somewhat less important than Flanders, but England was useful none the less, as it was stable, well-governed, relatively prosperous, eager for all other types of goods, on the route to Flanders, close to Spain and a producer of the one commodity of international trade for which Spain had a lasting need—cloth.

The shipowners and masters and merchants responded to the trade potential by developing practices suitable for its scale. Neither shipping nor mercantile organisation should be dismissed as backward or primitive simply because it was less sophisticated than the Italian. The question to pose is whether the men provided adequate means for sustaining trade of those dimensions and scale and allowing for expansion: and they did.

Shipping was supplied in plenty by the main ports of Spain and England and by the fishing ports between. Their resources might at times be limited but the demands of the routes, particularly the short direct route between England and northern Spain, were modest; small ships could be frequently and economically run between the two and there was an adequate supply of larger ships for the longer route to Portugal and Andalusia. Vessels of all nationalities were in fact used on the route, and especially those of the

Italian city-states, who provided a strong link between the north and the Mediterranean by way of Andalusia, but there is little evidence that England and Spain would have been unable to supply sufficient tonnage if these had been withdrawn at any time.

Details known of the routes, shipping, cargoes and merchants emphasise clearly the complex and fully international characteristics of medieval trade: an Italian vessel for example with a crew of sailors from several countries would be carrying Oriental, Mediterranean, Andalusian and Portuguese goods for Italian, English and Spanish merchants into Southampton or London; likewise Flemish ships or Dutch picked up Spanish goods in Bruges for Englishmen, and the trades between England, Gascony and Spain, or England, Portugal and Spain were closely entwined.

Mercantile organisation, like maritime, was suitable for the scale of the trade: there were no great commercial houses or monopoly companies and no marked advances in financial or commercial techniques, but it was not a primitive trade. No established merchant needed to travel with his goods, as the use of brokers, agents, factors, apprentices, or junior partners allowed widespread and valuable businesses to be run from a home base. Methods of credit, investment, exchange and insurance, often pioneered by Italians, were adopted when desirable, and since the Italians were present in most major ports and had the means for sophisticated financial dealings at their finger-tips, their agency was often used; there was at this time and in this trade no particular incentive to compete with or wrest their business from them. Italian organisation is of great interest for future commercial development and was essential in long-distance and luxury trade, but while some of its techniques were helpful to some of the merchants engaged in Anglo-Castilian trade many were not imperative in this or indeed many other European trades of modest distance and modestly priced goods.

Tables have been included to indicate the size of the trade, since some quantification is essential to give meaning to such adjectives as 'large', 'considerable', and 'modest', and to offer a more precise appreciation of trends and characteristics. The wealth of record information in English archives invites some such tabular analysis but the results must be used with caution. The main problem is the one well known to economic historians, that none of the sources which can be used was intended to supply information for a commercial survey, so that many essential details are missing or may be inaccurate or only partially declared depending on the interests, idiosyncrasies or laziness of the recording clerks. There are also gaps in record series, form and content of a series may change over the centuries, and discontinuation of a series or severe alteration of its content may make necessary a comparison of two dissimilar sources to obtain any overall picture at all. For instance one must judge Spanish activity in

London in the thirteenth century from the recognisance rolls and the *London Letter Books* but in the fifteenth century from the customs accounts. There is also the problem of precise identification of the trade: there was usually no reason to record Spanish trade separately, and Gascon and Portuguese names, cargoes and ships are sometimes difficult to disentangle from Spanish ones, especially in the highly individual rendering of alien names by some English clerks; also other nationalities carried some of the trade, and Spaniards picked up goods from other countries in several markets; moreover the English role in the trade is almost everywhere undervalued as it is usually impossible to identify the last ports of call and the destinations of so many of their ships. Such shortcomings do not totally invalidate the figures, but they mean that they must be treated with care and taken to indicate orders of magnitude and comparative importances rather than precise amounts. With these reservations they add sharper outlines to the picture drawn from the wealth of detail offered by more qualitative sources.

In the text common place and proper names have been modernised, but more unusual ones, or those of uncertain identification have been left in the form in which they most frequently appear.

The short appendix offers a selection of biographies of some of the masters and merchants about which most is known and who seem to be typical of certain groups.

NOTES TO INTRODUCTION

1 Pero Tafur, *Andancas e viajes de Pero Tafur por diversas partes del mundo avidos*, see the English translation *Pero Tafur, Travels and Adventures*, ed. M. Letts (London, 1926), p. 92.

2 I intend to look more closely at this problem elsewhere.

CHAPTER 1

The fortunes of the trade
1254–1369

With complementary markets and a body of able merchants and seamen the trade might be expected to flourish and expand, but its development was tightly tied to political and diplomatic activity in north-western Europe as well as to the general economic fortunes of the whole continent, and all too often the political, military, or dynastic interests of the English and Spanish rulers overrode the economic interests of their merchants. Not that the rulers were unaware of economic considerations, nor that they were unwilling to accept that part of their royal responsibilities as well as their self-interests lay in promoting the prosperity and well-being of their people, but very few economic groups or markets were strong enough to influence governments to the consistent promotion of their interests. More usually the importance of a particular market or trade was used to achieve political ends, and although commerce and industry might be allowed free development at times, and even artificially encouraged at others, if political interests seemed to demand it their needs would be sacrificed. Anglo-Castilian trade was no exception to this general pattern, and so its development must be viewed not only against the general European economic movements but also against the political actions of the English and Castilian kings.

The beginning and the end of the whole period here examined saw the two great peaks of medieval Anglo-Spanish trade; in the later thirteenth and again in the later fifteenth centuries the volume of trade rose rapidly in line with the general increase of European economic activity and was stimulated too by political alliance, close friendship and particularly good trading terms in the later period. Between these two times of fortune and prosperity the trade fluctuated, at times violently; again its movement was more or less in line with European movements, but it was overemphasised or distorted by the political relationships.

In the first half of the period four main phases can be discerned: there was friendship from 1254 to about 1290 which co-incided with the later-thirteenth-century expansion; there was a brief war-crisis from about 1290 to 1303 which temporarily upset trade; this was followed by a long period of unsettled but generally friendly neutrality until about 1350, during which trade continued at a high level at least into the thirties; then, after the brief disruptions of the Black Death and the battle of Les-Espagnols-sur-Mer the close friendship of 1351–69 made trade flourish again.

The alliance of 1254 and the following trade boom were foreshadowed by the marriage alliance in the previous century between Alfonso VIII and Henry II's daughter, and by the modest mercantile activity which followed. This friendship had not endured and in 1204 the 'Portuguese and other Spaniards' found it expedient to seek a safe-conduct from John for fear of trade disruption while Alfonso made claim to Gascony on the strength of Eleanor's dowry.[1] His motive, after such delay, is unclear, but perhaps seeing John's poor showing in 1202–4 he felt he had a real chance to take it, or perhaps he was creating a diversion for Philip-Augustus, his new son-in-law. John, however, was well able to deal with the Castilian threat and overwhelmed Alfonso's troops at Bourg-sur-Marée in the summer of 1206; some sort of reconciliation followed and the Castilian claim lay dormant for half a century.[2] No formal agreement of any kind seems to have been reached during this half-century despite several exchanges of envoys,[3] but neither was there any open breach, although some Castilians continued to trade with France during her scuffles with Henry III and some occasionally attacked Duchy subjects.[4] In fact at this time Castile's government lost much of its interest in northern affairs as its sights were firmly fixed on the reconquest of the south. Alfonso started the successful crusade with the victory at Nava de Tolosa in 1212. Cordoba fell in 1236, Murcia became a tributary State in 1241, Seville was taken in 1248. Since León was absorbed through inheritance in 1230 and the Basque Provinces were held by a Castilian vassal, by 1252 Castile had rapidly expanded nearly to the extent at which she remained until Ferdinand and Isabella took Granada. While Castile was thus expanding, her merchants were free to develop their trade where they wanted, and since this was a century of expanding commercial activity it is not surprising to find Spanish goods, ships and merchants frequenting English and Gascon ports. Spanish cloth, horses, wines, wax, furs, skins, leathers and cordage were bought for the King or sent to English harbours. The ship seized and robbed at Sandwich in 1227 gives a clear picture of the sorts of cargoes sent: it had aboard wine, grain, goatskins, skins of wildcat, hare, fox and lamb, cordwain, basan and thread.[5] If there were no Spanish ships available then the Spanish merchants used those of Bayonne.[6]

Spanish merchants travelled inland to Winchester and Boston for the great fairs of St Giles and St Botolph,[7] and the casual type of information we have on this and their presence in ports implies that their trade was carried on peacefully enough with the Castilians welcomed and with little need for formal licence or protection, except for those men of San Sebastián who fell foul of the seamen of the Cinque Ports and in 1237 thought it prudent to arm themselves with a five-year safe-conduct specifically for protection against Cinque Port marauders.[8] A similar situation appeared in Gascony: despite complaints of violence, Spanish merchants continued to take goods there,[9] and some Gascons had close enough links with the Basques to settle in San Sebastián.[10] Thus on the eve of the marriage alliance, Anglo-Spanish trade, almost entirely in the hands of the Spaniards, was modest, but frequent and well-established, and could only be improved by closer ties of political alliance.

The earliest events of the years 1252–4 cannot have given merchants confidence in the future of their trade. At his accession Alfonso X made a renewed claim to Gascony, probably simply to stop the claim failing through default rather than as a serious attempt at expansion in this direction for, while Henry III was pleading for financial aid against Alfonso's imminent invasion, Alfonso was in fact far away, engaged in the south. The claim once made, however, was a real danger to Henry as Alfonso became a rallying point for those Gascons, such as Gaston de Béarn, who were discontented with Montfort's rule in Gascony. Henry, struggling to hang on to his Angevin inheritance, lost no time in opening negotiations with Alfonso; not only to eliminate the threat to Gascony but also to provide himself with a worthy and dazzlingly strong-looking military ally against France.

The records of 1253–4 are full of references to the diplomatic moves which culminated in the treaty of 1 March 1254: the treaty was offensive and defensive, with promises of aid to Castile in Africa and leniency to the Gascons who had joined Alfonso; Henry's son Edward married Alfonso's sister Eleanor and the Gascon claim was given up in their favour.[11] Peace reigned. Terms regarding the release and restoration of property to disaffected Gascons were only slowly fulfilled, but were not made a pretext for hostility; even the rivalry of Alfonso and Richard of Cornwall over the Holy Roman Empire caused little problem, although Henry refused the support requested by Alfonso.[12] The links became stronger with Edward's accession: he willingly supported Alfonso's claim to the Empire at Richard's death;[13] he permitted his subjects to help Alfonso and arranged to build galleys to help him against the Moors in 1276;[14] because of the treaty he refused to aid France against Castile and did his best to mediate between the two;[15] he also sent men and money to help Alfonso at the end of his life in his civil war against his younger son Sancho over the inheritance of the Castilian throne.[16]

For these thirty years after 1254 Spanish merchants made the most of the friendship. Almost immediately the Castilian ambassadors successfully supported a claim for freedom for four years from the king's prise for Apparicius and Matthew de Bures and Juan Petri of Spain.[17] A few Castilians met difficulties in the Barons' war but found the king ready to order recompense wherever possible.[18] Others found local difficulties, but in cases of mistreatment also found they could rely on royal support, as in

1263 when the king rebuked the local officials at Southampton for charging unjust tolls, and then granted the Castilians a house of their own for seven years for residence in Southampton when trading there.[19] Further in 1267, those Castilians lodging with Nicholas Barbeflete in Southampton managed to obtain exemption from the town's murage dues for seven years.[20]

These grants suggest strongly that Southampton was the centre of Castilian activity and the port at which a small colony of Spanish merchants might be growing up; if so their activity must have been considerable as trade at Winchelsea where they had no privileges was far from negligible: in 1266–7 at least twelve Spanish ships were there—eight from Fuenterrabía, two from Castro Urdiales, and two from San Sebastián—and in 1268–9 a further eight entered—two of Fuenterrabía, five from Castro, and one from San Sebastián which entered twice.[21] The accounts for 1271–2 and 1272–3 show one and three ships there, all of Castro; that of 1274–5 indicates some nine Spanish shippers there from Castro, San Sebastián, Fuenterrabía, and Pontevedra.[22] The apparent decline in their numbers may be because Winchelsea's erosion problems were already forcing them to seek new harbours[23] or more likely because they were attracted by the privileged group growing up at Southampton.

Mercantile favours to Spaniards increased after the accession of Edward and Eleanor through whom petitions were often addressed by her fellow-countrymen. Long-term grants of protection were given to Pedro de Mundenard in 1276 and 1285,[24] and to Gundesalvus and Giles Martini in 1277.[25] These last were described as 'King's merchants', so were probably regular suppliers of the royal household and were important enough for Gundesalvus to be sent in 1278 to Castile on the king's business, either in some minor diplomatic capacity or possibly for household supplies.[26] Other Spaniards by this time were taking a minor part in the export of English wool.[27] The Spaniards could still count on royal inquiries into complaints of unjust taxation, this time at Portsmouth where four merchants aboard two ships felt aggrieved and the preamble in the letter of commission of oyer and terminer felt it worth while including the comment (probably found in the original petition) that because of the injustice the 'merchants and others have entirely withdrawn their trade from the said port to the great loss of the said town and the adjacent parts'.[28] A legal inquiry into the robbery of two Spaniards at Winchester in 1277 shows them still attracted by the fair and apparently using Southampton as its outport.[29] By 1285 Southampton offered enough business to at least one merchant, Juan de Mundenard, to encourage him to settle and become a burgess of the town in late October or early November of that year; he may in effect have become the permanent English agent of a family firm dealing in Southampton and London over the previous twelve years.[30]

Most merchants of any standing were likely to find themselves dealing in London as well as Southampton, and London was probably the most promising centre for Spanish trade, particularly in skins, furs and leather: the amount of Spanish and Portuguese trade there was so great that by 1283 special brokers were appointed to deal with the distribution.[31] Although there are no customs records yet to illuminate the movement into the port, the London letter books and recognisance rolls are invaluable for the history of the Spaniards' dealings once ashore. From 1276 to 1284 quite a number of the alien merchants in London who took the trouble to have their debts properly recorded and enrolled were Spaniards.[32] The decline in numbers after 1279 indicates that they found the method either inadequate or, more probably, no longer necessary once regular and trustworthy customers had been established. Certainly they had not left, as the first recognisance roll shows some taking immediate advantage of the passing of the Statute Merchant in 1285 and Spaniards' transactions form the largest single group of alien entries: of the 235 entries on the roll, 133 involved debts to Englishmen, then forty-four debts to Spaniards and three debts to merchants of Navarre, eighteen involved Gascons, sixteen Italians and thirteen men from south-western France.[33] It is interesting that only two of the nine Spanish merchants on the roll had formerly used the letter books and seems likely that those with established businesses found they ran smoothly enough and only newcomers felt the need for this protection. The two who had used the letter books were themselves apparently dealing with new customers, about whom they may not have felt too certain. Numbers decline in the later rolls as they did in the letter books, probably again because the method was found unnecessary once the newcomers' regular and trusted contacts were built up, although at this time deteriorating political relations may also have forced a partial withdrawal.

The London information provides the names of a group at least thirty strong dealing in England, often repeatedly, during these first fifteen years of Edward's reign. Burgos is clearly already one of the main centres from which they come with perhaps eight of them being from there, three were from Vitoria, one from Valmaseda and one from Zamora, with seven probably from the Ebro valley.[34] Several had built up strong enough businesses to weather the short crisis of Sancho's reign.

When Sancho took his throne in 1285 it was with no reason to love the English who had helped his father, but with some gratitude to the French for their support.[35] His distrust of England no doubt grew when he learned of Edward's overtures to Aragon and the betrothal of an English princess to the King of Aragon, and by 1290 he had made a firm alliance with the King of France. This involved Castile in the clash between England and France over Gascony in 1293–4 when the French demanded Castilian aid, while Edward tried in vain to bring Castile back to his side. Sancho's interest in the alliance, however, was to obtain French aid against the Moors, not to fight England, and he sent little help, but the breach between England and

Table 1   Recognisances of debts recorded in the London Letter Books, 1276–84.[1]

Date	Spain				South-west France				Low Countries				England				Elsewhere			
	No.	£	s	d	No.	£	s	d	No.	£	s	d	No.	£	s	d	No.	£	s	d
1276	5	177	10	0	12	154	9	4	2	48	0	0	15	139	7	6	5	76	13	0
1277	1	19	0	0	3	37	10	0	1	28	13	4	9	85	16	1	1	38	0	0
1278	24	715	9	0	8	282	5	4	3	83	16	0	7	51	3	6	2	145	0	0
1279	10	141	0	0	2	100	0	0	2	7	19	0	3	52	0	0	1	3	16	0
1280	9	31	19	8	3	19	19	8	2	19	17	0	19	295	5	0	2	13	0	0
1281	6	68	16	0	18	214	12	8	1	12	0	0	41	340	2	0	–	–		
1282	3	25	8	6	17	307	15	0	3	14	0	0	47	614	17	3	7	58	12	0
1283	7	82	0	0	33	471	14	7	1	4	10	0	65	652	5	2	8	251	16	5
1284	–	–			4	34	6	8	–	–			33	132	3	6	2	4	10	0

[1] *Letter Book 'A'*, passim. The number given is of recognisances entered in the book, not of merchants, of whom there are fewer as several had more than one debt recorded. The south-west of France is taken to include all the hinterland of Gascony and Montauban, Toulouse and Montpellier. The Low Countries include some men of Cambrai and St Omer. The distinction between men of Spain and south-west France is not always clear but I have taken as of Spain all those described as such, except Stephen Carwin who is elsewhere and more often said to be from Cahors. I include the Mundenards as Spaniards. For the drop in aliens enrolling debts there see Chapter 6, note 133.

Castile and the opportunity it gave for piracy was sufficient to disrupt trade.

The Gascons, as usual, complained of Basque violence in the Bay of Biscay, probably with more justification than usual,[36] and a truce to curtail this was drawn up between Bayonne and and Castile in 1293,[37] but this can have had little effect when the Anglo-French war broke out the same year. From that time the stream of grants to Spaniards in England dropped to a trickle, and their names disappear from the London letter books and recognisance rolls (although as suggested above this may be due to the changing methods of their business). Their ships were attacked, their goods were forfeit, letters of marque were issued against them in 1289 and 1293.[38] In 1292 a levy of 12d in the pound was made on all their goods in the Cinque Ports, London, Southampton and Portsmouth in an attempt to provide recompense for a Gascon who had lost goods and been imprisoned in Castile.[39] In 1294 an arrest was ordered of all their goods in Sandwich, Southampton and London which were to be sequestered until merchants of Bayonne who had been robbed by Castilians while in Portugal were satisfied of their claim: the goods found at London and Southampton were not many at that time and were valued at £4 0s 0d and £58 6s 9½d respectively, those at Sandwich were valued at £1,610 0s 4d but well over £935 worth (mainly iron) was claimed back by merchants of Bayonne at least one of whom stated that he had bought it from men of Spain.[40] The subsequent legal suit was long and complicated between the two sets of Bayonnese claimants and underlines the character of the time: some Englishmen and Bayonnese and Spanish merchants were continuing to trade peaceably and extensively together, while others on both sides were tempted to violence. The Count of Flanders was so concerned at the violence in the Channel that he requested safe-conducts for Spaniards in 1294 and 1297 and the King of Portugal also urged peace negotiations.[41] Some merchants protected themselves by buying individual letters of safe-conduct,[42] but others, such as Stephen Vallad' (i.e. of Valladolid) who was in London in 1289, and Goubert Gonel who was there in 1293 and 1298, and those Spaniards at Southampton in 1290 who complained loudly of the false weighing of the pesager seem to have relied on the general continuing goodwill of their traditional customers.[43]

The worst of the crisis should have been between 1293 when the Anglo-French war broke out and 1295 when Sancho was succeeded by his small son Ferdinand whose Regency Council was far too busy defending him against the claims of his uncles and the territorial ambitions of his neighbours to send any material aid to France at all, and Edward clearly felt that peace was a possibility by 1296.[44] No peace was made however, and the confusing situation continued.

On the one hand in 1296 the towns of the northern coast, Santander, Laredo, Castro Urdiales, Bermeo, Guetaría, San Sebastián and Fuenterrabía, with Vitoria formed a Hermandad and agreed to stop trading with England, Flanders and Bayonne while the war lasted,[45] and they gave a warm welcome to the French ambassadors in 1297 who came to request them not to harm France.[46] On the other hand the Lord of Biscay was, as usual, hostile to his overlord of Castile and willing to offer support and even fealty to his enemies. Diego Lopez de Haro V was called on by Edward in June 1294 for aid according to undertakings he had given, he was later asked to supply horses and had been lent 1,000 livres morlaines probably to secure further supplies, but which he cannot have expended as he was asked to repay it in 1300.[47] It is unlikely that he would have in any way hindered his subjects if they wished to continue trading with England.

Some merchants continued to be active in Gascony and even contributed to Edward's war coffers, although it is not clear if this was always willingly. Juan de Bytoria and Martín Gonzales had lent £586 and in 1296 were given a safe-conduct to come to the Exchequer to put their claim for repayment.[48] Edward ordered a further £2,000 to be repaid through the Frescobaldi in 1300—the exact number of Spanish merchants involved was not stated but between them they held seventeen letters of obligation.[49] Others, less lucky or influential, were still making claims in 1305 and 1308.[50] Although no specific reference is made to loans, Andrés Perez of Castrogeriz and his brother Pedro, the wealthy Burgos merchants, received their first letters of safe-conduct for the good services they had done the king in Gascony at this time.[51]

The early fourteenth century saw the recovery of the trade route and the first thirty years saw a time of particular prosperity, backed by reasonably stable diplomatic relations, although violence at sea continued to be a trouble. The treaty between England and France in 1303 formally restored peace with Castile too as she had been involved only as a French ally. Edward's attempt to marry the future Edward II with his Spanish cousin came to nothing but the exchanges of letters were cordial.[52] Edward II on his accession did regrettably little to further any alliance there: he ignored Ferdinand's appeal to the terms of the treaty of 1254 for help against the Moors;[53] and he made no move to win the friendship of the next Regency in 1312, leaving diplomatic activity there to the French. Not until the visit of Hugh le Despenser the Elder to Castile in 1319 were diplomatic channels reopened,[54] and not until 1324, when England was on the brink of another French war, was a rather late bid made for a Castilian treaty.[55] The guardians of Alfonso XI seemed disposed to listen despite an agreement already made in 1317 to marry Alfonso to Isabella, the third daughter of the French king. The returning English ambassadors gave full instructions to their successors about meeting the French challenge, and Castilian envoys arrived in England in 1325, one of them possibly being Andrés Perez, the Burgos merchant, who also agreed at this time to arrange a loan of £6,000 for Edward in Castile. These returned home in February to be followed by

English ambassadors with powers to arrange two marriages and a treaty.[56] Even after the end of the Gascon fighting Edward went on pressing for a marriage alliance, but perhaps he was being too importunate, or perhaps the Castilians could see only too well how weak his position was, or perhaps they really did suspect he was double-dealing and just about to arrange a French marriage for his son who was by then in France, for the answers become somewhat evasive.[57] The whole project collapsed finally at the invasion of Isabella and Mortimer.

Although no formal treaty was made in this period merchants could rely on the generally peaceful relations between the countries, and perhaps quite as important as an alliance from their point of view were the attempts made to calm the bitterness of the Basques and Gascons over losses sustained during the war years. Reprisals by a group of Gascons who had suffered had led to a situation where men of Bayonne and Biscay were again openly fighting even if their rulers were not.[58] Edward I had arranged a two-year truce in 1306, but this had obviously broken down even before Edward II suspended it in June 1307, and matters had clearly gone far beyond the odd case of piracy when in 1308 the men of Sandwich, Dover and Winchelsea had to be forbidden to fit out a squadron to help Bayonne attack Spaniards.[59] Both Edward and Ferdinand were aware of the problem and opened negotiations in the autumn of 1308 which resulted in a two-year truce in 1309 between their subjects in that area, and at last in 1311 a permanent peace treaty was agreed with lists of compensations to be paid by each side.[60]

Merchants not of Bayonne, such as those of Southampton robbed in 1309,[61] or such as Alerin le Norman,[62] had to struggle on alone, making individual claims for arrests of goods belonging to men of Santander when they failed to get justice in Spain; but these arrests led only to further confusion and bitter complaints from men of Biscay that their goods too were being unjustly sequestered.[63] Even the merchants of Bayonne found it hard to obtain full reparations under their treaty and cases were reopened by Arnald de St Martin and John de St Cryk who applied for attachments of Spanish goods at Southampton.[64] This brought immediate protest from Spaniards and their English customers alike; the arrests were stopped and general letters of protection for Spanish merchants were given at the request of Alfonso from May to Christmas 1315;[65] the men of Winchelsea felt their valuable trade with Spain so threatened that they themselves petitioned for protection for the Spaniards trading there;[66] and several Spaniards bought their own personal safe-conducts.[67] St Cryk was driven to obtain further rights of arrest in 1318,[68] but the province of Biscay had already done much to protect her men by then. In 1317 Bermeo had pleaded that she and all Biscay had a tradition of friendship and aid to England emphasising her absolute independence from Castile, so that her men should not be penalised for the offences of Castilians nor subjected to arrest aimed at them. This assertion was accepted by Edward, as it should have been since it was legally correct and was quite properly backed by letters from King Alfonso.[69] It was also backed by letters from Bayonne which is more suprising since the two areas were so often hostile, and only twenty years before Bermeo and Guetaria had joined the Hermandad with its agreement to stop trade to Bayonne and England. The assertion and its backing should no doubt be seen as a strong indication that Anglo-Biscayan trade was still important to contemporaries—the disturbances of two decades had been weathered and steps were being taken to see that the continued aggression of a few men did not do it any further harm. The attempts to reach harmony at last bore fruit, and the third decade saw the practice of reprisal and counter-reprisal die down as men were satisfied or let cases drop through inertia and frustration.

The relatively stable governmental relationship and the attempts to settle the worst disputes seem to have outweighed the disturbances, and although some merchants suffered the trade as a whole was recovering and soon flourishing.

A considerable number of Spaniards were again at Sandwich in 1303–5, although bearing in mind the willingness with which Cinque Port men were going to join the Bayonnese war squadron against Castile in 1308 there must have been some smouldering resentment among certain groups in the towns.[70] Southampton is clearly still one of the main centres for their activity. Luke Stuyit of Southampton, whose wine was stolen by Spaniards, claimed to recognise some of the offenders among the merchants staying in Southampton in 1308.[71] In 1308–9 at least two Spanish ships and possibly a third are revealed there by the customs accounts, and at least twelve Spanish shippers on these ships and others of Bayonne and France were importing cargoes of wool, iron, leather, thread and wax. Several of the Gascon and French ships had very similar cargoes of leathers and wool, and in fact the two Spanish ships' total cargo value of £337 was overshadowed by three ships of Bayonne and Réole with a total cargo value of £1,074 1s 8d. Also, while Spanish ships brought 93 sacks 10 bales of Spanish wool, Gascon, French and English ships brought 176 sacks 288 bales of it. The Spaniards in this account for October 1308 to August 1309 are not overwhelmingly active, yet their imports still account for 9 per cent of all alien imports. A very short account for 1310 shows two possible Spanish ships there, and one for 1310–11 shows about a dozen, from which Spaniards supplied about 20 per cent of the total value of alien imports, leathers, wools and iron being the main goods handled. Spanish merchants and a Spanish ship were also engaged in the wool trade there in 1311 and 1313.[72]

At London too their trade was recovering and references occur to their transactions in 1302, 1304, 1306–7, 1308, 1310, 1311 and 1312 as they brought and sold leathers, yarn, wool and cloth, and took in return wool and cloth.[73] Although the customs accounts are few, the appearance of Spaniards in them seems particularly low and it is quite possible that the Spaniards were using Sandwich and Southampton as their disembarkation ports and were travelling overland to London as they had done in the thirteenth century and were to do later.

The Ordinances of 1311 removed petty custom dues until 1322 so customs accounts cannot illuminate further recoveries in the trade, but records of safe-conducts and licences to trade show that the famine of 1316–17 boosted their trade,[74] and in London by 1318 special Spanish brokers were again appointed.[75]

By the third decade trade is clearly again very prosperous. At Sandwich a quarter of the ships arriving between February 1325 and January 1326 were Spanish (eighteen out of seventy-six) and since several of the non-Spanish ships were local fishing boats not handling long-distance freight the Spanish share of commercial shipping must have been higher than 25 per cent. This high proportion dropped in the following years but the Spaniards were still frequent visitors and important in overseas shipping movements: from January to September 1327 two out of twenty-six ships were Spanish, from September 1327 to the following year six out of fifty-one, and from September 1328 to January 1329 six out of twenty-three. Over the whole of the earlier period their imported merchandise was valued at £857 4s and for the whole of the later at £1,230 16s.[76] At Winchelsea at about the same time (June to September 1328) they made up perhaps one-fifth of the alien merchants importing goods subject to petty custom: of the hundred entries on the account fifteen certainly and five more possibly concerned Spaniards, but their goods were valued modestly at some £86 compared with £122 of fruit brought by six Portuguese.[77] By 1324 or shortly after Ferand Manion and and Pedro Lopez Manion found their interests in London permanent enough to take out citizenship;[78] and by 1331 the Spaniards in London formed a group large enough to request and important enough to be granted exemption from murage, pavage and pontage dues in the City.[79]

Clear evidence is also available that the Spaniards were beginning to trade in the west of England: the *Nostre Dame de Seint Andreu* (Santander) was at Exmouth in 1304, but they were more frequently seen in the 1320s at Exeter, when ships of Bermeo and Castro sailed in in 1320, 1323, 1324, and 1327;[80] a Peter Gerveys de Hispannia sold figs and raisins at Fowey in 1323;[81] the *Magdalene de Plesencia* at Bristol in 1324 was probably a Spanish ship and the *Sta María de Veremue*, there in 1325, certainly was.[82] Occasionally some called in on the south coast at Chichester.[83] Although there are too many gaps in the records to provide as clear a picture as one would like there are enough indications that, although it still centred firmly in the older centres of London, Sandwich and Southampton, trade was flourishing enough to spread outside these, and was well able to respond to changing market needs. Already the accounts for 1322–30 show that leathers and peltry have sunk low in the ranks of imports, iron was maintaining and possibly increasing its importance, and imports such as tallows, greases and the allied soaps, and oils and dyes so important for the cloth industry were already entering the picture strongly.

This trade was in fact also protected by a barrage of letters of safe-conduct and protection, thought necessary because of the memory of the last decade's arrests and the weak government and wars of this decade. A general safe-conduct for all Spaniards was obtained in 1322;[84] this was renewed for a further year from 23 August 1324 when Edward sought Spanish help, and again for a year from 5 March 1328 when Spanish merchants, probably taking advantage of England's approaches to Castile that year, asked for it to protect their position further.[85] In 1324 and 1328 Castilians joined other alien groups seeking confirmation of the Carta Mercatoria.[86] Biscay too obtained specific safe-conducts for her men in 1324 and 1326 when attempts were being made to obtain a Biscayan alliance.[87] Anxiety at the violence of the deposition and early Regency years also prompted a number of individual safe-conducts,[88] but these were only temporary fears and there was no disruption of trade.

Edward III's reign opened with very bright prospects for Anglo-Castilian trade: it was flourishing, the weakened contacts at Southampton and London were reforged, and there was in London the nucleus of a permanently settled colony, similar to those developing in French and Low Country ports in the fourteenth century. It was smaller than the one in Bruges, had not anything like the early charters granted by Bruges, but given favourable circumstances it is highly likely that the Spanish connection in London would have resulted in the growth of a small settlement there enjoying certain group exemptions or privileges. After forty years these prospects were shattered by Edward's political adventures, although for a time they had seemed to burn even brighter.

The spectre which overshadowed peaceful trade was the Anglo-French war which began in 1337, for which each side sought a Castilian alliance in order to neutralise or obtain the use of her navy, which with its regular squadrons could be immensely valuable to countries which relied on impressed merchantmen. The hard core of Castilian galleys was good for raiding parties, especially since it was backed and defended by sailing ships.[89] The other Iberian kingdoms too kept permanent squadrons but these were too far from the northern axis to give much help, although Portugal sent a few ships to England's aid in the later fourteenth century. England herself could in fact raise sufficient warlike men and shipping to transport her armies and to inflict considerable damage on her enemies, as the battles of Sluys and Les-Espagnols-sur-Mer had shown, and her naval prestige was fairly high, but France had a poorly organised fleet and could expect to benefit tremendously from free use of the Castilian fleet. Thus

England would have been satisfied with an arrangement to neutralise the shipping while France wanted its use.

Both England and France clearly and openly avowed their interest. Edward, in January 1336, tried to forestall Castilian naval aid to France and offered to pay for ships lent to him instead[90] but he failed and France had included in her treaty of 1337 with Castile clauses specifying the numbers of ships on which she could call.[91]

Castile's best plan at this point would seem to have been neutrality, as she had nothing to gain from provoking the hostility of either except the disruption of her Flemish trade route and a repetition of the violence of Sancho's and Ferdinand's reigns. But if she must make an alliance then it would indeed be far likelier with France: England could offer a good trading market and a safe passage to Flanders; France could offer these, a real hope of useful and immediate military aid and an end to Aragonese attempts to embroil France in her quarrels with Castile. With such an alliance Castile's best long-term policy would still seem to be aloofness, non-provocation of the English and non-involvement in the Anglo-French squabble, and this appears to have been the plan of Alfonso XI, who showed himself an astute diplomat in continuing to negotiate with both sides.

Edward and his Regents were fairly slow to act on the Castilian front. In 1328 attempts were made to settle piracy cases[92] and overtures were made to Biscayan towns in 1329, and also to the Biscayan rulers with a suggested marriage alliance;[93] possibly this was with a view to collecting allies if a claim were made to the French throne, then vacant. Envoys were sent again in 1330 and 1331 as part of a general embassy to the whole Penin-sula,[94] and Castile obligingly returned one of Edward II's murderers,[95] but negotiations did not become urgent until 1335 when it became clear that the Process of Agen had failed. Then Edward suggested a marriage be-tween his daughter and Alfonso's son.[96] In January 1336 Edward also made his bid for Castilian naval help, and by March some preliminary agreement had been reached,[97] but the French had been active too and by December 1336 had arranged a treaty which was ratified in 1337. It seemed that France had soundly beaten England at the diplomatic game, and when the dispute over Gascony came to a head in 1337 Castile was, on paper, fully committed to the French cause with an alliance which specifically demanded naval support. Professor Russell suggests that England's failure was partly due to her ignorance of Iberian politics,[98] but her ambassadors should have been reasonably informed since envoys had been sent to Castile in 1313, 1319, 1324, 1325, 1328, and 1331, and representatives of the northern provinces had been met even more frequently; also Gascon officials were near enough to gather Spanish news, and the Spanish colony in London had been used by the king and could presumably have given general advice and gathered up-to-date information for royal envoys.

England's failure was mainly due as he shows to the influence of the Francophile Castilian nobility, and to the greater potential strength of France as ally, and potential danger as enemy. Alfonso did not however prove a staunch French ally; he offered little help to French war preparations and raids in the next two years, and was still offering England hopes of a settlement in his letters of the spring of 1337, and by the envoy sent in the following winter.[99] Edward's reply of January 1338 shows Alfonso still keeping open negotiations for a peace treaty, although he refused to give in to Edward's thinly veiled threats of danger if Spaniards continued to trade with Flanders.[100] Edward played the diplomatic game too: he made sure that arrested Spaniards had their ships and goods returned[101] and ordered that Spaniards should be treated as friends on 25 January 1338.[102] He willingly gave in the winter of 1337–8 large numbers of safe-conducts, letters of protection, and licences for re-exports to Spanish merchants some of whom had already suffered at the hands of Englishmen.[103] This first brief period of confusion came to an end when Castile was included, as an ally of France, in the Anglo-French truce in the autumn of 1339.[104]

Although kings might still be writing friendly letters and avowing peaceful intentions, matters were clearly difficult for merchants. Technically the Spaniards were enemy aliens and much of their trade was with the Flemings, also enemy aliens; not surprisingly English officials and sailors felt fully justified in arresting Spanish ships and goods whenever they could, at least until the order of January 1338, and this was why Spaniards bought full safe-conducts.

Many were most unwilling to become involved in the political upheavals of the time and it is clear that some valued their English more than their Flemish trade: twenty Spanish masters claimed that they had refused to fight for the Count of Flanders and had deliberately left his lands to sail to England as a token of their friendship and desire to continue trading, but none the less they had trouble with the English navy and were seized by the admiral off Sandwich.[105] The unsettled background could cause dissension even within one ship as individual preferences for English or Flemish trade came into conflict: in 1337 a Spanish ship flying a French flag and in company with a Flemish vessel met an English ship in the Channel, the master and two sailors from the Spaniard came aboard the English ship—for reasons nowhere explained in the records; the sailors were apparently favourably disposed towards the English (or unfavourably disposed to their master) and warned the English of his warlike intentions so that the English detained him as a prisoner.[106] Despite Edward's protection of Spaniards it was found when Flanders pressed for compensation in 1339 on behalf of Spaniards robbed while sailing there that claims worth over £2,700 were still outstanding.[107] There seems little doubt that the English had shown that their ability to molest Spanish traders could cause severe worry; England's victory at Sluys in 1340, although it involved no Spanish losses, also underlined her naval capacity and in the next decade Edward's approaches to Spain met with more warmth, although Alfonso rushed into no obligations but played France and England carefully. At times he offered to mediate between the two in the hope of thereby obtaining help against the Moors.

Spanish envoys were received in 1341, and in 1342 further suggestions were made of a marriage alliance between Alfonso's heir Pedro and any of Edward's daughters.[108] Continuous efforts were made to keep relations smooth,[109] and in 1344 negotiations were far enough advanced for a showy embassy to go to Spain led by Derby and Arundel. Their suggestions that Edward would help at Algesiras and go on a pilgrimage to Santiago were welcomed.[110] Later envoys dealt with terms of a Bayonnese-Castilian peace,[111] and marriage terms[112] and the Castilian admiral promised to send ships to help Edward.[113] The French ambassadors competed ably with the English and Alfonso used this as a lever to force up Joanna's dowry.[114] The French (as in 1336) were successful: the Franco-Castilian alliance was re-affirmed in 1345 with the naval clauses clarified and a marriage arranged between Pedro and Blanche of Bourbon,[115] and the Castilian admiral agreed to serve France.

Yet Alfonso continued to negotiate with England. Although he was fully committed to the French side at the time of the battles of Crécy and Calais his help arrived too late and by January 1346 he had agreed to a marriage alliance with England.[116] The negotiations were completed and final arrangements made for Pedro's marriage to Joanna in the summer of 1348.[117] There seems little doubt that Alfonso had every intention of going through with this marriage: nothing could have been better for him than a foot in both camps, and moreover the English alliance might have strengthened his hand against his Francophile nobility, but Joanna's death by plague on her way to Castile ended this prospect and Edward's attempts to keep the negotiations alive met with failure.[118] This did not necessarily mean that Alfonso had had second thoughts, rather that he was again closely involved in the south and saw no need for hurry— after all at least six years had been taken over the previous arrangements.

The continuing negotiations between England and Castile meant that merchants trading between the two had a less dangerous task than might otherwise have been the case. There were also of course periods of peace during Anglo-French truces, and the Anglo-Flemish treaty, in which Edward promised to pay damages for harm done to Spaniards, lessened their burden.[119] There were also Bayonnese–Castilian truces to protect trade in the bay of Biscay[120] but this area remained perilous with political unease giving excuse and encouragement to those with a bent for piracy, and in 1341 and 1347 Bayonne utterly refused to be bound by Anglo-

French and Anglo-Castilian truces which did not specifically deal with 'her war'.[121]

Truces however, even if badly kept, meant that claims for damages could be filed, and Edward certainly did his best for merchants while he worked for his Castilian alliance: there were frequent orders for the restitution of Spanish goods, or for justice to be done to them, and in March 1345, while the Franco-Castilian treaty was renewed, he still saw fit to order that all arrests in reprisal for violences should stop.[122] This royal order repeated what must have been the preamble to the petition—that the arrest had caused much withdrawal of the Spanish trade from England and worse was feared—and, whether the petition was from the Spaniards or from the merchants of one of the English ports, it shows both a presumption that the Spanish trade with England was useful and well worth continuing and an awareness that eight years of war were beginning to upset the balance. The following month Edward initiated a big inquiry into offences against Spaniards since his accession twenty years before, an inquiry which seems to have been triggered off by an investigation into the recent seizure of three great ships of Spain loaded with iron off the Isle of Wight.[123] Then in June came the culmination of royal protection when it was proclaimed that the Spaniards were to be treated as if they were his own people.[124] Finally in October he specifically forbade a sea-keeping force to molest Spaniards.[125]

The merchants feared not simply the outright loss of goods and ships to marauders but also the cost in time, trouble and expenses of obtaining royal letters to extricate themselves from English harbours into which they might have been forced. Moreover once they had been seized by an Englishman eager for plunder, they might be accused of helping France: if they had simply been trading with France, their ships were usually released after any enemy goods still on board had been removed, but if they had taken part in military operations their ships were forfeit, as Juan de Motrico found,[126] and at times it must have been difficult and time consuming, if not impossible, to prove innocence. Many again found personal safe-conducts the answer, and in 1345 while Edward was at Zwin in July, the Spaniards obtained not only a general letter of protection but specific ones for at least twenty-three masters and their ships: this was for the summer fleet then at Flanders, and comprised ten ships of Castro, four of Guetaría, three of Bilbao, two of San Sebastián, and one each of Motrico, Plasencia, and Portugalete, and one unidentified.[127]

The scale of Spanish trade with England during this troubled period is impossible to assess, although there are plenty of references to its peaceful continuance. It was made clear in 1340 that, while occasional visitors were fair game for arrests, well established firms and agents were not: Spaniards 'making constant stay in the realm and continual traffic there' were exempt from the arrests ordered in London and Southampton to recompense

Thomas Symon of Sandwich for his loss of £300 at the hands of men of Santander and Castro.[128] The Manions were still active in London and ready to help compatriots.[129] Customs accounts do not survive in numbers large enough to afford much expansion of the picture, but the ministers' accounts record Spaniards in Cornwall in 1338–40, at Sandwich from 1344 to 1347, and possibly at Winchelsea in 1345–6;[130] the local accounts of Exeter record Spaniards in 1337–8 and 1345;[131] and there are a number of casual references in letters patent and close to their peaceful trading presence in England. The trade, which was built up to some importance before 1337, continued throughout this unsettled period. Although there may well have been some decline as a result of delays and inconveniences caused by arrest and searches, Edward did his best to see that the Spaniards were treated more than fairly, and serious losses came less often from government-sponsored or government-backed action than from the activity of pirates who were encouraged by the war-time situation and whom no medieval government was ever able adequately to control.

Pedro's reign, which at its start bid fair to bring this reasonably acceptable modus vivendi to a painful and abrupt halt, soon saw the trade prosper again in peace, although the economic aftermath of the Black Death kept it from reaching the peaks of earlier decades.

Alfonso XI's sudden death had cut short any further overtures to England which he might have been planning and the young Pedro was under pressure from his nobles and the Pope to fulfil the terms of the French treaty and marry Blanche of Bourbon. This he did. Edward must have had reasonably good intelligence reports of the way things were going and took immediate steps against Spain, either as a simple warning or just possibly because he really feared they were about to swing decisively to the French side. On 10 August he wrote to his archbishops desiring their prayers in the forthcoming struggle with Spain. Spain was stated to have ignored the arrangements for renewing the former alliance, to have attacked and killed English merchants, to have taken their goods and destroyed the king's shipping, to be threatening to destroy the English fleet, to dominate the English sea and even to invade the realm.[132] The confrontation, known as the battle of Les-Espagnols-sur-Mer, took place off Winchelsea on 31 August and gave rise to considerable controversy among the older naval historians, particularly about the extent of the English victory and whether or not Edward really believed the invasion rumour.[133]

The exact effect on Pedro and his government is unclear, and was probably not as great as Edward would have wished: it was another twelve years before Pedro made his alliance with England, but the effect on the Castilian merchants was immediate and profound as, horrified, they saw their worst fears realised. The attack was made during a truce and the fleet was entirely of merchant ships—it was in fact the normal summer trading fleet to Flanders, and there was little or no provocation; despite Edward's allegations there is no evidence of any intention to invade and very little likelihood that it would even have been seriously discussed in Castile; the men at arms aboard the fleet were, it seems, increased in Flanders but this was most probably in response to the rumours of warlike preparations in England and intended simply for self-defence.

The Spanish mercantile community responded in a direct way by negotiating their own twenty-year truce with England. This probably suited Edward very well: he had shown, as he had threatened Alfonso fourteen years before, that he could inflict heavy damage on Castilian shipping and beyond that he had no need to go. He need not impose crushing terms nor humiliate Castile nor demand a positive military alliance; all he needed was to make the new Castilian king wary of committing himself to giving too much help to France. The battle was in the nature of a warning shot across the bows to stop Pedro going any further, and in fact it was largely unnecessary because it soon became clear that Pedro disliked his Francophile nobility and his French wife, and preferred the life and culture of southern Spain to tight links with France.

On 11 November 1350 Edward appointed four men to treat for a perpetual peace with the Spaniards living in Flanders, these four being M. Andrew de Offord who was already versed in Castilian affairs over Joanna's marriage arrangements, the Captain of Calais and two merchants, Henry Pycard and John de Wesenham, both with regular contacts in Flanders. On 16 December in reply to a petition from the Spaniards at Sluys and Zwin he reaffirmed that Offord, Wesenham and another merchant, John Goldbeter, had powers to treat about the truce.[134] On 29 January he confirmed until Easter 1351 the safe-conducts which the Spaniards had arranged with Wesenham for their ships going home from Sluys, provided that they gave a complete list to the Mayor of the Wool Staple at Bruges: thirteen took advantage of this agreement and seven of them had the safe-conduct further extended to 5 June. The king then further extended it until 8 September to cover all manner of ships and men and goods of the Spanish coastal areas peacefully trading at the request of Juan Martín de Vergayre and Ferand Martín de la Camera, representatives of the Spaniards. Juan Martín appears to have had closer contacts than that with the English because a safe-conduct for him granted on 28 January 1351 mentions his great help to Edward at Calais.[135] A truce was finally arranged to come into force on 1 August 1351.[136] It was made between the men of England and those of Castile and Biscay; no damage was to be done by either side to the other; no alliance was to be made with nor help given to an enemy; the men could travel freely in each other's territory by land and sea and to any other realm, taking any goods they wished; special tribunals were to judge any infringements and such infringements were not to be made an excuse for invalidating the truce; Spaniards living abroad might be included if they wished, if not then they would be considered enemies (this was probably meant to deal with the Spaniards living in French ports) but those Spaniards included in the truce were not to be punished in any way for offences committed by Spaniards who were not; in wartime any goods, ships or men captured should be returned unless the men had given active aid to the enemy; Spanish fishermen were to be free to use Breton and English ports. This seems to have provided the exemplar for a similar commercial truce made with the Portuguese in 1353.[137]

In 1357 doubts about some terms were clarified—the Spaniards were allowed to carry French goods without forfeit provided that English goods carried by them were also not forfeit if taken into French ports[138] and this was reaffirmed when Edward confirmed the privileges of the Spaniards living at La Rochelle after he captured it in 1361.[139]

This general truce was backed up by separate arrangements as usual between Bayonne and Castile, and Bayonne and Biscay. Several short truces between them were followed by a firm peace in 1353, ratified by Edward in July 1354.[140] A few merchants played safe by buying personal safe-conducts in the early years of the truce,[141] but as it proved durable they found these a needless expense.

Throughout these arrangements were intended for purely commercial ends; they were initiated by the mercantile community and partly negotiated by the merchants themselves, but prosperity did not follow immediately on the truce's conclusion as the first few years were overshadowed by the effects of the Black Death. Figures for the cloth and wine trades indicate something of a recession until about 1355, although at least with the wine trade part of the trouble came from the reopened war,[142] but the Spaniards were certainly active before then.

It is particularly unfortunate that so few customs details survive, especially for London and Southampton, for the period of the truce. The Butlers' collection of the new cloth custom shows a ship of Castro exporting a little from London in 1353; and that a ship of Motrico and one of Castro took cloth from Weymouth in the winter of 1352–3.[143] In 1352 five Spanish shippers exported cloth from Southampton, and in 1353 two Spanish ships delivered iron, woad, brasil, linen and paper there.[144] The ministers' accounts show a few shippers present in the Cinque Ports, such as Miguel Larrosti of Bermeo with figs to sell at Rye in 1353, and Miguel Yvaynes and Juan Dyago at Winchelsea and Rye in 1357, and Ocho Senchis at Winchelsea in 1365.[145] Sandwich still attracted them: Lupone de Garcie unloaded 60 tuns of wine, and one Pedro de Castre brought four tons of Spanish iron in 1350; at least seven Spaniards imported wine and salt in exchange for cloth in November and December 1351 and in September 1352; ships of Bermeo and Castro were used there for the export of cloth in 1352 and at least eight Spanish shippers were taking cloth in the financial year 1352–3.[146] The local customs for Exeter record a few Spaniards sailing in for west country goods; one ship of Motrico and one of Castro were there in 1359, one of San Sebastián unloaded in 1361 and one of Bermeo in 1366.[147] The rather more complete accounts of the Keeper of the Ports in Cornwall show Plymouth and Falmouth to be familiar with Spanish wine ships and others unloaded at Mousehole, Fowey and Mountsbay.[148] In every year for which there is an account Spanish ships appeared, sometimes in considerable numbers, such as the five in 1352–3, six in 1358–9 and nine in 1361–2. Some of these may have intended their wines for England but not necessarily for Cornwall, and in March 1361 the king ordered customs collectors not to extort customs from Castilian wine ships driven into port by storm if none of the wine was unloaded for sale, and in the account for 1361–2 it is stated that the admiral forced prise from unwilling masters.[149]

The Butlers' accounts of wine imports show Castilians to be particularly active in the wine trade, unloading at London, Southampton and Sandwich as expected, also at Weymouth, Exeter and Bristol, and even at Hull and Boston, where there is little evidence of activity since the thirteenth century and the decline of the eastern cloth trade and the fairs.[150] They suggest that the trade, starting anyway from a firm basis established by the 1320s and maintained despite difficulties in the next two decades, was strong enough to penetrate some way beyond the busy southern areas once it was given encouragement. Figures are difficult to draw from these records, but it is clear that Spaniards were especially busy in 1351–4 and that they were also handling high tunnages in 1358–62 and 1366–7.[151] The accounts of the Constable of Bordeaux also indicate an increasing activity there from 1355 with the climax reached between September 1360 and September 1361 when sixty-nine Spanish ships, overwhelmingly Basque, picked up wine there.[152]

Such indications are frustrating: if the Spaniards were so active in Bordeaux, in the wine trade and in the west country ports where they had fewer traditional links, then their trade with London and Southampton must surely have been substantial; yet we have no means of discovering its scale. The Chancery records refer quite often to Spaniards but without interest in the size of their trade and not as often as in troubled times, because now there was less need for recourse to legal process. The firm friendship between England and Castile seems to have been sufficient to produce a framework for smoothly operating trade which rarely made the news. Certainly there were enquiries into robberies, especially after alleged wreck,[153] but fewer cases involved allegations of piracy or false seizure. Incidents of wreck, and even the presence of Spaniards in England, do not necessarily prove an intention to trade in England, since some Spaniards used English ports as emergency refuges during storms,[154] but most of the casual references state or imply intentions to trade in England. Those such as Sancho Piers de Moretta, Juan Piers de Arane and Juan Martyn of

Bermeo who bought safe-conducts in 1353 intended to use them in England.[155] The merchants of Bermeo who sought a licence to re-export their wines to Flanders in 1358 had certainly originally intended to sell in England;[156] and by this date Spanish wine was regularly listed with Gascon in price-fixing lists, although it was unfamiliar enough at Dartmouth to be arrested as sweet wine in 1366.[157]

The use of Southampton by the Spaniards is attested by the casual reference to the presence there of the *S Pedro* and *Sta María* both of Guetaría; at least two other ships with Spanish masters were there in 1353 when Italians had licences to use them for wool exports;[158] and in 1355 when shipping for Spain was short in London and Bristol the English exporter expected to find the ships in Southampton.[159]

At London there was clearly not a large permanent Spanish colony as Edward wrote to the Spanish colony in Bruges to establish the credentials of a merchant claiming to be Spanish, and to urge justice for certain Irishmen.[160] Yet there were still Spaniards who had settled in London, such as Dominic Ferandi there in 1357:[161] and Spanish merchants were bringing wine and iron there in the next decade.[162]

Bristol too was beginning to attract some Spaniards: Spanish yew for bowstaves had been imported in the 1280s,[163] but thereafter, although Bristol was a very active port and traded much with Gascony, references to Spanish goods, ships and men there are sparse. The Butlers' accounts show them taking wine with one ship in 1328–9 and two in 1330–1, then none until two possible Spaniards imported eleven and a half tuns in 1341; another ship put in there in 1344, three in 1346 and odd ones in 1351, 1353, 1355 and 1361, but this is a sparse scattering compared with Southampton or London in the same accounts.[164] A merchant from Seville exported wool there in 1353,[165] the *St Mary de Coronade* (possibly a Spanish vessel) was destined for Bristol with La Rochelle wines of Spanish and Genoese merchants,[166] and a ship of Castro was loaded there for Flanders in 1360.[167] Although some Portuguese merchants traded in Bristol, Spaniards seem to have found it too far from their busy Flemish and southern English routes to be much worth visiting until the western cloth industry was better developed, and even then they became and largely remained transporters for English merchants, with no wealthy Spaniards attracted there as they were to London.

This twenty-year period also saw a marked increase in the numbers of Englishmen and English ships going to Spain. It could almost be said to be a new development, as so few had gone before and so many references are found after 1350. Bartholomew Stygan hired a royal ship to go there in 1355;[168] and licences to export cloth westwards, bypassing the Calais staple, in 1363 and 1364 reveal some twenty-six English merchants from London and Hatfield Peverel in the east, through Winchester and Dorset to Somerset, Cornwall, Devon and Bristol in the west, seeking permission to take cloth to 'Gascony, Spain and other parts beyond the sea in the King's dominion in the south and west'.[169] Clearly Spain was now reckoned a normal trading area for Englishmen in the west, although exactly how many of the twenty-six went there is unclear; only five obtained licences for Spain alone. This probably indicates the beginning of the major factor in the English development of their Spanish trade: their need for increasing cloth markets; but licences to vintners, exempting them from currency export restrictions when they went to buy the new season's wines in 1364, indicate that Spain was also being placed alongside Gascony as a source of wine for men of Sandwich and Winchelsea.[170] From this time onwards too is clearly visible the interest of English shipmasters, particularly of Bristol, in the transport of Santiago pilgrims direct to Corunna.[171] By this time Englishmen were fully converted to active use of the route and were sailing and dealing alongside their Spanish fellows in numbers far greater than any that had gone before.

The trade was not backed by any politico-military arrangements until 1362, although clearly Edward and Pedro had tacitly accepted a friendly connection by accepting the truces of their subjects. By 1359 however a formal alliance with England was beginning to look attractive to Pedro as he was harassed by the claims of his illegitimate half-brother Enrique Trastamara, supported by France. Pedro responded to English overtures at last and the alliance was concluded in 1362. Only four years later Pedro needed to call on the Black Prince at Bordeaux to implement the treaty obligations, and the Black Prince's moves indicate how far the English undervalued the Castilian alliance by that time. Perhaps with so little Castilian aid ever having been given to France they had forgotten its potential danger: perhaps Edward's lack of grip on government and politics was already evident, perhaps too much was left to the Black Prince who was unduly influenced by his strong personal dislike of Pedro and his methods of government. Be that as it may the Black Prince scored a brilliant victory for Pedro at Nájera, but only after having forced the Basque Provinces from him—which would greatly weaken Pedro at home when it was publicly known—and only to throw away its advantages. Professor Russell's work has underlined the dismal failure of the diplomacy: the Black Prince, Edward and their advisers seemed blind to the advantage of having a grateful king on the Castilian throne and to the unlikelihood that Trastamara would ever come to favour them above the French king from whom he had already had such tangible aid and from whom he could expect still more. Their ambivalent policies left Pedro further weakened and with his assassination in March 1369 occurred the event most prejudicial to English interests in the south-west, and to Anglo-Spanish trade: for the first time the King of Castile was bound to France not only by alliance (Trastamara had concluded his own with France in November 1368), but also by recent gratitude and immediate self-interest, which was increased when England gave asylum to the Castilian court in exile and Lancaster married Pedro's legitimate heiress.

This turn of events brought twenty years of very flourishing trade to an abrupt halt. There had been some difficulties already in the preceding period while Pedro and Enrique fought their civil war: William Canynges and Ellis Spelly had tried to force compensation for their losses at the hands of Trastamara's men from Spanish merchants at Bristol in 1366;[172] by January 1368 John Vautort of London applied to arm his ship for its passage to Spain as he feared the effects of the civil war;[173] and Henry Herbury of London found that in December 1368 things were so bad that the master of the ship he sent from London for Spanish wines refused to go beyond Bordeaux for fear of the civil war.[174]

Pedro's death made things immeasurably worse; not only were past crimes not to be remedied but new ones were committed. By June 1369 sixteen merchants of Bristol and two of London claimed to have lost goods aboard four ships (one of these was the *Clement* lost in 1366) at the hands of Trastamaran supporters with no restitution forthcoming, and in August references was made to these grievances and to the imprisonment and death of English merchants.[175] It was urged that a mercantile truce and agreement on the lines of that of 1351 should be made. This had seemed a splendid solution before, but now the situation was vastly more hostile. The English failed to obtain justice, and the Spaniards, unable to face the risks and dangers, disappeared entirely from English harbours.

The fluctuations of the trade over the previous century or so show how difficult it would be to assess exactly how important political or economic factors were in determining its scale. The rise in the thirteenth and early fourteenth centuries coincided with both a general European trade surge and good Anglo-Castilian relations; the apparent slackening in the late forties and early fifties coincided with both the Black Death and unsettled war conditions; the upsurge of wine dealings in the fifties coincided with both a need to compensate for Bordeaux losses and a settlement of the political uncertainty. The hard times of the 1370s coincided with another plague period and a slump in England's general overseas trade, and also with severe political dislocation. Economic hardships would result in a slackening activity, but only political action could cause the almost overnight disappearance of Spanish names from all the surviving local and national customs accounts, from the ministers' accounts, and those of the Butlers and Constables of Bordeaux. The events of 1369–70 provide one of the clearest examples one could wish for of the utter disaster a political policy could spell for honest commercial endeavour.

34   The fortunes of the trade

NOTES TO CHAPTER 1

1   R.L.P. 1201–16, p. 44.
2   Eleanor possibly visited her brother, and the Spanish Chancellor had a safe-conduct for negotiations in 1206; Foedera, I, i, 96, 100.
3   There was probably an exchange in 1226, certainly in 1233, 1247, 1249; R.L.C. 1224–7, p. 117b; C.L.R. 1226–40, p. 214; ibid., 1245–51, pp. 117, 121, 125, 232.
4   Rôles Gascons, ed. Bémont, I, 31; C.C.R. 1237–42, p. 502; Diplomatic Documents, ed. Chaplais, I, 145. In 1224 Bayonne complained of incessant warfare by men of Ferdinand III but this seems to be the outcome not of formal war but of general uncontrolled violence in the Bay of Biscay.
5   C.R. 1227–31, p. 89.
6   Ibid., p. 466.
7   R.L.C. 1204–24, p. 620b; C.M.I., I, No. 94.
8   C.P.R. 1232–47, p. 192. This hostility went back at least as far as 1221; R.L.C. 1204–24, p. 461a.
9   Rôles Gascons, ed. Bémont, I, 802, 1715, 1727, 2724, 2754, 3349; C.L.R. 1226–40, p. 156; ibid., 1240–5, p. 155; C.P.R. 1232–47, p. 321; C.R. 1253–4, pp. 183, 259. Henry III was able to raise money and cordage from them.
10   Camino y Orella, Historia de la ciudad de San Sebastián, pp. 56–7.
11   Diplomatic Documents, ed. Chaplais, 270, 271; the negotiations have been studied in some detail in J. O. Baylen, 'John Maunsel and the Castilian treaty of 1254: a study of the clerical diplomat', Traditio, XVII (1961), pp. 482–91.
12   C.R. 1261–4, p. 172.
13   Foedera, I, ii, 523.
14   Ibid., 522; C.P.R. 1272—81, p. 128; Nicolas, Royal Navy, I, 285–6.
15   Treaty Rolls 1234–1325, ed. Chaplais, Nos. 155–60, 165, 170, 172, 175, 177, 179–84; Rôles Gascons, ed. Bémont, II, 501–2; C.C.R. 1279–88, p. 116.
16   Foedera, I, ii, 620; C.P.R. 1281–92, pp. 113, 122.
17   C.P.R. 1247—58, p. 457.
18   C.C.R. 1264–8, pp. 91, 98; C.L.R. 1260–7, pp. 141–2, 148.
19   C.P.R. 1258–66, p. 258.
20   C.P.R. 1266–72, p. 169.
21   P.R.O. SC6/1031/19, 20; two other unnamed ships brought more goods for men of Castro and San Sebastián.
22   Ibid., 1031/21, 22, 24.
23   J. A. Williamson, 'The geographical history of the Cinque Ports', History, new ser., XI (1926–7).
24   C.P.R. 1272–81, p. 184; ibid., 1281–92, p. 149.
25   C.P.R. 1272–81, p. 196. This may be the Giles Martini acting as attorney for a fellow-Spaniard in London in 1289 (Letter Book 'A', p. 119), and who had received a letter of protection for life in 1268 (C.P.R. 1266–72, p. 265).
26   C.Ch.Warr., I, 4.
27   See Chapter 3.
28   C.P.R. 1272–81, pp. 338, 341.
29   C.P.R. 1272–81, p. 284.
30   John Mundenard, Burgess of Southampton, dealing in leathers, wool and yarn in London in November 1285, is almost certainly the same man as John Mundenard of Castri Novi de Vallibus who was dealing there up to October 1285 (London Recognisance Rolls, No. 1). Mundenard was without doubt a Spaniard, as

the same roll makes clear that both Peter Fort of Castri Novi de Vallibus and Peter Garsie of Castri Novi are Spaniards. This John Mundenard is probably that man who, with his brothers Peter and Ernald, sold leather in London in 1278 (Letter Book 'A', p. 18); his career went back earlier than that as a John Mundenard of Castri Novi had a licence to export English wool in 1273 (C.P.R. 1272–81, p. 17, where his name is translated as of Newcastle); and he was selling leather in London in 1276 (Letter Book 'A', p. 8). Peter de Mundenard, called a merchant of Spain, had letters of protection in 1276 and 1285 (see note 24 above), had licences to export English wool in 1277 (C.Ch.R.V., 1277–1326, p. 3) and was selling (Spanish?) lambs' wool in London in 1283 with an agent there to help him (Letter Book 'A', p. 62).

31   Letter Book 'A', p. 206.

32   See Table 1.

33   London Record Office, Recognisance Rolls, I.

34   Williams, Medieval London, p. 182, identifies the Mundenard family of Castro Novo de Vallibus as coming from the Ebro valley.

35   For a detailed examination of his reign see Gaibros Riaña de Ballesteros, Historia del reínado de Sancho IV.

36   Some of the cases were not settled for thirty years; C.P.R., C.C.R. passim.

37   C.P.R. 1292–1301, p. 34.

38   C.C.R. 1288–96, p. 324; ibid., 1296–1302, pp. 32, 34; Rôles Gascons, ed Bémont, II, 1380, 1737, III, 2131, 4254.

39   C.P.R. 1281–92, p. 509.

40   C.C.R. 1288–96, pp. 364–5, 371, 397, 452.

41   Foedera, I, ii, 797, 815–16.

42   C.P.R. 1292–1301, p. 203.

43   Letter Book 'A', pp. 117, 148; Letter Book 'B', pp. 80–2; Rot. Parl., I, 47b; P.R.O. SC8/2236.

44   Rôles Gascons, ed Bémont, III, 4254; the Duke of Lancaster in Aquitaine was to issue no letters of marque if peace seemed possible, but if he saw no hope then he might grant such letters.

45   Printed in Benavides, Don Fernando IV de Castilla, II, 57.

46   Mazo Solano, 'Manifestaciones de la económia montañesa' in Aportación al estudio de la historia económica de la Montaña, pp. 171–2.

47   Rôles Gascons, ed. Bémont, III, 3388, 4468; C.P.R. 1292–1301, p. 491.

48   Ibid., p. 222; P.R.O. SC8/3997.

49   C.P.R. 1292–1301, p. 489.

50   Rôles Gascons, ed. Bémont, III, 4907, 4959, 4974, 4988; Gascon Rolls 1307–17, ed. Renouard, 202; P.R.O. SC8/13228.

51   Rôles Gascons, ed. Bémont III, 4395.

52   C.C.R. 1302–7, pp. 83, 458. She was in fact the daughter of his cousin, Sancho.

53   P.R.O. SC1/16/14; C47/27/8(13); Benavides, op. cit., II, 558.

54   C.C.R. 1318–23, p. 123; C.P.R. 1317–21, p. 262.

55   C.P.R. 1324–7, p. 52; C.C.R. 1323–7, pp. 313–14.

56   P.R.O. E30/1289; C.C.R. 1323–7, pp. 253, 344, 345, 346, 350–1; C.P.R. 1324–7, pp. 84, 88, 93, 103, 104.

57   C.C.R. 1323–7, pp. 515, 533, 556. It was at this time that Pedro de Lopez Manion and Ferand Manion, the Spanish merchants who took out London citizenship, were taken in the train of M. Peter de Galiciano to Spain; C.P.R. 1324–7, p. 181.

58 The raid on Marennes shows how far some Spaniards took the hostility; C.C.R. *1307–13*, p. 136.

59 C.P.R. *1301–7*, pp. 460–1; *Gascon Rolls 1307–17*, ed. Renouard, 105; C.C.R. *1307–13*, p. 130.

60 *Foedera*, II, i, 60, 71; *Gascon Rolls 1307–17*, ed. Renouard, 211, 289, 290, 298, 336, 562.

61 These were finally fully satisfied in 1314 with a payment of £50 from Castro Urdiales; C.P.R. *1307–13*, p. 243; C.C.R. *1307–13*, p. 383; *ibid.*, *1313–18*, p. 95.

62 C.C.R. *1307–13*, pp. 248, 488–9, 527, 582; *ibid.*, *1313–18*, pp. 301–2; arrests for him prompted Spanish complaints of injustice at Abbeville (P.R.O. SC8/14137).

63 C.P.R. *1313–17*, p. 34; P.R.O. SC8/11871.

64 C.C.R. *1313–18*, pp. 38–9, 162.

65 *Ibid.*, p. 231.

66 C.P.R. *1313–17*, p. 303.

67 *Ibid.*, pp. 213, 269, 299, 300, 363, 367, 374.

68 C.C.R. *1318–23*, pp. 47–8.

69 C.P.R. *1317–21*, pp. 53, 55; P.R.O. SC8/13463.

70 P.R.O. E122/124/13. As nationalities were rarely recorded it is not always easy to sort out Gascons and Portuguese from Spaniards. At this time Sandwich sought protection for eight Spanish ships from arrests by one Piers Dartiglouk of Bayonne (P.R.O. SC1/39(39)): a Peter de Artigalung claimed to be Reymund de Artigalung's attorney in 1303 in the continuing suit over the offences of 1293–4; C.C.R. *1302–7*, pp. 82–3.

71 C.P.R. *1307–13*, p. 124.

72 P.R.O. E122/136/8, 17, 21, 23, 25. The nationalities of a few men and ships remain uncertain. See Chapter 4 for the values of the imports.

73 P.R.O. E122/68/13, 18, 69/1, 2; *Letter Book 'B'*, pp. 113, 121, 133, 134, 139, 166; London Records Office, Recognisance Rolls, VI, VII.

74 C.P.R. *1313–17*, pp. 466, 624; C.C.R. *1313–18*, p. 452.

75 *Letter Book 'E'*, p. 97.

76 P.R.O. E122/124/29, 30.

77 P.R.O. E122/147/14.

78 *Letter Book 'E'*, p. 191; C.P.R. *1324–7*, p. 82. For their lives see Appendix.

79 *Letter Book 'E'*, p. 269.

80 Exeter City Library, loc. cust. accts. 32 Ed. I, 13–14, 16–17, 17–18, Ed. II, 20, Ed. II–1 Ed. III.

81 P.R.O. E122/39/6.

82 *Ibid.*, 15/3, 4.

83 *Ibid.*, 32/7, 8.

84 C.P.R. *1321–4*, p. 175.

85 *Ibid.*, *1324–7*, p. 16; *ibid.*, *1327–30*, p. 250; P.R.O. SC8/3559.

86 C.Ch.R. *1300–26*, p. 475; *ibid.*, *1327–41*, p. 89.

87 C.C.R. *1323–7*, pp. 313–14; C.P.R. *1324–7*, pp. 32, 306.

88 C.P.R. *1327–30*, pp. 241, 304, 397, 418, 493, 529.

89 Russell, *English Intervention in Spain and Portugal*, pp. 233–5.

90 C.C.R. *1333–7*, pp. 697–8.

91 Daumet, *Étude sur l'alliance de la France et de la Castile*, pp. 3–5.

92 C.C.R. *1327–30*, pp. 243, 371; P.R.O. SC1/38/6, 7, 8; *Archives municipales de Bayonne, livre d'établissements*, No. 301.

93 C.C.R. *1327–30*, p. 583; C.P.R. *1327–30*, p. 455.

94   C.C.R. 1330–3, pp. 137, 331.
95   Ibid., pp. 315–16, 322, 324–5; C.P.R. 1330–4, pp. 121, 148, 312.
96   C.P.R. 1334–8, p. 133; C.C.R. 1333–7, p. 501.
97   C.C.R. 1333–7, pp. 649, 697–8.
98   Russell, op. cit, pp. 6–7.
99   C.C.R. 1337–9, pp. 125, 235; C.P.R. 1334–8, p. 573.
100 C.C.R. 1337–9, p. 282; Alfonso's stated reason for not concluding a peace treaty with England was not his alliance with France, but that he was busy with his war against Portugal.
101 C.C.R. 1337–9, pp. 206–7, 208, 229, 284, 288, 303, 358; C.P.R. 1334–8, pp. 579, 580–1; ibid., 1338–41, p. 68.
102 C.C.R. 1337–9, p. 379.
103 C.P.R. 1334–8, pp. 520, 524–6, 529–30, 537, 546, 551, 554, 571, 573, 581; ibid., 1338–41, pp. 2, 5, 23. Men of Southampton arrested nine in the autumn of 1337 (C.P.R. 1334–8, p. 579) which possibly included some mentioned in C.C.R. 1337–9, p. 208. About twenty were also arrested off Sandwich.
104 C.C.R. 1339–41, pp. 636–7.
105 P.R.O. SC8/3313; see also C.C.R. 1337–9, pp. 206–7, 208 which may refer to this incident.
106 C.M.I., II, 1588.
107 C.C.R. 1339–41, p. 105; C.P.R. 1338–40, pp. 372–3, 387, 464.
108 C.C.R. 1341–3, pp. 245, 501, 554; C.P.R. 1340–3, p. 397.
109. C.C.R. 1343–6, pp. 39, 226, 231–2, 369, 383; C.P.R. 1343–5, p. 18.
110 Foedera, III, i, 8–9; C.C.R. 1343–6, p. 449; P.R.O. SC1/38/10, 55/98.
111 Foedera, III, i, 8–9, 12.
112 Ibid., III, i, 22, 26; C.C.R. 1343–6, pp. 448, 449, 484, 492; P.R.O. C76/19 m.2; SC1/37/126.
113 P.R.O. C76/19 m. 2; SC1/37/125; C.C.R. 1343–6, p. 456. Boccanegra also signed an agreement to serve the French on 11 January 1345 and made a firm agreement in 1347; he did not, however, serve France while the English negotiations continued; Russell, English Intervention in Spain and Portugal, p. 9; Daumet, Étude sur l'alliance de la France et de la Castille, pp. 17–18.
114 Foedera, III, i, 46–7.
115 Daumet, op. cit. pp. 12–14.
116 C.C.R. 1346–9, p. 42; C.P.R. 1345–8, pp. 38, 100.
117 Foedera, III, i, 148–9, 151, 153–6; C.P.R. 1348–50, pp. 24, 26, 40; P.R.O. C76/26 m. 19.
118 C.C.R. 1346–9, p. 590.
119 C.C.R. 1339–41, pp. 458–9, 625.
120 Foedera, II, ii, 1233, 1241; III, i, 12, 152, 166; C.C.R. 1343–6, p. 226.
121 P.R.O. C47/30/8(20); C.C.R. 1346–9, p. 405.
122 C.C.R. 1343–6, pp. 552–3.
123 C.P.R. 1343–5, pp. 503, 512; C.C.R. 1343–6, p. 333; P.R.O. C47/60/5(146); K.B. 27/336 Rex m. 34.
124 C.C.R. 1343–6, p. 589.
125 C.P.R. 1343–5, p. 555.
126 C.C.R. 1346—9, p. 14.
127 C.P.R. 1374–7 (with appendices for 1340 and 1345), pp. 507–8.
128 C.C.R. 1339–41, p. 512.
129 See Appendix.
130 P.R.O. SC6/816/11, 12; 894/24–6, 28–9; 1032/5.

131   Exeter City Library, loc. cust. accts., 10–11, 11–12, 19–20 Ed. III.

132   C.C.R. 1349–54, p. 266. The alliance mentioned must be a reference to the negotiations of 1348 in which the former marriage alliance of 1254 would have been discussed, as it was in 1344; C.C.R. 1343–6, p. 474.

133   See for instance Finot, Les Relations commerciales entre la Flandre et l'Espagne, pp. 63–74; Fernández Duro, La Marina, pp. 99–108; Labayru, Historia general del Señorío de Biscaya, II, 357; Nicolas, Royal Navy, II, 102–14; Maza Solano, 'Manifestaciónes de la economía montañesa', pp. 191–3.

134   P.R.O. C76/28 m.2.

135   Ibid., 29 mm.15, 8d.

136   Ibid., m.4; Foedera, III, i, 228–9. There seems to be no survival of a ratification by the Castilian king but neither did he refuse it or call upon his men to break the truce and help the French.

137   Foedera, III, i, 247, 264.

138   Ibid., 363, 380.

139   Ibid., 606, 607.

140   Foedera, III, i, 266–8, 270, 280.

141   C.P.R. 1350–4, pp. 238, 240; P.R.O. C76/30 mm.3, 9, 31 m.6.

142   Carus-Wilson and Coleman, England's Export Trade, p. 138; James, Wine Trade, pp. 19–22.

143   P.R.O. E101/457/22, 23,

144   P.R.O. E122/137/16.

145   P.R.O. SC6/1032/9–11.

146   Ibid., 895/1, 3; E101/457/22,23.

147   Exeter City Library, loc. cust. accts., 32–3, 34–5, 35–6, 39–40, 40–1 Ed. III.

148   P.R.O. SC6/817/1–10.

149   C.P.R. 1358–61, p. 567; P.R.O. SC6/817/8.

150   P.R.O. E101/80/4–7, 9, 11–20.

151   See Table 20.

152   P.R.O. E101/182/2; see Table 19.

153   C.P.R. 1354–8, pp. 500–1,546.

154   C.P.R. 1354–8, p. 522; ibid., 1358–61, p. 181.

155   Ibid., 1350–4, pp. 405–6, 421.

156   Ibid., 1358–61, p. 28.

157   C.C.R. 1364–8, p. 158.

158   Ibid., 1349–54, pp. 535, 544, 549.

159   Ibid., 1354–60, p. 118.

160   C.C.R. 1349–54, p. 470; ibid., 1354–60, p. 276.

161   Ibid., p. 367.

162   C.P.R. 1361–4, pp. 151, 431, 432, 524.

163   Sherborne, The Port of Bristol, pp. 8–9.

164   P.R.O. E101/78/3a–5, 8–14, 16, 18, 19; 79/1–3, 5, 8–9, 11–17, 19, 22–4, 80/1, 3–7, 9, 11–20.

165   C.C.R. 1349–54, p. 537.

166   C.P.R. 1350–4, p. 543.

167   Ibid., 1358–61, p. 410; C.C.R. 1360–4, p. 22.

168   C.P.R. 1354–8, p. 281.

169   C.C.R. 1360–4, p. 507; C.P.R. 1361–4, pp. 479, 480, 492, 496, 510, 521.

170   C.P.R. 1364–7, pp. 15–16, 59.

171   Ibid., 1367–70, pp. 122, 140, 212, 226, 228.

172 C.C.R. 1364–8, p. 255.
173 *Ibid.*, p. 361.
174 *Ibid.*, p. 458.
175 C.C.R. 1369–74, pp. 30, 112–13; P.R.O. SC8/4262, 6934.

CHAPTER 2

The fortunes of the trade
1370–1485

To men in 1369 Trastamara's usurpation did not look irreversible. He was still far from strong at home: Pedro's daughters, his heiresses, were safe: the Basque Provinces, Andalusia and particularly Galicia remained loyal to them; Aragon and Portugal threatened Trastamara's borders; the English alliance could still be called on by his opponents. Yet again England missed her chance and, turning her back on Castile to engage France, she left Trastamara to build up support and Pedro's daughters' supporters to despair of help.

The Spanish merchants clearly feared temporary losses but felt a permanent breach could be avoided and took steps very similar to those in 1350 to protect their trade. In July 1369, after the arrest of six Spanish ships at Sandwich from which compensation was to be exacted for Spelly and the other Bristol and London merchants, three representatives of the merchants, masters and sailors of Castile and Biscay (Andrés Piers López de Legheseval, Juan Martín de Lougha, Juan Gonsalez de la Caleza) were in London citing the twenty-year truce and asking for its observance and the release of the ships as it had not been their will that the English should be harmed. Edward avowed his intention of observing the truce but insisted on satisfaction for his men, satisfaction promised but not given by Biscay and by Pedro before his death. If compensation were made the truce would be observed, the ships released and to show he was not intending a free-for-all on the matter of arrests but that they should be under royal supervision, he agreed to do justice to Castilians harmed by the English.[1] Further negotiations by Juan Martín with three other companions brought Edward's agreement by 16 August that the ships arrested should be kept safely as security until the representatives had had time to consult with their colleagues unless the Spaniards concerned paid up voluntarily. The representatives had until 1 May to devise a means of amendment and meanwhile other Spanish ships might trade freely between Castile and Flanders as long as they gave no help to enemies. Any already helping the enemy against the wishes of the Spanish colony at Bruges would not be deemed a cause for breaking the truce. Similarly Englishmen were to have free passage to Castile and the Flemish courts were authorised to enforce Spanish observance of this.[2] But this time the merchants were disappointed. I can find no evidence that any agreement was reached by May, that the Spaniards submitted any further terms, or that compensation was ever paid. The twenty-year truce was certainly ignored before its expiry date: in February 1371 Spaniards and Frenchmen were publicly pronounced enemies and by April the ratification of the Anglo-Flemish treaty specifically forbade Flemings from carrying Spanish as well as French goods; Spanish ships began to be seized in the Channel.[3] Trade was abruptly severed.

Despite the confusion in Spain with the civil war, it must have become clear enough fairly early that for all Trastamara's insecurity his opponents were in no position to oust him. As *de facto* king he showed no sign of emulating his ablest predecessors, hunting with the hounds as well as running with the hare; instead he came down wholeheartedly on the French side. Not only was England his enemy by the terms of his treaty with France but the Lancaster marriage made her his dynastic enemy also. From now on Castile had a stake in the Anglo-French war, especially when attacks on France were made through Castile and Lancaster's side-aim was the military conquest of Castile for himself. Trastamara ardently, and even obsessively, supported France and did his best to hinder any Anglo-French rapprochement.[4] Above all he gave France the naval aid she demanded and the English coastal towns were devastated by raids hitherto outside their experience, such as those of 1377 in which Rye, Rottingdean, Lewes, Portsmouth, Dartmouth and Plymouth were attacked first and later severe raids were made on Poole, Hastings, Southampton, Dover and Winchelsea. Dr Sherborne has rightly pointed out that one should not speak of the English losing control of the Channel through this Franco-Castilian co-operation, since medieval naval warfare was not of the type to provide control, except in the very short term when a fleet was actually at sea, but the co-operation meant that English coasts might now be raided, or that her ships might at any time meet a well-organised and equipped enemy fleet which had more chance of inflicting severe damage than had the old French fleet.[5]

Some slight amelioration came with the death of Enrique in 1379 but his son Juan could not afford to lose the French alliance, so real improvement had to wait until, in 1388, Lancaster acknowledged his failure in Castile and began negotiations. Although he was unable to obtain a full Anglo-Castilian alliance as instructed since France had just taken care to renew hers, he made a satisfactory personal settlement and the dynastic question was settled by the marriage of his daughter by Costanza to Juan's son. This removed Castile's strongest motive for supporting France; what remained were treaty obligations and the mutual hostility engendered by twenty years of fighting, raiding, reprisal and counter-reprisal. This was to prove strong enough to prohibit political alliance for another seventy-eight years, but was too weak to prevent Spain's gradual return to a policy of least-help to France and the gradual rebuilding of Anglo-Castilian trade.

Lancaster's negotiations opened the way for this by asking for the right of free passage for merchants as well as pilgrims to Santiago.[6]

The abysmal political relations of these nineteen years had caused an almost complete breakdown of direct trade, but goods were still exchanged, contacts made and old ties kept up as long as possible through the ports and markets of Flanders and Portugal. Bristol's customs accounts show a few sailings to Spain before 1380, one by a Bristol ship with a Spanish master, three by Flemings and one by a Portuguese. This was one of the rare times when Bristol needed to freight neutrals badly and other Flemish ships were there in 1378–9, 1379–80 and 1381–2 sailing for Portugal. From 1378 Iberian trade was directed to Portugal but after 1388 Spain and Seville occurred more often as destinations[7] and the number of Portuguese ships used on the route declined as Anglo-Castilian friendship was restored. English trade and traders never deserted Portugal, as it was a useful market in its own right and as a staging post on the Andalusia run, but the vigour and interest in it seem to decrease once the Spanish ports were reopened.

Other surviving records confirm the absence of Spaniards after 1370. The Butlers' accounts show no wine arrivals; the Bordeaux accounts show them avoiding the port in sharp contrast to their activity in Pedro's reign; Chancery records furnish numerous instances of hostile contact but none of peaceful trade or safe-conducts. Apart from the few loyalist ship-masters coming to support Lancaster,[8] those working for Bristol men,[9] and the odd ship of Ribadeo at Bristol in 1383,[10] members of the Spanish mercantile community kept well away from English shores if they could.

That the Castilian merchants accepted Trastamara rather than a life of exile is not surprising. Exile brought irritating misunderstandings with English officials, as the Guetarían shipmasters supporting Lancaster found in 1373 (Spanish names implied an enemy to harassed or obtuse English officials), and personal ties to family, home town and native land were strong. There were also sound economic reasons: in exile the Spaniards would lose access to Spanish oil, and wine and iron; they would lose their French markets and reach Flemish and Portuguese ones only under risk of meeting the Trastamaran fleet which would regard them as traitors and rebels. By staying in Spain they lost their English market, but might channel goods for it through Portugal and Flanders, to which their sailings would be less risky. Unless a merchant had a special reason for attachment to the court in exile, his best and easiest path was to stay put: the merchants would have preferred an open English market as their attempts at negoti-ations in 1369 showed, but when they failed most accepted the political change, probably expecting it to be short-lived in any case. Some must have endured hardship and losses through seizure, but most probably prospered and some found that the fund of good-will built up in England was such that they could obtain favours from Englishmen despite the war.[11]

Lancaster's agreement of 1388, together with the constantly renewed Anglo-French truce made at Leulingham and Richard's French marriage meant that the last decade of the century offered a good chance of a trade recovery, although attempts to acquire an Anglo-Castilian alliance in 1391 and 1393 failed.[12] This decade opens a period, similar to that of the early fourteenth century, when the two countries were nominally enemies whenever the Anglo-French war broke out again, but they tried to alleviate matters with letters of protection and safe-conducts, and could always trade during truces. Castile's aid to France became slower and less and by the middle of the fifteenth century the naval clauses in the treaty were reviewed and lightened. As memories of the period 1370–88 faded and became the memories of grandfathers so peaceful trade became again normal. It should not be expected that the volume of trade would reach that of the early fourteenth century, as European trade in general had slackened, but England's flourishing cloth trade and demand for oil, wine and iron held great promise for the route.

The Bristol customs accounts show how important the Iberian route had already become before 1400 with about one quarter of the sailings going to Spain or Portugal carrying up to 40 per cent of her cloth exports.[13] The Spaniards were again active in the wine trade, spreading their business between London, Southampton, Sandwich, Winchelsea, Rye and Bristol, and their role was again of useful size; in 1392–3, 1393–4, and 1394–5 they handled 20, 14, and 22 per cent of alien wine imports.[14] By 1398 if not before English shipping was again at Seville and Cadiz.[15]

Henry IV did his best to smooth the path for new contacts with Castile. Once the truces with France (which included Spain) were renewed he sent off to and received ambassadors from Castile in 1400;[16] but lack of governmental control in the first years after his coup led to one of the worst periods known for English lawlessness at sea. Henry's earliest negotiations with Castile were to rectify piracies, indeed the Spaniards insisted that at least partial restitution must be made before any further steps could be taken towards peace.[17] In December 1402 the Spanish ambassador presented for consideration a list of twenty-nine offences by Englishmen, most committed in 1401 and 1402,[18] and the English produced a counter-claim for eleven offences by Spaniards.[19] It was not easy, however, to reimpose order in the Channel; even as the Spanish ambassador negotiated and as Henry accepted the justice of some of the claims and ordered restitution,[20] and despite the truce declared publicly and extended to June 1404 to allow time for negotiations,[21] English pirates seized at least seventeen more Spanish ships before the end of 1403.[22] Certainly the Spaniards came off worst in this period, and it is little wonder that Don Pero Niño's raids in 1405 were aimed against the English as much for their piracy against Spaniards as for the sake of the French alliance.[23]

Table 2   Castilian ships and goods taken by English pirates, 1403.[1]

Date taken	Ships and/or goods lost
Before 16 Jan.	Trinidad of Eyvyle (Seville)
9 Mar.	S Nicolas of Bilbao
17 Apr.	S Pedro of Ondárroa
17 Apr.	Ship with master Juan Ortez de Galaizde
17 Apr	Ship with master Feran Ve de Al de la Croun (Corunna)
17 Apr.	Sta María de Guetaría
11 May	Goods aboard a ship of Danzig
22 May	Goods aboard another unnamed ship.
May	A ship of Bilbao
May	Sta María de Ville Neve de Wyarson (Oyarzun)
29 June	Goods aboard a Portuguese ship
18 Oct.	S Pedro of Lequeitio
18 Oct.	S Julián
19 Oct.	S Juan of Laredo
19 Oct.	S Juan of Bermeo
19 Oct.	Sta María of Presance (Placencia?)
19 Oct.	Sta María of Deva
27 Oct.	S Nicolas of Orio
27 Oct.	Sta María of Bilbao
Oct.	S Pedro of Presance (Placencia?)

1   C.C.R. 1402–5, pp. 33, 56, 67, 69, 70, 94, 99, 100, 108, 203, 257; C.P.R. 1401–5, pp. 277, 281, 283, 357, 360–1, 363–4, 424–8; C.M.I., vol. vii, Nos. 251, 254, 270; P.R.O. SC8/9011, 10829, 11438, 11444, 11460, 11466, 11483, 11521, 11529, 11533, 11549, 11553, 11571, 12473.

Henry did his best to satisfy Spanish demands; he had England included in 1404 as Portugal's ally in her ten-year truce with Castile,[24] and encouraged his Gascon subjects to come to a peace settlement with the towns of the northern Spanish coast by December 1404.[25] These arrangements were upset by the renewed French war, in response to which Niño organised his raids but by 1408 Anglo-French truces had re-established peaceful relations. Ambassadors were exchanged again between England and Castile in 1409 and, although the expected permanent settlement did not materialise, yearly truces were arranged from 8 February 1410 until Henry's death and continued under Henry V until 1416;[26] this was made possible since, when the Franco-Castilian treaty terms were renegotiated in 1406, Castile was henceforth allowed to make short one-year truces without referring to France. Castile's desire for peace is also shown in a letter from the Queen of Castile to her brother in which she offered to mediate for peace between

England and France,[27] and she and Henry, in order to protect their merchants, exchanged up to sixty letters of safe-conduct a year.[28]

Despite that shocking spate of piracy, trade had continued. There are no possible overall figures for the period, but it is clear that London and Southampton, and now Bristol, continued to be the centres for the trade. The list of English complaints against the Castilians in 1402 had included cases of at least six Bristol ships and several more Bristol merchants, making by far the most important group; four of the ships carried oil, grain and osey, indicating southern trips, the Trinity was stated to be coming from Seville, the Mary was taken by Sevillan ships off the Algarve and one other was taken off Lisbon. At least three other ships sailed for Spain from Bristol in 1400 and the María of Bilbao arrived with iron; four left for Spain and two arrived from there between April and November 1402; and in the winter months of 1403–4 thirteen arrived and thirteen departed for Spain, most of these being of Bristol with a scattering of other English, Welsh and Irish ships and one from Deva.[29] Some merchants of Bilbao were finding their way to Bridgwater for cloth by now, probably on the way to Bristol.[30] On the south coast Dartmouth furnished ships for the Flanders–Castile route,[31] and, although the Spaniards did not care to visit Exeter until 1409, from then until 1414 one or two ships arrived from Deva each year.[32] Plymouth too continued to hang on to Spanish trade to some extent and in 1413 three Spanish ships took their wine of La Rochelle there.[33] For Southampton records are particularly sparse but there seem to have been Spanish shippers there in 1403–4,[34] two ships of Zumaya tied up in 1413,[35] and a ship of Seville delivered wine in 1414.[36] Further east, Sandwich seemed to have lost its attractions: the surviving accounts for 1405–7 (a war period) and 1413 show none.[37] London was still a main centre for visiting Spaniards: they imported wine of La Rochelle in 1400;[38] ships of Deva and Ondárroa were there in 1402;[39] a merchant of Burgos arrived in 1403;[40] the customs accounts show Spaniards there in 1400–1, and probable Spaniards unloading off Italian vessels in 1410;[41] merchants of Seville were carrying wine to London when dispossessed falsely under an inapplicable letter of marque in 1413;[42] and the Butlers' accounts show that after an absence in the war period 1405–8 they were concentrating their wine trade in London by 1413–14,[43] the wine probably being Spanish or Rochellais since they were not yet visiting Bordeaux.[44] By December 1413 there were twenty-eight Spanish merchants in England, close enough together in time and place (possibly all at one time in London) to buy together joint letters of safe-conduct from the new king, Henry V.[45]

Documentation is poor but it seems reasonable to conclude that the recovery witnessed in the last decade of the fourteenth century continued through the reign of Henry IV and into that of Henry V. It was then upset again by war. Henry's invasion of France prompted the Castilians to support the French at Harfleur, not surprisingly in view of the Castilian privileges there which might not (and in fact did not) continue under the English.

Henry's triumph in France, his recognition as Charles VI's heir, did not end Anglo-Castilian hostility because Castile supported the Dauphin and trade was interrupted when the Cortes voted money for a fleet to help him; but the forty ships promised operated only off the west coast of France, and English fears of a Spanish invasion in 1419 were ill founded, as were later ones in 1421.[46]

With the death of Henry V vigour left the military scene, and on the whole for the next forty years merchants could expect reasonably peaceful trading conditions under a series of truces and safe-conducts. Not until 1426 did Charles VII bother to send an embassy to Castile, and not until 1435 was the Franco-Castilian treaty confirmed; Charles' requests for aid in 1426 and 1428 met promises only, and a token in the form of a prohibition of trade with England.[47] This did indeed cause inconvenience to some Spanish merchants in 1429 since several found licences of exemption either expensive or difficult to buy, so that they could not use their English safe-conducts before the expiry dates, and their English guarantors were called on to explain why they were late, or had not been used to swell English trade and customs revenue.[48] But Juan was far from fully committed to the French cause and entertained English ambassadors in 1424, 1428 and 1429; and by 1430 reference was made to a possible renewal of Anglo-Castilian alliances.[49] In the event only a one-year truce was arranged to begin on 1 May 1431, and Juan wrote that he regretted he could do nothing more as he was still bound to France, but he offered to mediate between England and France.[50] By 1432 his representatives had also managed to arrange a two-year truce between the seamen of San Sebastián and Bayonne; the terms of the settlement show a determined effort to save trade from the ravages of war and piracy, with elaborate arrangements for hearing complaints in Fuenterrabía or St Jean de Luz and submitting difficult disputes to the Prior of St Mary's in Pamplona, and prohibiting attacks on neutrals within the approach waters to each port.[51]

At this point interest in diplomatic exchanges waned on both sides, partly because the Anglo-French war itself became desultory and no new moves were necessary, partly because it was clear that Juan was not going to support France wholeheartedly, partly because it had also become clear that he was not enthusiastic or strong enough to overcome his nobility's traditional preferences and break with France, and partly because Juan no longer needed to forestall a possibly Anglo-Aragonese alliance because he had arranged suitable truces with Aragon himself.

In 1441 trade was threatened again when Henry declared that he had evidence of Castilian plans to help the French against Bayonne and Bordeaux,[52] but there is little evidence of government enthusiasm for this and the presence of Juan's ambassador, Diego de Valera, in England in 1442 probably indicates a desire to prevent a complete breach:[53] it is quite likely however that some of the northern seamen were planning to take advantage of the war to despoil Gascon neighbours yet again. With peace re-established by the truce of Tours in 1444, Henry's government tried again to wean Castile to the English side in preparation for the next round of Anglo-French confrontation, but the ambassadors could achieve nothing more permanent than an Anglo-Castilian truce to last from 3 May 1448 until 31 January 1449 during which time reprisals were to stop and inquiries were to begin into unlawful seizures.[54]

Henry's fears of renewed French aggression were soon realised, but the renewal of the war showed how far Franco-Castilian co-operation had broken down, even if it had not yet deteriorated enough to allow an Anglo-Castilian alliance, and it also showed commercial rather than political consideration again coming forward. Juan II utterly refused to listen to the French request for aid, complaining of their unheralded breach of the truces which had led to his subjects losing ships at English hands; he also complained that the French had not helped him in his need; and he refused to allow reciprocal mercantile privileges for French merchants in Spain. The French ambassadors made equally bitter complaints to him, and the issue was aggravated by a dispute over the validity of safe-conducts issued by each side. Relations were further strained by the French failure to make good damages sustained by three Spanish ships which, happening to be at Bordeaux, had helped the French against Shrewsbury.[55]

After Juan's death in 1454 the Franco-Castilian treaty was renewed, but with modifications, and the irritations continued to increase. Safe-conducts were a bone of contention, and the Convention of Gannet of 1456 (about which little is known in detail) was meant to settle disputes in this field. The issue of safe-conducts was an important one in Anglo-Castilian trade because the English and Castilian sovereigns and their merchants had already evolved an effective and mutually beneficial system of trade under safe-conducts. The exchanges of up to sixty letters a year mentioned in 1410 had possibly been restricted by Franco-Castilian agreements of later years; certainly the adjustments in the treaty of 1454 decreed that the Castilians could give only twenty a year freely to the English, and after that they had to submit a list to the French for approval. Possibly it was this restriction which made the question of safe-conducts such a prickly one in Franco-Castilian relations.[56] The safe-conducts were not always honoured, but they offered a large degree of protection and also the legal right to damages if they were broken. The English kings at least made great efforts to uphold their value: Henry V made breach of safe-conduct a treasonable offence in 1414, and, although the act was repealed in 1435 because it was such a deterrent to English sea-keeping, it was re-enacted in 1450 when piracy reached a new peak.[57]

The safe-conducts issued by England were generally enrolled on the treaty rolls, or occasionally on the patent rolls,[58] and in 1441 it was enacted that all safe-conducts had to be formally enrolled to prevent forgeries.[59] There was no immediate increase in the Spanish numbers enrolled, nor in total enrolments, so the legislation seems to have been either badly enforced or unnecessary. There was a marked increase in the numbers of enrolled safe-conducts for Spaniards after 1455, owing possibly to an increase of trade as the Franco-Castilian links weakened yet further, possibly to increasing awareness of the use of safe-conducts after the discussions about them in the Franco-Castilian negotiations, but more likely to fears of violence and uncontrolled piracy in the Channel after England's loss of Gascony, and with her civil war at home.

The safe-conducts give some idea of the size of Spain's interest in England at the time. Although some may have been obtained simply to ensure safe passage past England to Flanders, they were an expensive method of protection[60] and for that it was probably safe enough to sail close to the French coast. Many were certainly used for voyages to England: in some cases at least the conditions of issue demanded this,[61] in others the ships can be traced coming to English ports, as when three Spanish ships for which safe-conducts were obtained in 1412 brought wine of La Rochelle into Plymouth in 1413,[62] and the Nicolas of Deva, with a safe-conduct bought in January 1413, sailed into London with wine the following May.[63] The safe-conducts enrolled in the Great Red Book of Bristol are those for ships then at Bristol and presenting their safe-conducts for inspection and record by town officials;[64] and when Spaniards were unable to use their safe-conducts their mainpernors were called on, sometimes years later, to establish why they had not been used.[65] Some merchants had to guarantee to unload all their goods in England,[66] others to unload enough to provide a stated minimum of customs and subsidy payments, which could be as high as £100;[67] checks were made to ensure fulfilment of the terms and the renewal for the María of Bilbao came only after William Soper had been asked what it had brought last time, and sworn it had been good for £49 of duties and would be worth more next time.[68] There is little doubt that the government intended safe-conducts to be used for English trade, to swell revenues for the Exchequer.

Statistics for trade cannot of course be taken from such a source: low numbers of enrolments do not necessarily mean little trade but may indicate reliance on truces, or willingness to run risks, and high numbers mean greater fears of violence, not necessarily more trade; moreover not all safe-conducts were properly enrolled in chancery, and although most used them in England, not all can be proved to have done so. None the less they indicate persistence and vigour on the route in the mid-century despite all political obstacles and economic troubles. The number of safe-conducts was fairly low in the early century,[69] but confirms regular contact in the years 1409–1416, which may be even greater as these were years of truce and safe-conducts really unnecessary. The war of 1418–22 clearly made safe-conducts impossible to get although clandestine trade may have continued—Devon men were allegedly well-disposed to Spaniards at this time.[70] The next decade was fairly active, and confirms the modest activity shown in the customs accounts for Southampton, Sandwich, Plymouth and London. The war of 1440–4 gave rise to an

Table 3   Safe-conducts enrolled for Spanish ships in the English Treaty Rolls, 1400–73.[1]

Date	Number[2]	Date	Number	Date	Number	Date	Number
1400	–	1419		1438	4	1457	22 (6)
1401	–	1420	–	1439	1 (1)	1458	18 (11)
1402	1	1421	–	1440	4 (1)	1459	9 (13)
1403	9	1422	–	1441	10 (3)	1460	6 (9)
1404	1	1423	2 (2)	1442	10 (11)	1461	21 (8)
1405	1	1424	6 (7)	1443	2 (17)	1462	31 (8)
1406	1	1425	10 (2)	1444	4 (8)	1463	10 (6)
1407	1	1426	10 (2)	1445	– (6)	1464	20 (1)
1408	–	1427	5	1446	3 (2)	1465	13 (2)
1409	9	1428	3	1447	– (3)	1466	15 (4)
1410	3? (1)	1429	3	1448	5 (1)	1467	11
1411	6	1430	10 (10)	1449	4 (2)	1468	–
1412	5 (5)	1431	4 (2)	1450	2 (1)	1469	–
1413	2 (2)	1432	11 (9)	1451	– (2)	1470	2[3]
1414	–	1433	10	1452	7 (1)	1471	2[3]
1415	3	1434	6 (6)	1453	9 (5)	1472	2[3]
1416	2	1435	– (3)	1454	5 (6)	1473	5[3]
1417	1	1436	1 (1)	1455	32 (5)		
1418	–	1437	–	1456	18 (19)		

[1] P.R.O. C76/84–157.

[2] The first number is that of newly enrolled letters, the number in brackets is of those still valid for nine months or more from previous years; thus in 1425 at least seventeen Spanish ships had safe-conducts to trade with England; several more might have a few weeks left to run.

[3] Few were given as these were years of alliance and only the very timid or those with very valuable cargoes would need an additional safe-conduct.

increase in safe-conducts instead of a stoppage as in 1418–22, which is an indication of how far commercial considerations had re-established themselves as Castilian friendship for France cooled. Over the next decade during truces and war the numbers are lower but steady and not apparently affected by the war of 1449–53, but then there is an upsurge in 1455, when over thirty ships a year might have safe-conducts.

No such enrolments deal with the Englishmen's trade in Spain, but presumably the Castilian rulers expected the sixty mentioned in 1410, or the twenty mentioned in 1454, to be taken up, and casual references in law-suits indicate Englishmen buying them. Robert Russel had one in 1423;[71] Davy Savage, factor for Soper, Fetplace and James of Southampton, was robbed of £500 of goods, imprisoned and asked for a ransom of £200 at Bilbao depite his safe-conduct;[72] and in 1449 John Hotot found his waved aside by a band of Biscayans.[73] Although the author of El Victorial complained that it was the English who were a warlike race and ignored royal safe-conduct,[74] the Castilians were not blameless of the same offence.

The English interest in the trade is partially reflected by the numbers of those between 1422 and 1440 willing to get safe-conducts for Spaniards and guarantee their good conduct.[75] About sixty per cent of the known guarantors were merchants and half of them came from London, merchants of Bristol and Southampton coming some way behind.[76] It seems reasonable to assume that these had business contacts with the Spanish merchants and seamen they sponsored, and since the position of guarantor could mean a risk of loss of a considerable sum of money and a certain amount of time, they probably expected to benefit from the ensuing trade, or from reciprocal action in Spain, or expected to be well paid. Their sponsorship implies good faith between this group of Englishmen and the Spaniards they helped, probably indicating regular contacts and that they knew each other well. The interest of the knights, gentlemen, clerks and others is less easy to understand, unless it was for monetary return, or they were members of the London Livery Companies providing contacts between the commercial and administrative worlds of the time.[77]

Other records confirm the persistence of the trade although its volume still cannot be estimated. In London, despite the activity implied by the sponsorship of Spanish merchants, the customs accounts show up little Spanish trade.[78] A few Spanish-sounding names turn up in several years; some of the iron and beaver skins imported probably came from Spain; some Spaniards, such as Alfonso Dies in 1437–8, shipped aboard Italian vessels; but not until 1456–7 do they show a Spanish ship tied up there, and not until 1462–3 do they show Spaniards to be frequent visitors.[79] Yet other records show the Spaniards constantly working there: some came overland from other ports, as did Francis Dyes who docked at Dover and came to London through Canterbury and Rochester,[80] or Alfonso Dies who journeyed back and forth between Southampton and London in 1443–4,[81] or Martín Ochoa and Antonio Ferández who unloaded their goods at Southampton and Sandwich and sent them up to London.[82] Some of those applying for safe-conducts were clearly already in London: Ochoa Darreveya went personally to Chancery and gave his own securities for a

safe-conduct for the *Nicolas of Bilbao* in 1425.[83] Mainpernors for two Deva
ships and another Spanish vessel successfully proved them to have been
in London in 1431 and 1432 by citing customs records now lost.[84] The
hosting returns for 1440 and 1443–4 show ten Spanish merchants in
London lodging with Riche and Chirche.[85] A Spaniard, Juan de Medina
born in Seville, took out letters of denization in 1454, but he may not have
been a merchant.[86] Sancho de Ordoigne had lived in Tower Ward from 1
September 1458 when he received his safe-conduct up to October 1459
when he claimed wines arrested as enemy merchandise, and had apparently no difficulty in finding substantial guarantors for £160 there in
Thomas Canynges, alderman and grocer and James Wells, draper.[87] Martín
Ochoa, active in his thriving business, was in London in 1459 when with
seventeen Londoners and two Italians he provided sureties for four
Genoese merchants.[88] The books of scrivenors Styfford and Thorp for 1457
and 1458 show some of the dealings of four Spanish merchants and one of
Navarre.[89] And the illegal trading activities of Francis Dyes while in
London show how far respectable London merchants were prepared to go
in breaking currency and trade regulations for their Spanish customers.[90]
Such indications, together with the number of Londoners willing to
guarantee Spanish good behaviour, and the casual references to English
activity in Spain—as when Thomas Acton applied for a safe-conduct for a
Spanish ship to get his goods home from Spain in 1438[91]—suggest a firm
and regular basis for the trade in the 1430s and 1440s, even if one must
accept on the evidence of the surviving customs records that it was modest
in scale; but it was a trade which was beginning to blossom in the 1450s.
    At Southampton too customs records indicate only modest numbers of
Spanish ships and men present but the contacts were regular, and were
probably supplemented with some English activity in Spain that does not
appear clearly in the records, which give no destinations or last ports of
call for shipping. There were at least four Spanish shippers there in
1424–5; four Spanish ships unloaded there in 1429–30; four more were
there in that year with the Spanish ambassador, and two English ships
brought large cargoes of iron belonging to men known to be interested in
Spanish trade and probably brought direct from Biscay. At least two
Spanish ships were there in 1432–3, two more in 1433–4 and two from
Deva in 1435–6. The accounts of 1437–40 and 1442–3 indicate a certain
withdrawal by Spaniards except as shippers on Italian vessels but there
was a Spanish ship in Southampton again in 1443–4, and also in 1447–8.
In 1448–9, 1450–1 and 1454–5 there were again only a few shippers on
Italian vessels, probably due to the disruptions during the Gascon war and
the civil wars, but from 1456 much more Spanish activity is evident; Juan
Pérez de Segura brings in his ship of San Sebastián, then the following year
there were four Spanish ships and in 1459–60 seven; in that year too, the
English ship *Le Glyn* seems destined for Spain.[92]

As with London supplementary evidence comes from other sources: mainpernors proved from now lost accounts that Antonio Ferández brought goods worth £100 in duties on a Portuguese ship and that Andrés de Burgous brought his ship of Motrico there in 1432.[93] The hosting returns show one and possibly three other Spaniards lodged with Emory in 1440–1, two others in 1443–4 and four in 1444–5.[94] Martín Sánchez de Valendis brought his goods in a Spanish ship to Southampton in 1444.[95] At least four Southampton men were mainpernors for Spaniards and three were active traders.[96] Davy Savage and John Clement of Southampton applied for a safe-conduct to get their goods home from Spain in 1432[97] and Antony de Kemade had strong links in Southampton and Andalusia in 1424.[98]

At Bristol the customs accounts are very disappointing compared with the survivals from Richard II and Edward IV's reigns but cases heard in the Exchequer concerning smuggling reveal shipments to and from Spain in 1419 and in 1432 when three sailings for Spain and one from were made by Spanish ships.[99] Henry Gardygan of Bristol was active in Spain in 1432–3[100] and there were a number of Bristol men helping Spaniards obtain safe-conducts and themselves holding licences to trade in Spain.[101]

For the lesser ports, Spaniards were still fairly regularly visiting Sandwich between 1430 and 1450, although not in great numbers and they were absent in 1433–4, 1436–7, 1439–40 and 1447–9; they were then, as in other ports, increasingly active in the next decade.[102] They were at Plymouth and Fowey in 1433 but were far more active there too from 1456.[103] Plymouth merchants themselves were also active in the trade again by 1454 when a group bought a safe-conduct to fetch their goods from Spain.[104] At Exeter, after trading regularly until the outbreak of war under Henry V, Spaniards withdrew completely and did not return until 1445–6; they withdrew again in 1449–55 to reappear in 1456 with the general expansion.[105] Exeter was either a port of peripheral interest, for which it was not worth running risks during times of political disruptions, or else the violence of some of the west country seamen during such times drove them away, and the merchants were not strong enough to protect their Spanish trade as in the larger ports.

The Butlers' accounts show similar trends. After a fairly busy period in 1414–16, Spaniards are absent from the surviving accounts between 1420 and 1440 but by 1456–7 were again engaged in bringing wines to London, Southampton, Bristol, Sandwich and Bridgwater in modest amounts.[106] They were not attracted back to Bordeaux even with truces to protect them until one arrived in 1444 and three more in 1448–9.[107]

On the whole this half-century offers a picture of modest trade; attractive and profitable enough to make many go to the trouble of buying safe-conducts with fairly onerous conditions. The most active centres were London and Southampton, with Bristol interested, Sandwich not out of the picture, Dartmouth men having to be restrained from continuing to trade even in wartime,[108] but the other west country ports finding Spanish trade somewhat slack.

Assessment of numbers involved or the value of the trade is not possible, as the information is so incomplete and almost all the trade in English hands escapes notice. Within the period there are clearly crises and disruptions, notably during the war years of Henry V's reign from 1416, and again at the loss of Gascony, but shortly after that, as the Franco-Castilian alliance lost its *raison d'être*, and Franco-Castilian irritations rose again to the surface, there was a sharp rise in Spanish activity in England, and probably of English in Spain, which leads straight into the expansion of Edward IV's reign.

The earliest years of the reign did not show a marked difference from the last ones of Henry VI's; violence was rife as Edward could not immediately restore the full force of royal authority, and Spain was still a French ally and no formal truce had yet been made. However, Spaniards continued to trade in London and elsewhere, and one, Juan de Consistorio, was to help victual Calais.[109] Not surprisingly they continued to buy safe-conducts for this trade in large numbers until the Anglo-Castilian treaty was ratified in 1467. Thereafter only in the rather unsettled period after 1469 did a few Spaniards, perhaps those of greatest timidity, or those with especially valuable cargoes, renew the practice. In these years (1461–7) for the first time considerable numbers of licences for Englishmen to trade in Spain were enrolled: there had always been a few of these but in the first nine months of Edward's reign (March to December 1461) fifty-eight Englishmen bought such licences and in 1462 a further twenty-five were issued.[110] Sometimes they were issued covering both Spain and France, which suggests that the reason for them was the new government's wish to monitor westward trade closely, particularly that with France where Edward's rival lived. These licences, like the safe-conducts, declined in number as peace looked more stable, and only for the brief troubled time immediately after 1470 did some men buy safe-conducts for ships of Gascony, Aquitaine, Brittany or Spain.[111]

Edward showed his determination to make alliance with Castile in 1463. He had just made a truce with France but no contemporary could have expected it to last for long so Edward followed the traditional pattern of wooing Castile, especially important in view of the fact that he was a usurper and France was ready to intrigue on behalf of Henry VI. Exchanges of ambassadors in the next two years culminated at last in a treaty of perpetual alliance made in 1466 and ratified in 1467—the first such treaty for over a century.[112]

This was a treaty with clear political objectives—the making of peace, and the promising of aid against rebels and enemies—but it also included very important commercial clauses. Merchants of one country were to trade in the other as if denizens of that country, with all the advantages and privileges of denizens. The most important aspect of this was of course the payment of lower customs dues and subsidies. The Spaniards in England no longer had to pay 2s on the tun of wine as other aliens did; they did not pay petty custom of 3d in the pound on their general imports and exports; they paid only 1s 2d on a broadcloth instead of 2s 9d, and similarly lower dues on cloth in grain; their cloth was not subject to extra subsidies on its value as was that of other aliens. They could also without let or hindrance lease their own houses, dispense with the supervision of English hosts and become brokers. These last three benefits were probably not as great as they might have been ten to fifteen years earlier as legislation curtailing alien activities had been less strictly enforced for some time. The English similarly paid lower dues in Castilian ports, but perhaps did not benefit from the terms as much as Spaniards because, as the French had complained in 1450, the ports of the Basque Provinces, with which the English did a considerable amount of trade, did not exact higher duties from aliens.[113] Also it did not save them from a general increase in local dues at Bilbao levied on all, although six Englishmen there in 1480 appealed to the terms of the treaty in an attempt to escape them.[114]

Enrique intended to have the treaty well observed and in 1468 and 1469 sent letters to the northern provinces ordering them to help the English against the French and forbidding their making agreements with French towns as this was against the treaty with England.[115] He was unable to fulfil his intentions: in April complaints were publicly voiced through the Cortes, which objected to such an alliance with a king who, they said, although magnificent and noble, had not a realm as powerful, old, and honourable as the French king's nor one potentially so advantageous.[116] Enrique gave in, negotiated with the French ambassadors and made another alliance with France that year. Edward's ambassadors, sent to Castile in March 1470, were unable to reverse the repudiation and in October Enrique complied with the terms of his new treaty and ordered his subjects to help France in restoring Henry VI to the English throne.[117] Edward did not publicly accept or acknowledge the repudiation; clearly the military clauses were inoperative, but the commercial ones were still honoured in England and orders to customs collectors exempting Spaniards from alien duties were never rescinded. The collectors were understandably confused about the position and those in Exeter and Sandwich, perhaps cautious men, tried to exact full dues from Spaniards in 1469,[118] but in other ports there was no such effort and the evidence of the enrolled accounts shows no such effort being called for.

With Henry on the throne Castile was again a friendly power and Henry graciously approved several appeals for restitution of goods lost at the hands of the English,[119] but Edward was soon back and persisted in behaving as if there had been no breach; in the orders to customs collectors

Spaniards were still to be charged as denizens, and, despite some confusion in 1473 when Southampton and Poole charged some as aliens,[120]
Edward never withdrew those instructions although he made no headway
in persuading Enrique to desert his French alliance. On the latter's death in
1474 his successors Ferdinand and Isabella were better disposed to England as France supported their Portuguese rival, and they renewed the
treaty of 1466 on 9 May 1475.[121] Negotiations for necessary reparations due
to piracy began in 1476 and the treaty was confirmed in 1477, although a
suggested marriage alliance between the Prince of Wales and Isabella, the
Catholic Monarchs' only daughter, were rejected.[122] However Ferdinand
and Isabella badly needed French peace and in order to obtain it they too
publicly repudiated the English treaty in 1478; but again this in no way
upset the Anglo-Castilian understanding. The attachment to France was
cool, since Ferdinand, as King of Aragon, still disputed with France over
Russillon and Cerdagne, but it was strong enough to withstand Edward's
overtures in 1479 and 1482.[123] However merchants continued to enjoy
their commercial privileges and few bothered to apply for safe-conducts,
trusting in the favour of the kings, and also in the Anglo-French truces
which covered most of this period. This honouring of commercial clauses
continued under Richard and Henry VII until the Treaty of Medina del
Campo carefully reversed them. The ease with which this was done is
surprising, but the Castilian monarchs soon realised to what they had
agreed and protested strongly, although vainly. That trade was not
affected by the reversal of the terms indicates the strength it had reached by
then.

As at other times when relations were basically good but subject to
periods of confusion, the Spanish provinces set about acquiring letters of
safe-conduct or protection for their merchants, presumably with the
approval of a benevolent Castilian government. On Enrique's first repudiation the provinces of the north coast from Guipúzcoa to Galicia negotiated
for their men a collective safe-conduct which began in March 1470.[124]
Guipúzcoa, Biscay, Old Castile, Asturias and Galicia renewed theirs in
1472, 1474 and 1475; Oviedo was mentioned separately in 1475; Seville,
the only southern area to take part in this practice, received a safe-conduct
for two years in 1472.[125] Once it became clear that Edward was permanently settled on the English throne and that he was adamant in observing the treaty terms and able to enforce their observance on a majority of
his subjects, these safe-conducts were no longer renewed. The English too
benefited from general safe-conducts: certainly Biscay and Guipúzcoa in
1474 and possibly others furnished reciprocal letters for English merchants visiting their areas.[126] Men of these provinces were given pensions
by Edward IV, perhaps for their negotiating such protection—these
included the provost of San Sebastián, and Sebastián de Olasabal, one of
the Guipúzcoan proctors, and the wealthy merchant Pedro Sans de Ven-

esse, who, with his son Juan, was granted £20 a year from the Bristol
customs receipts.[127] By 1481 the contacts between England and Guipúzcoa
had blossomed into a formal ten-year truce. There are references to earlier
leagues but these must be either the agreements of the fourteenth century
or the recent safe-conducts as no evidence has been found of a previous
truce in Edward's reign. The formal agreement was drawn up in London
on 9 March 1482 and besides guaranteeing free trade and prohibiting
armed ships of one area harming the ships of the other, it was agreed that
letters of marque given by the Castilian king against the English should not
be executed in Guipúzcoan ports and that those granted by Edward against
Castilians should similarly not be valid against Guipúzcoans.[128]

As if this were not enough to strengthen common ties and interests,
Edward showed further favour to certain Spanish merchants in his very
good terms for compensation to those harmed by the English, which
damage Edward persisted in treating as piracy rather than justifiable
aggression against an enemy. His compensation was granted in the way best
calculated to increase trade, it was to come from the customs and subsidies
they themselves paid in England, so that some merchants to all intents and
purposes traded customs-free. In December 1474 the Guipúzcoan proctors
had reached an agreement that Guipúzcoan merchants were to be allowed
11,000 crowns (less 600 already paid) by taking half the duties paid on
Guipúzcoan goods brought into England, and this was amended in August
1476 to include all Spanish goods coming to Southampton, Sandwich,
Bristol and London.[129] Individuals received similar grants: Pedro Neto in
December 1474 was to receive £200 from half the customs and subsidies of
all Spanish goods in Southampton, Sandwich and Bristol;[130] Juan López de
Ernyalde and Antonio de Olaysola in February 1475 were granted 1,000
marks on all Guipúzcoan goods brought to England, and were also allowed
to keep all customs and subsidies due on 4,000 quarters of corn for which
they had an export licence;[131] and Juan Pérez de Cantele of Bermeo
received a grant in November 1476 for 1,000 crowns from half the dues
from all Spanish goods brought through Dartmouth, Exeter, Plymouth and
Bridgwater.[132] Arnald Trussel of Bayonne who emigrated to San Sebastián also received a grant to trade customs-free for ten years to a maximum
of £100.[133] In 1481 after three years of negotiations a group of merchants
from Biscay received a similar grant of 5,000 crowns to begin once the
Guipúzcoans were satisfied.[134] They had eventually to wait some time
since John Payn's grant of 3,600 crowns from half the customs on Spanish
goods took priority over the Guipúzcoans' grant, when the Guipúzcoans
had received only £1,438, some £400 short of their total.[135] The Biscayans
were mollified by an immediate payment of £700 in part settlement.[136]
López's and Olaysola's compensation came in only slowly too but Olaysola and López's heir were granted cash payments in 1481 as final
settlements.[137]

Richard III followed his brother's policy of compensation through customs: Pedro de Salamanca received a grant on goods brought by men of Burgos, Valladolid and Medina to London and Southampton, and by Michaelmas 1485 had received £189 5s 7d.[138] A group of Spaniards with strong interests in Bruges and the Toulouse woad trade (Pedro de Salamanca, Sancho de Valmazeda, Diego de Cadagua, Pedro de Valladolid, Ferando de Carion, Martín de Ordogne, Alfonso Lyon, Gonsalis de Salamanca, Diego de Castro and Juan Pardo) received a grant of £250 on 20 August 1484 and, together with Martín de Maluenda, another of 400 marks in March 1485 from their customs in London and Southampton; they had been overpaid by Michaelmas 1485,[139] which may have been the cause of the accusation against Pedro de Salamanca that he had wrongfully kept some of the King's customs, for which he was pardoned in 1493.[140] Under Henry VII grants already held were honoured although no new ones were given, and only the group of Biscayan merchants seems not to have been fully paid, although their representative and his son received a personal grant of 8,000 crowns in 1485, of which £887 18s 7d was paid by Michaelmas 1488.[141]

This method of compensation seems a suitable and wise one, likely to increase trade by encouraging newcomers and maintaining the interest of regular traders by offering them customs concessions better than denizens' let alone other aliens'. However, although Edward's financial position may have made such anticipations of revenue essential, it seems to have been largely unnecessary for encouraging trade, as almost all those named in the grants of 1484–5, for example, can already be found trading through London, sometimes in large quantities, before 1484;[142] nor was the total amount of Spanish cloth exported from London boosted by it. Altogether in 1484–5, 1,721 ordinary broadcloths and some grained and half-grained cloth was exported under the grants, which was over half the cloth exported by Spaniards, but their total for that year was only 3,069 compared with 4,957 in the previous year and 4,976 in the following year when the grants had already expired. No doubt the grants were appreciated by the recipients and no doubt their interest in English trade was firmly maintained by them; no doubt too they were helpful in confirming the general conception of England as a country which welcomed Spanish traders and was willing to offer them good trading terms and generosity in their setbacks, but the particular terms of the grants themselves do not seem to have directly increased the trade, and the astute Henry VII saw no need to adopt his predecessors' perhaps over-generous methods.

The political protection and encouragement was very important in the trade, particularly as it came after a troubled period, and was bound to help stimulate a trade which was clearly complementary and profitable to both sides, but the expansion of the late fifteenth century was also part of a general European economic crest. Some old centres such as Bruges, some old routes such as the Italian ones in the eastern Mediterranean, some old commodities such as Hanseatic furs were in trouble by this time but other centres, routes and commodities were thriving and developing. This expansion of trade is particularly clear in England, where there is quantitative evidence lacking in so many other centres: English cloth exports began to rise some time between 1470 and 1480, while wool exports were still holding their own, and wine imports, although slower to expand, show a sustained increase after 1477.[143] Similar quantitative evidence is lacking for Spain, but all other evidence indicates increasing activity in traditional markets such as Flanders,[144] as well as vigorous exploration of new areas. Flourishing Anglo-Spanish trade was for neither area a symptom of energy being siphoned off from other areas, but part of an absolute expansion, with political and economic factors reinforcing each other.

The scale of Anglo-Spanish trade now must have surpassed that of the other two heydays under Edward I and Edward III although sources for the periods differ considerably so that no useful direct comparisons can be made. The customs records suggest that the value of imports by Spaniards in the late fifteenth century were much higher, possibly as much as a third or even a half higher, than previously, even allowing for inflation and lack of sources in the early period, and the English exports to Spain were vastly increased with the development of the cloth industry. The balance of the trade was more even, and this time not only was there great activity from Spanish merchants and shipping, but the English merchants and ships were deeply involved as well.

The Spanish privileges at this time provide the historian with a much clearer quantitative picture of some aspects of the trade although they obscure others. Spaniards no longer bought safe-conducts which provided such good information about the type and tonnage of their shipping; their wine trade disappeared from the Butlers' accounts as they no longer paid alien dues; their general trade with London disappeared from the accounts of petty customs collection, which were kept separately there from the subsidy rolls, and, since unfortunately the accident of time has preserved more petty custom accounts than subsidy rolls, details of their activity there are all too often unknown; but the specific isolation of their activities in other ports by collectors justifying their non-collection of alien dues from them partially compensates for this.

The Castilians' export of English cloth was becoming of major importance even by the death of Edward IV. Their exports rose from 2–4 per cent at first to 14–15 per cent of the total exports immediately before the treaty of Medina del Campo.[145] This did not make them as important a group as the Hansards, whose share rose from some 10–11 per cent up to 25–7 per cent, and to a peak of 38 per cent in 1487–8; but their rate of growth was about the same as their privileges and peace took effect, and these two groups between them took the lion's share of alien cloth exports. The Castilians were also particularly interested in the specialised exports of grained and half-grained cloth, virtually all of which went through London.

The amount exported by them was not synonymous by any means with the amount eventually reaching Castile for two main reasons: first the non-monopolistic form of Anglo-Castilian trade, so that many Englishmen and other aliens joined the Spaniards in taking cloth there, and secondly the strong Castilian links with Bruges, where several of those who were the biggest exporters from London and had favourable customs concessions traded heavily; no doubt some of their cloth was resold in Bruges where the Castilians might hope to undercut even the Englishmen's prices let alone those of their alien rivals, but most was probably sent to Castile. It is likely that there was a thriving triangular trade route similar to some of the Italians' routes, with Spanish shippers taking wool, woad and iron to Flanders and picking up a partial return cargo, then coming on to England to complete their cargo with cloth.

The Spanish wine trade was also worthy of serious consideration now: Spain itself was becoming a more important source of wine as the French trade was disrupted, but Spaniards also still carried wine of La Rochelle and Gascony. The figures for their wine trade are not as accessible as for their cloth trade, but in two years for which Spaniards were generally noted separately, 1474–5 and 1483–4, the Spanish merchants owned 19 per cent and 27 per cent respectively of the wine imports, and in other years, 1484–5 and 1486–7, enough of their trade was listed separately to indicate a considerable share. Most of their imports were through London and Southampton still, although occasionally Sandwich and Plymouth took moderate amounts.[146]

The value of their trade in merchandise other than wine and cloth varied somewhat from year to year and port to port but was on the whole modest when compared with that of the Hansards. However it should not be ignored, expecially when the essential nature of goods such as iron and wool-oils is considered. The figures for this trade are far from satisfactory and can give only a glimpse of a probable order of magnitude. First, they are incomplete, and become more so as customs collectors saved time and space by consolidating Spanish and English totals; figures for Sandwich and Southampton disappear early, and those for Bristol follow by 1485. Secondly, extensive estimates have to be made to reach any figures at all; the central figure is the recorded poundage, from which is deducted the value of alien cloth exports, and to which is added the value of Hanseatic goods which paid petty custom but not poundage. Thirdly, the figures include values for both imported and exported goods, and while tin, corn, hides and miscellaneous other goods were relatively unimportant in England's export trade compared with cloth and wool, they were exported by Englishmen and aliens other than Spaniards, who rarely took anything but cloth. Thus the values of Spanish goods are virtually of imports only.

Table 4 Spaniards' share of the value of miscellaneous goods (%) imported and exported from England, 1471–89.[1]

Date	London	Sandwich	Southampton	Poole	Exeter	Plymouth	Bristol
1471–72	–	2	–	–	–	3 (AT)	
1472–73	–	1	–	–	–	32 (AT)	13
1473–74	–	13	18	–	–	–	
1474–75	–	22	10	18	–	–	
1475–76	–	inc.		inc.		29 (AT)	
1476–77	4	–	9	inc.	15 + 12 (AT)	16 (AT) + 5 (JP)	
1477–78	4	8		–	13 (JP)	4	2
1478–79	3	2	1	7	11 (AT) + 6 (JP)	7 (JP)	–
1479–80	5	–	–	12	23 (AT) + 10 (JP)	3 (JP)	–
1480–81	5	inc.	inc.	4	4	8	2 (AT)
1481–82	5	11	inc.		–	inc.	10
1482–83	4	–	inc.		inc.	inc.	22
1483–84	11	inc.	inc.		inc.	–	15
1484–85	6	inc.	inc.	inc.	inc.	14	–
1485–86	inc.	–		inc.	inc.	9	inc.
1486–87		inc.	inc.	–		4	inc.
1487–88	inc.	–	inc.	3		inc.	inc.
1488–89	inc.		inc.	–	–	20	inc.

[1] P.R.O. E356/22, 23. (AT) and (JP) indicate goods carried under licences granted to Trussel and Pérez (notes 132 and 133). These were not necessarily Spanish goods or carried by Spanish factors. inc. indicates that Spanish trade is mentioned but included in a general total. A dash indicates that there is no mention of Spanish trade. A blank indicates a missing account, or (in the case of Southampton) years which are covered by the previous and succeeding accounts.

The figures do indicate something of the activity of Spanish merchants but not the role of the Spanish market in this miscellaneous trade, as they take no account of English owned goods imported from and exported there. The Castilians themselves, however, proved to be taking a very modest share of London's trade at 4 to 6 per cent, but made a bigger mark in the provincial ports where they might take 18 to 22 per cent as at Bristol, Sandwich and Southampton.

During this peak period London was without doubt the centre of the Spaniards' trade, dealing in the largest absolute amounts, and attracting the largest number of Spaniards. The 260 names occurring in the customs accounts during the reigns of Edward IV and Richard are over three times those found at Bristol, and over six times those trading through Southampton; moreover some of them were wealthy men handling cargoes much larger than their compatriots' at other ports.

Their ships were frequently there too: in 1471–2 of 160 recorded departing twenty-three were probably Spanish, in 1472–3 of 184 recorded thirteen were probably Spanish and a further eleven ships (six from the Low Countries, four English, and one Portuguese) took cargoes shipped entirely by Spaniards. In 1480–1 of 305 departures eighteen were Spanish and Spaniards exported on a further twelve ships; in May to July of 1483, of sixty-nine departures six were Spanish and five others took partial Spanish cargoes.[147] The number of Londoners actively concerned with overseas trade to Spain must have been at least twenty to thirty.[148]

After London, in the second rank, come Bristol, Southampton and Sandwich. Bristol saw most Spanish activity with one hundred Spanish shippers coming during Edward's reign, although of more modest fortune than those at London; and Spanish shipping was in a much more dominant position by the second half of the reign than at London: between April and September 1473 for instance out of forty-four arrivals seven were by Spanish ships and of thirty departures six were Spanish; in the same months of 1474 seven out of forty-two arrivals and four out of nineteen departures were by Spaniards and in April to July 1475 they accounted for twelve out of forty-seven arrivals and fourteen out of thirty-four departures. However from September 1479 to July 1480 of 123 arrivals only five and of fifty-two departures only five were Spanish, but there were very high numbers of arrivals from other English ports (twenty-two) and from Ireland (sixty-three), so that the Spanish share of continental trade was still great; in the account for the full year 1485–6 twenty-one out of a hundred arrivals (fifty-seven of which were from Ireland only) and nineteen out of seventy-nine departures (thirty-eight to Ireland only) were by Spaniards.[149] Their vessels by now were operating not only between England and Spain but also came in from Lisbon or Bordeaux and were supplementing the English voyages to Andalusia.

At Southampton some forty Spanish shippers were evident and several

Spanish ships might arrive in a year: between July and December 1464 five visited, and between September and May 1473 seven; in the year from Michaelmas 1487 ten, and possibly eleven, were Spanish.[150] Sandwich saw irregular activity: between September 1473 and November 1474 four out of eighty-nine arrivals were definitely Spanish ships and seven others had Spaniards' goods aboard, and of 43 departures one certainly and a further six possibly were Spanish. Between then and November 1475 six definite and three possible Spanish ships arrived out of 126 and four definite and three probable Spaniards departed out of sixty-nine; another three Spanish vessels were recorded at Faversham, and some Spanish merchants at Dover. After 1478 the Spaniards favoured Sandwich less, only one arriving that year, although two put in at Queenborough, and only two Spanish ships being recorded there in 1486–7 with a further two at Faversham.[151]

Plymouth and Exeter seem to have been overhauling Sandwich by now in Spanish eyes. Most accounts for Plymouth from 1456 show two or three ships there each year, and after 1478 between four and six a year called. Both Juan Pérez and Arnald Trussel used up much of their grants at Plymouth,[152] indeed Pérez's had, presumably at his request, been made applicable only to the four western ports of Plymouth, Exeter, Dartmouth and Bridgwater. Exeter too saw an annual scattering of Spanish ships from 1461 with as many as four in 1473–4, a number not reached again until 1483–4 when five came, and 1484–5 when seven put in; these local accounts probably all understate the trade, certainly that for 1480–1 does.[153] Expansion is visible too in other ports: at Chester the occasional Spanish ship or shipper importing wine or iron is recorded between 1464 and 1474, then from 1484 it became increasingly common for two, or three, or four Spanish ships to unload iron there;[154] other Spaniards began to visit the east coast again and reached Yarmouth and Hull.[155]

The English too were taking advantage of the general peace and special truces and agreements to trade in Spain. At least 180 Englishmen in the last decade of Edward's reign had cargoes shipped to and from Spain through Bristol and from two to ten English ships a year set out for or came from Spanish, usually Andalusian, ports. Chancery records, although unsuitable for numerical treatment, and self-selective in that they usually record when things went wrong, also show a great upsurge of information about English activity in Spain. The account of John Balsall shows them trying to break into direct African trade from Spain, as do the tantalisingly oblique references to their intended use of Sevillan pilots, and to their fleets off west Africa. By the end of Edward's reign there could have been found in all southern English ports men familiar with Spanish sailing conditions, Spanish customs and legal formalities, and the demands of Spanish markets.

Now that the Spanish trade was allowed to flourish freely, it not only soared but at last showed clearly both the changes from the thirteenth century and its complementary nature. Leathers and furs had gone for ever except for modest shipments of beaver. Iron and wine increased in importance with supplementary southern foods for the rich, and now immensely useful and large cargoes of southern oil and Toulousan woad and other dyes for the cloth industry were increasingly brought in return for finished and dyed cloth; Spain for England was the supplier of raw materials in return for manufactures.

Table 5   Comparative values of the import and export trades (to the nearest £) of Spanish merchants, 1472–89.[1]

Date	Imports	Exports
1472–73	330	3,216
1473–74	3,780	780
1474–75	8,727	3,458
1475–76	1,256	1,904
1476–77	4,403	2,438
1477–78	5,123	1,912
1478–79	4,173	2,604
1479–80	5,455	5,054
1480–81	6,881	6,274
1481–82	7,620	6,714
1482–83	6,466	5,570
1483–84	14,315	14,398
1484–85	8,470	8,644
1485–86	2,178	10,912
1486–87	11,232	5,770
1487–88	7,657	11,804
1488–89	988	15,918

[1] P.R.O. E356/22, 23. The figures must be viewed with great caution as indicators of the comparative import and export values of Spanish trade as a whole since values are only of those goods handled by Spaniards: English-owned trade is quite unrepresented. The import figures combine the stated values on which poundage was charged, and the value of wine imports, assessed at £4 the tun: poundage amounts are incomplete as often Spanish values were combined in one total with English and alien goods; they also include export values but as the Spaniards exported little but cloth, on which they did not pay poundage, this factor cannot greatly increase the inaccuracy among all the other estimates. The value of exports is of cloth; Professor Gray's estimate of £2 each has been adopted in the light of the few cases where cloth for Spain is valued in the customs accounts, although the market value was at least £3 and probably more.

The balance of the trade cannot be accurately assessed because of a lack of most of the necessary information and the large numbers of estimates demanded in the use even of the little we have. However, as long as it is remembered that they take no account of the complicated pattern of Channel trade, nor of the costs and profits of the shipping involved, simple comparisons can be made first of the values of goods imported and exported by Spaniards in all English ports between 1472 and 1489, and secondly of goods imported and exported by both Spaniards and Englishmen at Bristol between 1461 and 1487 on ships stated to be sailing to or from Spain. Such figures offer suggestions rather than conclusions, but indicate that the commodity trade was now reasonably balanced, with the balance probably beginning to tip in England's favour before 1490.

Table 6   Comparative values (to the nearest £) of the import and export trade with Spain at Bristol, 1461–93.[1]

Date	Imports	Exports
1461	463	643
1465–66	535	726
1469	246	40
1471	1,370	2,391
1472	390	–
1473	4,176	1,361
1474	2,661	436
1475	2,949	1,576
1476	537	957
1477–78	2,058	1,272
1479–80	1,992	2,258
1483	–	3,322
1485–86	2,605	4,406
1486–87	6,797	8,167
1492–93	9,267	6,838

[1] P.R.O. E122/19/1, 3, 4, 6, 8–11, 13, 14, 20/1, 5, 7. Only the last three accounts cover full years, some of the others cover a few months only. Details of their dates are as in Table 11.

Again caution is necessary in drawing conclusions: the trade is that by Englishmen and Spaniards stated in the accounts to be with Spain and no adjustments have been attempted to take into account (a) those goods such as woad stated to be from Spain but clearly from Toulouse; (b) goods on ships sailing to and from Portugal which may also have called in Spain; (c) the role of Spanish shipping in Portuguese and Gascon trade.

Cloth and wine are valued as in the previous table. Exports include, as well as broadcloths and others, a small amount of tin and a few hides.

Although the role of Spanish trade in the total volume of English trade cannot be assessed,[156] the Spanish connections were clearly valuable, with Spanish merchants exporting some 14 per cent of England's cloth and 60 to 70 per cent of her scarlets; and with between 4 and 11 per cent of

England's total cloth exports going to Spain through Bristol alone; with Spaniards providing or handling up to a quarter of England's wine, providing well over half and sometimes nearly all her iron imports and providing increasing quantities of oil and dyes.

This prosperity at the close of the medieval period was due largely to Edward's good sense and staunch determination to show friendship to Castile, and to the Catholic Monarchs' own determination to accept his overtures, although prudently remaining for a time formally allied to France. Edward's and Richard's reigns laid the firm foundations of tolerance, and mutual friendship and knowledge, on which Henry was able to build further, and negotiate both a new Spanish alliance and the marriage which Edward had wanted but failed to get. Henry was less generous to the merchants, depriving them of their customs privileges by restoring trading terms to those current thirty years before, before the treaty of 1466, and despite frequent representation from the Catholic Monarchs he refused to amend the clauses. However, that he was able to do this without in any way diminishing the trade simply serves to underline its strength, as does its continued growth in the face of his navigation laws.

Except for the development of the New World trade, the pattern of Anglo-Castilian trade under the early Tudors had been delineated centuries before, and its prosperity had been already promoted by the Tudors' predecessors. Given the general trade expansion of Europe in the early sixteenth century, and the close political relationships enforced by a political marriage, the English and Spanish merchants entered a period when they could expect nothing but a steadily increasing amount of trade on this route, steadily increasing intercourse between the two nations and a steadily increasing colony of each in the other's territory; none could have foreseen that after forty years or so of vigorous trade, religious and political rifts deeper than those of the fourteenth would turn rivalry to hostility and hatred, and turn the mercantile communities against each other as dynastic problems of the fourteenth century could never do. At the end of the fifteenth century it must have seemed that the years of insecurity were over, and that the trade of the English and Spanish merchants with each other and in the New World could do nothing but prosper in peace and goodwill.

NOTES TO CHAPTER 4

1   P.R.O. E30/255.
2   C.C.R. 1369–74, pp. 112–13.
3   C.C.R. 1369–74, pp. 277, 300–2, 307–8; C.P.R. 1370–4, p. 228. Merchandise originally Spanish but bought by and the legal property of Flemish merchants was returned to them; C.C.R. 1369–74, p. 385; C.P.R. 1370–4, p. 62.
4   Russell, *English Intervention in Spain and Portugal*, pp. 204ff; *Foedera*, III, ii, 1031–4, 1048, 1051–2.

5　Sherborne, 'The battle of La Rochelle and the war at sea 1372–5', *B.I.H.R.*, XLII (1969).

6　Russell, *op. cit.* pp. 500–7, 519–23.

7　See p. 85 and Table 9.

8　*C.C.R. 1369–74*, p. 488; P.R.O. SC8/10504; Russell, *op. cit.*, p. 182.

9　See Chapter 5, notes 117–19.

10　P.R.O. E122/16/15.

11　*C.P.R. 1388–92*, pp. 210, 382; P.R.O. 159/163 Recorda Trin. (Devon), 167 Recorda Mich. (Devon); E28/1, 27 Nov. 12 Ric. II.

12　*Foedera*, III, iv, 39–42, 44–5, 47, 74–6, 83, 85, 87, 95–8, 112–18; Russell, *op. cit.*, pp. 532–9.

13　See Tables 9 and 10.

14　See Table 20.

15　See Chapter 5, note 41; *Cal. Plea and Memo. Rolls of London*, III, pp. 194–7.

16　Nicolas, *Procs. and Ords. of the Privy Council*, I, 111.

17　P.R.O. C47/28/7(2); Hingeston, *Royal Letters of Henry IV*, I, 132.

18　P.R.O. C47/32/24. Two dated also from 1393 and 1399.

19　P.R.O. E175/28 (roll); an earlier document seems to be E101/43/1 giving the first three claims on E175/28, and three of those on C47/32/24 as well as French claims.

20　*C.C.R. 1402–5*, p. 57; *C.P.R. 1401–5*, p. 276.

21　*Foedera*, IV, i, 48, 61.

22　See Table 2.

23　Diez de Games, *El Victorial*, ed. Mato Carriazo; extracts about his particular desire to attack Poole as the home town of Harry Paye known to him as a ruthless despoiler of Spanish shipping are translated in *The Unconquered Knight*, ed. Evans, pp. 122–9.

24　*Foedera*, IV, i, 64, 65, 92; Hingeston, *Royal Letters of Henry IV*, I, 191.

25　Maza Solano, *op. cit.*, pp. 195–200. No source is cited for this document.

26　*Foedera*, IV, i, 156, 165–6, 168, 174, 180–1, 198–9, IV, ii, 67.

27　P.R.O. C47/30/9(8); the date of the letter is uncertain.

28　Nicolas, *Procs. and Ords. of the Privy Council*, II, 118–19.

29　P.R.O. E122/17/1, 4–6, 10.

30　*C.P.R. 1399–1401*, p. 520; *C.M.I.*, VII, No. 196.

31　*C.P.R. 1401–5*, p. 134.

32　Exeter City Library, loc. cust. accts., 3–14 Hen. IV, 1–4 Hen. V.

33　*C.P.R. 1413–16*, p. 36.

34　P.R.O. E122/139/4, 7.

35　*C.C.R. 1413–19*, pp. 13, 30.

36　P.R.O. E101/81/8.

37　P.R.O. E122/126/12, 14, 35–8, 127/1.

38　*C.C.R. 1399–1402*, pp. 52, 56.

39　*Ibid.*, p. 363, 367.

40　*C.C.R. 1402–5*, p. 206.

41　P.R.O. E122/72/4, 77/2.

42　*C.C.R. 1409–13*, p. 381.

43　P.R.O. E101/81/1, 3, 5, 8.

44　*Ibid.*, 184/19, 185/3, 7, 9, 11.

45　P.R.O. C76/96 m. 13.

46　Suárez Fernández, *Navegación y comercio*, pp. 96–7, app. doc. 20; Daumet,

Étude sur l'alliance de la France et de la Castille, pp. 74–6; C.C.R. 1413–19, p. 526; C.P.R. 1416–22, pp. 209, 270–1, 323–4.

47   Suárez Fernández, *op. cit.*, p. 100; Daumet, *op. cit.*, pp. 79–81, 85–6.

48   At least five failed to obtain Spanish licences: P.R.O. SC8/9064; C76/109 m.3, 110 m.10, 111 mm.3, 5; E159/205 Recorda Mich. m.25, 207 Recorda Trin. m.8d, 208 Recorda Mich. m.20 and Easter m.11, 210 Recorda Hil. m.9d, 214 Recorda Mich. m.32.

49   P.R.O. C76/110 m.4, 111 mm.1.6, 112 m.15, 113 mm.11, 12, 19, 20; Nicolas, *Procs. and Ords. of the Privy Council*, III, 319–21, IV, 30.

50   P.R.O. C76/113 mm.12–13; Daumet, *op. cit.*, p. 82.

51   Mugica, *Curiosidades históricas de San Sebastián*, II, 63–83.

52   Nicolas, *Procs. and Ords of the Privy Council*, V, 414–17.

53   P.R.O. SC8/13459; C76/125 m.15; he was on a general embassy to Burgundy, England and Dacia.

54   P.R.O. C76/127 m.2; C.C.R. 1447–54, p. 103; Suárez Fernández, *op. cit.*, app. doc. 28.

55   Suárez-Fernández, *op. cit.*, app. docs. 29, 30, 42; Daumet, *op. cit.*, pp. 89–90.

56   Suárez Fernández, *op. cit.*, pp. 117–18; Daumet, *op. cit.* pp. 95–101.

57   A summary of legislation on safe-conducts is given in the introduction to *The Great Red Book of Bristol* ed. Veale, pp. 5–7.

58   Examples of those not so enrolled can be found in P.R.O. E28/43, 44, 49, 73.

59   *Statutes of the Realm*, stat. 20 Hen. VI c.1.

60   Pedro Sans de Venesse promised William Isgar who obtained his safe-conduct £12 for every voyage made under it: P.R.O. C1/29/390.

61   P.R.O. E159/207 Recorda Trin. m.8d; these conditional clauses were not always recorded in the extract of the Treaty Rolls (in this case see C76/111 m.3) so may be much more common than appears.

62   P.R.O. C76/95 m.3; C.P.R. 1413–16, p. 36.

63   P.R.O. C76/95 m.2; E101/81/8.

64   *Great Red Book of Bristol*, ed. Veale, examples throughout volumes I and II of text.

65   P.R.O. E159/207 Recorda Trin. m.8d, 208 Recorda Easter m.11, 210 Recorda Hil. m.9d, 214 Recorda Mich. m.32.

66   P.R.O. C76/114 m.2, 124 m.22.

67   *Ibid.*, 109 m.3; E159/205 Recorda Mich. m.25.

68   P.R.O. E28/37(30) this appears to be during Henry VI's reign if compared with C76/124 m.22.

69   See Table 3.

70   C.M.I. VII, No. 552.

71   P.R.O. E28/43(25); C76/106 m.10.

72   P.R.O. C1/9/403.

73   P.R.O. E28/78 (24 Mar. 27 Hen. VI).

74   Diez de Games, *El Victorial*: extracts in *The Unconquered Knight*, ed. Evans, p. 182.

75   Before and after these dates details of the English sponsors are usually omitted.

76   P.R.O. C76/106—125. The occupations of the eighty-five mainpernors were as follows: merchants, 52; gentlemen 11; armigers, 4; clerks, 3; yeomen, 2; knights, 2; husbandman, 1; unknown, 10. The home areas of the merchants were as follows: London, 25; Bristol, 8; Devon, 5; Southampton, 4; Wiltshire, 3; Middlesex, 2; Somerset, 1; Kent, 1; Worcester, 1; Hull, 1; Lincolnshire, 1.

77   Miss Imray suggests that gentlemen made members of the Mercers' Company

were expected to use their contacts for the company's benefit: ' "Les bones gentes de la mercerye de Londres" ', *Studies in London History*, ed. Hollaender and Kellaway, pp. 166–7.

78 No provenance or destination for ships is given, which obscures some Spanish carrying trade, and all journeys by English ships to Spain.

79 P.R.O. E122/76/34, 77/3, 194/12, 14, 16, 203/4.

80 P.R.O. C1/22/119; this journey was made under his five-year safe-conduct issued in 1453, C76/136 m.14.

81 See Appendix.

82 See Appendix.

83 P.R.O. C76/107 m.3.

84 P.R.O. E159/208 Recorda Trin. mm. 3d, 8, 10, Easter m.10.

85 P.R.O. E179/144/45, 56; E101/128/30.

86 C.P.R. 1452–61, p. 199.

87 P.R.O. E159/236 Recorda Mich. m.3.

88 C.C.R. 1454–61, p. 332.

89 P.R.O. E101/128/36, 37.

90 See Appendix.

91 P.R.O. C76/120 m.2.

92. P.R.O. E122/140/62, 141/4, 21, 22, 25, 29, 31, 33, 35, 209/1, 8; Ms. S.P.B. 1429–30, 1433–4, 1438–9, 1448–9, 1450–1, 1454–5, 1455–6, 1457–8, 1459–60; *S.P.B. 1435–6*, ed. Foster.

93 P.R.O. E159/205 Recorda Mich. m.25; 208 Recorda Trin. m.10.

94 P.R.O. E101/128/31 m.9, 128/35; E179/173/105, 110.

95 C.P.R. 1441–46, p. 290.

96 P.R.O. C1/9/403, 16/656, 17/235.

97 P.R.O. C76/114 m.7.

98 Kemade or Kemate is described as of Southampton in 1424 when he and his brother John Gyles, living in Sanlúcar, obtain a safe-conduct for a Spanish ship, but as of Spain in 1432 when he obtains another and he then has two London mainpernors; P.R.O. C76/107 m.8, 114 m.2.

99 P.R.O. E159/197 Recorda Mich. m.14, 210 Recorda mich. mm. 34–5.

100 P.R.O. C1/12/51.

101 P.R.O. C76/93 m. 12, 108 mm.3, 5, 109 m.5, 110 m.9, 113 m.3, 114 mm.3, 6, 117 m.6, 139 m.4, 140 m.22.

102 P.R.O. SC6/895/13–15, 19, 20–3, 896/1–10; E122/127/18.

104 P.R.O. E122/113/3, 59, 60.

104 P.R.O. C76/136 m.11.

105 P.R.O. E122/40/30, 36; Exeter City Library, doc. cust. accts., *passim*.

106 P.R.O. E101/81/8, 12, 15, 16, 82/4.

107 B.L. Add. Ms. 15524; P.R.O. E101/195/19.

108 P.R.O. E28/83 (29 Aug. 31 Hen. VI).

109 P.R.O. C76/145 m.26; his letters were revoked because an enquiry showed he had preferred to stay in London doing his own business to going to Calais; *C.P.R. 1461–7*, p. 41.

110 P.R.O. C76/145, 146.

111 P.R.O. C76/156, 157, 158.

112 *Foedera*, v, ii, 140, 146.

113 Suárez Fernández, *Navegación y comercio*, pp. 200ff.

114 A. M. Bilbao, cajón 4, reg. 2, num. 68; A.G.S. R.G.S. 1480, fos. 86, 238; partly printed in García de Cortázar, *Vizcaya*, app. doc. No. 11, pp. 362ff.

115   Fernández Duro, La Marina, app. doc. No. 35; Soraluce y Zubizarreta, Historia general de Guipúzcoa, II, 174–5.
116   Cortes, III, 809–10.
117   Daumet, Étude sur l'alliance de la France et de l'Espagne, pp. 110–11, 114.
118   P.R.O. E122/40/11, 128/10.
119   P.R.O. C76/154 m.10; Foedera, V, ii, 180–2; Scofield, The Life and Reign of Edward IV, I, 553–4.
120   P.R.O. E122/142/8; E368/246 Stat. & Visu Mich. m.5.
121   Foedera, V, iii, 60.
122   Scofield, op. cit., II, 177–8; Foedera, V, iii, 73, 75–6; P.R.O. C76/160 m.17; 161 m.5; E30/559; B.L. Cotton Ms. Vesp. C xii, fos. 198–9.
123   Foedera, V, iii, 102–3, 117.
124   P.R.O. C76/154 m.10. Several individuals bought safe-conducts between the repudiation of March 1469 and the beginning of the general safe-conduct; C76/153 mm.3, 12, 14.
125   Ibid., 155 m.21, 157 m.2, 158 mm.2, 20.
126   B.L. Cotton Ms. Vespasian C xii, fos. 198–9, 205–6; P.R.O. E30/1661(1).
127   C.P.R. 1467–77, pp. 273, 422; ibid., 1476–85, pp. 258, 278, 323.
128   P.R.O. C76/165 m.15; B.L. Cotton Ms. Vespasian C xii, fos. 209–10; Foedera, V, iii, 117. Possibly the clause on letters of marque was stimulated by the vexatious litigation between John George and John Payn of Bristol and Pedro Ochoa of Deva; see Chapter 5, note 77.
129   C.P.R. 1467–77, pp. 480, 599.
130   Ibid., p. 474; he was fully satisfied by 1482—P.R.O. E356/22 m.10d.
131   P.R.O. C76/158 mm.4, 8; letters of execution were sent out in March 1475, C.C.R. 1468–76, Nos. 1389, 1422.
132   C.P.R. 1467–77, pp. 602–3; he was fully paid by 1480—P.R.O. E356/22 m.17d. He was probably a Frenchman from Cantal who emigrated to Spain.
133   C.P.R. 1467–77, p. 559; P.R.O. C76/155 m.12; he was fully paid by 1481—P.R.O. E356/22 m.10.
134   Foedera, V, iii, 106; C.P.R. 1476–85, pp. 208, 279; C.C.R. 1476–85, No. 765; P.R.O. E30/576, 577, 1291, 1383, 1410, 1698. Some of the merchants had had enquiries begun under Henry VI in 1470 (Foedera, V, ii, 180, 181; C.P.R. 1467–77, pp. 249, 317, 319, 353–4; P.R.O. C1/43/174–6, 46/334). Those who were unsatisfied and some new plainftiffs approached Edward in 1478 (P.R.O. E30/1416, 1693) and agreement was reached in 1481.
135   C.P.R. 1476–85, pp. 271, 330; P.R.O. E356/22 m.38d.
136   C.P.R. 1476–85, p. 248.
137   Ibid., p. 277.
138   C.P.R. 1476–85, p. 449; P.R.O. E356/22 mm.40, 47d, 23 m.36.
139   C.P.R. 1476–85, p. 531; P.R.O. E356/22 mm.40d, 72d, 23 m.36.
140   C.P.R. 1485–94, p. 418.
141   P.R.O. E356/23 mm.36d, 41d, 42, 42d.
142   P.R.O. E122/194/23–6, 162/5.
143   Carus-Wilson and Coleman, England's Export Trade, pp. 123, 139; James, Wine Trade, appendix 6.
144   The water bailiff's account for Sluys in 1486–7 shows that thirty-three out of the seventy-five ships there were Spanish: fourteen (1,840 tons) brought wool and iron, eleven (1,370 tons) wine and fruit, four (565 tons) brought oil, and four (526 tons) mainly salt; Gilliodts van Severen, Inventaire, VI, No. 1221.
145   For details of the cloth trade see Chapter 3.

146   For details of the wine trade see Chapter 4.
147   P.R.O. E122/194/19, 20, 24, 25, 162/5 (which is the control for 194/26).
148   See Chapter 7 for details of the English and Spanish merchants engaged in the trade.
149   P.R.O. E122/19/10, 10a, 11, 14, 20/5.
150   P.R.O. E122/142/3, 8, 10.
151   P.R.O. SC6/896/13, 14; E122/128/14, 15, 16, 129/3.
152   P.R.O. E122/113/59, 60, 114/1, 2, 4, 7, 7a, 9, 10, 11, 13, 16, 162/7.
153   Exeter City Library, loc. cust. accts. 1 Ed. IV–1 Hen. VII; P.R.O. E122/41/6.
154   *Chester Customs Accounts*, ed. Wilson, pp. 32–5.
155   P.R.O. E122/62/7, 152/11.
156   Too many estimates have to be made to make tabular detailed information worthwhile, but the total value of Spanish trade in and out would seem to amount to roughly between 6 and 15 per cent of the value of England's total import and export trade in the first decade of HenryVII's reign.

CHAPTER 3

Complementary markets *I*
England's exports to Castile

The goods exchanged by the two countries and the markets each offered for the absorption of the other's goods make the obvious starting point for the detailed analysis of their trade, as they show how attractive this was to merchants and on what its vitality rested. The encouragement of kings, and adequate supply of shipping, the existence of able and adventurous mercantile communities were the means by which the trade could develop and prosper and were enormously important, but without the sound underlying economic attractions of complementary markets they would have been of very limited use. England and Castile found one another's markets so useful and profitable that a hundred years of unsettled and often hostile political relations severed the direct trade for only a decade. Despite land wars, naval engagements, and uncontrolled piracy the trade persisted, developing and changing in response to changing conditions and flourishing whenever periods of truce and peace allowed.

The attractions for each were several. To Castile England offered a useful combination of essentials—fish, beans, or corn when local harvests were poor, and woollen cloths of several sorts from expensive scarlets and good broadcloths to modest kersies and kendals, and inexpensive Cornish cloths. Several of its major ports, and particularly Southampton, Sandwich and London, were sited on or very near the main Channel route to the other great cloth producers in the Low Countries. In the early fourteenth century, and again by the later fifteenth century England had a total population of perhaps three million people and at least one major city in London, with its population of about thirty-five thousand; this was fairly small when compared with the Low Countries, with several cities of that size and bigger with hinterlands stretching from the Baltic to Germany, but England offered a compact and relatively well ordered and governed society with a fairly large group in the population able to buy imported goods. Internal communications by road and water were good and the distribution of Spanish goods to a reasonably wealthy aristocracy, to prosperous merchant and landed groups, and to a growing industry was smooth. At fairs, and then at the ports, the Spaniards could find an able merchant community backed by relatively firmly established and centralised legal and administrative systems on which they might call if necessary.

To England Castile offered a wide variety of goods; the earliest sent were from the northern and central regions, a little wool, yarn and cloth, far more wines, iron, furs and skins; then when the south was conquered were added some manufactured goods from Moorish industries, yet more wine, quicksilver, fruits, dyes and the oil which became increasingly important as the English cloth industry grew. Moreover in the early period the Spaniards had adequate shipping to carry the trade themselves, yet did not develop any monopoly to exclude the English when they began to transport their own goods. As a selling market Castile was ideal for England's cloth industry: her total population of perhaps three millions in the thirteenth century and four and a half in the late fifteenth[1] was not large for her size, but was much bigger than Portugal's, the other Iberian kingdom easily accessible to the English. Castile had a wealthy aristocracy, given like others in Europe to conspicuous consumption, and a considerable number of big towns, especially in the south where prosperous ruling hierarchies were swelled by rich Italian merchants: all could afford foreign cloths. Several of these main towns were easily accessible by sea or within easy reach of the coast so that visiting merchants had little difficulty in prosecuting their business quickly. Castile had little cloth industry of its own so wanted both luxury and medium quality imports. Internal stability and organisation were less good than England's but royal protection was offered to merchants, and the local nobility too might offer local protection in the interests of their personal rents and dues, as did the Dukes of Medina Sidonia at Sanlúcar.

While such goods could be exchanged there was little danger of conflicting economic interests and the rivalry and competition if not outright conflict that might be expected since both were major wool producers and sold much of their output in Flanders and Italy did not occur. Little raw wool was ever exchanged and few merchants participated in the other's wool trade.

In the thirteenth century for instance, Martín John of Spain had apparently just one sack of wool at Southampton in 1265[2] and when the embargo on English wool exports to Flanders was in force from 1271 few Spaniards obtained licences for export: four did so for ninety-two sacks in 1271,[3] two for an unspecified amount in 1272[4] and six for 160 sacks in 1273 when licences were issued for 32,743 sacks altogether.[5] One further licence was given in 1277 for Pedro de Mundenard to export fifty from Boston and fifty from London.[6] The surviving customs particular accounts confirm that the Spaniards took almost no part in the trade, as no more than five possible Spaniards have been found between 1290 and 1310 exporting altogether sixteen sacks and sixteen cloves.[7]

Examples become even rarer after this time: thirty sacks were allowed to Pedro Guillelmi of Seville for export from Bristol in 1353 as long as he took it to Seville and not Flanders,[8] and the safe-conduct granted in 1403 to

Ochoa Sanzes de Placencia, master of the S *Pedro* noted that the cargo he took would include wool.[9] Other cases occur of Spaniards having wool in England [10] but some were the result of their claiming back Spanish wool stolen from them as they sailed to Flanders,[11] and the 112½ sacks exported from Southampton in 1475 under licence granted to Arnald Trussel then living in San Sebastián were probably meant for Italy.[12] Some of the Spaniards living in Bruges however dealt in English wool from Calais; Juan de Lopez was one of the Celys' best customers, often paying them through Pedro de Valladolid in London, and they also had business dealings with Diego de Castro and Gomez de Sorio,[13] but most were probably too busy dealing in their own wools.

As transporters Spaniards were useful at times for carrying English wool from England or Flanders to Italy. The Genoese fleet was adequate for their normal needs but as it did not run to a regular schedule like the Venetian state fleet and, as occasionally large amounts had to be shifted in a short time, sometimes none of their vessels was available and the Genoese used whatever was at hand. The Castilian shipping suited them admirably as the seamen were experienced on Atlantic and Mediterranean routes. In 1353 they probably needed to move more wool than usual following their customs-free export grant and they hired ships with masters from Guetaría, Bermeo, Castro Urdiales and Santander.[14] Again in 1394 some of the Genoese in London used a Spanish ship for their wool.[15] The Florentines had no navy until the taking of Porto Pisano in 1406 and until then were entirely dependent on others' shipping, usually Italian. In 1337 when the Bardi and Peruzzi societies had exceptionally large consignments of wool following their financial dealings with Edward III they were deprived of Genoese shipping since Genoa was an ally of France, and of Venetian since Venice refused to run her fleets north because of war dangers, so they fell back on Spanish shipping with masters from Bermeo, San Sebastián and Santander. Some merchants of Bilbao also felt it worth acquiring letters of protection for trading in Lombardy either at the instance of the Italians or because they could see for themselves the possibilities there.[16] When Florentine sailings ceased at the end of the fifteenth century the Spaniards again helped carry their English wool.[17] In carrying English wool from Flanders too the Spaniards enjoyed the support of the English growers who complained in 1344 that they were losing money because the ruler of Flanders had stopped Lombards, Genoans, Catalans and Spaniards from exporting English wools from Bruges.[18]

Any real hostility over wool was prevented by the timing of the rise and decline of Spanish and English wools on the international markets, and by the very different characteristics of the wool.

Spanish wool was exported towards the north from the twelfth century onwards[19] but the amount was modest and probably remained low until the conquest of the central uplands in the thirteenth century and the organisation of the Mesta, which received its major early charters in 1273 and 1276. It is highly unlikely that its production came anywhere near England's, which was running at between twenty-five and thirty-five thousand sacks a year for export at the turn of the thirteenth and fourteenth centuries. Unfortunately the lack of customs or similar records in Spain prevents assessment of the amounts produced for export, and its import at its destinations is little better attested. England's highest import of Spanish wool was in 1308–9 when 269 sacks and 298 bales entered Southampton, but England was a minor market and soon stopped taking any at all.[20] Lack of records in France and Flanders make it impossible to trace the stages by which the Spanish wool trade developed but its export seems to be modest until the mid-fifteenth century when it began to appear with more regularity in Brittany,[21] Dieppe and Rouen,[22] and La Rochelle.[23] Even in Flanders, despite frequent references to its presence, the records for 1484 show only 150,000 kilograms sent to Sluys[24] (the equivalent of no more than some 906 English sacks), while England was still sending 8,500 sacks annually to Calais. By 1486–7 half the Spanish ships arriving at Sluys (fourteen estimated at 1,840 tons out of a total of thirty-three making 4,301 tons) carried wool, but the exact amount is unknown as all carried iron in their cargoes too.[25]

Dr Munro's recent work on Burgundian trade confirms this picture of the relatively late arrival of Spanish wool in any quantity.[26] Clearly it was simply filling the gap left by the steady withdrawal of English wool and no rapid expansion occurred which actually pushed English wool out and caused anger in English growers.

The decline in English exports is clear after 1365: the embargoes, seizures, bankruptcies and high taxes damaged the trade but it was strong enough to recover, had not English cloth makers found the conditions stimulating. From the 1360s the rise of English-made cloth for export is marked despite temporary setbacks in about 1370 and in the mid-fifteenth century and increasing amounts of raw wool were withdrawn from Europe. England's total wool production was no doubt less than before 1350 but it was sufficient to keep the wool-growers, clothmakers and merchants satisfied and comfortably prosperous, and none at that time indicated that they felt in any way squeezed by Spanish production; Spanish wool was simply filling a gap left by England's changing trade.

The differing characteristics of the wool also prevented too much direct competition for the same buyers. Although English wool had several varieties, much of that exported was of good quality and wanted by makers of the finest textiles. While Spanish wools too included various grades they were usually less good than the English throughout the period and despite their widespread use it was not until the sixteenth century that improvements made English observers begin to worry.

The Spanish wool brought to London in the thirteenth century was the poorer sort used by burellers, chaloners and chapellers[27] and the cloth workers of France and Flanders considered it on a par with Scottish, Irish, Dutch, Flemish and northern English wools.[28] The changing character of the Flemish industry in the fourteenth century with a decline in the high-grade cloths produced reflects a change in the wools available as well as the decline in techniques with the move to the country areas.[29] It is clear too that the Italians, while still buying Spanish wools, wanted the more distant English wools despite their cost; the Datini papers indicate that Spanish wool at the end of the fourteenth century cost only a third of English wool, in the fifteenth century Pisan customs valued Spanish at half the English, and Spanish woollen cloths were reported to be worth one-sixth of those made from English wool.[30] Clearly the English must have justified the cost by offering better quality.

Improvements were encouraged by the Mesta, and the introduction of the north African merino sheep, which does not seem to have appeared in effective numbers before the mid-fourteenth century,[31] made careful cross-breeding possible, but quality improvement was a slow business and it was a long time before Spanish wool was a substitute for the best English wools.

The main disadvantage of Spanish wools, apart from the fact that the reddish or darkish wools probably made dyeing in clear light colours more difficult, was, as the writer of the 'Treatise concerning the Staple' reported, that the short wool produced less durable cloths than the finer, softer, and more easily felted English wool: 'the wolles of Spayn are of such kynds without the wolles of England be myxed with, it can make no clothe of it self for no durable weryng, to be nother reisid nor dressid, by cause it hath no staple'. However he conceded that, although 'In short tyme the wolle shall were awey unto the likness of worstedd', it did make fine-looking cloth which could sell at 12s or more the yard, and a mixture of the two wools 'makith such cloth that will tak a shynyng glosse with forcibly pressing, plesaunt to the jie, by cause the Spaynysh heyry woll kepe the pressyng, wher English woll of fyne staple will not'.[32]

The wools were mixed from a very early date and some of the early English restrictions on the use of Spanish wool were meant no doubt to prevent fraud against buyers wanting good hard-wearing cloths. The Ordinances of the Andover weavers denounced its use in kersies in 1262[33] and the Ordinances of the London weavers in 1300 showed a similar concern: the two wools were not to be worked together, and only Spanish wool was to be 'teynt en blecche'.[34] This last may be because occasional faulty balances of tannic acid and iron sulphate in some black dyes weakened fibres.[35] The London weavers were not scrupulous about obedience to the ordinances, and complained that the ordinances were out of date when they were accused of mixing the wools and an enquiry was held in 1321.[36] Since imports of Spanish wool disappear from about this time, and it seems on the few occasions it reaches England to be virtually unsaleable, the practice of mixing the wool here must have disappeared, but it continued elsewhere. The writer of the *Libelle of Englyshe Polycye* remarked on it in Flanders:

> . . . as in cheffe
> The wolle of Spayne hit cometh not to preffe
> But if it be tossed and menged well
> Amonges Englysshe wolle the gretter delle;
> For Spaynesche wolle in Flaundres draped is
> And ever hath be that mene have mynde of this.
> And yet woll is one the cheffe marchaundy
> That longeth to Spayne, who so woll aspye;
> Hit is of lytell valeue, trust unto me,
> Wyth Englysshe woll but if it menged be.[37]

The writer of the 'Treatise concerninge the Staple', about a hundred years later, subjected the practice not only to scrutiny but also to disapproval. In his view English wool should have been worked at home to provide work for Englishmen and he remarked that the 'English wolle myxid with Spaynysh wolle makyth soo great quantite of clothe that distroyth the sale of all English cloth' and again that 'all the Dowch tong, havyng our English wolle at ther pleasure, with Spaynysh wolle doth drape great quantite of cloth, which they sell in hurtyng the sale of English cloth'.

He makes it clear that at last some Englishmen were aware of Spain as a rival and competitor in the wool trade because her wools had improved in quality and increased in amount: 'now of late years peple comonly reportith: Spaynysh woll is almost as good as English woll, which may well be soo, by that Spayn hath housbondid ther wolle from wurse to better, and England from better to wurse, which must nedes cause theym the nygher to accord to oon godnes', 'albeit Spayn hath bettrid ther wolle by shifting of leirs and by housbondry, and within a fifty yers hath encreasid so moche wolle, which by a staple holden in Brugge in Flaunders sellyng six tymes more now than of old tyme'. While disagreeing with the Staple in their export of raw wool, he notes as one point of their defence: 'that Spanysh wolle is so encresid to fynes, goodness and so great plenty, that withowt they holp to sell our English wolle, elles non other reame shuld have nede to bye it in England'.[38] Following this acceptance that they had improved their wool he still notes that it was of a different sort from English long stapled wools which were still superb, and certainly Italian buyers agreed with him on that well into the sixteenth century.[39]

Thus until the sixteenth century there was little fear by the English of the Spaniards usurping their markets, their declining exports were of their own choosing, and their best wools were still essential to top-quality industries. On the only occasion when the English seem to be critical of Spanish wool in Flanders in petitions of 1420 and 1421, closer inspection shows they were concerned with interference with the cloth trade. Complaining that the sale of Scottish, Aragonese, Catalan, and Spanish wools there in increasing amounts was depressing English wool prices, they referred to an agreement whereby the Flemings agreed to buy only English wool, as long as the English did not send their cloth to Flanders. They demanded that the Flemings obey the agreement or allow the sale of English cloth and the emphasis of the petition and the royal reply that the king would ask that cloth be sold there indicate that it was the cloth merchants rather than wool merchants who were the real objectors to Flemish policy.[40]

If the European raw wool trade had only negative importance to Anglo-Castilian trade, the cloth trade had enormous positive importance. For her great variety of exports Castile wanted one main cargo from the northern countries—cloth. From Flanders and England (and also Italy) she absorbed large amounts, and the exports sent by England to Castile, as to all Iberia and the Mediterranean, were overwhelmingly cloth.

The types and qualities of the English cloth sent to Castile varied widely, particularly in the later part of the period. In this we see the main difference between the thirteenth and fifteenth century exports: in the early period they were restricted in type but the later English industry provided almost any type of woollen cloth which could be in demand on the Peninsula.

The thirteenth-century records are scant but are enough to show that Spain received far less variety in English cloth than in Flemish. A Castilian price-fixing list of 1268 referred only to English black cloth, English *pardo* (a dusky grey or brown), English grained cloth, and Lincoln scarlet out of forty-three varieties mentioned, of which eighteen came from the cloth-making areas of the Low Countries and north-eastern France, and twelve from local Spanish sources, with Segovia and Avila specifically mentioned.[41] In terms of quality the English cloth was good: the Lincoln scarlet at 5 *maravedís* the *vara* was the second most expensive, after Montpellier scarlet, and the English grained cloth at 3 *maravedís* also came among the six most expensive.[42] The black cloth came fairly close behind in the next dozen which cost between 10 *sueldos* and 2½ *maravedís*, and the *pardo* fell within the next dozen which cost between 6 and 10 *sueldos*; even this was higher than most of the Spanish cloths which made up eleven of the cheapest twelve cloths (costing under 4 *sueldos*).

The cargo stolen from Spaniards off the east coast of England in 1272 also refers to scarlets: scarlets and 'other cloths' from Stamford, Beverley, York, Louth, Northampton and Lincoln were taken.[43] The few Castilian customs accounts which cover a few northern ports for some months in 1293 show only three sorts imported—six pieces were black cloths costing 250 *maravedís* each, which put them in the fairly although not most expensive category, four were cheaper white cloths and one piece was vermilion.[44] At least twenty-five other areas, mostly Flemish and northern French, sent cloth. The tariff list for the Cuatro Villas for the late thirteenth century listed only one type of English cloth—the highest quality stamfords which might be dyed or undyed. It also listed twenty-five other towns and areas from which cloth came, all in France and the Low Countries and noted sixteen other types of cloth.[45] The emphasis in these documents, few as they are, is always on England as producer of top-quality cloths but in very small amounts compared with the Low Countries and France. The early English customs accounts add little to the picture: in 1303 Andrea Piers (possibly Andrés Pérez de Castrogeriz) and Dongarsea de Burgh' exported from Boston one cloth in grain, six in half-grain and fifty-three without grain. The grained cloths would be in the expensive range, but the ungrained cloth might have been costly black stamfords, or cheaper straits. The amounts for these two merchants were fairly high, but Spaniards appear only rarely in other customs accounts exporting cloth, so total amounts were probably low, as the Spanish records suggest. The provenance of the cloths is still the eastern urban centres as the robbery of 1272 indicated, such exports as are known being from Boston, London and Sandwich, and none at all from Southampton or Bristol.[46]

Castilian trade reflects, not unexpectedly, the subsequent developments of English industry: by the later fourteenth century change is apparent and by the later fifteenth complete. While top-quality cloths still found a ready market in Castile a wide variety of types and colours, dyed in a wide array of colours, had been added to them, and the trade had shifted from the east coast to the south and south-west.

This change is not wholly apparent in the earlier Castilian documentation. The price-fixing list of 1369 still mentions only three English types, but all this time among the cheaper categories.[47] English burnet and *inglés de las mayores* fell among the lower-medium-priced cloths costing 40 *maravedís* the *vara*, and *ingleses menores* were one of the cheapest at 20 the *vara*. In the same list scarlet from France and the Low Countries was priced at 90 to 150 *maravedís* the *vara* and most of the other cloth from the Low Countries (much of it burnet) cost from 50 to 100 the *vara*. The low cost of English burnet possibly indicates by how much English manufacturers could undercut those of Louvain or Ghent, the burnet of which was priced at 60 *maravedís*, but the greater difference between it and burnet of Douai at 80 *maravedís*, must be due too to a difference in quality.

English records of the same period are more informative: licences issued in 1364 permitting merchants to bypass the Calais staple for direct exports to Castile noted exports of Devon straits called 'Backes', Essex straits, and Cornish and Somerset cloth.[48] Later they show even more variety. A Spanish ship arrested in 1414 carried large cloths, dozens, dozens of straits called blankets, and worsteds;[49] and the customs records, although collectors often translated all cloths into equivalents of cloths of assize for accounting purposes, also show some of the rising variety. Welsh backes, straits and frieze cloth left London, Exeter and Southampton as well as Bristol; west country cloths—westrons—were carried through Southampton and London too, as well as Bristol; rolls of Exeter cloths went through Bristol; Bridgwater sent Taunton straits, Barnstaple dozens, Bridgwater straits, osetts and dozens; kendals, kersies, and white Southampton straits also found their outlet at Bristol and probably some of the Irish cloth found in Navarre had its outlet through that port. Cornishmen sent Tavistock cloth down to Huelva.

Most of this is evidence of supply rather than demand, but since the trade prospered, the English and Castilian agents and merchants must have been reading the demands of their markets correctly. Not only did merchants take cloth as pure speculation but it was also ordered from associates who knew exactly what was selling best in their locality. Few letters with such orders or information survive, and only one for this branch of trade, which makes it all the more interesting: in 1470 Juan de Medina of Lepe, near Huelva, wrote to Juan Seboll of Burgos in London and asked him, if he were going to send more cloth, to make them 'ferretes e quartillas de bys batera fynas e cordellates buenos e papeles e gays', a contemporary translation of which was 'musterdevillers and streyts of byswate fyne and good carseyes and white russett and grene gays'.[50] Clearly the narrower cloths of Bridgwater and coarser kerseys and russetts could find a good everyday market alongside broadcloths in Andalusia. The translation of 'ferretes', which means brass-coloured, by 'musterdevillers' is interesting as it indicates that even if the origin of the word is to be found in a place name—Muster de Villiers[51]—it had come by the fifteenth century to be associated with a particular colour by Englishmen.

Most cloths were sent out expertly dyed and finished ready for the tailor, and the English dyers, no doubt strongly encouraged by the merchants, showed themselves ready not only to copy foreign originals but also to experiment with shades to please the customer, and they could offer a wide range of shades.

Customs accounts give little information on dyes, as all the collectors were concerned with was whether or not the dyers used grain, in which case the cloth fell into a higher duty category. Other records are fuller: the Spanish ship arrested in 1414 had loaded cloths dyed red, murrey, black, green and blue (both bluet and plunket)[52] and John Balsall sold blue, red and dark green cloths in Andalusia in 1480–1 with blue apparently the dominant colour (of the twelve cloths of recorded colour eight were blues—one sad blue drab, three sad blues, and four plunkets).[53]

The accounts of cloth bought for the Navarrese royal household provide a detailed picture of the colours sent there and colours sent out to Castile may well have been very similar.[54] Bristol cloth provided the widest range with three shades of red (*rojo*, a plain red, *bermejo*, nearer vermilion, and *granza*, a tomato red dyed with madder), purplish-red murrey and a dark murrey; plain green, light green and dark green were sent and at least four shades of blue (azure, perse, dark perse and light perse); experiments produced violet and turquoise too; most of the English burnet came from Bristol, dark burnet was sold too, and grey and two intensities of black (the *prieto* probably less intense than the *negro*); there was also white, a little scarlet and some medley cloths. London colours were fewer: the three shades of red, green and light green, occasionally azure, often black, some grey; but it sent also most of the English scarlet cloth, indicating that already at the beginning of the fifteenth century London was the centre for expensive dyeing and finishing.[55] In terms of popularity the red shades were without doubt the leaders, with green second and being increasingly bought in the fifteenth century. Burnets and blacks were in fairly high regard, often as mourning cloths, and well behind came blues, whites and medleys, with greys rarely bought.[56] Professor Wolff's examination of English cloth reaching Toulouse between 1380 and 1450 confirms the range of colours and the good dyeing techniques which could produce several shades of a colour: he found the reds, pinks, blacks, greens and perse blues predominating but browns, murreys and medleys sent too.[57]

The one obvious set of shades missing is the yellow, but as the English could provide this in the later period they probably could in the earlier and that they did not was probably due to fashion. Yellows were not bought widely from elsewhere either in Navarre: of non-English cloths bought the greatest amounts were of cheaper white cloths from more local sources in Tarbes and Aragon, then came purchases of burnets and reds, close behind came greys and russetts, and not far behind blues and blacks. Far down the list came greens, which indicates that the Navarrese household saw England as its main supplier of good green cloth, and even further down came 'ferretes' with only seventy-eight *codos* bought over the whole period and all from Werwicq.

The Castilian royal household accounts for 1492–6[58] confirm that England was a predominant supplier of greens and reds—204½ *varas* of green were bought, 117 of reds (of which 104 were scarlets: sixty-five and two-thirds were dyed in grain, thirty-one murreys were dyed in grain and seven and a half crimsons were dyed in grain). Very small amounts of white and brown were also sent.

The high amount of grained cloth supplied by London emphasises yet again London's virtual monopoly of that export by the fifteenth century, but the customs accounts show that the export of grained cloths was by then a minor affair at under a hundred cloths a year. However it is also clear that the Castilians were particularly interested in such grained cloth as was available and came to dominate the trade by 1489. They were also interested in half-grained cloths.

The Navarrese and Castilian household accounts clearly show the main supply ports, although not necessarily the manufacturing centres, to be Bristol and London, with London gaining ground as the fifteenth century advanced. Indeed although Bristol merchants were very active in Spanish

Table 7 Grained cloths exported through London 1472–89.[1]

Date	No. exported by Castilians	Total exported
1472–73	21	49
1473–74	18	61
1474–75	18	37
1475–76	17	38
1476–77	42	70
1477–78	18	27
1478–79	27	59
1479–80	20	50
1480–81	67	120
1481–82	27	76
1482–83	32	66
1483–84	85	122
1484–85	52	77
1485–86	69	116
1486–87	20	26
1487–88	94	123
1488–89	92	140

[1] For sources and details see note to Table 8, p. 82.

trade their contacts with royal household buyers seem few, and probably it is the wealthy Burgos merchants with their large businesses in Bruges and London who were the main household suppliers. The Navarrese accounts also mention cloth of 'Acestre', possibly Exeter.[59] Eastern ports, now that the eastern cloth industry had languished, have no importance.

Although the accounts are not the best sources for the purpose, they do shed some light on the quality of English cloth since prices may be taken as a crude reflection of this. Although they vary according to costs of raw wool, production and transport, the bargaining ability of individuals and the state of the market, wide and constant divergences for these causes, with the possible exception of wool prices, were unlikely.

The prices paid in Navarre, omitting scarlets, ranged from 10s to over 70s the *codo*.[60] The cheapest, usually bought for linings, came from the close sources of Aragon and western France and cost from 10s to 24s the *codo*. Bristol cloth was obviously much better and cost generally between 36s and 38s although some was bought for 24s and some for 56s; London cloth was usually more expensive at about 40s the *codo*. Some Low Country cloth from Werwicq and Courtrai also fell in this range but most of it and all of the Norman cloth cost more, mostly over 50s and much over 70s. A difference of 10s the *codo* could be explained by the difference in

Table 8   Half-grained cloths exported through London 1472–89.[1]

Date	No. exported by Castilians	Total exported
1472–73	3	25
1473–74	$\frac{1}{2}$	53
1474–75	2	25
1475–76	5	19
1476–77	14	19
1477–78	9	22
1478–79	7	57
1479–80	6	61
1480–81	14	46
1481–82	4	39
1482–83	1	33
1483–84	18	66
1484–85	16	37
1485–86	43	83
1486–87	23	33
1487–88	65	133
1488–89	43	75

[1] P.R.O. E356/22, 23. For these years Spanish trade is recorded separately owing to their customs privileges under the treaty of 1466; see below, p. 87. Exports through other ports were usually nil and never more than four cloths a year; the unit is the cloth of assize. Grained cloths were those dyed with kermes dye (*grana*) and half-grained those using some kermes (for example in violet colours). As this most expensive dye was used only on top-quality cloths, known as scarlets, gradually scarlets and grained cloths became synonymous. Their quality and value was always considered sufficient to stand higher export dues: in 1303 cloths without grain, in half-grain and in grain were rated at 1s 0d, 1s 6d, 2s 0d respectively, and in 1347 at 1s 2d, 1s 9d, 2s 4d for denizens and 1s 9d, 2s 7d, 3s 6d for aliens; Carus-Wilson, *Medieval Merchant Venturers*, pp. 218–20; Carus-Wilson and Coleman, *England's Export Trade*, pp. 14–15.

the costs of raw wool if the Low Countries used English wool, but that the household readily spent twice as much on some cloths as others must indicate a difference in quality. England could without difficulty provide both the cheapest linings and the dearest scarlets, but she was used by the Navarrese royal house mainly as a source of medium price, medium quality cloth. This again accords with Professor Wolff's findings for Toulouse where most of the English cloth was of good medium quality.

English supplies to Isabella's court were of a somewhat different character. Three-quarters of the London cloth was very slightly cheaper than that
of Courtrai and Rouen, not enough to suggest a lower quality but possibly
due to cheaper production costs; the rest were scarlets which competed in
price, and presumably in quality, with the finest and most expensive
Florentine woollens, fifty-two *varas* of which were also dyed in grain and
eighty-two *varas* of which were black but just as costly.

In the thirteenth century English cloth could not have competed with
Flemish and French cloth for variety (M. Laurent emphasised the wide
range and variety of colours still offered by Brabant and Flanders in the
fourteenth century[61] and M. Dollinger noted that a Hansard later that
century handled some forty sorts of cloth from that area[62]); but by the early
fifteenth century she offered a dozen types of cloth from a dozen or more
centres in at least twenty shades to Iberia, and the permutations of type,
quality and colour provided a choice quite as wide as that of Continental
suppliers.

England's ability to supply finished cloth of good quality at this time
needs emphasis, since her dyeing and finishing skills have been under-
estimated by many historians writing on sixteenth-century trade.
Although most modern writers now point out that England was sending
finished cloth to her markets in Spain, France, Italy—and Central Europe
and Russia through the Baltic—the suggestion is often made that this was
because those areas demanded lower standards of finishing than did the
Low Countries, and so would take cloth produced by an English industry
as yet in its infancy.

The emphasis in this general picture should be changed. There is no
doubt that in the sixteenth century much of England's exported cloth, and
nearly all that to the Low Countries, was unfinished; and the weight of
evidence, albeit that some of it comes from biased sources, points to an
inadequate English dyeing industry in the later sixteenth century; but it is
also clear that in the fifteenth century many of her exports were finished,
and that London coloured cloth was suitable for Spanish royal courts.
Indeed the continued export of fully finished cloth to Spain in the sixteenth century underlines English skills, since Spain was not a backward
country but the richest in Europe with an elaborate, sophisticated and
luxury-loving courtly and aristocratic life, Spanish buyers could afford the
best and had easy access to Antwerp cloths, yet would still buy English
finished cloth.

The change in England's exports took place under the twin pressures of
the demands of the Antwerp buyers and the acquiescence of the Merchant
Adventurers in their demands.

Low Country markets had always been a problem to English cloth
merchants as Flemings tried to protect their declining industries from
competition by prohibiting imports of English cloth. They failed in their

attempts to oust it, but Antwerp, growing into an international mart, and as England's other markets met difficulties, found itself in the position of England's main Continental outlet, and as such could promote the interests of its own originally small finishing industry.[63] Restrictions which mattered little in fifteenth-century conditions distorted the pattern of England's exports once Antwerp became so important and once the Merchant Adventurers achieved a monopoly position and were found to be quite happy to export unfinished cloth despite objections from English dyers and some attempts at prohibitive legislation by the English government. Behind its protective barriers the Antwerp industry reached high standards, but English finishing was still good and could still find a market for decades to come, not only in backward areas but also in those used to good cloths and able to buy Antwerp ones too. However it is clear that all was far from well with the dyeing industry by the late sixteenth century, and although more work needs to be done on a detailed chronology of the fortunes of the industry before firm conclusions are reached, it is most probable that the lack of numbers, and apparent lesser skills and lack of technical advance then, was due not to England's immaturity in dyeing but to a decline from previous higher standards forced on her by the characteristics of the Antwerp market.

The quantities of English cloth in Castile, and its relationship to the amounts sent by other manufacturing areas is far less well attested than the range of types.

In the thirteenth century it was low. The small numbers of references to it compared with the vast number to Flemish and northern French cloths suggest this and customs accounts confirm it. In the Spanish accounts for 1293 English cloth imports accounted for only eleven pieces worth 2,060 *maravedís* out of a total import of 3,906 pieces worth nearly 900,000 *maravedís* of which most came from Valenciennes (1,820 pieces), St Omer (853 pieces) and Narbonne (305 pieces) while Ypres sent 102 pieces, Ghent eighteen and Bruges and Malines eight each. English accounts show sixty cloths exported from Boston in 1303, nine from Sandwich in 1304–5 and one half-cloth from London in 1308 by Spaniards.[64] Other records for these ports and Southampton and Bristol for this decade show no other Spanish exports, nor do any others before the specific cloth duty was imposed in 1347. Admittedly the accounts are far from complete and English cloth might have been more frequently taken or acquired from foreign markets, but it is clear that amounts were very small compared with the known activity of the Spaniards in the import trade. As they took such little interest in the wool trade it is difficult to see how they could have found adequate return cargoes from England and the presumption must be that they often exported bullion to Spain, or went on to Flanders to buy cloth there.

In the later fourteenth century the export accounts for Bristol offer some quantitative data although their use also presents problems.[65] The Iberian trade has to be taken as a whole as often Spain and Portugal cannot be distinguished in the accounts: the collectors seem to have used 'Spain' and 'Portugal' as interchangeable terms and in 1379–82 all ships for Iberia are recorded as leaving for Portugal, while in 1382–3 all are recorded as for Spain, and in 1387 all are recorded as for Portugal again. There was no reason for the destination to have changed in those years, and it is more likely that the Bristol community, which had been vigorously pushing into Spain before 1369, having found one of their growing markets removed from direct access, reached it through the smaller Portugal. Portugal could have absorbed some cloth but could also pass on some at most periods to the larger Castilian market. Thus to Bristol merchants Spain and Portugal might be seen as all one. After the peace arrangements in 1388 it is more usual to find the two differentiated and increasing emphasis on 'Spain'. Once free intercourse was again possible it was the larger Castile that attracted the Bristol merchants.

Table 9 Sailings for Iberia from Bristol, 1376–1404.[1]

Date	Total exits	for Portugal	for Spain
1376–77	20	–	1
1377–78	37	–	4
1378–79	48	9[2]	1
1379–80	57	12	–
1380–81	46	17	1
1381–82	48	8	–
1382–83	66	–	16
1386–87	41	9	–
1390–91	83	20	6
1391–92	33	2	5
1395–96		no destinations given	
1398–99	106	–	22
1399–1400	37	–	3
1401–02	39	2	4
1403–04	52	–	13

[1] P.R.O. E122/15/8, 16/4, 5, 9, 11, 13, 15, 17, 19, 21, 22, 23, 30, 34; 17/1, 4, 5, 6, 9, 10, 40/12. The accounts run from Michaelmas to Michaelmas with the following exceptions:
    1386–87: 16 January – Michaelmas
    1391–92: Michaelmas – 20 January
    1398–99: 23 May – Michaelmas
    1401–02: 15 April – 10 November
    1403–04: 16 October – 25 March
[2] In the subsidy account one of these is said to sail to Spain.

The amount of cloth taken on these voyages was fairly high, although the Iberian market was not yet in Richard II's reign of overwhelming importance, and Gascony and Ireland remained in some years the main single markets. None the less despite robberies, imprisonments and piracy, both during the Spanish civil wars and after, the Iberian connection was proving increasingly valuable and might take a quarter to a third of Bristol's exports. These exports of Bristol alone to Iberia between 1377 and 1399 accounted usually for between 3 and 9 per cent, and once for 17 per cent, of England's total recorded cloth exports.

Table 10   Cloth exports from Bristol, 1376–1404.[1]

Date	Total No. exported	No. to Spain	No. to Portugal	% to Iberia
1376–77	630	31	–	5
1377–78	3,620	852	–	24
1378–79	3,142	65	1,176	40
1379–80	4,103	–	839	20
1380–81	2,671	127	698	31
1381–82	2,576	–	508	20
1382–83	4,068	1,155	–	28
1386–87	3,074	–	398	13
1390–91	7,017	195	1,887	30
1391–92	1,369	106	69	13
1398–99	8,150	1,643	–	20
1399–1400	3,499	401	–	12
1401–02	2,445	256	44	12
1403–04	2,070	309	–	15

[1] The unit is the cloth of assize. The dates are as for Table 9.

Whether these figures accurately reflect the importance of Iberia to the English export trade as a whole is more difficult to establish. On the one hand the records of total exports are incomplete, especially and most importantly in the case of London;[66] on the other the total of cloth sent to Iberia was also higher, perhaps much higher, as other ports were active and London was particularly attractive to the Spaniards themselves. It may well be that Iberia was already absorbing 10 per cent of England's cloth in some years.

How much of Castile's imports by now came from England is more difficult to discover. The Navarrese accounts indicate that there English supplies were important: in 1412 and 1413 England appears as the largest single household supplier. In 1412 purchases of English cloth reached 926 codos and seven pieces, of French cloth 431 codos and sixteen pieces, of

Aragonese 226 *codos*, of Low Country cloth fifty-six *codos*, of Tolosan twelve *codos* and of Mallorcan five pieces; in 1413 purchases of English came to 729 *codos* thirty-four pieces, of French to 618 *codos* and forty-one pieces, of Low Country cloth to 464 *codos* and half a piece, of Aragonese to nine *codos* and of Mallorcan to thirteen pieces.[67] England thus supplied some 50 per cent of the recorded cloth in 1412 and 40 per cent in 1413. Her share of the Castilian royal purchases at that time and of the general market was probably less as Castile had strong traditional links with Flanders, whereas Navarre had no coastline and was more likely to look to her Gascon neighbour and to England, some of whose cloth reached Navarre through the hands of merchants from Bayonne and Bordeaux.

By this time English merchants were pushing harder into Iberia and there is no reason to doubt a continuing increase in the amounts of cloth sent to Castile in the fifteenth century, at least until the general recession in mid-century, and it is probable that the Spanish trade suffered much less from that than did others; but it is not until the reigns of Edward IV and Henry VII that there is enough material for further quantitative assessments.

Bristol's prosperity by then had become heavily dependent on Iberia, partly owing to the loss of Gascony. All the surviving accounts show large percentages of her cloth exports sent to Iberia with Spain clearly taking the lion's share, but only three accounts cover full years: in 1485–6, 57 per cent of exports were sent to Spain and 22 per cent to Portugal, in 1486–7 the percentages were 70 and 17 respectively and in 1492–3 they were 58 and 26.

Unfortunately accounts from other ports do not offer this degree of detail; they indicate increasing numbers of Spanish ships and shippers in port but give no destinations for the English ships leaving port, some of which were certainly going to Spain.

The enrolled customs accounts assume importance between 1472 and 1489 since many of the Castilian exports are specifically listed in them. From 1466 Castilians paid only denizen rates on their goods,[68] but in the early years of the agreement the Exchequer clerks made no special mention of them, possibly because their numbers were still modest, or the clerks felt it unnecessary; however after the treaty had been called into question following the repudiation by Enrique IV, the re-adoption of Henry VI and the resultant confusion about how Spaniards should be charged,[69] Edward IV's clerks settled on the general practice of noting their presence and usually but not invariably recording their trade separately. This continued until the Treaty of Medina del Campo cancelled the customs privileges.

The accounts show that between 1472 and 1489 Castilians shipped an increasing amount of English cloth and their share of total exports rose, with some fluctuations, from between 2 and 4 per cent to over 14 per cent, and they formed the third largest exporting group after the English and

Table 11   Cloth exports from Bristol, 1461–93.[1]

Date	Total	No. to Spain	% to Spain	No. to Portugal	% to Portugal	% to Iberia
1461	741	318	43	–	–	43
1465–66	2,862	313	11	1,601	56	67
1469	746	19	3	277	39	42
1471	1,854	1,133	61	107	5	66
1473	2,444	639	26	1,087	45	71
1474	571	184	32	206	36	68
1475	911	597	65	85	9	74
1476	454	440	97	–	–	97
1477–78	2,689	563	21	311	11	32
1479–80	2,556	1,035	41	478	15	56
1483	3,034	1,540	51	910	30	81
1485–86	3,646	2,084	57	814	22	79
1486–87	5,387	3,779	70	920	17	87
1492–93	5,683	3,283	58	1,505	26	84

[1] P.R.O. E122/18/39, 19/1, 3, 4, 6, 8, 10, 10a, 11, 13, 14, 20/1, 5, 7, 9. The unit is the cloth of assize. The dates of the accounts are as follows:

1461: 26 March – Michaelmas	1476: 18 July – 20 September
1465–66: Michaelmas – 14 May	1477–78: 1 November – Easter
1469: 26 August – 14 November	1479–80: Michaelmas – 1 July
1471: 29 March – Michaelmas	1483: 20 July – Michaelmas
1473: 18 April – Michaelmas	1485–86 ⎱
1474: 10 April – 9 September	1486–87 ⎰ Michaelmas – Michaelmas
1475: 9 April – 18 July (despite heading) 1492–93	

Hansards. The Castilians were never as important a group as the Hansards but their exports were usually about a quarter of theirs and at times rose to a half, and the rate of growth of their activity was the same as the Hansards' as Table 12 indicates. The figures show very clearly that London was their main centre, and here they handled by the 1480s generally between 14 and 22 per cent of alien exports. They were also active at Bristol and here they usually handled between 80 and 100 per cent of alien exports. At Plymouth they also took a high proportion of alien exports, generally over 75 and often over 90 per cent, but dropping to about 60 per cent after 1485. In Exeter where they were also busy exporters they usually took a smaller share—between about 20 and 55 per cent although it was once 75 per cent. In Southampton, as in London, they were working alongside numerous other aliens and their share of alien exports there was only between 8 and 24 per cent.

In London many of the Spaniards had close contacts with the Spanish merchants in Bruges, and sometimes acted as their agents. Some of their cloth could easily be sold in Bruges and never reach Castile, but the proportion was probably never high since cloth was, after all, what Cas-

Table 12   Cloth exports from England, 1471–89.[1]

Date	Total exports	By Hansards	By Castilians	By other aliens	Castilian % of alien exports	Castilian % of total exports
1471–72	34,076	3,202	1,051	15,818	5	3
1472–73	35,197	4,084	1,608	7,410	12	5
1473–74	43,548	1,949	390	19,979	2	1
1474–75	31,171	4,215	1,729	9,144	11	5
1475–76	41,163	10,160	952	6,301	5	2
1476–77	46,009	8,865	1,219	11,598	6	3
1477–78	39,048	6,314	956	3,279	9	2
1478–79	67,270	12,217	1,302	10,783	5	2
1479–80	55,604	11,581	2,527	9,104	11	5
1480–81	64,081	15,568	3,136	7,068	13	6
1481–82	66,958	14,573	3,357	10,452	12	5
1482–83	35,019	8,213	2,785	7,177	15	8
1483–84	50,846	13,649	7,199	5,316	28	14
1484–85	46,713	14,770	4,322	6,556	17	9
1485–86	57,282	14,628	5,456	3,593	23	10
1486–87	33,529	9,022	2,885	2,504	20	9
1487–88	47,564	14,390	5,902	9,543	20	12
1488–89	53,521	14,905	7,959	5,687	28	15

[1] P.R.O. E356/22, 23. Totals are as in Carus-Wilson and Coleman, England's Export Trade, where the exact dates of the accounts are given. The unit is the cloth of assize. Grained and half-grained cloths are included in the totals. Exports under licences of Arnald Trussel and Juan Pérez (see Table 13) are not included under the Castilians' total. Figures have been supplemented for some ports from particular accounts as in Table 13.

tilians sought in Bruges as well as England in return for their iron, oils and wool. However it does mean that the amount of cloth exported by Spaniards from England cannot be assumed to have all gone directly to Spain. On the other hand the enrolled accounts offer no information whatsoever on cloth shipped to Spain by Englishmen, and this must have been considerable as Bristol, Southampton and London men were well entrenched in Andalusian trade. This English participation underlines one important difference from Hanseatic trade: the Castilians had no monopoly of Iberian trade; aliens (including Englishmen) had free access and were even encouraged. It is thus possible and even likely that English exports to Castile not only made up for but passed any losses from Castilian sales in Flanders. What this meant in terms of Castile's share of England's cloth is still uncertain but suggestions can be made: in 1485–6, 1486–7 and 1492–3, 4, 11 and 6 per cent of England's exports were sent to Spain through Bristol alone; in 1485–6 and 1486–7 Castilians exported 8 and 6

Complementary markets

Table 13   Cloth exports by Spaniards, port by port, 1472–89.[1]

	1471–72	1472–73	1473–74	1474–75	1475–76	1476–77
Bridgwater	–	–	–	10	(141)	(273)
Bristol	–	245*	16*	58*	–	–
Exeter	–	–	–	–	–	123 + (88)
Ipswich	–	–	–	–	20	–
London	1,018*	1,300	328	1,220	932	997
Plymouth	–	–	–	–	(228)	15 + (75)
Poole	–	–	2	–	inc.	–
Sandwich	33	–	2	6	–	–
Southampton	–	63	42	435	←	84

	1477–78	1478–79	1479–80	1480–81	1481–82	1482–83
Bridgwater	9 + (308)	–	(89)	(226)	(12)	59
Bristol	103	–	–	(391)	609	558
Exeter	(261)	(144)	(403)	111*	379	167
Ipswich	–	–	–	–	–	–
London	772	1,071	2,460	2,802	2,060	1,930
Plymouth	71	142 + (9)	67 + (7)	173	284	31
Poole	1	inc.	–	–	8	4
Sandwich	–	3	–	–	–	22
Southampton	←→	86	–	50	17	14

	1483–84	1484–85	1485–86	1486–87	1487–88	1488–89
Bridgwater	38	12	40*	–	–	inc.
Bristol	721	–	60*	399*	inc.	inc.
Exeter	544	372	inc.	99	127	187
Ipswich	–	–	–	–	–	–
London	4,957	3,069	5,088	2,127	5,592	7,495
Plymouth	670	786	178	187	61	124
Poole	–	inc.	–	–	–	27
Sandwich	–	–	–	–	–	–
Southampton	269	83	90	73	122	126

[1] P.R.O. E356/22, 23. Details as in Table 12.

Asterisked figures are supplemented by particular accounts. Numbers in brackets are those cloths exported under licences of Arnald Trussel and Juan Perez, former Gascons living in Spain, by alien and denizen but rarely Spanish factors. 'Inc.' shows that Spanish cloth is included in a general denizen total. Arrows show that cloths for these years are included in the previous and later years' accounts.

Northern ports are not listed, as Spaniards' exports from them are negligible.

per cent of England's exports from London alone; to these must be added their exports from southern and western ports and English exports to

Spain from all ports except Bristol (already accounted for). Clearly Spain must have been absorbing well over 10 per cent a year, and probably between 15 and 20 per cent, and the Castilians themselves were handling at least 15 per cent in the early years of Henry's reign. Castile had clearly become a useful client for English cloth producers, and these had at last ensured that England could provide welcome return cargoes for as many ships as Spain liked to send.

There were several sound reasons for this steady penetration of Castile by English cloth from the fourteenth century—geographical, traditional, and economic.

Castile was close, particularly to the developing west country areas. The Basque Provinces were particularly close to the already well-used Anglo-Gascon route and, since land-transport difficulties and costs made any internal journey of more than about a hundred miles a major undertaking, the north of Spain was as accessible to southern Englishmen as were the Midlands. Navigation was simple: a straightforward, often repeated cross-Channel run as for Gascony, followed by a coastal journey, although increasingly sailors favoured a route across the Bay of Biscay itself. Indeed a coastal journey could easily be made all the way to Andalusia and back and this route was widely known to be practicable since the Italians began their regular runs in the thirteenth century.

Tradition was another simple factor. Political and commercial contacts stretched back into the twelfth century. Spanish merchants and shipping with their wine, leathers, horses, iron and fruits were common in English ports, and when Englishmen needed to sell more cloth than Flanders would take, it was natural to look to Castile as an outlet.

Moreover the lack of a well-developed cloth industry in Castile made her particularly receptive to increasing English imports. Although there was reference to Spanish cloth in England in 1214 and 1219, and some was good enough for export to Portugal in the thirteenth century,[70] the industry seems not to have developed much beyond local importance, despite some centres of considerable size. Not until the fifteenth century do demands for protection indicate industrial consciousness, and even then little was done until the following century. This relatively slow development of the industry despite far better supplies of raw materials, with oil and dyes as well as wool, than Flanders and England was partly due to Castile's late unification—while Flanders reached her zenith as a specialist urban production area, much of Castile was still frontier territory with the main concerns of her population being war, conquest and the occupation and exploitation of vast tracts of land as speedily as possible. It was no doubt also due to the quality of Castilian wool and partly to the many vested interests in the export of the wool. The aristocratic wool producers were satisfied with the already efficient disposal of their wool-clips; the Mesta naturally approved the continuation of raw wool exports; the Crown still

saw them as an easy means of tapping revenue; the wealthy Burgos merchants saw their fortunes as founded on the wool trade; and while Bilbaon
ship-owners were not dependent on wool-carrying it was a considerable
part of their business. While the antipathy towards gild organisation in
Castile had probably been overstated it remained a further factor in limiting the development of pressure groups in favour of home industry,
although England's industrial history shows that gild organisation in the
cloth industry could be stultifying and her rural industry reached considerable heights without it.

Similar pressures were present in England in the thirteenth and early
fourteenth centuries: English wool was exported in great amounts for the
specialised Flemish and Italian industries, and the wool-growers, wool
merchants, the government and its Italian bankers all had reason to
encourage raw wool exports. No doubt this emphasis on exports helped to
explain the agonising unemployment of some of the older urban cloth
centres. In England, however, there were differences too: there was a
tradition of high-quality cloth working; England was a reasonably unified
and prosperous country with a relatively strongly developed town and
gild organisation; her aristocracy was already less dominant than Castile's;
there was no monopoly organisation like the Mesta (the Staple Company
was a later development, a protectionist organisation for a declining
trade); and, most important of all, there were political pressures at work in
the fourteenth century to upset the combination of pressures for raw wool
exports. Wartime efforts to undermine Flemish prosperity by offering
asylum to skilled workers were of minor importance, but by placing
embargoes on wool exports, by wartime taxation and loans on and in wool,
the government gave unforeseen protection to the English cloth industry
which, although in difficulties in the old centres, was developing in the
country. This enabled home producers to undercut Flemish products
made of English wool. Nothing comparable happened in Castile to upset
the wool trade and its population continued to rely on foreign
centres—Flemish, Brabantine, Italian and English—to supply its need for
better quality cloths.

The English penetration of the Castilian market was aided by Flemish
difficulties due to the French war and civil disturbances. Flanders had
been one of Castile's main suppliers and when she encountered difficulties which affected the amount and type of production this would be
reflected in Castile. M. Laurent postulated a decline in the amount of
Flemish cloth on the French, Aragonese and Mediterranean markets,
while Brabantine cloth rose,[71] but M. Verlinden questioned whether the
increase of Brabantine cloth in Castile was similarly at the expense of
Flemish.[72] Unfortunately, in the absence of customs accounts or similar
records the information is inconclusive as it deals necessarily with the
range of types present and not with quantity. Flemish cloth certainly did

not disappear, and with such strong mutual trade interests, it is likely that Flemish cloth would remain longer in its Castilian market than elsewhere, but the war, urban dissension, the withdrawal of some English wool, the increased price of the rest and the shift to Spanish wools must have left part of the former market unsatisfied. Thus a gap appeared which Brabantine and English cloth could fill.

The development of the English industry with a good surplus for export led to a need for reassessment of overseas markets. The traditional Flemish market wanted wool and tried to limit the amount of competitive English cloth sent there.[73] The English merchants accordingly began vigorously to seek other markets for cloth. In the later fourteenth and early fifteenth centuries they pushed into the Baltic, Scandinavia and then Iceland; they and their ships became more frequent visitors to northern Spain, Portugal and Andalusia; and they even tried to push directly into the Mediterranean. At first they had considerable success in the north and west but by the mid-fifteenth century, although their cloth remained popular, they and their ships had been pushed back from the north. Similarly, although their cloth was welcome in the Mediterranean their ships had been expelled at once by the Italians. But in the Spanish Peninsula not only was their cloth popular but they could successfully maintain an active role in shipping and selling.

A major contribution to this continuing activity there was the absence of any monopolistic commercial organisation in Castile. The Hanseatic towns had developed a tradition of collective action to exclude the alien and protect their interests; thus, although the English made rapid and thorough advances in the later fourteenth and early fifteenth centuries at a time of internal Hanseatic strife, once the ranks closed again they found themselves pushed out not only of the Baltic but from Iceland too.[74] The Italian city States relied for their wealth on mercantile activity and here too the merchants could rely on firm political and military support for any action they took against unwelcome intruders, and they used force against the English ships.[75] Nothing comparable happened in Castile. Some towns had occasionally formed *hermandades* for mutual support, such as the one in 1296 between the northern ports by which they agreed to limit trade with England while the war lasted,[76] but the *hermandades*, although they might sometimes promote such *ad hoc* and temporary trade restrictions did nothing in general to exclude aliens from playing as big a part as they wished in the coastal trade. The Spanish ports were strategically placed on an important European trade route, and all ships on it had to pass along the coasts and especially close through the Gibraltar Straits, but the ports showed no desire to control such trade, and indeed might have found it impossible. It was a very large area to police, the historical particularism of north and south might have made it difficult for northern and southern ports to find real points of agreement, and, most important of all, the south had been opened up and developed commercially in the first place by aliens, particularly Italians, with the encouragement of Castilian kings, and these now held a firmly established position there. In these circumstances Castile was, and remained, wide open to foreign activity, and the English found no commercial obstructions, only temporary setbacks during political confrontations.

The exact nature of the buyers of English cloth, and whether the English benefited from an increase in the absolute demand for foreign cloth in any section of the market or simply took up slack left by a decrease in other supplies, remains a problem.

The top end of the market offers least trouble: the royal households, the nobility, the richest clergy and perhaps the richest Andalusian–Italian merchants were long used to buying foreign cloth, and indeed only they would be able to afford the most costly stamfords and scarlets. They also are the ones to have left most records, and the accounts for Isabella's court for instance show it as a heavy consumer of the most expensive English cloths. The Castilian dominance in the exports of English grained cloth also imply that they saw a ready market for these.

Much of England's medium-price and medium-quality cloth was also acceptable to this sector for normal day wear and household liveries. Again Isabella's accounts show the medium quality being bought, but the Navarrese accounts show in detail what the cloth might be used for.[77] There it provided the royal family with gowns, jackets, sleeves, and hose, as well as gown-linings; Exeter or Chester red was lined with Aragonese white, or a gown of Montpellier perse blue was lined with Bristol red, and London black made mourning clothes for the queen and infantes. It was given as gifts, wages or for liveries to many in the household from a countess, or the knights at the queen's coronation, or the ambassadors setting out for Castile, to jugglers, trumpeters, and pages, and even masons and carpenters; it also made saddle cloths and caparisons for the horses. On the other hand it was used for gifts for important personages such as the Bishop of Bayonne, the visiting secretary of the Queen of Sicily, and Bristol cloths of various colours were sent to the Queen of Castile in 1421.

English cloth was no doubt also used by the prosperous but not superlatively wealthy groups, similar to those found buying it in Toulouse by Professor Wolff, the gentlefolk rather than the nobility, the lesser bishops and the officials of the smaller towns.

It is just possible that there was a widening market for foreign cloth, despite the lower late medieval population. Less detailed work has as yet been done on Castilian wages and living standards than on those of other countries, and it is in any case a subject fraught everywhere with difficulties and controversy, but it is clear that Castile suffered from similar economic disruptions after the Black Death to other European countries, and needed similar legislation to keep down prices and wages. Perhaps there was an alleviation of pressure on resources and a slightly wider-based prosperity, especially as the wool, oil and wine exports increased. Possibly a few more families had a little more money free to indulge in buying luxuries like foreign cloth.

One thing must of course be emphasised, and that is that although English cloths may be spoken of as medium priced (or even cheap, in the cases of kersies, dozens and straits), they were far superior to the local products in softness, fineness, durability, brilliance or subtlety of colouring, and were far more costly. They remained a luxury product fit for court dress, and for daily wear by the wealthy when fashionable velvets, brocades, and damasks were unsuitable; as such they were available to only a small section of the whole population when new. Moreover the volume of England's exports confirms that the amounts would be available to a restricted group: an English broadcloth would make perhaps two gowns (or perhaps only one elaborate gown with full sweeping train and sleeves) and at that rate England's total exports in the later Middle Ages of some sixty thousand cloths a year might clothe only one hundred and twenty thousand people a year with new gowns. The 2,084 cloths sent from Bristol to Castile in 1485–6 might make some four thousand gowns, thus clothing considerable numbers in the upper groups but unlikely to penetrate far down in a total population of perhaps four and a half million. It is less, then, to increased demand at the lower end of the market than at the upper that one should look.

Although there can never have been a time in human history when some individual or group was not indulging in what is now called conspicuous consumption, it seems to be generally agreed that in the fifteenth century Europe entered a period when it was particularly evident. Life was becoming more civilised, more sophisticated, less rough and ready, and within that framework larger retinues had to be better clothed, gifts and largesse had to be widely handed out, more furniture had to be better hung, draped and covered, and the fantastic extremes of fashion, which were also changing with startling rapidity for the times, had to be adopted by those concerned with improving or maintaining status. It is thus possible that as well as benefiting from the Flemish difficulties, the English cloth trade might have benefited from more demand, as the richest bought more in an age of display and exaggeration, and those on the edge of medieval affluence may have experienced enough prosperity to have some money to spare for elegance. The mass of the populace however, even if marginally better off, would still have no money for such extravagance.

An examination of England's export trade is not quite complete without reference to the other commodities found in cargoes for Spain, although these were minor compared with cloth.

Hides were some of the earliest English exports to be taxed but these were of little interest to Spain with her own good supplies, although some Spanish shipmasters carried them for Bristol and Irish merchants in the mid-fourteenth century,[78] and John Bailly and John Esterfield of Bristol thought they could find buyers for small shipments of tanned hides and calf-skins sent to Spain in 1480.[79]

Tin was an important English contribution to European life, and the mines of Devon and Cornwall were more important than those of Saxony and Bohemia until the better exploitation of those in the later fifteenth century.[80] Little however went direct to Spain despite the close links between western ports and the Peninsula. This was due to the controls on tin distribution: at times it was made a staple commodity as in 1343 and 1363,[81] and at all times there was a royal right of pre-emption, often granted under licence to particular merchants—usually Italians—who then exported it through Southampton and London. That exported by Englishmen was often taken to Bruges, which was a busy centre for the tin trade,[82] and the Castilians could have picked up there any supplements to their own production which they needed for bronze and pewter-making, artillery, bell-solder, metal protection or manuscript illumination.[83] So far only four instances of direct Castilian exports have been found for the fifteenth century.[84]

Lead, mined in the Mendips, was little exported as England did not produce a surplus, but occasional small shipments were made by Spaniards from western ports.[85]

A variety of manufactured metal and cloth goods went to Spain in very small quantities: they were no more than miscellanea carried to fill up cargo space, or because an individual spotted a bargain, or because it was all a seaman could find or afford to use his space allowance. England's tin deposits made her a major exponent of pewter making, strictly controlled by the London Pewterers' Gild even outside the capital. Pewter, tin or laton mugs, plates, basins, ewers, saucers and candalabra, along with shipments of the vaguer 'tin vessels' or 'pewter vessels' were bought in small amounts for the Castilian market.[86] Belts, caps, hose, points, purses, Winchester coverlets, cushions and benchcovers of cloth and leather were occasionally sent,[87] as were made-up mantles, usually from Bristol.[88] Alabaster tables—probably portable altars or reredoses[89]—also sometimes went through Bristol at the end of the fifteenth century.[90]

Cargo space was also occasionally filled with feathers for arrow flights,[91] potash,[92] candles[93] or tallow.[94]

More immediately useful to Castile were the food supplements that England could send. This was not a regular trade but peaked at times of emergency and disappeared for long periods in between. Corn was the most important of these; a few beans were also sent,[95] and fish surprisingly frequently in the fourteenth century.

The corn trade often indicates the superiority of sea over land transport for bulky cargoes and underlines the extreme dependence on local weather conditions, rather than proving that a country was specialising in food production or that the importing country was chronically badly off. However in the case of Spain there do seem to have been increasing problems in corn production, and while it was often Castile that supplied England in emergency in the early period, the balance tipped the other way in the fifteenth century.[96] The important corn areas of southern Spain depended on the intensive Moorish agricultural methods, which the Castilians did not manage to sustain at their former high level so that Andalusia became less useful, although not negligible as a corn-producing area. Elsewhere in Spain much of the land was too poor for good arable farming, in some areas the protection of Mesta pasture lands made it difficult to bring marginal areas into cultivation, and other areas, particularly the north, while not over populated were at least very highly populated by the standards of the time so that there was constant pressure on supplies.[97] If a bad season came on top of that supplements might have to be sought quite far afield.

England sent corn to Spain in two main periods—before the Black Death, and between 1470 and 1480 when population was beginning to rise again, pastoral lands were at their maximum, and a series of bad harvests led to misery.

In the first period, at least four English merchants received licences in 1333–4 to export 1,900 quarters of corn to Gascony, Ireland, Scotland or Spain, but how much reached Spain is uncertain, and two Spaniards who also exported corn at that time took theirs to Gascony.[98]

Ten years later Spain was among those friendly countries to whom corn exports were permitted, and in 1346 several Castilians bought export licences: Juan Durango and Juan Boun were to export on a ship from Castro; Lopez Johannis could buy 1,000 quarters north of Boston, 500 at Southampton and Portsmouth, and 500 in Somerset and Dorset, and his letter certifying delivery in Spain of the corn from Portsmouth still survives; other Spaniards again supplied Gascony.[99] Licences were not always applied for and accusations of smuggling corn to Spain were made in 1390 and 1392 against merchants of Bristol and Gloucestershire.[100]

In the fifteenth century English corn exports to Spain coincide fairly closely with the dates given by Dr MacKay for the widespread shortages in Castile.[101] In 1414 two London grocers bought licences to export corn to Spain or Portugal;[102] in the fairly localised southern shortages of 1421 and 1423–6 England offered no help; nor was she able to help in the greater problem of 1434–8 because she herself was short and had to turn to Baltic suppliers;[103] and then in 1441 she turned to Castile for help.[104] The southern shortages of 1447 and 1455 seem to have made no call on England but the Andalusian dearth of 1461–2 triggered off a response and in 1463 a Gascon received permission to take 300 quarters to Spain, and William

Wodehouse and Richard Whitington, regular traders with Andalusia over the previous decade, who presumably saw the shortage at first hand, received permission to take fifty weys to Andalusia.[105]

Castile then entered a long period of difficulty from 1465 to 1473, and immediately after this, in 1473–5, English corn exports for Castile became frequent. The timing seems a little late but it may be that England was always seen as a last resort called on at the end of a crisis, or that the amounts sent were just sufficient alongside other supplies to cover the shortage in those years and prevent too many complaints, or that England was supplying only the chronic deficits of Biscay while the rest of Castile was recovering.

At this time the customs accounts for 1473 show 995 quarters and 6 bushels sent by Spanish shippers through Southampton and Sandwich and 193 weys sent by Englishmen to Spain from Bristol. In 1474 Bristol sent another fifty-seven weys worth £38, and Spaniards shipped through Sandwich and Faversham 4,124 quarters worth £986 5s. In 1475 Bristol sent the large amount of 541 weys worth over £360 and Spaniards shipped through Sandwich, Faversham and Poole 5,358 quarters of corn and twenty-five of barley worth £1,411 15s. The next year some Spaniards exported a little under a licence granted to John Sudbury.[106]

The particular customs accounts are not complete by any means for this period, and licences granted to permit corn exports show the Spaniards to be even more heavily engaged than do the accounts. They do not always give a destination for the corn, nor is there proof that they were all used but the sudden Spanish interest coming close to a known period of scarcity suggests that the Spaniards were stimulated by home needs and probably used the licences to the limit.

In 1474 the first licence was issued in January for an unspecified amount to be sent to Spain within three months; then came licences for 700 quarters to be sent specifically to Spain, for 4,750 to be exported by Spaniards aboard Spanish ships, for 250 to be exported by a Spanish merchant, and for 200 to be exported by Portuguese merchants; English and Breton shippers were licensed for only 800 quarters. In 1475 the Spaniards were even more active: they obtained licences for 11,930 quarters, of which 8,800 were specifically said to be exportable to Spain; a further 13,700 quarters were exported by English, Breton and Burgundian shippers, some of which might have reached Spain. By 1476 the Spanish crisis was clearly over and Spanish licences almost disappeared: one for 200 quarters was obtained in 1476, another for fifty in 1477. Occasionally licences for modest amounts were obtained after 1480: in 1481 Spaniards had licences to export 1,000 quarters, in 1482 licences were granted for 1,600 quarters to go straight to Spain because of the great shortage there, but only 500 quarters were licensed for Biscay in 1484 and 600 for Spaniards to take to any foreign parts in 1485.[107] Clearly

English supplements were still useful but not on the scale of 1474–1475.

The English exports of fish to Castile are slightly surprising as the Basques were able fishermen, who early ventured far out to sea in search of whales, took care in the 1351 agreement with Edward III to safeguard access to English ports while fishing off the coasts, and were also found fishing off Irish coasts. However, particularly in the mid-fourteenth century, there was a market demand which the Devon and Cornish merchants expected to supply. In 1364 English merchants acquired licences to send to Spain 200 tons of fish and 40 tons of hake from Fowey, Mousehole, and Plymouth.[108] Thereafter throughout the fifteenth century modest amounts of pilchards, seapike, cod, skate, whiting, ling and lampreys, as well as herring and hake, were not infrequently sent, usually from Plymouth, but also at times from Bristol and Bridgwater, and in 1484 Martín Geldo intended to use Sandwich for his exports of herring.[109]

It is abundantly clear that although England could become a useful supplier of basic foodstuffs in emergency, particularly for the northern coastal areas, and although she could provide a little tin and lead, some manufactured articles and odd shipments of tallow or feathers, it was her manufactured cloth which formed the vast bulk of cargoes for Castile. Other goods were economically insignificant in comparison, and the value of the Castilian market to the English exporter lay solely in its ability to absorb large quantities of English cloth while offering a wide variety of essential goods for the return cargo.

NOTES TO CHAPTER 3

1   The assessments of medieval populations are notoriously difficult to make. I have used here the brief but clear comments in Perez, *La Revolution des 'Comunidades' de Castile*, pp. 18–19; Vicens Vives, *Manual de historia económica de España*, pp. 223–4 adds information for the earlier medieval period and the towns. For later figures see also Braudel, *The Mediterranean and the Mediterranean World*, I, 395, 404–8.

2   C.R. 1264–8, p. 98.

3   C.P.R. 1266–72, p. 593; Arnaud Blaunk and Bonamy de Baylac, merchants of Spain, 50; Martin de Anglare, merchant of Spain, 33; Gerard de Rosillun (possibly the same called of Spain in the *London Letter Books*), 9. The names are not Spanish.

4   *Ibid.*, pp. 691, 704: Nicholas de Garsie, John de Audon.

5   *Ibid.*, 1272–81, pp. 14, 17, 22, 24–6: William Garsi of Spain, 20; John Mundenard (probably Spanish see Chapter 1, note 30), 20; Nicholas de Garsie of Burgos, 40; Dominge Martine of Burgos, 20; John Darys of Spain, 20; Peter de Navarre of Spain, 40, For an analysis of the licences see Schaube, 'Der Wollausfuhr Englands vom Jahre 1273', V.S.W.G., VI (1908), and the comments on this by Lloyd, *The English Wool Trade in the Middle Ages*, pp. 32–3, 40, 48.

6   C.Ch.R.V. 1277–1326, p. 3; as Peter de Monte Anardi, merchant of Spain.

7   P.R.O. E122/6/5, 68/13, 124/13, 136/3.

8   C.C.R. 1349–54, p. 537; see also Beardwood, Alien Merchants in England, p. 159, n. 2.

9   P.R.O. C76/87 m.17.

10 P.R.O. SC6/896/10.

11 C.C.R. 1476–85, No. 1222.

12 C.P.R. 1467–77, p. 559; P.R.O. E356/22 m.63.

13 Cely Letters, ed. Hanham, Nos. 26, 31, 41, 157, 201–2, 204–13, 215, 217–18, 220–1, 225, 231, 234–5, 237–9, 241, 243. De Lopez is not specifically described as of Spain and may have been born in Flanders, but undoubtedly was of Spanish descent and worked with Spanish contacts.

14 Ruddock, Italian Merchants in Southampton, p. 42; C.C.R. 1349–54, pp. 535, 544, 549; C.P.R. 1350–4, p. 472.

15 C.C.R. 1392–6, pp. 49, 366.

16 Ruddock, op. cit., pp. 30–1, 57; C.P.R. 1334–8, pp. 537, 543, 554.

17 M. E. Mallet, 'Anglo-Florentine commercial relations 1465–1491', Ec. H. R., 2nd ser., vol. xv (1962), p. 263.

18 Rot. Parl., II, 149a; for carrying examples see C.C.R. 1389–92, p. 250; ibid., 1392–6, p. 477; C.P.R. 1391–6, pp. 441–2, 521.

19 Henry II tried to ban its import to England in 1172; Klein, The Mesta, p. 34.

20 P.R.O. E122/136/8; for Spanish wool in England see Chapter 4.

21 Touchard, Le Commerce maritime breton, p. 63.

22 Mollat, Le Commerce martime normand, pp. 18, 54, 58, 113.

23 Trocmé and Delafosse, Le Commerce rochelais, pp. 85–90.

24 Finot, Les Relations commerciales entre la Flandre et l'Espagne, p.223.

25 Gilliodts van Severen, Inventaire, VI, 1221.

26 Munro, Wool, Cloth and Gold, pp. 4–5.

27 See Chapter 4.

28 Power, 'The wool trade in the fifteenth century', in Studies in English Trade, ed. Power and Postan, p. 43 and n. 15; Castro, 'Unos aranceles de aduanas del siglo XIII', Revista de Filología Española, vol. 8 (1921), p. 5.

29 Laurent, La Draperie des Pays-Bas en France, p. 205; van Houtte, 'The rise and decline of the market of Bruges', Ec.H.R., 2nd ser., XIX (1966), pp. 37–8.

30 Cited by Mallett, 'Anglo-Florentine commercial relations', Ec.H.R., 2nd ser., XV (1962), p. 257.

31 Lopez, 'The origin of the merino sheep', The Joshua Starr Memorial Volume, pp. 161–8.

32 'A Treatise concerninge the Staple and the Commodities of this Realme', in Tudor Economic Documents, ed. Tawney and Power, III, 102, 114.

33 Gross, The Gild Merchant, II, 4.

34 Munimenta Gildhallae Londoniensis, ed. Riley, II, Liber Custumarum, part 1, p. 125.

35 The less hard-wearing and darker Spanish wools may have been considered both safer and easier to dye by this method.

36 Munimenta, p. 423.

37 Libelle, ed. Warner, lines 98–107.

38 'Treatise concerninge the Staple', loc. cit., pp. 98, 102, 114.

39 One example of Italian approval is cited in Lipson, History of the Woollen and Worsted Industries, p. 215; Bowden, The Wool Trade in Tudor and Stuart England, indicates how the wool increased in amount, but decreased in quality, when sheep were brought off the hills and pastured in enclosed lowland fields.

40 Rot. Parl., IV, 126a, 146b.

41 Cortes, I, 65–7.

42 The vara was just short of a yard at about 33 inches.

43 Newcastle-upon-Tyne Records Committee. Publications, II: Northumberland Pleas from the Curia Regis and Assize Rolls, 1198–1272, ed. Hamilton Thompson, p. 212.

44 The accounts are printed in Gaibrois Riaña de Ballesteros, Historia del reinado de Sancho IV, I, iii ff. The information on cloth has been summarised by Gual Camarena, 'El comercio de telas en el siglo XIII hispano', Anuario de Historia Económica y Social, I (1968), pp. 85–106.

45 Castro, 'Unos aranceles', loc. cit., p. 10.

46 P.R.O. E122/ 5/7, 15/1, 3, 4, 69/2, 124/13, 136/8, 17, 21. The cloth of aliens was recorded as they paid 3d in the £ on the value of all goods imported and exported under the terms of the Carta Mercatoria.

47 Cortes, II, 172–3. The adjectives may refer to quality or size: menores may be straits or short cloths while de las mayores may indicate full broadcloths. However Ypres menor at 45 maravedís and Bruselas menores at 50 were more expensive than inglés de las mayores let alone ingleses menores.

48 C.P.R. 1361–4, pp. 480, 492, 496, 521.

49 P.R.O. E159/191 Recorda Mich. m.24d.

50 C.C.R. 1468–76, No. 709; the transcript there of the Castilian text is incomplete, omitting the word 'papeles'. The letter was enrolled in Chancery as proof of ownership of wines sent to Seboll but stolen en route.

51 Beck, Draper's Dictionary.

52 See note 49 above.

53 Reddaway and Ruddock, 'The accounts of John Balsall', Camden Miscellany XXIII.

54 The surviving accounts have been briefly calendared in Archivo General de Navarra. Catálogo de la Sección de Comptos. Documentos, ed. Castro and Idoate. The accounts of cloth purchases are far from complete but enough survive for the period 1390–1420 to suggest tentative broad conclusions.

55 The Brokage Book of Southampton, 1443–4, ed. Coleman, I, xxxii and n. 4.

56 A.G.N. Catálogo, ed. Castro and Idoate, vols. 20–32 passim. The amounts bought were as follows: reds (including seventeen codos of murrey), 1,078 codos and eight pieces; greens, 537 codos and four pieces; burnets, 319 codos and two pieces; blacks, 216 codos and two pieces; whites, 180½ codos, two pieces and one cloth; blues, 162 codos; medleys, 141¼ codos and two pieces; greys, forty-two codos. Again it must be emphasised that the accounts are incomplete. The codo is equivalent to a cubit (about 18 to 22 inches).

57 Wolff, 'English cloth in Toulouse (1380–1450)', Ec.H.R., 2nd ser., II (1950).

58 Cloth details have been abstracted by de la Torre, 'Telas extranjeras en la corte de los reyes católicos', in VI Congreso de Historia de la Corona de Aragon, 1959.

59 A.G.N. Catálogo, ed. Castro and Idoate, vols. 28ff; the editors take 'dacestre' to be a Chester, but a southern port with greater known contact with Spain seems more likely.

60 The prices are given as they appear, in libra, sueldo and dinero, the Navarrese money of account.

61 Laurent, La Draperie des Pays-Bas en France, pp. 211–18.

62 Dollinger, The German Hansa, pp. 248–9.

63 It was minor in the early fifteenth century, but by 1516 textile workers formed

the third main craft gild; van der Wee, *The Growth of the Antwerp Market*, II, 51n. 137, 70, 133.

64   P.R.O. E122/5/7, 69/2, 124/13.

65   Most ports' accounts fail to give any destination for shipping, and even when they do as at Bristol it is only the first or main destination and many ships for Andalusia for instance called at Portugal, or ships for Portugal might go on to Andalusia.

66   Carus-Wilson and Coleman, *England's Export Trade*, pp. 80–7.

67   *A.G.N. Catálogo*, ed. Castro and Idoate, vols. 29, 30 *passim*. These are the only years for which there are enough surviving records to prompt comparisons and even so the records are not complete. Moreover they illuminate only one aspect of the market. The *codo* measured about a cubit so the the amounts are relatively small—England's recorded sales for 1412 reaching little over nineteen whole cloths.

68   *Foedera*, V, ii, 140–2, 146–9.

69   P.R.O. E122/40/11, 128/10, 12 show confusion at Exeter and Sandwich.

70   See Chapter 4, note 208; Carmen Carlé, 'Mercaderes en Castilla, 1252–1512', *Cuadernos de Historia de España*, XXI–XXII (1954), p. 196; *Cortes*, I, 65–7.

71   Laurent, *op. cit.*, pp. 181–3.

72   Verlinden, 'Draps de Pays-Bas et du Nord de la France en Espagne au XIVe siècle', *Le Moyen Âge*, 3rd ser., VII (1937).

73   *Rot. Parl.*, IV, 126a, 146b.

74   Postan, 'England and the Hanse', and Carus-Wilson, 'The Iceland trade', both in *Studies in English Trade*, ed. Power and Postan.

75   They were willing to accept some English commercial activity there as long as the merchants shipped on Italian vessels.

76   Printed in Benavides, *Don Fernando IV de Castilla*, II, No. lvii.

77   *A.G.N. Catálogo*, ed. Castro and Idoate, vols. 20–43 *passim*.

78   *C.P.R. 1354–8*, p. 73; *C.C.R. 1360–4*, p. 22.

79   P.R.O. E122/19/14.

80   Lewis, *The Stannaries*, pp. 39–40; Hedges, *Tin in Social and Economic History*, p. 16; Nef, 'Mining and metallurgy in medieval civilisation', *Camb. Ec. Hist*, II, 488.

81   *Foedera*, III, i, 142; *Rot. Parl.*, II, 246–52.

82   Lewis, *op. cit.*, pp. 58–63.

83   For its various uses see Hedges, *op. cit.*, pp. 104–9; Salzman, *Building in England*, pp. 294–5, 308; Theophilus, *On Divers Arts*, ed. Hawthorne and Smith, p. 37.

84   *C.C.R. 1409–13*, p. 167; P.R.O. C76/159 m.23, 168 m.24; E122/20/1; E159/205 Recorda Mich. m.25.

85   P.R.O. E122/19/11.

86   P.R.O. E122/19/8, 10, 41/8, 111/60, 114/9, 142/3; E159/208 Recorda Trin. m.8.

87   E159/205 Recorda Mich. m.25; 208 Recorda Trin. m.8.

88   P.R.O. E122/19/13, 14, 26/13.

89   English alabaster work was well known in Europe; Salzman, *English Industries*, pp. 96–9.

90   P.R.O. E122/19/13.

91   *Ibid.*, 136/21.

92   *Ibid.*, 5/7.

93   *Ibid.*, 41/6, 114/9.

94   *Ibid.*, 19/8, 10, 13, 14, 128/14; C76/159 m.27.

95   These were sent from the west between 1477 and 1482; P.R.O. C76/165 m.10, 166 mm.5, 12, 19; E122/19/13, 14.

96   Gras, *Corn Market*, appendix B, shows that England imported more in the fourteenth century than the fifteenth.

97   García de Cortázar, *Vizcaya*, pp. 84, 92–9, found that Biscay needed constant help from the areas to its south, Andalusia and France.

98   C.P.R. *1330–4*, p. 419, 487, 542; *ibid.*, *1334–8*, p. 80; C.C.R. *1333–7*, pp. 98–9.

99   C.P.R. *1345–8*, pp. 58, 198, 201, 206, 213; C.C.R. *1346–9*, p. 116; P.R.O. SC1/42(7).

100   P.R.O. E159/166 Recorda Mich., Hil., Easter for Somerset; 168 Recorda Hil. for Gloucester.

101   MacKay, 'Population movements and pogroms in fifteenth century Castile', *Past and Present*, No. 55 (1972), pp. 56–8. The several crises in Andalusia would have aggravated the northern problems too.

102   P.R.O. C76/97 m.26.

103   Postan, 'England and the Hanse', *Studies in English Trade*, ed. Power and Postan, p. 140.

104   See Chapter 4, note 135.

105   P.R.O. C76/147 mm.11, 12.

106   P.R.O. E122/19/10, 10a, 11, 128/14, 15, 142/8; E356/22 mm.55, 56.

107   P.R.O. C76/157 m.1; 158 mm.3–8, 10, 27; 159 mm.4, 13, 15, 20, 22–9; 160 m.9; 161 m.2; 165 mm.9, 10, 14; 169 m.2; 221 m.1.

108   C.P.R. *1361–4*, p. 496.

109   P.R.O. E122/114/4, 9, 10, 11, 16; E122/19/14, 26/13; C76/168 m.13.

Complementary markets   *II*
England's imports from Castile

Compared with England's monotonous although valuable cloth exports to Castile, imports from there showed considerable variety, especially after the addition of Andalusia. The writer of the *Libelle of Englyshe Polycye* listed them for the mid fifteenth century:

> Bene fygues, raysyns, wyne, bastarde, and dates,
> And lycorys, Syvyle oyle and also grayne,
> Whyte Castell sope and wax is not in vayne,
> Iren, wolle, wadmole, gotefel, kydefel also,
> (For poyntmakers full nedefull be the ii)
> Saffron, quiksilver . . .[1]

A Flemish commodity list of the late thirteenth century was even more painstaking and went through the Peninsula province by province: Castile provided grain, wax, cordwain, basan, yarn, wool, skins, quicksilver, tallow, wine, cummin, anise, almonds and iron; Léon provided the same except iron; Galicia was poorer but sent lard, quicksilver, wine, wax and wool; Andalusia exported honey, olive oil, figs, raisins, skins, wax and leather; Navarre, like Aragon, produced yarn, cordwain, basan, skins, sailcloth, licorice and almonds, and Aragon added rice and saffron; Portugal's goods were similar to Andalusia's.[2]

All the goods and others were brought to England at one time or another, and break down into four main categories: first, raw materials for the cloth industry in England; secondly metal goods and military supplies: thirdly foodstuffs and wines; fourthly furs, leathers, and miscellaneous luxuries.

Since most were considered necessities they met with the approval of the writer of the *Libelle* who criticised so bitterly the trifles brought by the Venetians and Florentines. His complaint about Spanish trade was simply that the English were failing to profit from it fully. He pointed out that

> . . . Spaynes marchandy
> Is into Flaundres shypped full craftylye.
> Unto Bruges as to here staple fayre.

and that Spaniards picked up there return cargoes of cloth, which irritated him because

... ye Flemmyngis, yf ye be not wrothe,
The grete substaunce of youre clothe at the fulle
Ye wot ye make hit of oure Englissh wolle.
Thanne may hit not synke in mannes brayne
But that hit most, this marchaundy of Spayne,
Bothe oute and inne by oure coostes passe?
He that seyth nay in wytte is lyche an asse.
Thus if thys see werre kepte, I dare well sayne,
Wee shulde have pease with tho growndes tweyne;
For Spayne and Flaundres is as yche othere brothere,
And nethere may well lyve wythowghten othere.[3]

The writer is perhaps a little too pessimistic in tone, but he had a legitimate complaint—Anglo-Spanish trade had been very lively and profitable in the past, and would be again before the end of the fifteenth century, but at his time the volume was lower and goods were being exchanged through middlemen at Bruges, or being carried by Italians.[4] However his sea-keeping solution would probably not have helped greatly given the techniques and efficiency of medieval navies: it was difficult for any fleet of the time to dominate even a narrow strait permanently and that would have been the only way to force changes in a trade route. In fact as political relationships between England and Spain improved and English civil disturbance was held at bay, the Spaniards were again attracted into English harbours and Englishmen ever more frequently sailed to Spain.

The first group of goods—raw materials for the cloth industry—is the most obviously complementary one: here Castile produced the primary goods, shipped them to the specialist manufacturing areas (Flanders and Italy as well as England) and loaded return cargoes of finished cloth.

The main constituent, wool, was clearly not needed in England although a little was sent in the early period[5] particularly through South-ampton,[6] but also into London.[7] The imports slackened rapidly under Edward II and thereafter Spanish wools and yarns were wholly missing in cargoes meant for England. In fact a casual phrase in a safe-conduct enrolment for a Spanish ship in 1425 indicates that merchants were forbidden to bring Spanish wool,[8] and the small amounts of it found in England were, as far as one can tell, the results of wrecks or piracy against ships on their way to Flanders. Some of the seized wool may have been used locally, but several men preferred to re-export to Zeeland, Normandy, Brittany or Calais where it clearly found more favour and buyers:[9] Walter Fetplace and Piers James complained that their Spanish wool would fetch only £30 in England and were prepared to spend over £57 on getting it to Calais, where, presumably once they were in touch with the Flemish market, they hoped to cover such expense.[10]

Much more important for the industry were Spanish supplies of dyes. The most expensive was the kermes, or scarlet grain dye. Some of that on

Spanish ships may have been from Barbary,[11] some probably came from Portugal and was picked up at Lisbon on the way from Andalusia, but Seville grain or Spanish grain is also specifically mentioned and probably most of that brought on Spanish ships or English ships coming from Spain

Table 14   Imports of Spanish wool, 1267–1331.[1]

Date	Amount	Value	Entrance port
1267–68	24 sacks		Winchelsea
1268–69	10 sacks		Winchelsea
1270–75	nil		Winchelsea
1307	5 sarplars 2 pokes	£24 0s 0d	London
1307–08		over £2 10s 0d	Sandwich
1308–09	268 sacks 298 bales	approx. £400–£450	Southampton
1310	3 sacks	£2 10s 0d	Southampton
1310–11	87 sacks 81 bales	£108 16s 8d	Southampton
1325–26	nil		Sandwich
1326	10 sacks 30 bales	£17 0s 0d	Southampton
1327–28	nil		Sandwich
1328–29		£1 0s 0d	Sandwich
1330–31	3 bales	£2 0s 0d	Southampton

[1] P.R.O. SC6/1031/19–24; E122/69/1, 124/18, 29, 30, 136/8, 17, 21, 29, 137/5. The customs accounts are fairly sparse for the period so no doubt more did arrive.

was of Spanish origin. The Book of Rates of 1507 indicates that it was cheaper than Portuguese grain, assessing it at three-quarters of the latter's price, but whether the difference is due to quality or some other cause is nowhere made plain. It is not easy to judge from the fifteenth-century customs accounts values whether the grain is likely to be Portuguese or Spanish, as there seems to have been little convention in the valuations and the estimates given varied enormously, as with most of the more expensive goods,[12] In London in 1437 grain was valued at £5 the hundred, but in 1431–2 at £10—possibly here the difference could be that in 1431–2 it was already powdered. At Southampton in 1455 it was valued at £8 and at Bristol in 1485–6 at the rate of £8 6s 8d. the hundred. Yet in Bristol too it was imported in relatively huge amounts—by the ton, pipe and hogshead rather than the hundred or bale—and if these are the normally sized tons then it was being assessed at the rate of only £1 or £2 the hundred.[13]

The cheaper red dye, brasil, more often used in leather dyeing, was an East Indian dye, and the few shipments on Spanish vessels were re-exports from Italian ports or Seville.[14] The reddish-brown or reddish-purple orchell dye was reintroduced from the east to Italy in the fourteenth century and the difficulties in eastern trade in the fifteenth encouraged the development of western sources of the necessary lichens, one good source being the Canary Islands. Spain thus contributed further to the English dyeing industry, although the orchell trade became a virtual monopoly of the Genoese in Andalusia.[15] These shipped it to Southampton and London on their own ships, on Portuguese ones and on vessels with Guipúzcoan and Andalusian masters; they also carried it for the few Spaniards who dealt in it, such as Juan de Valladolid who had twenty-four bales of it transhipped to an Italian carrack at Corunna for delivery in Southampton; some Englishmen, such as William Rowley of Bristol, bought their supplies in Spain and shipped it home without further Italian aid.[16] However by 1464 the use of orchell was forbidden on high-quality cloth as it faded so quickly[17] and it never became an important cloth dye. A similar dye made from lichens was cork,[18] but this and madder came mainly from Germanic and Norwegian sources and rarely appeared on Spanish ships.[19]

For yellow dyes weld or saffron could be used: weld also rarely appeared in Spanish shipments,[20] but saffron came more frequently, although it was more often intended as a flavouring than a dye as few English cloths were dyed yellow shades, and it was very expensive.[21]

For blue colours woad became the most important dye, and it became increasingly part of cargoes loaded on to Spanish ships. The earliest specialist woad-producing areas had been Picardy and then Brabant; later Lombardy entered the field and much of that brought aboard Genoese ships was from there. In the fifteenth century the Toulouse fields became extremely important and it was this trade, with its outlet at Bordeaux or even the Basque ports themselves, that the Spaniards began to take part in to such a large extent. The reference to 'Spanish woad' in the *Treatise concerninge the Staple* simply indicates how inseparably linked Castilian transporters had become with the trade:[22] while there is no reason why woad should not be grown in parts of Spain, there is no evidence that it was grown there commercially, and indeed the Toulousan merchants saw Castile as another possible outlet for their own product. They made very serious attempts to move into it in 1458 and 1459 when the English market had been temporarily disrupted but made little headway before about 1475 as there was then no cloth industry to speak of there. After 1475 Castilian activity in the Toulousan woad trade increased markedly, a little of the woad being sent to Castile for the nascent industry, but most of it carried by Castilian ships for their compatriots or Italians to the greedy markets of England and Flanders.[23] In Southampton most of the woad unloaded still came off Italian carracks and galleys and the very full account for 1487–8 shows even then that Castilians were not involved there.[24] Nor did they consider it worth shipping into Sandwich or the Devon and Cornish ports, although they unloaded expensive grain there. Bristol was another matter: although gaps in the records make annual totals impossible to give, the amounts were clearly large, reflecting both Bristol's natural westward trade and her position as both cloth-making centre and distribution centre for the Midlands.

Table 15   Imports of woad to Bristol, 1461–93.[1]

Date	Value (£)		Date	Value (£)	
1461	–	–	1475	476	185
1465–66	22	42	1476	42	–
1469	–	–	1477–78	–	1,333
1471	629	275	1479–80	424	2,551[2]
1472	290	–	1485–86	581	647[2]
1473	1,369	399	1486–87	2,258	426
1474	967	245	1492–93	2,912	247

[1] Details of the accounts as for Table 11. The woad is valued at £5 the pipe. The first column is of woad said to be from Spain, nearly all on Spanish ships, the second is of that said to be from Gascony.

[2] In these two years Spanish ships carried £387 and £400 worth from Gascony too.

Woad was always one of the three major imports by Spaniards, the other two being iron and wool-oil. The summer months of 1473 and 1474 were particularly good, as were the years 1485–6 and 1486–7 for Spanish carriers. At £5 the pipe it was not a cheap dye, but compared with scarlet, assessed even at the low Bristol figures of £10 the pipe, it was much more likely to colour the gowns of people of 'middling sort'. At Bristol the Spaniards were almost entirely woad transporters for English merchants, a markedly different situation from that in London. Lack of poundage records for the city make it impossible to trace Spanish imports there but other records show merchants of Burgos and Avila who were deeply involved in the Toulousan–Bruges trade extending their marketing to London: Pedro de Salamanca sold thirty-two bales there for £47 19s 6d in 1483, and he and Diego de Bernuy disputed the ownership of certain bales of woad in London in 1490.[25] Bernuy, Castro, and Maluenda are names occurring frequently in the Toulousan trade of the late fifteenth century,[26] and all were also trading in London.

The mordants supplied by the Castilians were small in amount. Potash for fixing woad came occasionally in small amounts in the early period,[27] but England generally used her own or Baltic supplies. Alum appeared from time to time and became more useful after the Genoese loss of their

Asia Minor sources. It was the most important imported mordant for England and several Spanish shipments arrived in the early fourteenth century: Juan de San Sebastián and Ferand Garcye brought some to Sandwich in 1305–6 in very mixed cargoes with fruits, nuts, leathers and vinegar.[28] There was then a long gap until a ship of Bermeo was robbed of 157 bales of rock alum in 1402, and Martín Ochoa took two barrels of it into London in 1432 with a cargo of iron.[29] Then in Edward IV's reign Castilians began to carry it more regularly albeit in small quantity: they took it to Southampton in 1471 and 1484, to Sandwich in 1475, to Topsham in 1477 and to Bristol in 1475, 1476 and 1477.[30] Some may have been from the Barbary coast, some already from the Papal sources at Tolfa, but some no doubt was from their own deposits in the south, either near Cordova at Niebla on the banks of the Rio Tinto or at Mazarrón south of Cartagena where the deposits were mined from 1462. Spanish alum had been known and used all over Europe in the thirteenth and fourteenth centuries[31] but its use sharply declined when the Genoese organisation of their monopoly at Foglia was complete, the Spaniards could not compete in quality or quantity and were not needed as transporters. Only when the Asia Minor monopoly failed were their deposits again useful on a European scale.

Far more important than their contribution in mordants was their contribution of oil. The best olive oil was used for cooking, but as it aged it was used in leather tawing and for clothmaking. It was needed for soaking the scoured wool fibres before carding or combing to help prevent fibres breaking and to keep them together both then and during spinning. Rancid butter or pig fat could be used as a substitute but was not as good and much more unpleasant to handle than Mediterranean oil. The writer of the *Treatise concerninge the Staple* saw wool-oil as the only good reason for which England need hang on to the trade with Spain, and sighed that, if only England had had oil of her own 'than wolde England sette nought be Spayn'.[32] In fact good oil was also obtained from Portugal and Italy, so Spain was not quite in the monopoly position implied by the *Treatise*, but it was a major producer—Portugal was smaller and the Italian trade was by then somewhat reduced. The large landowners of Andalusia found the agricultural methods used for sheep-rearing, vine- and olive-growing preferable to the intensive methods necessary for other crops, and their good oil supplies had been one of the main attractions for the Genoese who settled in Seville and whose ships could pick up supplies for England and Flanders. The oil was so widely needed that all who could dealt in it, but the three main active groups were the English, Spanish and Italian merchants. Spanish ships were bringing substantial amounts into the southern ports by the end of Edward II's reign: to Sandwich in 1325–6 came various oils and greases worth £77 14s although only £6 worth was actually called *oleum*; in 1327–9 however *oleum* was worth £148 and other greases were worth no more than £97.[33] Thereafter greases, tallows and fats appear far more rarely and olive oil becomes supreme. It was probably the oil above all that persuaded more and more Englishmen to take their ships down to Andalusia from the mid fourteenth century; by 1364 a trading licence noted that the return cargo from Spain would be of oil as well as of iron, salt and wine, implying an intention of sailing south,[34] and Bristol and London merchants were trading in Seville before 1369 despite the dangers of the civil war.[35]

During hostilities Portuguese supplies became more important but much Spanish oil, good Seville oil, continued to be brought on Italian vessels to Southampton and London, and of course it could be acquired through Bruges. In peacetime however nothing could be more convenient than shipping out to Spain direct a cargo of cloth and loading the necessary wool-oil for the return trip. The Bristol customs accounts for the later fifteenth century show that English and Spanish ships brought just over half Bristol's oil imports from Portugal, and the rest came from Andalusia: most ships from the south carried some, and some carried little else. The *Mary Redclyffe* in from Seville in 1473 carried 134 tons of oil worth £536 with 146 tuns of wine, and soap and sugar worth £36 10s; the *Trinity* the same year brought 141½ tons of oil worth £566 with 81 tuns of wine, and soaps, grain, vinegar, almonds, wax, rice and iron worth altogether £90 1s. Other ships such as the *Bastyan of Plymouth*, the *Christofer of Tenby* and

Table 16   Imports of oil to Bristol, 1465–93.[1]

Date	from Spain		from Portugal	
	tons	£	tons	£
1465–66	–	–	115	460
1469	½	2	121	484
1471	85	340	–	–
1472	–	–	–	–
1473	275	1,101	–	–
1474	2	8	130	520
1475	162½	650	63½	254
1477–78	206¾	827	¼	1
1479–80	42¼	169	230	920
1485–86	69¼	277	194	776
1486–87	78¼	313	166¾	667
1492–93	322¼	1,289	148½	594

[1] The details of the accounts are as in Table 11. Only the last three accounts cover full years so there is distortion in the other years.

the *Mary Cliffe* in 1475 brought only oil from Andalusia, but in smaller amounts at between 42 and 58 tons each—perhaps at least the first two were instances of smaller carvels or barges being sent out. In Bristol oil was one of the three most important imports at this time and was doubtless important elsewhere, but records are less good. In Southampton in mid-century fifty, a hundred or two hundred tons, probably picked up at least in part in Andalusia, would come in on Genoese carracks. In London lack of poundage records obscures imports by Spaniards and Englishmen, but petty customs accounts show few oil imports by Portuguese, and legal and other records confirm the picture of London supplies being Spanish rather than Portuguese and obtained in Spain and Bruges by English merchants.

Oil was a necessity, and was steadily sought, and in the sixteenth century Thomas Howell of Bristol could make some 40 per cent profit on it,[36] yet the meagre figures we have suggest less profit in the fifteenth. The customs valuation of £4 the ton is of course grossly low, and selling prices were about double that, fluctuating according to quality and demand,[37] yet at times they would have to have been much higher than that to offer any profit at all: in 1433 John Chirche's factor bought eight tons in Seville at £10 each[38] and it would have cost him at least £1 a ton freightage and handling and customs charges. Thomas Hay on the other hand may have made some 15 per cent profit on the three tons his factor bought cheaply at £5 3s 4d each in Seville during a civil disturbance.[39] Unless the selling price fluctuated more than the records so far reveal, it is possible that oil may at times have qualified as a 'loss leader'.

Soap, increasingly desirable for personal and linen washing in the civilised fifteenth century, was also beginning to be used in the cloth industry for cleansing before finishing, although the older methods using fuller's earth or urine continued for some time. Castilian soap, both black, white and smigmate, was a common cargo constituent from the south or could be bought from Bruges—Thomas Catworth, a London grocer, ordered six pipes worth £40 from there in 1428, and Thomas Wattes, also a London grocer, still preferred to get it there even when direct trade with Spain was flourishing in 1472.[40] The white soap was the most refined and was entirely for personal use—an expensive comfort: rates in 1507 valued it at £10 the ton, while assessing black soap at only £3. The soap and smigmate coming to Bristol in the fifteenth century was almost entirely of this cheap variety with its custom valuation falling between £3 6s 8d and £4 the ton and although eight tons brought in 1479–80 cost £6 13s 4d the ton this was still far below white soap prices. Probably even at this price relatively little was used in the cloth industry until England herself could produce soap sufficiently cheaply in the sixteenth century.

Also for the cloth industry were the small shipments of combs. Some were wooden ones, but others in the fifteenth century were of iron—products of the versatile Bilbaon iron-makers no doubt. They were probably intended for the early wool-combing process, but some in the later period might have been intended to replace teazles in the raising of the nap, a practice which was forbidden by Edward IV.[41]

There is no doubt that Andalusia with its oils and dyes, and also occasional mordants and soaps, was important to England's cloth industry. It had no monopoly of such goods, but it was nearer than Italy, and probably had a larger area for supplies than Portugal, although the latter remained very important at Bristol for oil imports; moreover the oils and dyes could easily be picked up in Bruges, or collected off Italian vessels. But in peacetime it was very convenient for shipments of cloth to be made direct to Spain and the essential raw materials picked up and brought back directly for sale to the cloth producers. In the commercial rivalry and complaints of the sixteenth century it is of England's dependence on Spain for good oil that economic critics wrote with despair.

Of the second group of commodities—metals and military supplies—it was above all the iron which was consistently important.

Throughout the later medieval period the iron mines of Biscay and Guipúzcoa provided one of the most important Spanish imports into England. Catalonian and Asturian deposits were fairly good but far outstripped by those of the Basque Provinces, which in European terms came second in importance of production and international commerce only to those of the much larger area of Styria and the Palatinate. Professor Sprandel suggested that it was royal encouragement that stimulated Guipúzcoa's early development,[42] but Biscayan iron, of an even better quality than Guipúzcoan and without such stimulation, was no later in development and is even mentioned as early as the eleventh century.[43] These very early workings are obscure but it is clear that in both provinces iron working was well under way by 1200 and the international trade was well established by the middle of that century, when Henry III's agents bought it and steady shipments were sent into Winchelsea.[44]

The particularly good seams in Biscay ran north-west to south-east from the border with Santander and had a focal point near Somorrostro about twelve kilometres north-west of Bilbao, and Bilbao's increasing dominance of the whole province at the expense of Bermeo is clearly partly due to its favourable position for the iron trade as well as its merchants' skilful manipulation of the transport needs of the wool trade. The shipping used in the iron trade with England is not particularly reliable evidence of the relative importance of the two provinces but it may be significant of Biscayan dominance that it was Biscayan shipping rather than Guipúzcoan that furnished most of the iron for England: of the fourteen Basque ships bringing iron to Sandwich between February 1325 and January 1326 all were from Biscay and Castro Urdiales, and of the seven bringing iron between January 1327 and January 1329 at least four were Biscayan and only two Guipúzcoan.[45] Whatever the balance between the two however, by the fifteenth century English merchants knew that they could obtain first class iron at Bilbao or San Sebastián or Rentería.

The Basque ore had three advantages given medieval extraction and working techniques. First it came in compact masses fairly near the surface making open-cast mining possible in many places. Secondly it was rich, containing some 48–58 per cent iron, and, since extraction efficiency varied enormously from perhaps 5 to a claimed 73 per cent, but settling usually around 17 to 25 per cent, this meant that the richer the ore the more easily extractable was a reasonable amount of iron, and the better for the profits of the producers.[46] Thirdly its low phosphor content enabled good malleable iron to be produced easily and while many European areas were wholly satisfied with local supplies for the mundane work of edging agricultural tools, binding cartwheels, making harness pieces and so on, the specialist workers wanted a better quality iron for the chains, anchors, pins and nails of shipbuilding, for the tie-bars, clamps, glazing bars and stanchions of the splendid lay and ecclesiastical buildings, and for the decorative locks, hinges, candle and torch holders, metal grilles, and tomb railings which adorned them, and this high quality iron Spain could supply. The fifteenth-century writer of *Le Debat des Heraulx d'Armes de France et d'Engleterre* delightedly pointed out that 'you have iron in England and we have abundance of it in France but the best iron that there is for shipbuilding is the iron of Biscay in Spain since it bends but does not easily break. Now we dwell near Biscay and are allies of Spain so we can procure it readily and cheaply. But for your part you cannot procure it except by means of safe-conduct and with great difficulty.'[47]

But despite these difficulties, and although England supplemented her supplies with increasing amounts of Swedish osmund from the fourteenth century, Spanish iron was still much sought and used all over England. A great deal of it went to royal works—for castle building, siege weapons and shipbuilding, as the accounts of Edward III's buildings[48] or the account for the building of the galley *La Philipe* show.[49] Probably some of the specialist gilds, such as the wiredrawers of Coventry or Bristol, used it. Wealthy landowners, castle dwellers and soldiers would find it necessary, and so did religious institutions even as far north as Durham Abbey.[50] In some coastal areas it would have been as cheap as or even cheaper than English supplies if they had to bear high land transport costs, but else-where there might be a considerable gap in prices. Thorold Rogers' price index indicates that in the early fourteenth century its price was fairly stable at 4s to 4s 4d the hundredweight with a drift down to 3s to 3s 10d between 1344 and 1354 probably due to increasing supplies or possibly to steady supplies meeting a lower demand in the plague years. At that time unspecified iron, which might be English or foreign, varied wildly in price between 2s and 7s 6d the hundredweight. After 1354 Spanish iron prices rose sharply, like most other prices after the Black Death, and they stayed high at about 5s 6d to 7s 6d for the next century, probably sustained by difficulties in getting the iron in some of the worst phases of the Hundred Years War. In the better climate after about 1456 the price dropped back to

4s to 5s the hundredweight until the Tudor price rise began to take hold by 1525 and had nearly trebled prices by mid-century.

The customs records consistently undervalue the iron in market terms at £2 to £2 10s the ton, this probably being originally the purchase price in Spain sworn to by the merchant or his agent, but Southampton used an assessment of £4, which other documents show to have been the wholesale price at the ports even if inland consumers had to pay more. A London vintner accused of concealing usurious loans in 1415 and 1417 did it by spurious dealings in Spanish iron, buying back iron for £4 a ton from men to whom he had previously sold it for £5 10s the ton.[51] Thirty tons of iron landed at London by Simon Weston from a Spanish ship without payment of customs or subsidies in 1432 were forfeited and appraised at £4 the ton at which price Weston agreed to buy it back.[52] A claim made in 1439 for losses of iron—possibly Spanish—at the hands of a merchant of Bayonne fifteen years previously alleged that 11½ tons were worth 100 marks, or just over £5 16s the ton,[53] but a claim made in 1440 by Juan Martín de Luxaro for goods stolen by men of Sir Nicholas Carreu priced the 180 tons of iron loaded at Bilbao and lost at £4 6s 8d each.[54] The sales of some 217½ tons of the 257 tons brought to Southampton in 1441 by Martín Ochoa, Thorold Gonsalve and Martín Pagas, made in amounts varying from over thirty-seven tons to a little over ten hundredweight, were made at about £4 the ton giving or taking a few pence for discount or friendship.[55] These prices seem to have held up into Edward IV's reign but the drift downwards can be seen in the complaint of Robert Gowdby, a London draper, that he bought 40 tons of Spanish iron for £4 8d the ton from another draper, William Capell, on condition of delivery before next St George's day, but Capell failed to bring it until the summer by which time the price of iron had fallen by 16s 8d a ton; but when Gowdby refused to accept it Capell began a suit of debt against him.[56] These port prices were lower than Rogers' figures, but inland things were different. The cellarers and bursars of Durham Abbey steadily bought Spanish iron, usually at 6½d to 8½d a stone (about £4 6s 8d to £5 13s 4d a ton) although between 1470 and 1475 and in 1488–9, when supplies should have been good and prices dropping, they had to pay 9d or more. Clearly extra transport costs and middlemen's profits in getting it to Newcastle and then to the abbey took their toll, yet despite the cost the abbey continued to see a few tons a year as essential even though local Weardale iron could be bought at 2d to 5d the stone (£2 13s 4d to £3 6s 8d the ton).[57]

The vast majority of iron shipments sent to England, Flanders and other northern ports were measured in tons, pipes or quintals, and even detailed lists of sales to English merchants, such as those by John Emory's guests in 1440–1, show iron sold simply by the ton, hundredweight, quarter and pound.[58] This probably means that it was being shipped in rough bloom form, after smelting but before being worked into useful articles or even bars, but the records are not precise on this point. Spain in fact exported iron as vein, mass or worked, and it is not clear which was found the most profitable way,[59] but although Pedro Pardo and his associates of Burgos preferred vein for their exports to Italy,[60] this was unnecessarily bulky and the Basque iron workers objected to the loss of work. Moreover in England there is no reference to indicate ore imports, nor evidence of large number of bloomeries growing up around the ports to deal with an inflow of ore. It seems certain that these bulk imports were not worked iron either, which would have appealed to the Basque ironworkers, but less to the merchants since worked iron was taxed in Biscay, and not at all to iron workers in England and Bayonne, who periodically objected formally to such worked iron or took the law into their own hands and pitched it into the Severn.[61] The evidence from Rogers' price index is minimal but the one clear example of Spanish wrought-iron prices it at 13s 6d the hundredweight (£13 10s the ton) in 1421, far and away above normal prices. The bulk imports by ton, pipe and quintal valued at £4 to £5 the ton must have been roughly smelted blooms, or at most roughly shaped bars.

Occasionally more precise information is given on the form of the iron cargoes: Spanish merchants in London in 1338 had rods of long iron, pieces of pointed iron, iron plate, cut iron and iron welded in gobbets;[62] iron plates were aboard a Spanish ship wrecked in 1357;[63] the cargo forcibly taken from Furtinus Vanes of Bermeo in 1404 included iron bars;[64] and in 1459 at Southampton the *Katerina of Guipúzcoa* unloaded 13,395 'endys' of iron, making 116 tons.[65] As this was a deliberately chosen term and 11 tons and a pipe of iron were unloaded from that ship too, and the iron on three accompanying ships was recorded in tons, pipes and hundredweights as usual, it is likely that the shipments were visibly different. The 'endys' were counted as well as weighed and were probably a fairly uniform size of small bar. This form for Spanish iron occurs again in London in Henry VII's reign,[66] and was commonly used by John Smythe of Bristol in drawing up his accounts in the sixteenth century, but he still sold his iron by weight.[67]

Some iron was imported as nails, usually to Southampton or London, but sometimes to Bristol, Exeter, Sandwich or Plymouth.[68] Local smiths in England were of course the main suppliers of nails but clearly if Spanish smiths produced a surplus, they could be fairly sure of finding a merchant to export it and a sale in England. The imports were modest: from ten to thirty thousand in a year is usual, although Southampton accepted fifty-seven thousand in 1434 and fifty-two thousand in 1460; values were correspondingly modest, usually between £1 and £6, with the fifty-seven thousand at Southampton valued at £9.[69] Various types were sent: prices varied between 1s 6d and 3s 4d the thousand, probably indicating a variation in size; specific mention is sometimes made to small nails, clench nails, board nails, 'hachnaylls' and nails 'de teloat'.[70] Other manufactured articles included girders, rakes, prongs and shears,[71] a few anchors[72] and iron combs.[73] Some arms and armour (swords, brigandines, crossbows, helmets and even guns[74]) were sent but this was a negligible trade although Bilbao was already known as an arms-producing centre by the late fifteenth century. Very occasionally the iron was further processed and arrived as steel.[75]

The importance of the iron trade in Anglo-Castilian trade is clear and references to it abound; indeed in the *Commodyties of England* Fortescue wrote that Biscay had 'moost plentye of Iron of ony contrey of the worlde', clearly considering it far more important than eastern areas for iron supplies.[76] Firm figures however can be found for only a few ports for limited times.

In Winchelsea in 1267–8 the 148 quintals which arrived were overshadowed in value and volume by the 353 tuns of wine also brought by Spaniards,[77] but in Sandwich in 1294 when Spanish goods were arrested, nine merchants of Bayonne claimed back well over five thousand quintals (about 250 tons) of iron worth over £900 some of which was specifically claimed to have, and all of which probably had, been bought off the Spaniards already.[78] In Southampton in 1310–11 over 80 tons valued at £133 was bought by Spaniards but the total value of their imports amounted to £1,199, leathers still accounting for over £700.[79] Yet in Sandwich fifteen years later iron was their main article of commerce: their iron was valued at £550 out of a total merchandise value of £857 with almonds and fruit forming the next most valuable shipments at £110, then in the two years 1327–9 iron was worth £635 out of a total value of £1,230 for imports, with oils, tallow and soaps forming the second important group worth £281 and kermes dye the third at £150.[80] Tonnage is not given in these accounts but if the later customs valuation of £2 the ton is taken then tonnage was fairly high at 275 in 1325–6 and 317 in 1327–9. Sandwich continued to take considerable amounts of iron from Spaniards: 101½ tons in 1343–4, 214 in 1344–5, 67½ for part of 1345–6, and 110½ in 1346–7, but in these cases values are not given, so accurate comparison with the earlier years is not possible.[81]

After the troubles of the 1370s, when imports must have decreased sharply and probably temporarily disappeared, iron continued as a major import, and in 1390–1 London received 156 tons aboard Spanish ships.[82] The fifteenth-century customs accounts, although sparse for the first half of the century, are enough to show imports continuing at a good level. London took 496 tons from three Spanish ships in April and June 1431;[83] Southampton took 101 tons in 1432, 107 in 1433–4, 432 in 1435–6, and the hosting returns in 1440–1 show 257 tons brought by three Spaniards alone;[84] Sandwich took 357 tons in 1457–8,[85] while London again took 215 tons in 1456–7,[86] and Southampton 268 tons in 1459–60.[87] Bristol took a fairly high tonnage for the rest of the century, with iron vying with woad and oil for the role of the most valuable cargo brought from Spain. Here iron brought by Englishmen can be seen as well as that brought by Spaniards, but in all other ports amounts of iron from Spain may well be under-estimated as Spanish iron brought by Englishmen is impossible to identify with certainty. In estimating totals it has been assumed that iron brought in by Spanish ships and by Spanish merchants is Spanish since with their excellent supplies it is highly unlikely that they would have handled Breton or Gascon iron, which occurred in small quantity and inferior quality. Iron aboard Gascon ships has not been included, although most of it might be from Spain, and the Gascons could be very active. They were particularly so in London in the mid fifteenth century, importing 592 tons in 1442–3, 154 tons in 1445–6, and 686 tons in 1449–50;[88] indeed the

Table 17 Imports of iron (tons) to Bristol, 1461–93.[1]

Date	Spanish	Total	Date	Spanish	Total
1461	175	175	1475	381	383
1465–66	97	124	1476	190	190
1469	78	95	1477–78	80	80
1471	100	137	1479–80	114	131
1473	248	270	1485–86	214	295
1474	483	501	1486–87	411	411
			1492–93	648	697

[1] Details of the accounts as for Table 11. Spanish iron includes only that on ships stated to be from Spain. The rest is almost all imported in fact on Spanish ships said to be in from Bordeaux or La Rochelle and is almost certainly also Spanish. The occasional ton or pipe imported on English ships from Bordeaux or Chepstow is similarly almost certainly Spanish.

Commodyties of England notes iron as one of the main imports from Gascony through Bayonne,[89] but the proximity of the Spanish Basque supplies would make it surprising if considerable amounts were not from there. No inclusion can be made of Spanish iron reaching England through the Low Countries, although clearly such shipments were made: Italians for example brought 239 tons of iron in 1450 along with 500 lb of Spanish grain from Flanders, and it is quite possible that both were bought there from members of the Spanish and Basque nations in Bruges; in 1456 Spanish merchants imported iron on Low Country vessels, possible indi-cating a reshipment from Flanders, although it could be direct from Spain; small amounts of iron specifically described as Spanish were sent into Boston on ships of Veer between 1467 and 1483.[90] Perhaps some was being used as ballast but it was clearly eminently saleable ballast in England. An estimate of the average annual Spanish iron import to England for the mid fifteenth century of about 800 or even 1,000 tons would not be outrageous, since any of the four main ports engaged in Spanish trade was likely to take between 200 and 400 tons from Spanish shippers alone, and these supplies might well be supplemented by imports by Englishmen and even on Gascon and Flemish ships there. Moreover additional amounts of 20 or 30 tons a year might be coming into any one of the western ports such as Exeter, Plymouth or Bridgwater.[91]

The treaty concessions and period of peace under Edward IV and Richard III brought increased trade, helping to produce the downward drift of prices, and annual imports of Spanish iron rose to well over 2,500 and probably well over 3,000 tons. Bristol alone in 1492–3 imported over 648 tons of Spanish iron, but the highest amounts are recorded in London; there Spanish merchants alone imported 2,099 tons in 1487–8, 2,532 tons in 1490–1, and 1,614 tons in 1494–5.[92] At this time too imports of Spanish iron to the smaller western ports, now including Chester, were rising sometimes to 100 tons a year.[93]

Such a scale of imports was clearly enormously important to England, whose own output has been estimated at 900–1,200 tons a year in the later thirteenth century, which might have fallen in the fourteenth century and not appreciably risen in the fifteenth.[94] Periods of hostility with Spain, if such had occurred, would have been troublesome, as it would not have been easy to develop Swedish, German and French supplies to this level quickly. Such eastern iron rarely came into western or southern ports (whose small supplements to their Spanish supplies came from Brittany or Gascony) and the customs accounts for London and the eastern ports show imports of osmund and of irons from Liège or Central Europe seldom to have reached 100 tons a year in any one port.[95]

An English market taking iron on this scale must have been important to the Basques too, but in the absence of production figures for the area just how important remains unclear.

M. Bautier and Professor Sprandel, both using the fragmentary export figures for Sancho IV's reign, have suggested for the later thirteenth century annual seaborne exports of 4,000–5,000 tonnes and 62,000 cwt respectively.[96] These known export figures will not easily bear the weight given them in making these estimates,[97] and yet the export of some 7,800 quintals which they show for three ports only, for periods of eight, three and two months only is fairly high, and an annual seaborne export from the Basque Provinces of up to 3,000 tons would not be wholly unreasonable.

By the later fifteenth century Spanish production had certainly increased and might account for a major part of western European production; Professor Sprandel suggests that it was about one-third of an estimated total European production of perhaps 40,000 tons.[98] If such assessments come near the truth, then seaborne exports of 4,000–6,000 tons a year would be quite possible from the Basque Provinces. England's imports of 2,500–3,000 tons or more in a year, together with imports in Flanders, France[99] and Italy, could offer confirmation for this scale of activity.

Dr García de Cortázar's work on Biscay in the fifteenth century is tantalising, since he shows that there are figures concerning iron production, but the imponderables in them are too great for any accurate conclusions to be drawn. The iron of Biscay was taxed at 16 old *dineros* the quintal worked, and the tax was farmed for 63,000 *maravedís* in 1406 and for between 104,000 and 182,000 *maravedís* in the last quarter of the fifteenth century. Two sixteenth-century estimates exist—for 300,000 quintals of worked iron produced in Biscay and Guipúzcoa in 1545 and for 1,000,000 quintals of iron produced in 1525—both being difficult to trust, interpret or reconcile.[100] On such slight foundations it would indeed be rash to base production figures: contemporary estimates are notoriously unreliable, it is always risky to base production figures on tax returns, especially when currency relationships were unstable, as in fifteenth-century Spain, and when it is not clear exactly what stage in production is meant.[101]

The fortunes of the Anglo-Castilian iron trade fluctuated according to political and general economic movements in Europe: England was probably a very important customer in the thirteenth and early fourteenth centuries, but the Hundred Years War probably enhanced the importance of Flanders and France, although England did her best to provide safe-conducts and encouragement for the Spanish trade at most periods. Then in the later fifteenth century England became important again, and by 1490 when an ordinance forbade the buying of iron from the exchange in Bilbao for resale until the iron fleet was satisfied and had left, it clearly considered that London and Flanders were the two main markets with first call on exports.[102]

The Middle Ages have been called the age of wood, and to some extent there is justification in this:[103] compared with modern times, and because of the difficulty of extraction with medieval techniques, the amount of iron used was relatively small and its cost compared with other goods comparatively high so that all that could be made of wood, stone or leather for everyday use was so made. However it was indispensable, and the richest social groups concerned with warfare, shipbuilding, castle- and church-building and elegant decoration made sufficient demand for high grade iron to promote and maintain a large-scale international trade in it.

The other metal supplied by Spain was quicksilver: Spanish mercury had been known from the fourth century B.C. and, although there were undoubtedly long gaps in production, in the later Middle Ages it was still the most important European supply centre. The main deposits were at Almadén, about 150 km north-east of Seville; these were first ceded to the Knights of Calatrava in 1168, regranted to them to be held jointly with the Crown after they had been retaken from the Moors in 1212, and then granted to the Order alone in 1320,[104] but by the later fifteenth century, like much else in Andalusia, its export was in the hands of a Genoese firm. Mercury was no bulk cargo, and was needed in modest amounts by specialist workers: it was used in small amounts to harden the tin–copper or tin–lead amalgam making pewter and also in the final polishing of pewter. It was immensely useful to the painter, illuminator and gilder: vermilion pigment could be made from its ore; the base layer on metals before gilding was often a mixture of argol, salt, water and mercury; it was used in milling gold and silver before those were used in painting and gilding; and because of the ease with which it amalgamated with gold and silver could be used to recover these from old gilded works.[105]

Imports to England were on a suitably modest scale. It appeared frequently on Castilian ships in English harbours in the thirteenth and fourteenth centuries; the largest single shipment made seems to have been the sixty bags worth £200 stolen from a ship wrecked off England in 1277,[106] and usually single shippers brought much less—amounts worth £3 or £6 as at Sandwich in 1304–5,[107] or the nine bales worth £8 at Southampton in 1310, and shipments worth £15 and £17 there the following year.[108] From the mid fourteenth century it disappears from Castilian ships, nor does it appear on English ships coming back from Andalusia; henceforth England's imports are in the hands of the Genoese.[109]

As for military supplies, the iron itself formed the greatest part, but was supplemented by the armour, arms, anchors and chains sent ready made from Biscay. Besides these came some cordage for Henry III's soldiers' crossbows,[110] and the straight Spanish yew for bowstaves,[111] but volume and value of both were minor, as England could not allow herself to be dependent on a potential enemy for such supplies particularly as for these, unlike iron, home and Gascon supplies would suffice. Nor was Castile willing to allow free export of military materials.

Various export prohibitions also covered Spanish horses for much of the period, but exemptions could be bought and Spanish horses were eagerly sought by English kings. The reputation of the Spanish horse was doubtless based on the stamina and speed of Arab horses bred in Castile and the other Iberian kingdoms and for a century and a half up to the outbreak of the Hundred Years War English kings had sent to Spain and Navarre as well as Sicily and Lombardy for their livestock. In 1214 King John gave Thomas Briton 200 marks to buy Spanish horses for him, in July of the same year Walter Vinetarium of Bristol had a safe-conduct to go to Spain for some (although it was not said whether these were for the king or not) and in the winter of 1214–15 John had eight Spanish horses in his stables.[112] Henry III also sent to Spain for horses,[113] and so did Edward I, who was prepared in 1281 to spend 1,000 marks on them.[114] Missions to Spain for horses were even more frequent under Edward II, who, although he impressed contemporaries with a lack of enthusiasm for warlike pursuits, certainly enjoyed his hunting and clearly wanted good mounts for it. In 1308 William de Guerenum was sent to Spain for thirty;[115] in 1310 William de Tholosa went there for more and in 1312 was also sent abroad for horses, although whether to Spain or not is not clear; in 1313 he was sent to Spain and Navarre for thirty and in 1314 again to Spain;[116] the king's sergeant Dominic de Runcevalle was sent there for six in 1310 and had bought two for 50 marks by December;[117] in 1317 a merchant of Caen or Condom was ordered to buy horses and armour in France, Gascony, Navarre and Spain;[118] and Hugh le Despenser was to bring back destriers and other horses if he went to Spain in 1319.[119] Some time during his reign Edward also entrusted the Spanish merchant Andrés Pérez de Castrogeriz and his associate Gonsalvus Guderitz with 1,000 marks to buy horses in Spain, but both Edward II and Pérez died before the deal was complete and Edward III's man Arnold Garsy de St John was sent out in 1332–3 to recover the money from Guderitz and Perez's heirs and buy fifty horses with it. Prices were higher than expected, because he was able to buy only twenty-three for £715 13s 4d.[120] Clearly most Spanish horses reaching England were ordered, mostly for the royal stables, but some may have been brought as a speculative venture since Domyngus Joun in London in 1311 was known as 'mercator equorum de Ispannia' yet so far as we know had no dealings with the king,[121] and Juan de Bures de Ispannia in 1304 brought to Sandwich three horses worth £23.[122] Arnald Garsy's imports are the last example of large numbers of Spanish horses being brought; in 1334 he and three others went to Spain and other foreign parts for horses and other goods and to carry out other royal business,[123] but after that kings ceased to send to Spain for bloodstock.

This marked change was caused by a coincidence of several pressures. The Castilian monarchy had for a long time issued intermittent prohibitions against export of horses[124] which they needed themselves for their Moorish and Iberian wars, but had allowed licences to export to the English kings among others; these licences were less easy to obtain however once Castile became a firm ally of France and the Hundred Years War became more bitter. Yet that cause alone would not have stopped exports as early as the 1330s, and possibly decreasing English demand was as important. Edward II's large introduction of Spanish blood to his stables and careful breeding may have limited the need felt by Edward III's stablemen for new Spanish stock. Also changes in the English army may have affected demand: the emphasis on archers and foot soldiers probably reduced the demand for warhorses a little, although the cavalry was never superseded and a good warhorse remained essential for any knight; possibly the heavier plate armour favoured from the later thirteenth century demanded larger, heavier horses than those with Spanish blood—the really heavy warhorse of this period was reckoned to cost up to £100 but Spanish horses do not seem to have come so expensive and were perhaps lighter. Some were none the less destriers and several of the orders for Spanish horses stipulated they should be warhorses, and Garsy's account makes it clear that he brought home seven destriers, ten coursers and two horses, but all were cheaper than £100. Two destriers were worth £60 each, two £50 each and three £40 each, while two coursers cost £40 each and the others ranged from £10 to £25; the horses cost £10 and £24. Clearly there was little difference between the top-quality horses and the poorer courser or the good courser and poorer destrier as far as prices went. Even if the warhorses were not up to the heaviest rider they were probably still popular for hunting, but in France they also remained popular as warhorses well into the fourteenth century despite the increasing weight of armour.[125] Possibly in England it was as much Edward II's breeding plans as the changing army composition, changing armour and political hostility which led to the end of imports.

Spain could also supply essentials to the navy in modest amounts, but again England could not allow dependence on a French ally, and imported most of her supplements from the greater supplies of the Baltic, except for the malleable iron so useful for shipbuilding which had to come in large part from Spain. Spain occasionally sent rosin, pitch, tar and bitumen, either from her own forests or picked up in Gascon ports from Landes.[126] Canvas, sailcloth and cordage were not unusual in fifteenth-century Spanish cargoes, some being picked up in Brittany and the Channel Isles, but some coming from Biscay which had plenty to spare by the sixteenth century.[127] Most of the cork needed for floats and buoys came from Portugal but a little came from Seville.[128] Basque shipbuilding enjoyed a good reputation by the late fifteenth century and ships themselves were a major article of commerce in the sixteenth century but few as yet were sold to English merchants; an isolated example is of the *Nicholas of Winchelsea*, late of Bilbao, being run by Henry Gray in 1484.[129] The Crown was more interested than the merchants, or perhaps information survives better for these transactions: Henry IV asked his half-sister, the Queen of Castile, to sell him her ship the *Sta María*, then at San Sebastián,[130] and Edward IV, rebuilding a navy, bought at least five Spanish ships between 1471 and 1484.[131]

However, Spanish exports to England of essential military and naval commodities were minor, except in the case of iron, which was of paramount importance. England was heavily dependent on foreign (and especially Spanish) supplies of this essential in the fifteenth century and the writer of the *Discourse of the Common Weal* was still complaining in 1549 that England could produce less than half the iron she needed, and had to import supplements, and often arms and armour itself: England, he says, had to import certain goods essential to life 'as yron and salte, for that is within the Realme, (yet of both is not halfe sufficient for the same) oiles, tarre, pitche, rosing, wherof we have none at all . . . for thoughe god is bountifull vnto vs and sendeth vs manie great commodities, yet we could not live with owt the commodities of others. And, for an ensample, of yron [and] salt, thoughe we have competentlie therof, yet we have not the iii part to suffice the Realme.'[132]

The third group of imports, foodstuffs and wines, while not generally necessary for subsistence, was essential for palatable meals, and the writer of the *Libelle*, moving in circles which used spices, sweeteners, Mediterranean fruits and wines as a matter of course, saw them as nothing but beneficial, although his dislike of the Venetian and Florentine trade did lead him to criticise their import of eastern spices and sweet wine.

Corn was one of the real necessities which was occasionally brought in the earlier period. A Castilian merchant provided 120 quarters for royal use in 1255, some was brought from Ajo near Santander in 1309 for Bayonne, and later Bermeo seems to have been the outlet port.[133] In the savage famine years of 1315–17 England looked to Spain as well as Genoa and Sicily for provisions: in 1317 Laurence de Poyhane, master of the S *Julián of San Sebastián* was to fetch corn and a letter was sent on behalf of Antonio Pessagno of Genoa to the rulers of Castile asking them to let his servants export up to 1,000 raised bushels of wheat; this wheat would presumably have come from Andalusia, where the Genoese were established and which at this time was still a useful corn producer.[134] Some of the safe-conducts given to other Italians to bring corn could well have covered exports made through their agents in Andalusia, too. Thereafter Spanish corn was rarely imported, although a safe-conduct of 1441 mentions corn as a possible cargo from Spain.[135] English growers were in general not in favour of foreign imports; there were complaints of ruin following imports of cheap corn, and in 1463 protection was offered to English suppliers by forbidding all imports unless scarcity pushed English prices above a specified level.[136]

Salt too was an essential in which there early developed an international trade, England had its own good supplies but supplemented them from the Bay of Bourgneuf, from which by the mid fourteenth century came two-thirds to three-quarters of her salt imports.[137] The Bay's nearness was a clear advantage over the good Iberian sources. Castilian deposits were found at Anaña in Alava, near Cuenca, and in the southern areas near Jaén, Cordoba, Seville and Cadiz; in Portugal the deposits at Setubal were good. Salt was mentioned as a possible return cargo from Spain in 1364 and was occasionally brought into all southern English ports on Spanish ships,[138] although it is not made clear whether it was Spanish salt or picked up at the Bay en route.

Foreign flavourings are on the border between luxury and necessity: the wealthy considered them indispensable and their recipes rely on a heavy use of several at a time, but the poor can rarely have tasted them. The Spaniards provided mainly three European flavourings—cummin, licorice and saffron—and rarely touched the expensive oriental spices which were the Italians' monopoly.

Cummin was carried most frequently in the thirteenth and fourteenth centuries and in 1283 and 1289 was included in the list of typical Spanish imports for which there was to be a special broker in London.[139] It was probably a bequest from Moorish cookery and some supplies may have been from North Africa. Like most flavourings and spices, its customs valuation did not become quickly conventionalised and indeed fluctuated widely, but its value on the whole declined through the fifteenth century: it was valued in Bristol in 1404 at 17s the 100 lb, in 1475 at 10s and in 1478 at 6s 8d. At the same time shipments declined in frequency. Since the scarcity was not leading to rising prices it seems that cummin was dropping out of favour.

Licorice, for medicinal use, began to be more frequently imported by Spaniards in the fifteenth century and was fairly widely dealt in by Gascons too. Again customs valuations varied but seem to be dropping in the later century, possibly this time because of increasing supplies with the expanding Iberian trade, rather than with lack of demand. At Bristol its valuation dropped from 5s the bale in 1466 and 1469 to 3s 4d in the following decade, and at Southampton it dropped from 6s 8d the bale in 1434 to 2s 6d in 1464. Both cummin and licorice were fairly cheap to buy: Durham Abbey for instance paid a little over a penny a pound for cummin in the fourteenth century, and about fourpence a pound for licorice in the fifteenth, while pepper would cost 2s.[140]

Vastly more expensive then these was saffron, which was grown in and imported from Italy, Valencia and Aragon as well as in the areas around Toledo, Jaén and Guadalajara. Occasionally Aragonese saffron was carried by Castilians, such as the 5 lb carried in 1440 by Juan Martín de Luxaro from Bilbao,[141] but usually no provenance is given. Most of the imports by Spaniards are on Basque ships along with cargoes of iron, beaverskins, rosin and nails, so it is unlikely to have been from the Jaén fields and was more probably from the central areas, with perhaps other Aragonese supplements travelling up the Ebro valley. Customs valuations again vary and are lower than market prices at 10s to 6s 8d the pound, while the Durham Abbey Cellarers and Bursars usually paid between 9s and 13s 4d although sometimes as much as £1 the pound.

Sweetening, mostly in the form of honey, but increasingly in the form of sugar, was fairly often brought by Spaniards. Honey was produced all over Europe, including England, but steady supplements of dozens or scores of tons a year were brought in from Basque and Gascon ports. This may indicate that England's climate did not enable her to produce as much as she wanted, but possibly indicates that then as now there were people of discriminating palates who enjoyed the taste of Pyrenean honeys.

Estimated at £2 10s the ton by the customs collectors of the fifteenth century, honey was cheap compared with sugar, assessed at £40 the ton. Much of England's sugar was handled by Italians and brought from Mediterranean and North African sources, but enough was grown in western Europe and the newly exploited Atlantic islands in the fifteenth century for sugar to feature frequently in Bristol's Iberian trade. Most came

Table 18   Imports of sugar to Bristol, 1465–93.[1]

Date	Lisbon	Madeira	Spain	Seville	Huelva	Andalusia	Sanlúcar
1465–66	3	–	–	–	–	–	–
1469	15½	–	–	–	–	–	–
1473	–	–	–	8¼	–	–	–
1474	10	–	–	–	–	–	–
1475	1	–	–	–	–	–	–
1476	–	–	2	–	–	–	–
1479–80	234¼	–	–	50	–	–	–
1485–86	60¾	232½	–	4	19	1	–
1486–87	7	–	–	6	–	½	–
1492–93	766	–	–	3	–	–	11

[1] The details of the accounts are as for Table 11. The unit is the hundredweight (the *caisse* used in some accounts is the equivalent of the hundredweight). The provenances are the ports and areas from which the ships are stated to have come in the accounts and indicate loading points rather than production areas.

from Portugal; Castilian supplies from the Canaries either could not compete with Portuguese ones from Madeira or were more used at home.

Fruits, both dried and fresh, and nuts were welcome additions to the English diet. Figs, raisins and (more rarely) dates found a seasonal market and could not be easily sold after winter, as Nicholas Palmer of Bristol pointed out: he claimed that Moses Conterin was refusing to accept a return cargo from Andalusia of figs and raisins which he had ordered, because the ship had been delayed by storm and arrived too late for him to sell them profitably.[142] Such fruits were far from a Spanish monopoly and large amounts came in from Portugal or on Italian vessels from the Mediterranean, but fairly steady, moderate amounts were brought from Spain and household accounts sometimes refer to the fruit bought specifically as Seville figs, or Spanish raisins.[143] The nuts brought were usually almonds but the reference to 'small nuts' may indicate a filbert-type also.[144] Of fresh fruit the sharp oranges often used in medicine were those most frequently brought, and they were almost a commonplace in small amounts among Iberian, particularly Portuguese, cargoes to London and Southampton in the fifteenth century; but like all fresh fruit they were troublesome if weather was treacherous and delays occurred and some were already described as *debil'* on arrival. Pomegranates, which had been the main fruit bought for the ailing Queen Eleanor in 1289, became rarer, and lemons and apples were rarer still.[145]

Other foods brought in small quantities were mostly from the south: vinegar, rice, olives, onions, whalemeat in the earlier period and tunny fish in the later provided change for the upper classes.

Larger in bulk and value were the wines aboard Spanish ships. Spanish wines were exported from the thirteenth century onwards to France, Flanders and England, and were well appreciated in all places. Spaniards had been bringing wines into England at least as early as 1227–8[146] and they continued to be an important part of their trade from north and south, as well as of their carrying trade from the Mediterranean and Gascony. The price-fixing lists of the second half of the fourteenth century clearly show that they were considered as good quality as Gascon wines: Spanish, Gascon and Osey wines were fixed at the maximum retail price of 6d a gallon or 100s a tun, while best Rochelle was not to exceed 4d,[147] and at least one recipient of an annual royal gift of two tuns of wine preferred it to be Spanish.[148] In practice however, after the years immediately following the Black Death, the wine often failed to reach Gascon prices, as sales by the king's ministers in Cornwall show. In 1351–2 and 1361–2 it was sold at the same price as Gascon—£5 6s 8d and £4 the tun respectively, but in 1352–3 it fetched only £2 3s 4d to £4 the tun while Gascon fetched £3 6s 8d to £6, and after 1380 it sold for £2 the tun while Gascon was £3. Generally Spanish wines remained more expensive then wines of Rochelle, but in the last decade of the century there were years when they fell even below that. However by 1405 they were back among the higher prices at £5 the tun.[149] Prices of course fluctuated widely depending on the supplies of the year, and the time of the year they were sold, since by summer wines were old and weak and prices would drop, and once the new wines came in the old were virtually unsaleable. There would probably be some difference too according to reputation, and even to the quality of particular shipments, although the whole system of vineyard status and vintage was missing at this period. That Spanish wines were so often lower priced than Gascon implies lack of quality or lack of popularity in the south-west, unless much of that sold was wine forfeited from Spanish enemies after 1369 and thus saleable at less than market prices, but this seems unlikely. The Trastamaran troubles decreased the supply of Spanish wines in England but some still got through: in 1370 London forbade the keeping of Spanish and Gascon wines in the same cellar as Rhenish in an attempt to stop fraudulent mixing[150] and in 1374 Walter Broun of Norwich had 14 tuns of white Spanish wine, now too old and weak to sell advantageously in England, but worth re-exporting to Prussia, presumably for pickling.[151]

Although most of the wines are called simply Spanish, a few details emerge from the records. The wines were both white and red but white seems to have predominated. The Cornish royal officials sometimes called the white they handled 'Rubidage'; this usually came in on northern ships so is almost certainly from the northern coast, and is possibly a corruption of Ribadeo, or of Ribadavia, which furnished popular wines in England in the sixteenth century.[152] Basque wines appeared: 20 tuns of red Biscay were brought to Southampton in 1441 by Martín Ochoa, and Englishmen bought wines in Bilbao in 1458 and Fuenterrabía in 1467;[153] but some came from the areas of the Rioja, Logroño and Navarrete through the Basque ports too, so it is not usually clear exactly which wines the Basque ships were carrying.

Wines from Castro Urdiales were mentioned as early as 1237 when 12 tuns were bought at Southampton for Henry III;[154] again these probably came from Biscay, or the inland areas. Galician wines from Vivero are recorded from the second half of the fourteenth century and the Flemish commodity list mentioned wines as a Galician export even before that; it seems that this was an area exploited mainly for the Flemish taste, since most of the references in English records to Vivero wines are to their being plundered on the way to Flanders. In 1402 for instance 150 tuns were taken off a bark of Corunna, and 84 tuns off a ship of Bermeo;[155] however the Genoese merchants who used a ship from Zeeland to pick up 85½ tuns of Galician wines at Betanzos, near Corunna, intended to sell it in England.[156]

Some of the Spanish wines, probably those from the south, were difficult to classify, and in 1366 some were arrested with wines of Osey and the Algarve at Dartmouth by the mayor and bailiffs on a royal order to impound sweet wines. The Dartmouth burgesses who owned them alleged that this was a deliberate and malicious move to upset their trade on the part of the officials, and their petition for release was granted by the king in a letter stating that it was 'not the king's intent that such wines should be called or reputed sweet wines'.[157] However some of the southern wines certainly were sweet: in 1406 'sweet wines of Lepe' were brought into England;[158] yet on the other hand neither the 120 tuns of wine of 'Lupe' seized off Cornwall in 1382, nor the 85 tuns brought from Lepe for London by Juan Rodriguez of Seville in 1413 were called sweet,[159] and the large amount of Andalusian wine shipped into Bristol in the late fifteenth century was not taxed as sweet. The wine however must have been naturally strong, if not fortified, and Chaucer, whose family were vintners, and who must have known well the qualities of wines, issues a strong warning against the heady Lepe wines through the lips of the Pardoner:

Now kepe yow fro the white and fro the red
And namely fro the white wyn of Lepe,
That is to selle in Fysshstrete or in Chepe.
This wyn of Spaigne crepeth subtilly
In otheres wynes, growynge faste by,
Of which ther ryseth swich fumositee
That whan a man hath dronken draughtes thre,

And weneth that he be at hoom in Chepe,
He is in Spaigne, right at the toune of Lepe—
Nat at the Rochele, ne at Burdeux toun;
And thanne wol he seye 'Sampsoun, Sampsoun!'[160]

The Castilians certainly carried, and in some cases produced their own, romney, malmsey and bastard, which were sweet wines;[161] they also carried from the Mediterranean wines of Majorca and Greece in 1402,[162] wines of Caprik',[163] and creci wines originally made in Greece but copied in Italy.[164]

Spanish wines were clearly popular enough to be one of the earliest cargoes sought in Spain by the English themselves, as well as by Flemish and Italian dealers for the English market. Richard Kempe, one of the earliest English masters we know of going to Spain, was hired by Portuguese merchants to fetch Portuguese and Spanish wines and olive oil in 1338.[165] English vintners receiving licences to export bullion for the new season's wines in 1364 were empowered to use them in Spain as well as Gascony, and some certainly did so.[166] Four years later Robert Stotter and William Gyse, owners of the Cog Thomas of Hoke, and Henry Herbury sent the ship from London to Spain for wines.[167] Unfortunately their voyage highlights the danger that not only the Anglo–Spanish wine trade but all Anglo–Spanish trade was running into at that time—the master and merchants aboard feared to go beyond Bordeaux because of the violence of the Spanish civil war. Herbury however felt their fears were unjustified and sued the owners for default. After the troubles of the civil war were behind them, the English merchants continued to trade in Spanish wines, and the customs accounts for Bristol show how heavily engaged they had become by then in Andalusia.

The total amount of Spanish wine offered on the English market at any time is impossible to assess, as provenance of wines is so rarely given. Those on ships from the south of Spain may fairly be assumed to be mainly Spanish in origin, but those on some ships from the north might also be of La Rochelle or even Gascony.

Lack of good records at La Rochelle leaves its role unclear, but it is possible that at that time its wine periodically bulked large in Spanish cargoes since the Spaniards were well established there commercially, and La Rochelle had long been a main exporting centre for the wines of the Aunis and Poitou, which were popular in Flanders and had been in England until the loss of all England's French territories except Gascony acted as a forcing house for the latter's wine trade. The earliest reference to Spaniards carrying wines of La Rochelle to England seems to be that of 1298 when the Sta María of Castro Urdiales was plundered when bringing 220 tuns for burgesses of La Rochelle[168] but doubtless this was not the first instance. Later in 1336 ships of San Sebastián and of Castro were loaded with Rochelle wines;[169] in 1353 the St Mary la Coronade was to carry them to

Bristol for Spanish and Genoese merchants,[170] in 1361 three merchants of
Bermeo loaded 80 tuns of white wine there for London aboard the *S Juan of
Bilbao*,[171] and in 1356–7 and 1361–2 the Haveners of Cornwall recorded
prise taken in Rochelle wines from Spanish ships.[172] The total number of
known instances of Spaniards carrying this wine is low and it is dangerous
to generalise from such a small number, but it may be more than a coincidence that several of them fall in the period 1350–69, and it may indicate
a conscious effort by Spanish shippers to compensate for the severe depre-
ssion in the Gascon trade.[173]

Castilian activity in the Gascon trade is better recorded but was rarely
more than modest, and usually negligible; the ambivalent, nearly
love–hate, relationship between Gascon and Basque probably inhibited
the development of trading in the earlier period, and the instability during
the Hundred Years War made it difficult later. Probably there was some
trading in the thirteenth century when relations were good between
Alfonso X and Edward I, and some of the 353 tuns of wine taken into
Winchelsea in 1267–8[174] might have been picked up in Gascony; certainly
Spanish merchants were in Gascony at the end of the century, and some
were plying between Flanders and Gascony in 1302,[175] but not until the
survival of registers of the Constable of Bordeaux can the size of their role
be clearly seen. Between 1303 and 1308 ships of Fuenterrabía, San Sebastián, Bermeo, Castro Urdiales, Laredo, Santander, Ribadeo and Corunna
loaded there, but their numbers were small at twenty-four out of a total of
well over 2,800 in the five years, and they carried a total of only 1,977 tuns
when the average annual export was well over 90,000 tuns.[176] During the
decades of the mid fourteenth century, when contacts between England
and Spain were increasingly friendly, they played a larger role in a smaller
trade. They arrived in increasing numbers after the truce of 1351, and in
the year and a half between December 1359 and July 1361 the climax came
with eighty-four of the 480 departing ships being Spanish; they took
mainly the spring wines and in March and April alone thirty-seven of the
ships loaded were Castilian, taking a total of 4,106 tuns at a time when
annual exports had sunk to under 30,000 tuns.[177] Since the total exports
had sunk so far it is unlikely that there was any real shortage of traditional
shipping for it, and the increasing Spanish activity was due to their own
pushing initiative, offering merchants competitive terms.

Much of the Gascon wine carried by Spaniards cannot be proved to have
come to England, since customs accounts are scarce and the Butlers'
accounts which survive in greater numbers record only aliens' wines and
not those of English merchants merely transported by aliens—and most of
the Spanish activity fell into the latter category. Of the 103 Spanish ships
leaving Gascony between 1355 and 1361 only three can be certainly seen
unloading in England.[178] There was of course plenty of scope for them to
take the wines elsewhere for English or other merchants, as England took

only half Bordeaux's exports then.[179] England's demand for wine was still
high but she did not monopolise Gascon trade which could flow freely to
Flanders or elsewhere. The Butlers' accounts do show considerable numbers of Spanish ships arriving in England with alien wine aboard and, since
so few of these can be traced in Bordeaux when the two sets of records
coincide in survival, the wine must have been from Spain, La Rochelle or
other western sources; it is most likely that much of it was from the
Spaniards' own vineyards.

Table 19 Spanish activity in the Gascon wine trade, 1303–1483.[1]

Date	No. of Spanish ships loaded	Total ships loaded	Tuns aboard Spanish ships	Total tuns exported
1303	6	289	619	30,709
1303–04	3	588	195	55,393
1304–05	6	1,020	318	86,233
1305–06				97,848
1306–07	3	617	356	93,452
1307–08	4	783	285	85,172
1308–09	–	772	–	102,724
1310–11	1	615	48	51,351
1318–20	3	?	162	?
1355–56	6	152	646	14,411
1356–57	7	244	888	20,200
1357–58	7	221	509	27,838
1359–60	15	137	1,659	14,722
1360–61	69	343	7,306	26,797
1444–45	1	136	115	12,000[2]
1448–49	3	160	146	12,000[2]
1482–83	8	306	?	?

[1] P.R.O. E101/158/2, 5, 10, 160/3, 7, 8, 161/3, 162/1, 4, 5, 6, 164/12 (this, for 1318–
1320, is fragmentary only so no totals are available), 173/4, 182/2, 195/19;
B.L. Add. Ms. 15524 (for 1444–5); *Archives Historiques du Département de la
Gironde*, L (1915) (for 1482–3). The few surviving accounts for 1320–55 and the
many for 1372–1444 show no Spaniards at all at Bordeaux.
[2] Approximate figures.

The Butlers' accounts allow some assessment of the Spanish role in the
alien wine trade. Until 1351 the scale of their activity was modest although
Spanish arrivals were not uncommon: in 1328–9 and 1329–30 Spanish
ships carried 250 tuns and 294 tuns respectively for other aliens when total
alien imports were 7,386 tuns and 6,067 tuns; in 1330–1 a Spaniard
unloaded 23 tuns out of an alien total of 634, and another Spanish ship
brought Englishmen's wines to Winchelsea; in 1333–4 26 tuns certainly

and 71 possibly were owned by Spaniards and a further 71 were brought
for aliens while the alien total was 6,196 tuns; and in 1336–7 they carried
403 tuns out of an alien total of 2,146 tuns. This modest role continued in
the next decade.[180] There was then a brief absence in the years of the Black
Death and the first war years with France, but then they moved in in larger
numbers, and also owned considerable percentages of the alien wines
brought—32 per cent in 1352–3, 16 per cent in 1353–4 and then 30 per cent
in 1366–7; and at times their ships carried substantial amounts for other
aliens, making the total they handled in some way as importers and
carriers, very high in some years.[181]

Table 20   Wines handled by Spaniards, 1349–95.[1]

Date	Total alien tunnage	Spanish-owned wines	% of total owned by Spaniards	Others' wines carried by Spaniards	Total % handled by Spaniards
1349–50	1,815	–	–	–	–
1350–51	2,169	60	3	–	3
1351–52	1,051	216	21	–	21
1352–53	2,646	864	33	117	37
1353–54	2,389	362	16	310	28
1354–55	1,829	229	13	–	13
1355–56	1,799	110	6	–	6
1357–58	2,052	40	2	53	5
1358–59	1,640	30	2	214	15
1359–60	1,809	175	10	72	15
1360–61	1,437	123	9	205	23
1361–62	2,856	249	9	69	11
1363–64	1,493	147	10	34	12
1364–65	1,454	81	6	–	6
1366–67	1,150	340	30	–	30
1367–68	1,177	70	6	–	6
1370–71	817	–	–	–	–
1371–72	1,174	–	–	–	–
1378–79	2,017	–	–	–	–
1379–80	1,285	–	–	–	–
1380–81	1,185	–	–	–	–
1381–82	1,392	–	–	–	–
1392–93	1,927	86	4	177	14
1393–94	4,868	59	1	385	9
1394–95	3,947	62	2	486	14

[1] P.R.O. E101/80/3–7, 9, 11–20, 22–3, 25; the unit is the tun. Totals include
Rhenish wine; very little of this wine is stated to be Gascon.

The Trastamaran hostility after 1369 broke into the trade quite dramat-

ically and the accounts both of the Constables of Bordeaux and the Butlers
show a total disappearance of Spanish ships and merchants for a decade.
The accounts of the Cornish ministers confirm this disappearance until
1382. For England this was most unfortunate, as exports of wines from
Bordeaux became abysmally low[182] and she had now lost her supplements
from Spain and Rochelle.

With peace in the last decade of the fourteenth century Spaniards clearly
began to reclaim their carrying role, and in the fifteenth century a scattering of ships continued in the trade despite the political instability, and
after the loss of Gascony—when England badly needed alter-
natives—their activity increased.[183] The customs accounts and various
legal documents confirm this picture of continuing but modest Spanish
activity, and the Constables' accounts show that again very little of the
wine was Gascon; not until 1444–5 do they record one ship, the S Mark of
San Sebastián, and the account for 1448–9 shows only three, all from
Fuenterrabía—it seems to have been only the very nearest Basque ports
which bothered with it. Other records however show a master from Santander collecting wines there for London in 1416, and a little later Spanish
merchants used a carvel from Bridgwater to transport their Gascon
wines;[184] none the less their interest was not heavily engaged there, not
even by 1482–3 when the first French account shows only eight ships.

The Bristol customs accounts for Edward IV's reign by their last ports of
call of incoming vessels confirm this low Spanish interest in Gascony until
the early years of Henry VII.[185] Until then what wines the Spaniards
brought were mainly from their own northern areas and they left not
only Gascony but also Andalusia to the English, and the Portuguese trade
to the Portuguese and English. Quite clearly Englishmen had come to rely
heavily in the west on Iberia to offset Gascon losses.

The nascent Spanish activity in Gascony was temporarily disrupted by
the Navigation Acts of 1485 and 1490 but already they had an alternative
and pushed vigorously into the Andalusian trade. It proved fairly easy to
buy exemption licences from the Navigation Acts however, and by 1492
Spaniards were strongly active not only in Andalusia but also again in
Gascony, not only keeping their share but improving it.

To Bristol this Iberian trade was very important with 20 to 30 per cent of
her wines (which were a fifth to a quarter of England's total imports)
coming from Spain alone.

Southampton and London can offer no supplementary information:
only two very short tunnage accounts survive for London and these show
no Spaniards,[186] although the enrolled customs accounts show them to
have been very busy there; in Southampton no last ports of call are given
although Spaniards are certainly importing wine there.[187]

The treaty of 1466 led to Spanish-owned wines, of whatever origin, often
being listed separately in the enrolled customs accounts, and where this

Table 21 Imports of wine to Bristol, 1461–93.[1]

Date	Gascony		Spain		Andalusia		Portugal		Mediterranean		France		British outports	
1461	—	—	4	—	—	—	—	—	—	—	—	—	—	20
1465–66	—	247	46	—	—	—	—	549	—	—	—	—	—	31
1469	—	—	—	—	—	—	—	3	—	—	—	—	—	—
1471	31	8	27	—	—	227	—	44	—	—	—	—	—	11
1473	—	146	12	9	—	—	—	—	—	—	—	60	—	3
1474	—	57	22	18	—	—	—	—	—	—	—	—	—	24
1475	67	227	59	—	20	—	—	40	—	—	—	4	—	77
1477–78	—	499	1	11	—	172	—	179	—	—	—	—	—	23
1479–80	22	807	36	—	81	79	—	195	—	—	—	58	—	39
1485–86	494	151	24	—	39	189	92	117	—	90	—	—	—	15
1486–87	—	400	24	—	239	434	82	191	—	—	—	—	—	11
1492–93	758	441	16	47	440	239	9	459	—	—	—	—	—	151

[1] The unit is the tun. Figures in the left columns are tuns aboard Spanish vessels, those in the right tuns on all other vessels. The details of dates of the accounts are as in Table 11. The place-name is the ship's stated last port of call.

occurs the scale of the interest of the Spanish merchants appears.[188] Until 1474 Spanish importance was slight, unless some wines were included without specification in general totals, thus making the peak of 1474–5 less sudden than it seems. Indeed the peak itself may be false as, if the

Table 22   Spanish-owned wines brought to England, 1472–89.[1]

Date	Total wine imports	Amount brought by Spaniards[2]	Spaniards' % of total
1472–73	5,646	24	0
1473–74	4,159	18	0
1474–75	5,366	1,040	19
1475–76	4,272	143+	3+
1476–77	6,820	178	3
1477–78	5,934	97+	2+
1478–79	8,599	235+	3+
1479–80	7,371	7+	0+
1480–81	8,473	50+	1+
1481–82	6,172	84+	1+
1482–83	5,575	336+	6+
1483–84	7,024	1,900+	27+
1484–85	7,183	1,257+	18+
1485–86	6,013	25+	0+
1486–87	7,081	661+	9+
1487–88	6,352	175+	3+
1488–89	10,599	268+	3+

[1] P.R.O. E356/22, 23. Where accounts do not run from Michaelmas to Michaelmas they have been included under the year in which most of the account falls. The amounts are to the nearest tun and include sweet wines.

[2] The figures in this column are for ports where Spanish wine was separately itemised. These amounts are usually incomplete because in most years the clerks in some ports combined totals of denizen and Spanish wines into one figure. Where this happens in ports unimportant for Spanish activity it may make little difference; where it happens in Bristol, London or Southampton it may obscure considerable tunnage. Years where such combined totals are given are marked with a plus sign. For details see Table 23.

Southampton imports (shown in Table 23) fell evenly in 1474–6, Spanish imports would be nearer 12 per cent in both years. The rise might however have been a true one, stimulated by lack of English shipping during an abortive expedition to France. Thereafter the Spanish role was again modest but probably rose steadily to reach the peak of 1483–5 although the stages are obscured by the habit of clerks of combining Spanish and denizen totals for many ports. The drop immediately after 1485–6 may be partly due to this habit, although as a glance at the figures for each port shows their activity in their main centres certainly did fall off. None the less they still contributed wine under licence, and they might well have been recovering their position just at the time when the end of their customs concessions eliminates their special mention in the records, as the

Table 23   Spanish-owned wines brought to England, port by port, 1472–89.[1]

	1472–73	1473–74	1474–75	1475–76	1476–77	1477–78
Bridgwater	–	–	–	*	–	–
Bristol	–		Account missing			55
Exeter and Dartmouth	–	–	–	–	35	*
Ipswich	–	–	–	–	–	12
London	–	–	120	143	35	30
Plymouth	–	–	–	–	–	–
Poole	–	–	–	–	–	–
Sandwich	24	–	98	–	–	–
Southampton	–	18	825	←[2]	108	←[2]

	1478–79	1479–80	1480–81	1481–82	1482–83	1483–84
Bridgwater	–	–	–	–	–	40
Bristol	–	–	–	1	86	95
Exeter and Dartmouth	*	*	–	–	*	*
Ipswich	–	–	–	–	–	–
London	107	7	50	77	225	1,600
Plymouth	4	–	–	4	2	148
Poole	–	–	–	–	–	–
Sandwich	–	–	–	2	23	17
Southampton	124	–	*	*	*	*

	1484–85	1485–86	1486–87	1487–88	1488–89	
Bridgwater	6	–	–	–	*	
Bristol	–	–	*	*	152	
Exeter and Dartmouth	*	*	*	*	*	
Ipswich	–	–	–	–	–	
London	1,083	*	580	175	*	
Plymouth	141	25	5	*	116	
Poole	*	–	–	–	–	
Sandwich	27	–	–	–	–	
Southampton	*	*	76	*	*	

[1] P.R.O. E356/22, 23; the unit is the tun. Wine imported under the licence of the former Gascon Arnald Trussel is not included unless said to be by Spanish factors.

In asterisked years Castilians imported wine but their totals are not recorded separately.

[2] These accounts run from 29 September 1474 to 2 November 1476 and from 3 November 1476 to 20 June 1478.

Bristol particular accounts seem to indicate. A comparison of the Bristol particular accounts and the enrolled ones indicates just how inadequate the latter are for an assessment of the true Spanish role in the wine trade.[189] In the enrolment for 1485–6 there is no indication whatsoever that Spaniards had any connection with the 1,217 tuns imported there, but the particular account shows that 228 tuns came from Andalusia, 38 tuns from northern Spain, a further 676 tuns were carried on Spanish vessels and moreover Spanish merchants had owned 32 tuns of it which the enrolling clerk had not thought it worth noting; in all well over 900 tuns owed something to Spanish enterprise. A similar although not so sharp contrast was found the following year when the enrolling clerk simply noted 1,265 tuns brought by denizens and Spaniards, but the particular account shows Spanish merchants shipping 21 tuns, Murcia and Andalusia providing 671 tuns, northern Spain 24 tuns, while Spanish ships brought another 20 tuns from Lisbon. The amount is smaller than in the previous year out of a higher total import of 1,330 tuns, but Spain and the Spaniards are still very important despite the Navigation Act's effect on the Gascon trade.

In general one can be certain that Spanish wines had been long-established in England as in France and Flanders, that they were of good quality and reasonably popular, but their quantity was insignificant as long as England was importing 15,000 to 20,000 tuns a year and the Gascon trade was going well. However, when disruption dogged this trade in the mid fourteenth century, Spanish activity began to increase in it and alongside it, and, when in the fifteenth century England's total imports sank to 10,000 tuns a year and then after the loss of Gascony often to less than 5,000, their activity relatively assumed ever more importance. It is clear from the records, for all their shortcomings, that as a source of wine Spain never compensated for the Gascon loss. With the final loss of all its French territories the days of plentiful and cheap wines were over for England, but the south of Spain could produce and send enough to establish a new taste for stronger wines and before long Spanish sack was able to be the fashionable and popular drink.

The last group of goods to consider is that related to clothing, comfort and display, which include furs, leathers and silks and various manufactured articles.

Leathers were the most important component of this group, and fine, soft Cordovan leather or cordwain remained a byword for luxury long after the Spaniards had ceased to bring it. Its reputation rested on the skills of the Moorish craftsmen in Cordoba, and from the first years of the Reconquest Spanish merchants made the most of the manufactures in the new territories and brought large amounts of cordwain to northern markets; it could make up the greater part of a cargo, as in 1277 when a Spanish ship wrecked was alleged to be carrying 100 bales of cordwain worth £1,600 sterling, while the rest of the cargo was worth only £940.[190] Also sent to

England was basan, a lower-quality leather made from sheepskin and sometimes already dyed red, and baldred, a cheaper white leather. Goatskins and cow hides were imported for tougher goods and, although some of the hides might have been from the north where there was good grazing land, some were noted as good Seville hides and many others came aboard ships along with cargoes of figs and raisins from the south. Much of the leather sent however was called just that—*allutum*—without any further qualification.

When special brokers were appointed in London in 1283 and 1289 to deal with Spanish and Portuguese imports, these were listed as leather, basan, goatskins, baldred, cummin and other goods,[191] and most of the debts to Spanish merchants in London at that time were for leather. Of the fifty-four debts in the *Letter Books* between 1276 and 1286 for which the commodity sold is recorded, thirty-eight were for sales of leathers to cordwainers and curriers,[192] and the recognisance roll for 1284-5 shows that fifteen debts, amounting to £223 13s, were owed to Spaniards by leather merchants while twenty debts by chaloners amounted only to £137 17s 9d.[193] Imports of leathers are frequently mentioned in customs accounts particularly for south-eastern ports up to about 1325 and leathers accounted for £740 of the £1,099 worth of Spaniards' goods customed at Southampton in 1310–11, but somewhat later accounts for Sandwich show a marked drop. Although these accounts are for only two ports and four years, other records of all types show that they reflect a decisive change in the character of the Spanish goods sent into England at about this time (Table 24).

The fashionable continued to wear soft Spanish leather, and Chaucer's Sir Topaz showed his extravagance by his Spanish shoe leather, but the Spaniards were no longer supplying it. The techniques were quickly copied elsewhere and it seems clear that the Castilians allowed the Moorish industry to run down, so that imports in the later fourteenth and fifteenth centuries came on Portuguese and Gascon ships or on Italian ones bringing their own cordwain from Pisa and Genoa or picking it up in Malaga and Valencia[194] and it became extremely rare to find leather shipped from Spain to England.[195].

Allied to the leather trade, but always much feebler, was the Spanish fur trade. Furs were fashionable, a sign of wealth and also a near necessity for comfort in medieval winters, and all who could lined their robes, cloaks, hats, gloves, shoes and bed coverings with furs even if they were scraps or fourth-hand. Furs were obtainable locally everywhere in Europe including England, but as always exotic foreign furs or thicker, better furs from colder climates could command high prices in the international markets. Spain's cold upland winters and proximity to Africa allowed her to play a modest part in the trade in the thirteenth century. Most of the imports to England were simply called peltry, but this clearly included wild cat, civet

Table 24   Variety and values (£) of Spaniards' imports at Southampton and Sandwich, 1310–11 and 1325–29.[1]

	Leathers	Peltry	Wool and yarn	Iron	Oils, soap, etc.	Kermes	Mercury	Fruit and nuts	Rest
Southampton									
1310–11	704	16	126	133	–	–	40	19	61
Sandwich									
1325–26	55	27	–	550	111	–	–	110	4
1327–28	25	3	–	142	39	–	–	40	7
1328–29	6	12	1	493	242	150	6	43	21

[1] P.R.O. E122/136/21, 124/29–30. A few of the names at Southampton are doubtfully identified but the great majority are certainly Spaniards.

cat, hare, fox, goat, rabbit, lamb, wolf, beaver and squirrel.[196] The most frequently sent however were rabbit, lamb and beaver, and the total scale, small enough in the thirteenth century, slackened enormously, like the leather trade in the fourteenth.

The soft and glossy coney skins were worth importing and fairly popular[197] since the rabbit was not well established in England until the second half of the thirteenth century,[198] and then for a time was preserved as a game animal. Imports were generally to the south-east from London to Southampton and shipments might reach the thousands; in 1274–5 10,300 were sent into Winchelsea by Spaniards, and three London skinners owed at least £30 for coney skins in 1278;[199] but often the skins are mentioned simply as part of a total cargo as when in 1308 one Rodrigo brought to Sandwich a cargo of coney skins, iron, quicksilver, grease, hare and wolf skins, cordwain, basan and leather worth altogether £102.[200]

Skins of young lambs, sometimes even of unborn lambs,[201] were highly thought of for trimmings and some of the best came from Bougie, which gave its name to the skins known as 'budge'.[202] The budge on Spanish ships in the thirteenth may be from Bougie or Spanish, that of later periods was probably all from Spain as her wool production increased and often it is called Spanish lamb, Spanish budge or Spanish shanks.

Beaver skins were less a fashion fur than a hard-wearing weatherproof skin for outer clothing,[203] and the longer fibres could be used in felt hat making. English beaver seems to be already rare by the thirteenth century and Spanish beaver was steadily imported in small amounts throughout the period, without undergoing the permanent diminution of other fur trades. Amounts sent to Bristol in the fifteenth century illustrate the modest size of the trade: few ships brought more than two to four loads valued at £2 each, and the *María of Fuenterrabía*, which brought twenty-five loads in 1475, was exceptional. Total recorded imports for the whole of Edward's and Richard's reigns were sixty-four loads, but the first two years of Henry's reign, when the accounts also were for full years, show a brisker trade with forty-four-and-a-half loads brought.[204]

The clearly perceptible changes in the fur trade are first a decline from the variety of the early years to a predominance of rabbit, lamb and beaver by the early fourteenth century, then a new disappearance of coney skins and a general diminution in the scale of the trade. Miss Veale's work on the fur trade indicates the main pressures on it: in the thirteenth and four-teenth centuries the fashionable world began to clothe itself over-whelmingly in squirrel, which Spain did not have in abundance; increas-ing home supplies of coney skins made import less necessary and the fur less fashionable, so that it was common enough by 1363 to be considered most suitable for the middling to lower classes;[205] then Spain, like most other Mediterranean suppliers, could not compete with the efficient organisation of the fine and abundant Baltic fur supplies by the Hanseatic towns, which fed the fashion for squirrel, and which accounted for 80 to 90 per cent of all England's fur imports by the late fourteenth century.[206] The steady supply of lambskins on the other hand was helped by the Mesta dominance in Castile and increased grazing was provided by cutting back yet more forest, hitherto the sources of the small amounts of other furs. By the late fifteenth century fashions were changing again: stiffer furs in rich dark colours were demanded and, as the sables were becoming very expensive with the over-trapping and clearing in northern forests, black lambskins which Spain provided became more sought after. By the sixteenth century fewer furs were worn but those wanted were the exotic, and Spain could again find a market for her civet or North African skins; but the Spanish peltry trade was never again more than negligible.[207]

Occasional references were made to Spanish cloth; the households of King John and Henry III used it in 1214 and 1218–19 but the prices—£7 10s for five—do not imply high quality,[208] and they then disappear from the market. Silk making was a thriving Moorish industry but does not seem to have well survived the Castilian take-over and imports to England generally came from Italy or Aragon. Only occasionally is it mentioned on Spanish ships: the large amount worth £1,000 belonging to Francis Dyes or Juan Rodriguez, both Andalusians, may be of local make or from outside Castile as it was aboard a Venetian galley;[209] smaller imports were made in Bristol after 1485.[210] The linen, sail-cloth, canvas and baize occasionally brought in small quantities were probably picked up in Brittany or Flanders.

Carpets, for decorating tables, benches and walls rather than floors, were appreciated by the English upper classes, whose demand for luxurious and fashionable surroundings increased in the fifteenth century. The Italian merchants were able to find an easy market for Barbary carpets, and Spanish carpets too began to appear in inventories at the end of the fourteenth century.[211] These may have come from Salamanca, where a carpet industry throve, or from a continuation of the Moorish industry in Andalusia. The two fardells of carpets brought to London in 1432 by John Chirche on a ship of Deva, along with a cargo of iron and steel and nails, clearly came from a northern outlet and were possibly products of Salamanca.[212] From southern lands came the three great carpets worth £6 13s 4d each brought by Antonio Ferández to Southampton in November 1428.[213] His wares seem to have been very popular because in May 1429 he obtained a safe-conduct for a year to bring to England two carpet-workers and their servants, and he renewed his licence for a further two years in 1430.[214] These may have been meant simply as expert repairers for carpets already brought, but it is more likely Feránndez intended to set up a small workshop of skilled craftsmen in the middle of his market; unfortunately it has been impossible to discover the success of the enterprise.

Occasional shipments of paper, possibly of Andalusian origin, would please the scholars and clerks among the Spaniards' clients.[215] Felt hats aboard a Deva ship may have come from the industries of Segovia or Toledo, but may equally well be from Flanders.[216] Golden Moorish pottery was famous in the fourteenth century and as early as 1289 a Spanish ship brought some for Queen Eleanor but it did not appear on others or on English ones coming from Spain; it seems that the Castilians let this industry too run down and imports were generally in the hands of the Italians, who picked it up in the Balearic islands, Malaga or Valencia.[217] The frankincense at Exeter in Richard III's reign may have been a re-export of eastern provenance, or a cheaper substitute which could have been made from Spanish resin.[218] Wax too was a commodity for the upper classes and the religious, for seals and candles. From the thirteenth century, when wax was bought for Henry III from Spanish merchants in England,[219] small shipments were frequently brought on Spanish or English ships from Spain. Spain had not a large surplus of wax but enough for modest supplements for England's needs.

More dazzling, but negligible in trading terms were jewels and jewelled goods from Spain. Juan Seboll brought 10 lb of coral and 5 lb of Venetian gold into Dover in December 1474 and Pascuall Sole of Spain brought 600 yards of silk, 80 lb of coral and 10 lb of gold wire the following April,[220] but these seem to be the only Spaniards to try the speculative trade in raw materials for the London goldsmiths and they had to rely on oriental and African materials, probably bought from Italians. The Spanish jewelled goods mentioned in England were all in royal hands and were probably the result of gifts, dowry or plunder and had nothing to do with trade at all: Richard II and Henry VI pawned a silvered, gilded and enamelled Spanish table (probably a portable altar or reredos),[221] a Spanish saddle, Spanish stirrups of gem-encrusted gold,[222] a jewel laden gold 'palet' (possibly a sort of head-dress)[223] and a sword with scabbard, hilt and pommel of gold inlaid with balas, sapphires and pearls.[224]

On the same extravagant scale and just as negligible in the general pattern of the trade were the animals for English menageries: the monkeys brought to Bristol and London,[225] and the lions intended for Henry VI and Edward IV.[226]

Spain had sufficient goods and a sufficient variety of them to offer in return for England's cloth to make the fact that she and England were both major wool-producing countries unimportant, and although most of the goods could be supplied from other sources in Portugal and Italy, the size, proximity and ease of access of Castilian markets ensured steady and regular trade. Only the artificial interruptions of war and politics could distort this and then only temporarily.

The approval of the writer of the *Libelle of Englyshe Polycye* was clearly justified too. Most of the imports were useful, and some were essential to

England's economic as well as social life. The criticism he made of the trade was simply that it was not bringing England as much profit as it should because too much was going to Flanders, and should be forcibly brought into English harbours. This, given the pattern of European trade and the variety of goods involved, was impossible, but, as the conditions of the late fifteenth century showed, there was room for much expansion of the trade, although English shipping and English merchants since the mid fourteenth century had already been playing a very active part in the transport and marketing of the commodities.

NOTES TO CHAPTER 4

1 *Libelle*, ed. Warner, lines 53–8.

2 Gilliodts van Severen, *Etaple*, I, 14. M. van Houtte suggests a later, fourteenth-century, dating; 'Bruges et Anvers, marchés "nationaux" ou "internationaux" du XIVe au XVIe siècle', *Revue du Nord*, vol. 34 (1952), p. 89 n.l.

3 *Libelle*, ed. Warner, lines 58–60, 77–87.

4 A Commons petition of 1439 directed against the Italians also complained that Spanish, Portuguese, and Breton trade had fallen and ascribed it to over-activity by the Italians; *Rot. Parl.*, V, 31b. But Italian carrying was a symptom not the cause of the problem.

5 For general comment on the wool trade see Chapter 3.

6 See Table 14.

7 *Letter Book 'A'*, *passim*.

8 P.R.O. C76/107 m.1.

9 P.R.O. E28/38(27); E122/184/3 file 5; E159/235 Rec. Mich. m. 35; C76/119 m. 4.

10 P.R.O. SC8/5863, 5504: they complained when they were robbed and had still to answer for the custom duties.

11 *C.P.R. 1401–5*, p. 131.

12 The customs valuations can be useful for purposes of comparison in some cases but are of little use for market prices: they were assessed on the buying prices abroad, on the oath or letter of the owner, but they tended to become fixed and conventional, and by the later fifteenth century were usually about half the market price here.

13 Twelve pipes valued at £120; one ton and a hogshead at £25; a hogshead at £5; and three hundreds at £3; P.R.O. E122/19/13, 14.

14 P.R.O. E122/137/16; its use in cloth dyeing was forbidden at times (Carus–Wilson, *Medieval Merchant Ventures*, pp. 218–19).

15 Pérez Embid, 'Navigation et commerce dans le port de Seville au bas moyen âge', *Le Moyen Âge*, vol. 24 (1969), pp. 488–9.

16 P.R.O. E122/194/12, 20, 20/7; C1/43/177.

17 *Statutes of the Realm*, 1 Ric. III c. 8.

18 The use of this too was restricted; *ibid.* 4 Ed. IV c. 1, 1 Ric. III c. 8.

19 They occasionally picked up madder in Flanders; P.R.O. E122/142/10, 19/14.

20 P.R.O. E122/137/16.

21 For saffron see p. 24.

22 *Tudor Economic Documents*, ed. Tawney and Power, III, 109. Biscay as a source of 'moche woode' is also noted by Fortescue, *Commodyties*, ed. Payne.

23 For Spanish participation in the trade, see Caster, *Le Commerce du pastel*,

pp. 91–121, 138–40; Wolff, *Commerce et marchands de Toulouse*, pp. 118, 124–9, 247–52.

24   P.R.O. E122/142/10.
25   P.R.O. C1/67/307, 85/28.
26   Caster, *Le Commerce du pastel*, pp. 91–121, 138–40.
27   P.R.O. E122/124/13.
28   *Ibid.*
29   C.P.R. *1401–5*, p. 131; E159/208 Recorda Easter m. 12d.
30   *S.P.B. Edward IV*, ed. Quinn and Ruddock, I, 89; Ms. S.P.B. 1484–5, Lib. Comm. (unfol.), 17 Nov.; P.R.O. E122/128/15; Exeter City Library, loc. cust. accts. 17–18 Ed. IV; P.R.O. E122/19/11, 13, 18/39.
31   L. Liagre, 'Le commerce de l'alun en Flanders au moyen âge', *Le Moyen Âge* LXI (1955), pp. 181, 197–9; Delumeau, *L'Alun de Rome*, pp. 16, 38.
32   *Tudor Economic Documents*, ed. Tawney and Power, III, 99.
33   P.R.O. E122/124/29, 30. See Table 24.
34   C.P.R. *1361–4*, p. 492.
35   C.C.R. *1369–74*, pp. 30, 112–13.
36   Connell-Smith, 'The ledger of Thomas Howell', *Ec.H.R.*, 2nd ser., III (1950–1), p. 366.
37   C.P.R. *1388–92*, pp. 173–4; P.R.O. C1/60/5.
38   *Ibid.*, 11/204.
39   *Ibid.*, 44/253.
40   *Cal. Plea and Memo. Rolls of London*, IV, 215; C.P.R. *1467–77*, p. 307.
41   P.R.O. SC6/896/13; E122/19/10a, 11, 14; *Statutes of the Realm*, 4 Ed. IV c. 1.
42   Sprandel, *Das Eisengewerbe*, p. 94.
43   Churruca, *Minería, industria y comercio del País Vasco*, p. 6.
44   C.P.R. *1247–58*, p. 348; P.R.O. SC6/1031/19–24.
45   P.R.O. E122/124/29, 30: the ships were as follows. In 1325–6: from Bermeo, seven ships with iron worth £242 10s 0d; from Castro, five with £221 0s 0d; from Lequeitio, two with £27 0s 0d; from Gaudr' (?), one with £30 0s 0d. In 1327–9: from Bermeo, three ships with iron worth £294 0s 0d; from San Sebastián, two with £147 0s 0d; from Castro, one with £74 0s 0d; unknown, one with £55 10s 0d.
46   Sprandel, *op. cit.*, pp. 262–3; Schubert, *Iron and Steel Industry*, p. 139 and n. 3.
47   Pyne (ed.), *England and France in the Fifteenth Century*, p. 52.
48   Salzman, *Building in England*, pp. 286–7.
49   Nicolas, *Royal Navy*, II, 469–73.
50   Thorold Rogers, *A History of Agriculture*, II, 455–70; III, 346–54 shows its wide use over England.
51   *Cal. of Plea and Memo. Rolls of London*, IV, 99, 101.
52   P.R.O. E159/208 Recorda Trin. m. 3d.
53   P.R.O. E28/63 (4 Sept. 18 Hen. VI).
54   *Ibid.* (20 Apr. 18 Hen. VI).
55   P.R.O. E101/128/31.
56   P.R.O. C1/66/238.
57   *Accounts of Durham Abbey*, ed. Fowler; I am indebted to Dr G. V. Scammell for lending me his transcripts of unpublished parts of the accounts.
58   P.R.O. E101/128/31. The English quintal was about a hundredweight but there were fifteen Spanish quintals to the English ton as it was fixed at 144 lb. in Bilbao in 1452; García de Cortázar, *Vizcaya*, p. 134, n. 46, and see P.R.O. E122/142/2; E159/208 Recorda Trin. m.8; Salzman, *Trade*, p. 409 citing Arnold's Chronicle.

59   García de Cortázar, *op. cit.*, pp. 142–3.

60   *Ibid.*, p. 147, n. 90.

61   *Rôles Gascons*, ed. Bémont, III, 3882; P.R.O. C1/45/127, 64/1146—the Englishmen may however be objecting to the import of any Spanish iron, worked or unworked.

62   *Cal. of Plea and Memo. Rolls of London*, I, 149.

63   *C.P.R. 1354–8*, p. 546.

64   *Ibid.*, *1401–5*, p. 431.

65   Ms. S.P.B. 1459–60, Lib. Comm. (unfol.), 3 Oct. There were usually between 106 and 123 'endys' to the ton and their value in the customs accounts—usually under £3 the ton—does not suggest expensively wrought iron: P.R.O. E122/194/15.

66   P.R.O. E122/78/7, 9, 79/5. These were about 120 to the ton.

67   *The Ledger of John Smythe*, ed. Vanes, pp. 87–9, 168–9, 192–3, 213–14, 235–6, 265–6, 301. These were usually 93 to 102 to the ton.

68   The earliest reference is to their being taken from a ship of Lequeitio in 1403; P.R.O. SC8/11549.

69   P.R.O. E122/141/4, 142/3; Ms. S.P.B. 1429–30, 1433–4, 1455–6, 1457–8, 1459–60; *S.P.B. 1435–6*, ed. Foster, pp. 37, 53; *S.P.B. Edward IV*, ed. Quinn and Ruddock, II, 165.

70   P.R.O. E159/208 Recorda Trin. m.10 (clench); E122/19/11 (board); E122/142/3 (small and 'hachnaylles'); Ms. S.P.B. 1459–60 ('de teloat'—as yet unidentified).

71   Ms. S.P.B. 1459–60.

72   P.R.O. E122/114/13, 71/13, 194/12.

73   See note 41 above.

74   *C.P.R. 1354–8*, p. 546 (swords); *S.P.B. Edward IV*, ed. Quinn and Ruddock, II, 146 (brigandines and helmets); P.R.O. E122/19/11 (brigandines, crossbows, guns); E122/41/5a (eight guns worth £4).

75   P.R.O. E122/114/13, 141/4; SC8/11549, 14742; E159/208 Recorda Easter m.10, Trin. m.8.

76   Fortescue, *Commodyties*, ed. Payne.

77   P.R.O. SC6/1031/19.

78   See Chapter 1, note 40.

79   P.R.O. E122/136/21.

80   *Ibid.*, 124/29, 30.

81   P.R.O. SC6/894/24–6, 28–9; the names of importers are not always easy to allocate to areas, and some of the iron may be carried by Gascons.

82   P.R.O. E122/71/16.

83   P.R.O. E159/208 Recorda Trin. mm. 3d, 8, 10; Easter mm. 10, 10d, 12d. It also took 152 tons off English and Gascon ships from the Basque direction in the winter of 1431–2 (E122/77/1).

84   P.R.O. E122/141/21–2; Ms. S.P.B. 1433–4, fo. 16; *S.P.B. 1435–6*, ed. Foster, pp. 37, 53, 55; P.R.O. E101/128/31.

85   P.R.O. SC6/896/10.

86   P.R.O. E122/203/4.

87   Ms. S.P.B. 1459–60, Lib. Comm.

88   P.R.O. E122/77/4, 203/3, 73/23.

89   Fortescue, *Commodyties*, ed. Payne.

90   P.R.O. E122/73/25, 203/4, 10/8, 9, 11, 13, 20, 22.

91   P.R.O. E122/26/6, 40/10, 113/59, 114/2; Exeter City Library, loc. cust. accts. 1–2 Ed. IV.

92   P.R.O. E122/20/9, 78/7, 9, 79/5.

93 P.R.O. E122/26/13, 41/6, 114/16; *Chester Customs Accounts*, ed. Wilson.

94 Dr Schubert suggested 900 tons (*Iron and Steel Industry*, p. 109); Professor Sprandel favours the higher figure (*Eisengewerbe*, pp. 274–5).

95 I intend to look more closely at the general pattern of England's iron imports elsewhere.

96 Bautier, 'Notes sur le commerce du fer en Europe occidentale du XIIIe au XVIe siècle', *Revue d'Histoire de la Sidérurgie*, I, iv (1960) pp. 17–18; Sprandel, *op. cit.*, pp. 268–9, 274–5. Both these works have brought together very valuable information on the iron production and trade of the Middle Ages.

97 They appear in Gaibrois Riaña de Ballesteros, *Historia del reinado de Sancho IV*, I, pp. xvii ff. They cover the ports of Oyarte (3,235 quintals in three months), Orio (4,347 quintals in eight months), Segura (217 quintals in two months). The definition of the quintal offers some difficulty: it is generally taken to be the equivalent of a hundredweight, but by the fifteenth century the Basque quintal was of 144 lb. and thus it took only 15 to the ton and not 20; see note 58 above.

98 Sprandel, *op. cit.*, p. 277.

99 England may have benefited from Ferdinand's attempt to stop Basque iron exports going to France, now his enemy.

100 García de Cortázar, *Vizcaya*, pp. 133–8.

101 On one set of assumptions the figures may confirm the suggestion of 4,000–5,000 tons available for commerce: taking the quintal at 15 to the ton, and the *maravedí* at 10 *dineros* the farmers would expect production of 4,266 to 7,500 tons to break even. How much of this was exported or used at home, how much had been already exported as ore, and whether 'worked' meant roughly smelted or fully worked is unclear. If Spanish production rose fourfold in the late fifteenth and early sixteenth century then the sixteenth-century estimates may indicate 4,000–5,000 tons worked, and a total production, possibly of ore only, of about 16,000 tons in the fifteenth century.

102 García de Cortázar, *Vizcaya*, appendix 34, p. 423.

103 Professor Sprandel comments on this aspect of comparative costs, 'La production du fer au moyen âge', *Annales: économies, sociétés et civilisations*, 24 (1969), pp. 315ff.

104 *Enciclopedia universel ilustrada*, under 'Almadén'.

105 Theophilus, *On Divers Arts*, ed. Hawthorne and Smith, pp. 34–5, 40, 110–13, 145–6.

106 *Cases concerning the Law Merchant*, ed. Hall, III, 137–40.

107 P.R.O. E122/124/13.

108 *Ibid.*, 136/21.

109 Pérez Embid, 'Navigation et commerce ... de Seville', *Le Moyen Âge*, vol. 24 (1969), pp. 488–9; Heers, *Gênes au XVe siècle*, pp. 487, 490.

110 *Rôles Gascons*, ed. Bémont, I, 2724, 2754, 3349; Michel, *Histoire . . . de Bordeaux*, I, 156.

111 Sherborne, *The Port of Bristol*, pp. 8–9; P.R.O. E122/19/13; C1/22/195.

112 P.L.C. 1204–24, pp. 163b, 176b, 190b, 192a; R.L.P. 1201–16, p. 117b.

113 *Rôles Gascons*, ed. Bémont, I, 302, 825; C.P.R. 1232–47, pp. 310, 362; C.C.R. 1237–42, pp. 500, 529.

114 C.P.R. 1281–92, p. 11; *Rôles Gascons*, ed. Bémont, III, 2064, 4468–9; C.C.R. 1296–1302, p. 378.

115 C.P.R. 1307–13, p. 82; *Cal. Chanc. Warr.* p. 273.

116 C.P.R. 1307–13, pp. 204, 437, 557; *ibid.*, 1313–17, p. 102; C.C.R. 1307–13, p. 569.

117 C.P.R. 1307–13, p. 291; Gascon Rolls, 1307–17, ed. Renouard, Nos. 456–7.

118 C.P.R. 1313–17, p. 643; ibid., 1317–21, p. 60.

119 C.C.R. 1318–23, p. 123.

120 C.C.R. 1330–3, p. 423; C.P.R. 1330–4, p. 364; P.R.O. E101/101/10—a detailed account of the horses by type, colour and price.

121 London Record Office, Recognisance Rolls VII.

122 P.R.O. E122/124/13.

123 C.P.R. 1334–8, p. 52.

124 See for example Cortes, I, 225, 348.

125 Renouard, 'Un sujet de recherches: l'exportation de chevaux de la péninsule ibérique en France et en Angleterre au moyen âge', Homenaje a Jaime Vicens Vives, vol. I.

126 P.R.O. E122/19/1, 14, 114/13, 128/14, 15, 142/10, 194/12; SC6/896/14.

127 E122/41/5a, 114/13, 128/14, 142/10, 162/7; Guiard y Larrauri, Historia de la Noble Villa de Bilbao, I, 502–3.

128 P.R.O. E122/19/13, 14, 142/10; SC6/895/13.

129 P.R.O. C76/169 m.16.

130 Nicolas, Procs. and Ords. of the Privy Council, II, 24–6.

131 Richmond, 'English naval power in the fifteenth century', History, LII, (1967), pp. 12–15.

132 A Discourse of the Common Weal of this Realm of England, ed. Lamond, pp. 42, 61.

133 C.L.R. 1251–60, p. 217; C.C.R. 1307–13, p. 231; Exeter City Library, loc. cust. accts. 13–14, 16–17 Ed. II.

134 C.P.R. 1313–17, pp. 466, 624; C.C.R. 1313–18, p. 452.

135 P.R.O. C76/123 m.12, 124 m.22.

136 Gras, Corn Market, p. 148.

137 Bridbury, England and the Salt Trade, p. 114.

138 C.P.R. 1361–4, pp. 480, 492; P.R.O. E122/17/10, 19/10a, 40/30, 114/2, 124/29, 126/3; Exeter City Library, loc. cust. accts. 16–17 Ed. II, 32–3 Ed. III, 13 Ed. IV.

139 Letter Book 'A', pp. 206–7.

140 Account Rolls of Durham Abbey, ed. Fowler, passim.

141 P.R.O. E28/63 (20 Apr. 18 Hen. VI).

142 P.R.O. C1/48/114.

143 Account Rolls of Durham Abbey, ed. Fowler, II, 510; P.R.O. C47/4/5; R.L.C. 1204–24, p. 352b.

144 P.R.O. E159/208 Recorda Trin. m.8.

145 P.R.O. C47/4/5; C.P.R. 1401–5, p. 431.

146 C.R. 1227–31, pp. 71, 89; see R.L.C. 1224–7, p. 203b.

147 Statutes of the Realm, 5 Ric. II stat. 1 c. 4. Ordinances had already fixed it at these prices in 1358; C.C.R. 1354–60, pp. 539–40.

148 C.P.R. 1374—7, p. 298.

149 P.R.O. SC6/816/11–12, 817/2–5, 7–10, 818/1, 2, 11, 819/2, 3, 15; E122/40/13, 19.

150 Letter Book 'G', p. 272. This followed an order of 1362 to keep even Spanish and Gascon wines apart; ibid., p. 138. Adulterers of wine used Spanish wines both as the old base needing improvement, and the new wine to add strength to old; Cal. Plea and Memo. Rolls of London, IV, 212.

151 C.C.R. 1374–7, p. 11.

152 Huetz de Lemps, 'Apogeo y decadencia de un viñedo de calidad: el de Ribadavia', Anuario de Historia Económica y Social, I (1968), pp. 207–25. A wine

called 'Ryptage' is described by Fortescue as Portuguese in the mid fifteenth century; *Commodyties*, ed. Payne.

153   P.R.O. E101/128/31; C1/28/473, 44/160. Some allegedly Gascon wines were picked up by a Plymouth ship in Fuenterrabía in 1453–4, *C.C.R. 1447–54*, pp. 502–3; *C.P.R. 1452–61*, p. 168.

154   *C.L.R. 1226–40*, p. 253.

155   P.R.O. C47/32/24.

156   P.R.O. E28/84 (10 May 32 Hen. VI).

157   *C.C.R. 1364–8*, p. 158.

158   *C.C.R. 1405–9*, p. 166. Lepe is about twenty kilometres due west of Huelva.

159   P.R.O. SC6/818/11; *C.C.R. 1409–13*, p. 381.

160   *The Works of Geoffrey Chaucer*, ed. Robinson, lines 562–72 of the Pardoner's Tale.

161   P.R.O. E159/236 Recorda Mich. m.3; *C.C.R. 1468–76*, No. 709.

162   *C.P.R. 1401–5*, p. 131.

163   *C.C.R. 1454–61*, p. 85.

164   P.R.O. SC6/817/4.

165   *C.P.R. 1338–40*, p. 1.

166   *Ibid., 1364–7*, pp. 15–16, 59.

167   *C.C.R. 1364–8*, p. 458.

168   *C.P.R. 1292–1301*, p. 376.

169   *Ibid., 1334–8*, pp. 367, 377.

170   *Ibid., 1350–4*, p. 543.

171   *Ibid., 1361–4*, p. 151; *C.C.R. 1360–4*, p. 4.

172   P.R.O. SC6/817/8.

173   James, *Wine Trade*, pp. 19–25. The period 1351–69 was one of friendship and expanding trade between England and Castile; see Chapter 1.

174   P.R.O. SC6/1031/19.

175   *C.M.I.*, I, 2412.

176   P.R.O. E101/158/2, 5, 10, 160/3, 7, 8, 161/13, 162/4. There were no Castilians in 1308–9, and only one in 1310–11, 162/6, 163/1, 3, 4. For totals see James, *op. cit.*, p. 32.

177   P.R.O. E101/173/4, 182/2; the ships came from the following towns: San Sebastián, nineteen; Motrico, nineteen; Bermeo, fifteen; Castro, nine; Fuenterrabía, four; Guetaría, four; Lequeitio, three; Bilbao, three; Deva, two; Santander, two; Plasencia, San Vicente de la Barquera, Ondárroa and Ayo one each.

178   P.R.O. E101/80/7, 9, 11–15. The records are not complete.

179   James, *Wine Trade*, p. 20.

180   P.R.O. E101/78/3a, 4, 4a, 9, 12, 13, 16, 18, 19, 79/8, 12, 15, 19, 24.

181   It must again be emphasised that this takes no account of their role as carriers for the English.

182   James, *op. cit.*, pp. 26–7.

183   P.R.O. E101/81/1, 3, 5, 8, 12, 15, 16, 82/4, 5, 7, 14, 20, 22, 23: Spaniards are omitted from records of alien trade after 1466 unless they carried for other aliens. Their ships appear as follows in the Butlers' accounts:

1403 –	1408 –	1417 –	1436 –	1456 2	1463 9?	1480 –
1404 1	1413 4	1418 –	1437 –	1457 7	1464 3	1485 –
1405 –	1414 4	1425 –	1438 –	1460 –	1475 5 or 3	1486 –
1406 –	1415 3	1426 –	1439 –	1461 –	1476 1?	
1407 –	1416 2	1427 –	1440 –	1462 2?	1479 –	

184   P.R.O. SC8/15047; C76/98 m.3; C1/59/51.

185 It may have been the suddenness rather than the size of the Spanish involvement in Gascony which prompted the Navigation Acts.

186 P.R.O. E122/194/16–18; Aug.–Sept. 1463, Nov.–May 1465–6.

187 P.R.O. E122/142/1 (4 tuns), 142/3 (185 tuns), 142/8 (148 tuns,), 142/10 (174 tuns).

188 The figures again give no indication of the amount of Spanish wine brought in by Englishmen or other aliens, nor of any Spanish carrying trade.

189 P.R.O. E122/20/5, 7; E356/23 m.1.

190 *Cases concerning the Law Merchant*, ed. Hall, III, 137–40.

191 *Letter Book 'A'*, pp. 206–7.

192 *Ibid.*, *passim.*

193 London Record Office, Recognisance Rolls, I.

194 See for examples E122/17/10, 71/16, 77/1, 3, 125/12, 126/5, 16, 38, 141/21.

195 Two isolated examples occurred at Bristol in 1404 and 1432, E122/17/10, E159/210 Recorda Mich. m.35.

196 *C.R. 1227–31*, p. 89; P.R.O. E122/124/18, 136/21.

197 In 1236 some were bought for Henry III; *C.R. 1234–7*, p. 479.

198 Veale, *The English Fur Trade*, app. B.

199 P.R.O. SC6/1031/24; *Letter Book 'A'*, p. 21.

200 P.R.O. E122/124/18.

201 A hundred 'abortise' were brought to Southampton in 1311; E122/136/21.

202 Veale, *op. cit.*, p. 216.

203 *Ibid.*, p. 14.

204 P.R.O. E122/19/1, 3, 4, 6–11, 13, 14, 20/5, 7.

205 *Statutes of the Realm*, 37 Ed. III c. 9.

206 Veale, *op. cit.*, pp. 69–70.

207 *Ibid.*, 135–6, 140–1: the rich would even wear rabbit again if it was black, or silver-grey; *ibid.*, p. 176.

208 *R.L.C. 1204–24*, pp. 175a, 384b, 408a.

209 P.R.O. E159/235 Recorda Mich. m.54, Hil. m.11.

210 P.R.O. E122/20/5, 7.

211 *C.M.I.*, VI, 237; *C.P.R. 1401–5*, pp. 408–9.

212 P.R.O. E159/208 Recorda Easter m.12d.

213 *Ibid.*, 205 Recorda Mich. m. 25.

214 P.R.O. C76/111 m.5, 113 m.6.

215 P.R.O. E122/137/16, 71/16, 194/24.

216 Ms. S.P.B. 1459–60 Lib. Comm. (unfol.), 3 Dec.

217 P.R.O. C47/4/5; Ruddock, *Italian Merchants in Southampton*, p. 76.

218 Exeter City Library, loc. cust. accts. 1–2 Ric. III, 2 Ric. III–1 Hen. VII.

219 *C.P.R. 1247–58*, p. 7; *C.L.R. 1245–51*, p. 179; *ibid.*, 1251–60, p. 217; *ibid.*, 1267–72, Nos. 1675, 2311.

220 P.R.O. E122/128/15.

221 *C.P.R. 1381–5*, p. 149; P.R.O. E28/61 (25 Jun. Hen. VI)—the table was finally sold in 1439 for 400 marks.

222 *C.P.R. 1381–5*, p. 149; *ibid.*, 1388–92, p. 314; the stirrups alone were pawned for £682 13s 4d.

223 *C.P.R. 1381–5*, p. 149; *Letter Book 'H'*, p. 160, n.2.

224 *C.P.R. 1385–9*, p. 478; P.R.O. E28/79 (20 Dec. 28 Hen. VI).

225 P.R.O. E122/16/21, 71/13, 16.

226 P.R.O. E28/66 (13 Feb. 19 Hen. VI); Quinn, 'Edward IV and exploration', *Mariners Mirror*, XXI (1935), 277–8.

CHAPTER 5

The shipping:
supply and operation

The characteristics of the shipping in Anglo-Castilian trade underline again how closely the trade was enmeshed in the wider European patterns of commerce. There were of course many direct sailings between England and Castile but there were also more complex voyages touching several countries on the Channel and Atlantic routes and reaching into the Mediterranean or to North Africa. There was little idiosyncratic about the Anglo-Castilian carrying operations.

The nationalities of the shipping involved in the trade reflect this complex pattern: the Castilians and, a little later, the English provided much of it, but they did not monopolise it and Gascony, France, the Low Countries, Portugal and the Italian city States played a part. Such Gascon shipping as was used was mostly used in the earlier period and generally came from Bayonne, although occasionally from St Jean de Luz. The inevitably close contacts of the Basque and Gascon areas, when not hostile, can be seen in the career of Arnold de Bearritz who was master of the *Sta María of Fuenterrabía*, which was wrecked bringing Navarrese goods to England.[1] Breton shipping was rare before the later fifteenth century when a few vessels sailed between Bristol and Spain or the Algarve.[2] The shipping of the Low Countries plied both between Spain and Flanders, and Flanders and London carrying Spanish goods there, and ships of Bruges, Sluys, Zeeland, Kampen and Ziericksee had been used by Bristol merchants to carry their Spanish trade when Anglo-Castilian relations were at their worst between 1377 and 1382.[3] A Dutch vessel from Amsterdam was sent by London merchants through the Straits of Gibraltar in Henry IV's reign.[4] Hansard shipping also carried Spanish goods between London and Flanders at times, and some had sailed directly to Spain in the early fifteenth century,[5] but after the Hansard retreat from the Bay of Biscay in the face of Castilian hostility it played no part in Anglo-Castilian trade in western waters. Portuguese shipping was scarcer than might be expected, probably because for much of the period Portugal and Spain were at war, but it was occasionally used in the early fifteenth century, and had been extensively used at Bristol from about 1370 until the end of the century.[6]

Far more important, mainly for the trade of Andalusia with England, were the great Italian vessels. Genoese carracks generally called at Seville or Cadiz on their way north and many of the Florentine galleys in the

Maps 2–5 Main directions of sea trade

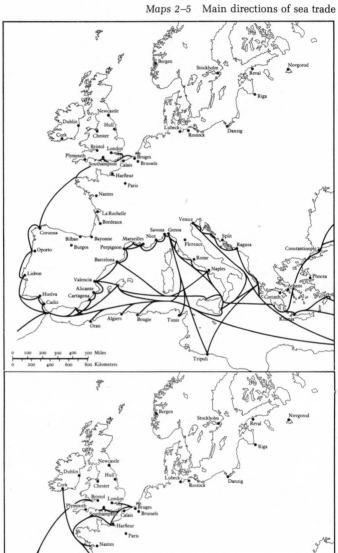

Italian

Spanish

Hanseatic

English

fifteenth century followed suit. Thus, part of the wine, oil, dyes and fruit aboard Italian ships was of Spanish origin although belonging to Italian houses, and Spanish merchants and Spanish crewmen also transported their Spanish goods aboard Italian ships. These rarely called at northern ports, completing their cargoes at Lisbon if not before, and sailing direct from Finisterre to Brittany and on to England and Flanders. Their role as carriers of Spanish trade was so obvious to contemporaries that in times of difficulty and contracting trade, complaints against it were made, as in 1429 when attempts were made to prohibit their carrying of goods originating west of Gibraltar.[7]

Of the Spanish shipping used the overwhelming majority came from the Basque Provinces. These had helped in southern areas during the Reconquest, but military activity quickly gave way to economic and Basque shipping soon predominated in Spanish commercial shipping in north and south. Early in the fourteenth century Basques became common sights in many Balearic, Valencian, Aragonese, French and Italian ports and even visited Ragusa, Rhodes and Chios, and only in the later fifteenth century did their Mediterranean activity decrease with the Turkish advance and the attraction of increasing Atlantic and Channel trade.[8] Their great maritime activity stemmed from a long history of fishing, the demands of their rulers, the stimulation of contact with the Italian sea routes, and a hinterland rich in exportable goods—Basque iron, Rioja wines, and wools from the pastures of Estremadura, La Mancha and Toledo. Their shipbuilding resources were abundant with chestnut, beech and oak for timber and charcoal, and replanting and preservation orders ensured continuous supplies.[9] The local iron supplies were particularly suitable for shipbuilding; ropemaking was of high quality from the thirteenth century; and the forests supplied resin and pitch for caulking. By 1402 Bilbao, Bermeo and San Sebastián were noted as the most important northern Spanish shipbuilding ports.

The English records of all types confirm the remarkable dominance of Basque vessels among those sailing the Channel. They show that the two main Guipúzcoan ports supplying ships were San Sebastián with its exceptionally sheltered harbour and Fuenterrabía, both of which were important in the thirteenth century and continued to be so throughout the period; but many ships of Pasajes and Rentería (especially in the fifteenth century) and of Orio, Zarauz, Zumaya, Guetaría, Motrico and Deva also came into English ports, Deva being the most important and certainly the only one to provide merchants of any substance in the English trade. In Biscay the main centre was at first Bermeo, a town early described as a port, which soon developed a *Cofradía de Mareantes* and in 1296 received privileges for its merchants similar to those given the Gascons and Genoese at Seville. As the leading town of the province its representatives usually led the negotiations with Gascony. It flourished well into the

Map 6   The Basque Provinces and Santander

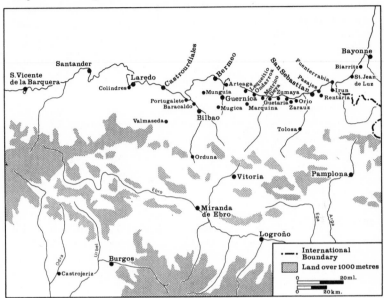

fourteenth century but lost its pre-eminence to Bilbao in the fifteenth. Bilbao received its town charter in 1300 and grew apace aided by its sheltered harbour, iron supplies and good position at the junction of three rivers and roads, and by the later century was strong enough to withstand its only danger—pressure from the merchants of Burgos trying to break its near-monopoly of transport to Flanders.[10] As in Guipúzcoa, so in Biscay many smaller ports supplemented the merchant marine: Ondárroa, Lequeitio and Portugalete sent ships in the fourteenth and fifteenth centuries, and Murueta and Mundaca sent masters and merchants but not apparently ships.

Further west the province of Santander backed its shipping with reasonable building supplies and a hinterland supplying a considerable variety of goods, although lacking the Basque mineral resources. Its shipping was concentrated in the Cuatro Villas, Castro Urdiales, Santander, Laredo and S Vicente de la Barquera and outside these, unlike the Basque Provinces, there was little activity at all—at least as far as English trade was concerned.[11] Castro was the most active in English trade, and perhaps should be considered rather with the Biscayan ports, since it was geographically close and indeed part of fifteenth-century Biscay until formally separated in 1471.[12] Its shipping was often present in English ports in the thirteenth and early fourteenth centuries but thereafter came less, and in 1430 the town blamed massacres, wars, civil disturbances, two fires and robbery by the English for its decline;[13] to these should be added its proximity to Bilbao, to whose vigorous rise it, like Bermeo, succumbed. Ships and merchants from the other three towns were sometimes found trading to England but their shipping seems to have specialised more in the Flemish trade and contacts with England were more often than not by chance or violence.

Further west still there was less shipbuilding, owning and investment. Occasionally ships of Ribadesella, Ribadeo, Avilés, Vivero, Corunna, Pontevedra, Noya and Vigo could be found but their numbers suggest a commercial community not involved in overseas business on anything like the Basque scale. Their shipbuilding resources were not as good nor their hinterland as rich, although the Flemish commodity list noted some variety. The scarcity of references to Galician shipping in English records is however surprising in view of the importance of Corunna as a disembarkation point for English pilgrims on their way to Santiago de Compostella. This was a popular shrine attracting men of all classes from the ordinary souls crowding most west country ships to scholars like William Wey, and there was even discussion of a visit by Edward III.[14] The journey was straightforward and could take as little as four days in fair weather[15] and many licences to transport pilgrims were granted in spring and summer months.[16] The shrine was important enough to the English for freedom of passage for pilgrims to be protected in the negotiations between Lancaster and the King of Castile in 1389,[17] yet the pilgrim activity was clearly insufficient to stimulate Galician shipping and English vessels overwhelmingly predominated.

Southern shipping on Channel routes was even rarer, but not missing altogether: ships from Seville called at England as early as 1304 and a few continued to come in the fourteenth and fifteenth centuries,[18] supported in the latter half of the fifteenth by odd vessels from Sanlúcar, Cadiz and Lepe.[19]

This immense predominance of northern over southern shipping in Channel ports might be expected but its clear dominance in the south[20] too requires some explanation. Andalusian shipping was not held back by poor building resources, because although these were not as good as the Basque they were fully adequate for the royal dockyards at Seville, and for the Andalusian fleets which challenged the Portuguese off Africa. It was not held back by a poor hinterland: at the Reconquest Castile took over a well farmed land with developed industries, and although the expulsion of the Moors, slow colonisation from the north and the emphasis of the Military Orders and nobility on the simplest exploitation of their vast estates meant the loss of techniques and labour for the industries and intensive cultivation of the Moors, the production of raw materials remained immensely valuable. Merchants from all over Europe were attracted by the production of corn, fruit, wine, wax, wool, leather and hides, mercury, oil and grain, and by the produce of the Canaries and West Africa which increasingly came through the ports. Conditions were favourable for profitable trade and that the local population played a relatively small part in it was due largely to the early establishment of privileged Italian commercial colonies on whom the Castilian king had relied at the Reconquest for any exploitation of the area at all, given the small local Spanish population then there. Once they were established and busily active in the export of oil, mercury and wine it was difficult for the local population to oust them, and perhaps few wished to do so. The Italians were quite happy to transport the goods of Andalusians too and so these merchants could be content with a position subordinate to the Italians' yet also prosperous while the southern trade prospered. They were accustomed to see the world come to them and felt little need to go out to meet the world in traditional markets; but when newer, exciting, quasi-military opportunities arose for trade and piracy on Atlantic and African routes Andalusian seamen were among the foremost to take them, encouraged by the Andalusian nobility.

Of English shipping used on the route most came from the southern half of England as one would expect. Few of the east-coast ports north of London had any regular contact with Spain after the thirteenth century except for some pilgrim transporting,[21] as their sights were set on north-eastern markets where they could easily sell the wool and cloth of their hinterlands. Neither did ports north of Bristol maintain Spanish contacts, looking more to Ireland, although occasionally as far as Bordeaux. The ports between London and Bristol furnished ships, but only from the fourteenth century.

Despite London's importance as a market for Spanish goods her own shipping was apparently less used than one would expect. Londoners exporting cloth to Spain in 1364 and 1369 chartered ships from Bristol, Plymouth and Spain,[22] and this practice continued in the next century when Londoners used and obtained safe-conducts for west country and Spanish ships.[23] Some owners were sending ships by the later fourteenth century, and the *Vyncent of London* set off in 1398.[24] Some transported pilgrims in Henry VI's reign[25] and may at other times have sailed in the same waters for purely commercial purposes. John Chirche of London sent two of his ships to Lisbon in 1437 and 1441[26] and as he was fairly active in Spanish trade too almost certainly sent them to Spain; possibly the two unnamed ships for which he had a licence to trade in Spain in 1430 were his own.[27] Later the *Marie Folkys of London* was sent to Spain,[28] a London ship was taken by Spanish pirates off Guipúzcoa in 1477,[29] and the *George of London* sailed into Bristol from Seville in 1480.[30] These cannot have been the only London ships engaged but the dearth of shipping detail in the customs accounts obscures further identifications.

Shipping from the Cinque Ports was little represented despite the early importance of Winchelsea and Sandwich for the trade. The activity of these ports had always been more military than commercial and all too often references to them in an Anglo-Spanish context are to their lawlessness. Moreover the English participation in the carrying of overseas trade coincided with the beginning of the decline of the Cinque Ports through erosion or silting. Sandwich alone retained importance as an outport for London but provided little shipping, although one of her ships and one of Dover were licensed for Spanish trade in the fifteenth century.[31]

At Southampton the question of identification arises again, as the customs accounts lack detail of home ports and last ports of call. Certainly one was hired as early as 1338 to go to Spain and Portugal for wine,[32] and doubtless others followed, but evidence is lacking, and certainly Southampton merchants, like the Andalusians, often relied on foreign shipping to carry their goods.

The Dorset ports of Melcombe and Poole and Weymouth attracted a little Spanish trade, but all references to their shipping on the Anglo-Spanish routes refer only to the carrying of pilgrims to Corunna.[33]

The shipping of Devon and Cornwall was much more closely involved. It was hired by the London merchants, was particularly heavily used in the pilgrim transport,[34] and the ships of Plymouth and Dartmouth were sailing down to Andalusia again as soon as the Trastamaran troubles were over.[35] The west country customs accounts show English and apparently local ships engaged in the Spanish trade and the more detailed Bristol accounts show ships of Fowey, Dartmouth, Plymouth, Bideford and Barnstaple unloading Spanish cargoes there. These also note ships of Chepstow, Swansea, Milford, Caerleon and Tenby engaged in small numbers, and ships of Wells, Coventry and Taunton too, in addition to considerable numbers from Bristol itself.

Only from these Bristol accounts can any estimation of the relative shares of the Spanish and English shipping in the trade be made. Other sources make it quite clear that the Spaniards predominated in the thirteenth century, and English ships, except for the one at Corunna in 1234 apparently there by accident,[36] do not seem to have ventured that far before 1311.[37] In the mid century their numbers increased steadily but were upset by the Trastamaran troubles. By the late fourteenth century, despite the after-effects of these troubles, considerable numbers of Bristol ships were sailing to Spain and Portugal. Indeed they dominated the city's Iberian trade, three English ships being active to one alien. Until 1380 Portuguese ships had held their own but between Michaelmas 1380 and Michaelmas 1400, 121 departures and arrivals are recorded for Iberia and of these ninety were by Bristol ships, nine by other English and Welsh ships, seventeen by Portuguese, three by Flemish and two by Spanish ships.[38] Eighty years later changes had taken place at Bristol. Castilian shipping had enormously increased; many more sailings were specifically said to be for

Spain and fewer for Portugal. In Edward IV's reign the ratio of English to foreign ships on the route to Spain was now 1 : 2½. Of the voyages to and from Spain ninety-two were by Spaniards, all but four from Biscay and Guipúzcoa, twenty-eight were by Bristol ships, nine by ships of other English ports and four by those of other alien ports. The Castilian shipping was particularly strong on the northern Spanish route, and most of the long-distance trade with Andalusia was left to the Bristol ships. In the Portuguese trade the activity was still similar to that for the whole Iberian trade earlier: thirty-nine of the sailings were by English ships, fourteen by Portuguese and two by other aliens. However this English dominance in the Portuguese and Andalusian trades was already threatened early in Henry VII's reign as more Castilians broke into it.[39]

The balance of the shipping in the trade as a whole will remain unclear but it is likely that the Castilians throughout the period carried most although their share varied from time to time.

The rulers of each country considered their own shipping inadequate at times and tried to exclude alien shipping from their trade. In 1381 and 1390 Englishmen were ordered to use English ships in an attempt to increase the navy, said to be sadly diminished,[40] but it cannot have been Spanish competition which was responsible since in 1397 and 1398 similar orders were given in Castile and the English were specifically included among the aliens who must use Spanish shipping—'asi genoveses como placentinos catalanes franceses o ingleses que cargasen en Cadiz o Sevilla'.[41] Probably in both areas the general slackening of trade in the late fourteenth century was leaving some shipping idle, but it may be in the Spanish case that English merchants seeking cloth markets were pushing more vigorously than for some years into a Spain with which there was now a reasonably peaceful relationship.

The fears of inadequate shipping persisted in the war period of the fifteenth century: in 1436 the Spanish Cortes was concerned at the lack of great ships to protect the convoys to Flanders,[42] and in 1439 the English government ordered that neutrals' goods taken from enemy ships should be forfeit, since the practice of returning them had discouraged English ship-owners, masters and builders as they could no longer hope for quick returns from loot.[43] At the end of the century Henry VII again promulgated Navigation Acts,[44] this time probably with more justification against the Spaniards who were becoming much more obvious in the Gascon wine and woad trade, at least at Bristol. However Ferdinand and Isabella did not see the Spanish shipping industry as thriving and virtually repeated the orders of 1398, forbade the export of ships and encouraged bigger ships with bounties.[45]

On the whole the promulgation of such orders so close in time to those in the other country suggests that neither was in danger of being swamped by the other, and, even in the later fifteenth century, increasing Spanish

activity may have been a symptom rather than a cause of the visible
situation: given the commercial expansion of the late fifteenth century it is
likely that the supply of shipping lagged behind the booming opportunities which merchants could see for trade, so that they became aware of
a shortage and put it down to their own inadequate numbers due to alien
competition rather than noticing a total shortfall. In such a situation the
Spanish shipping was filling a gap, not pushing out the English shipping,
and the ease with which Castilians bought exemptions from the Navigation Act indicates that they were filling a need.[46]

A great variety of vessels was used on the route, but all were of traditional types. The Biscayan shipyards, although so well placed to appreci-
ate northern and southern types, and renowned building centres, none
the less produced no innovations, and the one marked change in
the period—the carvel—seems to owe relatively little to Biscayan enterprise.

The majority of vessels given a name at all were called *nefs* or *naves*, a
general term covering many types, but also with a more precise meaning of
a fairly large sailing vessel with a round hull and square sails, although
later a mixture of square and lateen might be used. Sometimes the term is
used in conjunction with another, such as *balinger* or *barge* which may
indicate, as with the *nef carvelle*, or *carvela redonda* noted by M. Bernard,
a mixture of styles which blurred distinctions.[47]

The larger northern cog was used in the fourteenth century, as with the
'*S Marie Cog of Castro*', which unloaded 130 tons of cargo at Exeter in
1338,[48] and the '*navis vocat' La Rodecogg of Bristol*' which sailed to
Portugal in 1382, and the Flemish cogs used for Spain from Bristol about
the same time.[49] The cogs disappeared in the fifteenth century, a similar
trend to that in the Mediterranean where the Basque cogs also disappeared
at that time.[50]

A few Spanish hulks appear in the fifteenth century,[51] which may
indicate a copying of Hanseatic types after their penetration of the west,
but there was also one isolated example of a Spanish hulk—the *holac* of
Fuenterrabía—at Winchelsea as early as 1266.[52]

More frequently used were barges, most being used on the shorter
journeys between England and Biscay or Guipúzcoa but some coming
from Barbary, Seville and Portugal.[53] Most unloaded less than forty tons of
cargo although others carried 150 or 120 tons, and the small size accords
with Miss Burwash's findings for sea-going barges.[54] Balingers appeared
in the mid fifteenth century and some seem to have been larger than
those recorded by Miss Burwash, reaching 100 tons and even 300 or 500
tons[55]—not only to a Chancery clerk (undoubtedly a thorough landsman)
but also to his informant (more probably with sea-going connections) there
seems to have been nothing obviously incongruous in calling a 500-ton
vessel a balinger. Small crayers and spinnaces unloading between 10 and

40 tons and 8 and 20 tons came into western ports, generally from the Basque provinces too.[56]

In the middle of the fifteenth century the carvel began to make its appearance on this route. The earliest reference is to the '*Carvela Mary de Seynt Sebastian*' which came into Exeter in 1457 with wine. In 1462 and 1463 more carvels came into Exeter and Bristol and in 1466 to Bridgwater and Plymouth.[57] The carvel was developed from the Portuguese caravelle with its carvel planking, lateen rigging, and smaller and more slender hull. Its greater manoeuvrability suited it well to the demands of African exploration and it was used not only by the Portuguese but by their Andalusian rivals. Although southern styles must have been as well known to the northerner as his were to the southerner, and although carvel planking was used on northern ships before the end of the fourteenth century,[58] not until the second half of the fifteenth was a vessel developed distinctive enough to warrant a new name. It was not necessarily closely like the caravelle, and the use of the terms *nef carvel* or *carvella redonda* suggests a composite style.[59] The size of those working in England was usually under 100 tons and their increased use in the later century reflects the general increase in the use of smaller ships then.

Some distinctive Mediterranean types were of course used in the southern Spanish trade. The great carracks and fast galleys of the Genoese and Florentines—owned, commanded and operated by Italians, largely for Italians—usually called at Seville, Cadiz and Lisbon between the Mediterranean and England or Flanders and so might carry substantial amounts of Spanish produce, and take English cloth to Andalusia.

On the whole the types of vessels are what one would expect. The biggest and most expensive Italian types were well known in Spanish and English ports but were unnecessary and would not have paid for themselves so were not copied. The bulk-carrying hulks and cogs could be used but the use was limited, possibly because very large and slow carriers were less easily defended on dangerous Channel passages. On the other hand fairly large nefs, barges and balingers were frequently used for the fairly bulky cargoes of iron, wine and oil, and the differences between these and some of the cogs must have been slight. Smaller carvels were useful for frequent fast runs on which they were filled to capacity each time, and even very small crayers and spinnaces could be used. In fact anything which could put to sea could be used at some time on the route since there were long passages and short, bulky cargoes, and less bulky, expensive ones.

The sizes of the ships set problems: there were various methods of assessing ships' cargo-carrying capabilities, and a ship's tonnage expanded or contracted according to who was interested in it and for what purpose, and according to whether the eye which gauged it was experienced or not. The English and Spanish seamen used wine measures to define tonnage but these were not the same size: the English tun was reckoned at 2240 lb including the cask for weight, or at 40 cubic feet for freight for some goods. The Biscayan *tonel* is reckoned to have been about 1.7 cubic metres, which was close to the 60 cubic feet of the actual tun cask with the wasted space around it, but the Castilian was 1.4 cubic metres; there were roughly ten Biscayan *toneles* to twelve Castilian; the *tonel* seems to have been smaller than a *tonelada* which was nearer to the English tun.[60] The differences make comparisons difficult but a series of tonnages from one set of records probably is based on the same term of reference throughout, and the English treaty rolls afford such a series with the lists of safe-conducts granted to alien ships in the fifteenth century.[61] These include those for some 350 Spanish ships between 1400 and 1485, most granted by Henry VI. The majority were of moderate size, three-quarters being of 200 tons or less, a further fifty-four being under 300 tons, a further twenty-nine between 300 and 400 tons and ten over 400 tons. These tonnages correspond with those found by M. Heers for Basque shipping in the Mediterranean for this century, but both these groups of figures are much higher than those found by Mlle Carrère for Basque shipping at Barcelona 1439–42:[62] of forty tonnages found by M. Heers thirty-three were under 330 tonnes (three of these were under 190 tonnes), five were between 330 and 475 tonnes and two over 475 tonnes.[63] Most of those at Barcelona were noted as *barca* and were between 60 and 220 *botes*, and one *nau* was of 300 *botes*.[64] The reason for the sharp difference is not clear.

There are perceptible changes in the sizes of the Spanish ships: an increase occurred in large ones in the fifth and sixth decades, and not only are there more examples of large ships of 400 or 500 tons but the size of the smallest receiving safe-conducts rose from around 80 to 100 tons, and in some years nothing under 220 tons was recorded. Thereafter a decline in size set in, but the movement is obscured after 1467 when Spaniards no longer needed safe-conducts and drop out of the records.[65] This decline in size is in line with trends in other areas and branches of trade at this time: the Spanish ships sailing to Flanders were between 100 and 200 tons—of the thirty-three recorded at Sluys in 1486–7, twenty-five were between 100 and 199 tons, five were under 100 and three were of 200 tons;[66] Dr Scammell found English east coast shipping declining in size;[67] M. Braudel cites the statement of Andrea Satler in Bruges in 1478 that small ships had quite driven out large, and presents other evidence for a drop in size then.[68]

Information about the English tonnage in Spanish trade is more scattered but indicates similar trends to those above. A few licences to trade abroad show Englishmen using ships of up to 400 tons, but the group issued for trade with Spain or France between 1458 and 1462 shows that most by that time were under 150 tons.[69] William Worcester's list of William Canynges' ships is often cited to show the large size of English ships since one was 400 tons, one 500, and one an exceptional 900 tons, but it also shows that seven of the ten were under 250 tons, and his list of ten other Bristol ships in 1480 indicates a decline in size, with five of the ten under 100 tons and the largest 360 tons.[70]

The tonnages underline again that neither Spanish nor English ships, with the exception of Canynges' *Mary and John*, rivalled the great carracks of 800 to 1,000 tons. They had moved towards larger sizes in the early fifteenth century, but for security reasons, since until the widespread use of artillery a large ship was virtually unassailable by smaller ones. The sound commercial reason for liking them was cheapness for bulky goods especially over long distances, but on the Anglo-Spanish route this would not offset their disadvantages, which were large capital outlay, great losses if anything went wrong, and longer turn-round times in port during which they earned no money. Once the Channel became safer in the later fifteenth century demands of security were less important, and the smaller, faster ship came into its own again: the larger Castilian ships which still existed and any Ferdinand and Isabella encouraged with their bounties might carry Flemish wool or break into the American trade. The difficulty of quickly filling large ships is suggested by a comparison of the stated tonnages in safe-conducts—many being between 100 and 200 tons, with the cargoes unloaded in England—many being well under 100 tons; no cargoes came near the size of Canynges' *Mary and John* and Martín Ochoa's ships unloaded in Southampton between 27 and 116 tons although the smallest for which he had a safe-conduct was 120 tons and the largest was 400 tons.[71] However other ships unloaded cargoes near their stated capacity,[72] and the underloading may be more apparent than real, especially in Southampton or London where ships might unload only part of a cargo before sailing on to Sandwich, London or Flanders despite some stipulations about complete unloading in safe-conducts.

The total tonnage involved in the trade, like the total English or Spanish tonnage available, is impossible to determine but it might have been high since in the decade 1455–65 Spanish ships totalling 28,000 tons obtained safe-conducts from the English kings.

Investment in shipping was widespread despite the very real hazards and expense of constant refitting, wreck, mutiny, piracy and war. The last two were particular problems in the Channel during the disruptions of the Hundred Years War. Piracy became endemic and reached spectacular peaks when governments were weak: in 1402 the Castilian ambassador presented a list of twenty-nine cases of unremedied piracy and during negotiations saw his countrymen lose a further seventeen ships and goods from Prussian and Portuguese ships.[73] Another spate of piracy occurred in the middle of the century when Henry VI lost control and the royal sea-keeping fleet itself was among the worst offenders.[74] The temptation to steal was indulged not only on the high seas but even when a ship was safe in harbour.[75] The worst dangers of war could be offset with a safe-conduct, and if a ship was taken by pirates or against the safe-conduct the owners could sue for restitution and many did so successfully; but costs could be great and delays long, especially if a weak government could not enforce execution of its sentences. Juan Martín de Luxaro complained of the problems in 1440, although his case was not one of the longest known by any means: he declared he had been suing for eight months before Parliament, king, and Council, had had three letters of privy seal and a sergeant at arms sent to order restitution of his goods, had spent £150 so far and had nothing back from the offender, Baron Carreu; in 1442 £79 was still outstanding from the value of the goods and costs.[76] The English had similar problems at times: John Payn and John George of Bristol lost a ship despite safe-conduct under a letter of marque at Deva in 1475, they sued unsuccessfully in Spain until 1482, during which time George had died at Medina del Campo, and Payn eventually obtained a grant from the English king levyable on the customs and subsidies already granted to Guipúzcoan merchants; by that time his costs amounted to 1,600 crowns, over three-quarters of the size of the original loss.[77]

Seizure as a legitimate prize of war of course meant total loss, but enforced war service could also cost large sums, and Thomas Martin of London reckoned it had cost him £486 to serve the king instead of making his voyage to Spain in 1458.[78] However, if the need for shipping was not too pressing, the king might be persuaded to exempt ships already loaded, as he did in the case of several ready to sail to Spain in 1398.[79]

None the less ship-owning remained attractive. Provided all went well, returns soon covered initial outlay, perhaps within a year,[80] and in most cases ships did arrive safely and the risks were well worth taking. For small investors among the sea-going community it was particularly enticing as its profits could offer a chance to prosper and enter the merchant ranks and from there even the landed or administrative groups. A merchant-owner could expect lower freight charges for his goods. Any owner expected a share of loot taken. Ships and shipping shares were easily purchased, quickly realisable and worthwhile inheritances. It made an important and rich industry supported by the capital of all classes and some men sank as much into shipping as others into land. The social pattern of investment in shipping on the Anglo-Spanish route follows the general pattern already indicated by Dr Scammell.[81]

Royal ships, when not needed for war or royal transport, were hired out to merchants: Bartholomew Stygan took Edward III's *Welifare* to Bermeo, and Fetplace and other Southampton men hired Henry V's *Petit Holyghost* for a voyage to Portugal.[82] The Queen of Castile's ship loaded goods at London in 1410 and another of hers was hired by Agostino Lomellini of Seville in 1412 to transport his goods to England.[83]

The nobility too promoted shipping. Their motive for owning ships was partly military and for prestige, but they were only too willing to make additional profits with commercial voyages as well as piracy. In England Warwick and Howard had the biggest and best-known private fleets, but many of the lesser nobility and gentry followed their lead, and Dr Scammell found some seventy owners of this class between 1450 and 1550.[84] The Castilian nobles, particularly in Andalusia, were similarly attracted to shipping.[85] Diego López de Stúñiga, Baron of Spain, was recorded as the owner of a ship of Bilbao bringing goods of Lombards living in Seville to England;[86] two ships belonging to the Constable of Castile were given safe-conducts for trade with England in 1409;[87] the *Sta María of Deva*, which belonged to Pedro de Monsalva, the king's brother's treasurer, came with the ambassadorial squadron in 1409 and was given a safe-conduct but the extract in the treaty roll is too short to show whether it included the right to trade.[88] Later the Marquis of Villena, one of the new nobility and a favourite of Enrique IV, had one of his ships seized despite its safe-conduct while on a normal trading voyage to England.[89] The Dukes of Medina Sidonia and other southern aristocrats had the additional incentive of African exploration for ship-owning and looked south, but the *S Antonio of Spain* for which Medina Sidonia sought an English safe-conduct in 1463 may have been one of his own which he was sending to trade in the north.[90] Lesser nobility too sent their ships to trade with England, men such as Fernando Perre Dandrate, knight, recorded as obtaining a safe-conduct for his fifty-tonner the *Marie of Carence* in 1456.[91]

The greatest amount of investment however came from the commercial and sea-going communities. An important group of owners were the masters who owned or partly owned the ships they sailed, and there is no dearth of men described as 'master and owner', men such as Martín de Langueren, master and owner of the *Sta Katerina of San Sebastián* with a safe-conduct in 1412,[92] or Martín de Antiaga of Bilbao master and owner of the *S Bartolomeo* bringing wines from Lepe to London in 1470.[93] For merchants there was a strong advantage in a master being owner, and for other ship-owners in his being a co-owner, because he became personally interested in the speedy success of the voyage, ironing out delays swiftly, keeping the ship running smoothly at all costs.

The merchants who invested in shipping probably formed the largest group in England, and maybe in Spain too, although the references to master-owners are particularly frequent on Basque ships. Certainly numbers of Spanish merchants are described as owners, from the early-fourteenth-century merchant-owners of the *Maudelyn of Spain* to men such as Sancho Ortiz of Bilbao, Juan Divarola of Navarre, Salbatus Martín Danscue, provost of Fuenterrabía, in the fifteenth.[94] Some men would probably have found it difficult to say where their main interest lay if, like Martín and Pedro Ochoa of Deva, they commanded and owned ships and often unloaded whole cargoes in their own names.[95] Many of the English merchants owned or part-owned the ships they used to Spain: Ellis Spelly, Thomas Sampson, William Spaynell, the Rowley family, among others at Bristol owned shares or whole ships,[96] and Canynges and Straunge owned fleets of ten and twelve.[97] Other Englishmen and Spaniards were multiple owners too, although not on the Bristol scale. John Chirche of London, mercer, owned four or five;[98] John Hawley of Dartmouth owned at least three ships in 1379 and two ships in 1386;[99] two Basques in the Mediterranean owned at least two each;[100] Martín Ochoa probably owned two;[101] Juan Divarola of Navarre owned three ships and a barge.[102] But most ship-owning was on a more modest scale and few owned more than one ship or its equivalent in shares.

This practice of holding shares was widespread all over Europe as it spread the risks of loss at sea as well as the costs of building. The costs per ton of commercial shipbuilding are not well documented but were commonly accepted as a strain on a man's financial resources.[103] The Italians and Hansards carried the division of ships into shares to its furthest extent, but in England and Spain, as ships were smaller, so shares were larger, rarely a greater proportion than thirds or quarters, although occasionally eighths are mentioned in England,[104] and two references to twenty-fourths of Spanish ships can be found.[105] Possibly these were instances of owners needing ready cash quickly, although one of the examples is of a master of Ondárroa transferring the share to a sailor while in the Mediterranean. The many safe-conducts in the English treaty rolls which record three to five possible masters for a ship probably indicate instances of shared ownership among practising seamen any of whom might command the ship, or just possibly that there was a pool of qualified and experienced masters on whom an owner might call.

Geographically as well as socially, owning was widespread, although the vast majority of owners came from coastal districts, and most invested in the shipping of their home ports. Some however came from inland, and the ships of Taunton, Berkeley, Coventry and Wells sailing between Bristol and Spain indicate inland merchants' investments,[106] and similarly in Spain, men of Burgos, Santiago and Pamplona in Navarre invested in shipping.[107] Some men invested in foreign vessels: Basques were joint owners with Italians in the Mediterranean, and Londoners with Portuguese in the Atlantic.[108] There were of course commercial advantages in a ship's being able thus to sail under two flags, and M. Bernard has described one method of achieving this by fictitious sales in Gascony in the fifteenth century;[109] but with multi-national ownership such a stratagem would be unnecessary.

The manning of the ships, English and Spanish, differed little from that of the sixteenth century described by Dr Scammell,[110] except that even fewer details survive. The operating on this route, as in most of the northern areas, was the responsibility of the master: he had to provide and control an adequate crew, see that the ship was adequately victualled and navigated, and ensure that cargoes were safely delivered at time and place specified in the charter-parties. He was not helped here, as he was in the south, by a patron or governor; although in the later period he could expect to have a purser to deal with many of the financial and cargo details, and professional pilots for unfamiliar and dangerous waters. Occasionally Castilian ships had patrons or governors aboard, usually when there was an indication of Mediterranean sailing, but sometimes it seems the terminology was picked up without the organisation: the Biscayan patrons on three barges bringing malmsey in 1403 seem to be nothing more than the usual masters,[111] but the two ships of Bilbao for which the Count of Niebla sought safe-conduct in 1426 carried governors and masters.[112]

The vast majority of masters came from the same area if not the same port as the ship they commanded, but occasionally there are references to inland men becoming active masters, such as Urtonus Sanxhers of Vitoria,[113] and the widespread activity of the Basques led to their command of Italian[114] or Andalusian ships, as when Pedro Martín of Berme commanded the *Sta María of Seville* in 1391;[115] more rarely the opposite occured,as when Martín de Martyns of Cadiz commanded a ship of Bermeo which was plundered by the English of Italian goods between Sluys and Brittany.[116] The employment of an alien master had advantages if he was well acquainted with the foreign harbours and markets for which he was bound, and the Bristol merchants employed some Spanish exiles after 1369: the owners of the *Juliana* employed Diego Fernández in 1377 when she went to Spain, then John de Vay, a Portuguese, in 1379, and Juan Sánchez, probably another Castilian, in 1380.[117] Likewise the *St Anthony of Bristol* was taken to Portugal by Fernándo López in March 1379, although when she came back she was called the *St Anthony of Lisbon*, which may indicate clerical error, a recent sale, or even joint ownership.[118] The practice is not found outside Bristol, nor there outside this period, except that Juan Sánchez was still working for his Bristol employers twenty years later when he commanded the *Katherine of Bristol*.[119] Whatever the advantages of aliens it appears to have been easier to find suitable compatriots.

Most of the masters were, or soon became, men of modest substance: they were also owners, part-owners, or sons of owners, as were Richard Spaynell of Bristol and Pedro Ochoa of Deva.[120] All had opportunities for trade on their own account, and some dealt in large amounts in their own names (although in some cases they may be acting as agents for others, they were not simple employees since they appear as the shippers with full responsibility for all customs and duties): Juan Roys, master, unloaded 68 tons of iron in his name at London in 1391;[121] Juan de Gatery (Guetaría) unloaded 35 tons of iron there in 1463;[122] and Martín and Pedro Ochoa while masters of their ships unloaded and sold large cargoes of wine and iron.[123] Similar examples could be cited many times over;[124] even smaller amounts, a ton of iron or a single cloth, multiplied in several ports throughout a year may be part of a much more substantial business.

The master did not necessarily trade alone and commonly the customs accounts record goods shipped by the master *cum sociis suis*.[125] Often the amounts are small and may indicate an association of the master with some of his crew, and sometimes this is made clear: in 1447 at Sandwich the shippers of a cargo unloaded (24 tons and a barrel of iron, two barrels of nails, and one pipe of wine) were Ferrando de Rysaball 'm'r' et marinar' suis'.[126] Merchants too found partnership with a master useful; thus Martín de Fuenterrabía master of the *María of Spain* partnered a merchant in the export of sixty dozens of whites and russets from Exeter in 1462, and the master of the *Nicolas of Saragossa* partnered another in the export of thirteen cloths and import of 12 tons of iron in 1481.[127] Often it is impossible to identify the master's associates but the practice shows that the master was active in commerce as well as navigation and sought after as a partner for his experience in many markets.

The master might also be used as an agent or factor by a merchant, but normally this would be to supervise the transport rather than the sale of goods as the masters were unwilling to keep their ships longer than necessary in port.[128]

The master's first responsibility however was the running of his ship. The size of the crew he needed varied according to the size, type and efficiency of the vessel, and the safe-conducts for Spanish ships in the fifteenth century indicate this variety without providing the means for anything but the roughest analysis. Generally ships under 100 tons took less than forty men, ships up to 200 tons between thirty and forty men, ships up to 300 usually required fifty to sixty men and the biggest between 400 and 500 tons demanded eighty to a hundred men, but there are wildly divergent crew sizes apparent too. One ship of 200 tons might take forty men while another needed eighty, a ship of 450 tons might require sixty or a hundred; put another way, a crew of sixty might operate anything from 100 to 450 tons. Such variations depended on whether oarsmen were needed, how many masts and sails the ship carried, whether rigging was square, lateen or mixed, whether extra men for defence were carried, and how long the journey was to be, but unfortunately there is not enough information in the safe-conducts to indicate exactly how the numbers changed. The numbers are high compared with, say, Hanseatic crews, which M. Dollinger found to be usually one man for twelve tons;[129] the Spanish proportion is rather unstable but normally is about one man for four to six tons, with the worst ratio at one to one and a half, and the most efficient at one to seven. This difference may be partly due to different rigging and a higher proportion of lateen rigging on Spanish ships, but must also be largely due to defence: the Hansards operated fairly large ships in relatively peaceful waters while the Spaniards were running smaller ships in the dangerous Channel.[130]

Again, as with the masters, most of the crew whose locality is given come from the coastal areas, and in Spain particularly from the Basque Provinces, probably with a steady flow from inland attracted by the mobility of sea-going communities and the possibility of making their fortune. Many doubtless worked all their lives on ships of their own nation but others took whatever opportunities presented themselves and the result was ships with very mixed crews. Two ships from Barcelona at Haverfordwest in 1342 were worked by sailors from Catalonia, Castile, Portugal, Bayonne, England, Flanders, Genoa and Lombardy;[131] Ellis Spelly of Bristol had employed four or five Spaniards aboard his ships, but had run against the disadvantage that some Irishmen had taken this as an excuse to arrest his ship as an enemy vessel.[132] Sometimes captured seamen were pressed into service, and in 1373 sixteen Castilians were released from the Tower on condition that they served aboard Edward III's new galley;[133] perhaps they were sympathisers with the Castilian court in exile and not averse to the change. A steady number of Spaniards also served aboard Italian carracks and galleys sailing north from Andalusia[134] and in the Mediterranean.

Such a mixture of nationalities can have offered few practical difficulties since sailing terms and techniques were everywhere similar and small differences could be quickly picked up. Common seafaring problems and conditions gave rise to similar codes of conduct and discipline for most of western Europe by the thirteenth century, and the Laws of Oléron provided one source for sea codes from the Baltic to the Mediterranean and embodied many terms as applicable to Spanish seafaring life as to English. The laws and subsequent codes indicate both the general responsibilities of the master and the conditions in which the crew should work, and, although in many cases the practice may have fallen short of the ideal, if the management of a ship was kept even moderately close to the codes, a sailor aboard a merchant ship could expect fair discipline, acceptable food and wages, reasonable care if sick or injured, a fair deal for dependants on his death, and an opportunity for personal trading. Although natural dangers were ever present, the lot of the medieval sailor was a good deal less harsh than that of later sailors, especially aboard men of war.

Specialists among the crew are occasionally mentioned in the fourteenth century and increase rapidly in the fifteenth. A smith on a Spanish barge was unfortunately killed by English attackers in 1402,[135] but the countermaster and shipwright on Pedro Sanchy's ship at Southampton in 1460 worked and made use of their cargo space in more peaceful times.[136] A more authoritative person aboard was the purser, who in 1453 on the *Julian of Bristol* could reserve five tons of cargo space for his use;[137] and the recent publication of the accounts of John Balsall, purser of the *Trinity of Bristol*, shows how busy he was paying the crew, local pilots, for repairs and victuals, and local duties as well as acting as factor for some of the merchants exporting cloth on the ship.[138] The most important person aboard for the safety of the ship was the pilot, if carried. Many masters were capable of navigating in the open sea and probably into many of the ports they entered, but some long-distance pilots, and more local ones, were employed; charter-parties indicate that the payment of these was in some cases the merchants' responsibility and not that of the master.[139] A pilot's job was exacting and severe penalties were laid down in the Laws of Oléron if his negligence lost the ship: whether the English pilot Lodomannus de Mergate, hired by the merchants, suffered them by losing the *S Juan of Bilbao* off Sheppey is uncertain,[140] but the Spanish pilots involved in a dispute over wreck off Flanders in 1456 expected only loss of salary.[141] Spanish pilots were frequently found working along the Channel on French,[142] Spanish[143] and Italian vessels and are increasingly obvious from about the third decade of the fifteenth century. Alessandro Moro, patron of a Venetian ship, was unfortunate in that his Spanish pilot was arrested as an enemy alien when ashore for recreation at Southampton and he had to wait for the man's release before finishing the voyage,[144] but usually no trouble was made and Spanish pilots of Basque origin or family often appear among shippers aboard Italian vessels.[145] Like Moro's pilot, many of these were long-distance pilots working between Andalusia and Flanders or England, men such as Juan de Bormeo and Alvero de Ryo who brought a Venetian carrack from Cadiz to within sight of the Flemish coast in 1456 and won full payment of salary when it was wrecked because then the responsibility for the ship was the local pilot's.[146] Again, in 1466, four Castilians called as witnesses before a court at Middelburg were said to be used to sailing the sea daily as pilots, bringing Genoese and Catalan ships north: two were men in their forties and two in their sixties, indicating that age and experience rather than a youthful constitution were the requisites of a pilot.[147]

The confirmation of the ordinances of the *Colegio* of Biscayan pilots at Cadiz towards the end of the fifteenth century described it as established from time immemorial.[148] This takes it back at least to the early fifteenth century and, although none of the English records refer to such an institution, the frequency of reference to pilots of Guetaría, San Sebastián and other northern ports piloting Mediterranean vessels from the south and along the Channel indicates that it was thriving by mid-century. English merchants knew that skilled pilots could be found in Andalusia not only for the north but also for African expeditions and by 1480 were eager to employ them. These Spanish pilots and others were forbidden by Ferdinand and Isabella, who had just made the Treaty of Toledo with Portugal, to help the English fleet then planning to sail south,[149] but Edward's attempt to obtain retrospective Papal approval for an English voyage to Africa about this time, John II of Portugal's protests in 1482 about English activity off Africa, and the difficulty of the Reyes Católicos in controlling their Andalusian nobility and particularly the Dukes of Medina Sidonia, who had had rights on the African coast as far as Cape Bojador since 1449, suggest that the English did sail and quite possibly took Spanish pilots with them.[150]

The form of information used by the pilots and masters remains a topic for debate. No charts survive for the fifteenth century, although, as has been pointed out, there must have been some precedent for the work of the *Casa de Contratación* at Seville in the early sixteenth;[151] probably most navigators however found the information of a rutter more useful in tidal Atlantic and Channel waters. Existing rutters give much information for approaches to Spanish harbours as well as northern coasts: visible land-marks, compass directions, type and depth of bottom, depths of water at harbour entrances at high and low water, distances between ports, are all given.[152] Coastal navigation was doubtless the most accurate method but the frequent coasting journeys done did not mean that medieval seamen were incapable of open sea navigation—the astrolabe, compass and sounding line provided an adequate system for this, and many ships ran straight across the Bay of Biscay—but simply that for many the balance of advantage lay in favour of staying close to shore with its shelter, supplies and opportunities for small-scale trade.

Charter-parties specified the responsibilities of the masters on particular voyages but few survive for Anglo-Spanish trade. One of 1392 shows Thomas Lynne, master of John Hawley of Dartmouth's barge, agreeing with Italian merchants at Seville that he would be responsible for sup-plying the sailors, victuals, ship's gear, lighters in port where necessary and lighting aboard fore and aft, while the merchants caulked the cabin, provided the pilot from Seville and would pay for petty pilotage and towage if needed.[153] The charter-party further stipulated that loading was to be finished in four weeks, the ship would then go to Sanlúcar, then Southampton to spend four days unloading before going on to London to complete unloading in a further twenty-five days. Freight was to be paid at $4\frac{1}{2}$ gold francs the ton with 25 francs gratuity. Any flotsam, jetsam, or plunder was to be shared between the master and crew on one hand and the merchants on the other. The master and crew undertook to defend the merchants' goods, and default on either side carried a penalty of 300 *doubles*. Such agreements did not prevent a master calling at ports en route, but most of them make clear that the main merchants were not interested in ships as 'travelling bazaars', in M. Braudel's phrase, but in selling goods at a particular destination, although in some cases alter-natives were allowed. The *Julian of Bristol* was to sail to Lisbon, to Ireland, back to Plymouth and on to either France or Holland, probably depending on what market information and what cargoes the merchants picked up en route;[154] the *Sta María of Santander* was freighted for Southampton and Sandwich, and then Flanders but only if there was peace between England and France;[155] the goods aboard the *S Juan of Pasajes* were to be unloaded at Saltes or Barrameda, depending on how the weather stood and which she arrived at first.[156]

There was no attempt to stipulate the length of the voyage itself of course as wind and weather made such a difference to the relatively clumsy ships and masters might have to wait for favourable winds. Provided the weather set fair, however, merchants could expect to reach the west of England from northern Spain in under a week, and London in ten to twelve days,[157] although faster crossings were made: William Wey went from Plymouth to Corunna in four days in May, the Florentine galleys reckoned to cross from northern Spain to south-west England in three to four days, and the run from Sluys to Laredo could be done in under a week.[158] The journey from Andalusia to England probably took two and a half to three weeks but the round trip between Bristol and Andalusia generally took some three or four months including calls at Lisbon and probably at least two southern ports. Unless the weather was really poor what took most time was the turn-round period in port, loading, unloading, refitting, looking for more cargo, documenting, weighing and customing goods. For the shipowner this was an unproductive time, which was why charter-parties were so particular about the time spent in port and why lawsuits followed if merchants transgressed. The port time allowed was generally three to four weeks in most trades, although the Florentines allowed a short ten days in Flanders but forty-five in Southampton,[159] and Juan de Medina using the *S Bartolomeo* from Lepe to London in 1470 was allowed thirty-one days to pay freightage.[160] The English customs accounts show that five weeks was not unusual, and that one or two days were possible.[161] The ownership of the goods would influence port times: if goods were consigned to a resident factor he could immediately unload and warehouse them, but if they belonged to a merchant with few contacts they might have to be sold from the ship, as were Philip Wawton's cloths in the *Mary Assh* at Sanlúcar in 1478.[162]

Freightage was stipulated in the charter-parties, and variations might be expected according to the length of voyage and the risk of war at any one time, but something fairly near a standard rate between England and either north or south Spain seems to have obtained. In 1441 £1 the ton was charged for bringing iron and wine from the north to Southampton;[163] in 1470 Genoese goods in Andalusia were sent to Southampton on the *St James of Seville* for 21s 0d the ton;[164] in 1467 or 1468 Thomas Basset arranged for John Goo to bring his wines from Fuenterrabía to Southampton for £1 the tun, but that included transport six miles into Fuenterrabía first;[165] on the other hand in 1453 Thomas Martin alleged he had lost 28s 0d the ton freightage on a voyage from London to Spain; as he was attempting to claim compensation from the Exchequer he might be exaggerating, but charges in 1453 might have risen because of war risks.[166]

These rates correspond closely with those found by Dr James for the Gascon wine ships at this date, she also found about a 100 per cent rise over the late-fourteenth-century charges because of rising war risks, and charges for Spanish trade seem to have risen likewise, as Thomas Lynne had agreed to freightage of $4\frac{1}{2}$ gold francs the ton from Andalusia in 1392, which at 2s 0d sterling the franc would be only 9s 0d.[167]

The owners kept their ships moving right through the winter on this route, and found no lack of merchants ready to take the weather risk. Slow and clumsy though the vessels were in the thirteenth century, eight Spanish ships unloaded at Winchelsea in December 1266.[168] At Sandwich in 1329 six Spaniards came in in January.[169] At Bristol there were three departures for and one arrival from Spain in December 1403, two departures and ten arrivals in January 1404, and five departures and one arrival in February, and some of these were clearly dealing in Andalusia.[170] In 1477–8 a similar pattern emerges there: in December three arrivals from Portugal, two from the Algarve, and one from Seville, in January another from Seville; in 1479–80 three arrivals from Portugal in December, one from Seville in January, and another at the beginning of March.[171] There was a slackening of movement for winter but never a cessation even in the early period.

The seamen took the risks they had to in the face of nature, but minimised the risk from man wherever they could. Safe-conducts were one method of protection, and convoy sailing was another. The size of convoys might be large: Spanish ones for Flanders in the fourteenth century might reach forty ships,[172] English ones from Bordeaux in the fifteenth neared fifty,[173] Hanseatic ones once they ventured down to the Bay for salt rose to thirty, forty, fifty and above.[174] Yet as these rose in size the Spanish seem to fall: the Cortes complained in 1436 that masters were taking their ships piecemeal out of the fleets (now only of ten to twenty ships) once away from the coast,[175] but their remedy was not to enforce convoy discipline but to build bigger ships for protection. The convoy system did not however fit Anglo-Spanish trade as it did Hispano-Flemish trade as there was no one seasonal commodity like the wool clip to transport, and, while some masters might accompany a Flemish convoy on the first part of their journey, they would soon peel off, and others probably preferred to avoid a convoy limited to the speed of the slowest and from which in any case ships could be cut out and plundered.[176] Thus the ships sailing between England and Spain sailed singly or at most in groups of three or four,[177] and if one of the group was delayed, as was Martín de Lucerra by a suit in Admiralty by William Folkys when ready to sail with a group from the Thames, then the others sailed without him.[178]

Insurance also minimised risks and costs but as this usually applied to the cargoes rather than ships it has been dealt with as part of the merchants' organisation.

This pattern of shipping and the developments within it were similar to those on most of the northern and some of the southern routes outside those dominated by the great Italian and Hanseatic fleets. There was enough variety of commodity and distance in the trade to encourage and justify the use of almost every type and size of vessel of any seafaring nation, although most on the direct route were English and Basque ships of moderate size. The Spaniards dominated the trade until the mid fourteenth century, were joined by the English then who were dominant at Bristol, but in the fifteenth century the Spaniards remained very active, and increased their activity in London and also Bristol.

The changes in the size and types of vessels used were in line with those for other northern trades, and the patterns of investment too were similar. Operating methods too were common with other northern routes; little use was made of Mediterranean manning with which the Spaniards must have been very familiar. Such conformity is not surprising, since the Anglo-Castilian route was in no way isolated from the other routes of northern Europe and its scale made no unusual demands on the resources of the countries.

NOTES TO CHAPTER 5

1   C.P.R. 1307–13, p. 367.

2   P.R.O. E122/19/10a, 13, 14. For the growing Breton vigour at sea see Touchard, Le Commerce maritime breton, pp. 210–14, 224; Mollat, Le Commerce maritime normand, pp. 14–15; Mathorez, 'Notes sur les rapports de Nantes avec l'Espagne', Bulletin Hispanique, XIV (1912), pp. 119–20, 125–6.

3   P.R.O. E122/194/20, 26, 162/5, 15/8, 16/4, 5, 9, 13.

4   P.R.O. C76/95 mm. 13, 21.

5   C.P.R. 1401–5, p. 424; C.C.R. 1402–5, pp. 70, 94, 108; P.R.O. SC8/11529, 11553.

6   C.P.R. 1401–5, p. 281; P.R.O. E122/16/5, 9, 11, 13, 17, 19; see pp. 85, 156.

7   Rot. Parl., v, 31b.

8   See particularly Heers, 'Le commerce des Basques en Mediterranée au XVe siècle', Bulletin Hispanique, LVII (1955).

9   García de Cortázar, Vizcaya, pp. 103–7; for general comments on the Basque ship-building industry see Guiard y Larrauri, La industria naval Vizcaína.

10   See among others García de Cortázar, op. cit., pp. 214–26; Smith, The Spanish Guild Merchant, pp. 67–70; Maréchal, 'La colonie espagnole de Bruges du 14e au 16e siècle', Revue du Nord, XXXV (1953), pp. 13–18.

11   Very rarely men of Colindres were mentioned: C.P.R. 1436–41, p. 411; P.R.O. E28/66 (19 Feb. 19 Hen. VI); C76/123 m.6, 124 m.18, 126 m.16, 135 m.15.

12   García de Cortázar, Vizcaya, pp. 64–5.

13   Cortes, III, 91.

14   C.P.R. 1367–70, p. 140; William Wey, Itineraries; C.C.R. 1343–6, pp. 449, 484; P.R.O. SC1/38/10.

15 William Wey, *Itineraries*, p. 153.

16 Storrs, 'Jacobean pilgrims from England from the early twelfth to the late fifteenth century', especially pp. 31, 44, 47.

17 Russell, *English Intervention in Spain and Portugal*, pp. 523, 534.

18 C.P.R. 1301–7, p. 286; C.C.R. 1389–92, p. 250; *ibid*, 1402–5, p. 33; *ibid*, 1405–9, pp. 21, 24; P.R.O. E101/80/25; C76/149 m.9.

19 Sanlúcar: P.R.O. C76/149 m.9; Cadiz: C.P.R. 1436–41, pp. 535, 575; P.R.O. C76/120 m.4, 124 m.2; E28/66 (13 Feb. 19 Hen. VI); Lepe: Exeter City Library, loc. cust. accts., 1-2 Ric. III, 2 Ric. III–1 Hen. VII; Andalusia: P.R.O. C76/145 m.20.

20 This has been established by Heers, 'Le commerce des Basques', *Bulletin Hispanique*, LVII (1963); Mollat, 'Deux études relatives aux constructions navales à Barcelone et à Palma de Majorque au XIVe siècle', *Homenaje a Jaime Vicens Vives*, I; Carrère, 'Le droit d'ancrage et le mouvement du port de Barcelone au milieu du XVe siècle', *Estudios de Historia Moderna*, III (1953).

21 *Foedera*, v, i, 1, 4, 5, 7, 29, 65.

22 C.C.R. 1369–74, p. 30.

23 *Ibid.*, 1461–8, p. 347; *ibid.*, 1468–76, No. 1039; P.R.O. C76/106 m.8, 107 m.8, 108 m.4, 109 m.4; E159/208 Recorda Mich. m.20; E122/19/8.

24 C.C.R. 1396–9, pp. 328, 329.

25 *Foedera*, v, i, 4.

26 P.R.O. C76/119 m.5, 123 m.18 (the *Margaret* or *St Margaret* is shown to be his in C.P.R. 1429–36, p. 512; *ibid*, 1436–41, p. 349).

27 P.R.O. C76/112 m.8.

28 P.R.O. C1/57/48–50, 59/169–70, 62/419–20.

29 Gorosabal, *Memorias sobre las guerras y tratados de Guipúzcoa con Inglaterra*, pp. 54–5.

30 P.R.O. E122/19/14.

31 P.R.O. C76/140 m.6, 145 m.36.

32 C.P.R. 1338–40, p. 1; the *Anne of Hampton* went on to Spain from Bayonne in the fifteenth century, P.R.O. C1/26/300.

33 *Foedera*, v, i, 4, 5, 7; C.P.R. 1391–6, p. 602.

34 A large number of licences for the later fourteenth and early fifteenth centuries appear in *Foedera*, the C.P.R. and the *Deputy Keepers' Reports*, vols. 44, 48.

35 C.P.R. 1369–74, p. 30; *Cal. Plea and Memo. Rolls of London*, III, 194–7.

36 C.P.R. 1232–47, p. 68.

37 *Ibid.*, 1307–13, p. 375. The next chronological example is that of 1338; *ibid*, 1338–40, p. 1.

38 P.R.O. E122/15/8, 16/2, 5, 9, 11, 13, 15, 17, 19, 21, 23, 30, 34, 17/1.

39 P.R.O. E122/19/1, 3, 4, 6, 7, 8, 10, 10a, 11, 13, 14, 20/1, 5, 7; the division between Portuguese and Spanish trade is less than it looks as Andalusian-bound ships often called at Lisbon en route.

40 *Statutes of the Realm*, 5 Ric. II st. 1 c. 3, 6 Ric. II st. 1 c. 8, 14 Ric. II c. 6.

41 Guiard, *La industria naval Vizcaína*, pp. 3, 8–9, app. 1; Colmeiro, *Historia de la economía politica en España*, I, 461.

42 *Cortes*, III, 263–4.

43 *Statutes of the Realm*, 18 Hen. VI c. 8.

44 *Ibid*, 4 Hen. VII c. 10.

45 García de Cortázar, *Vizcaya*, pp. 172–3, 190–1.

46 C.P.R. 1485–94, p. 340; C.C.R. 1485–1500, No. 558.

47 The *Nicholas of Biscay* ship or balinger (C.P.R. 1452–61, p. 281); the *Julián of San Sebastián* ship or barge (P.R.O. C76/108 m.4); Bernard, 'Les types de navires

ibériques et leur influence sur la construction navale dans les ports du sud-ouest de la France', *Actes du 5e Colloque International d'Histoire Maritime*, ed. Mollat and Adam.

48   Exeter City Library, loc. cust. accts. 11–12 Ed. III.

49   P.R.O. E122/16/11, 13.

50   Mollat, 'Constructions . . . à Barcelone . . .', *loc. cit.*, pp. 563–5.

51   P.R.O. E28/42 (10 Jun. 1 Hen. VI), *ibid*, 49 (26 Feb. 5 Hen. VI); E122/114/14.

52   P.R.O. SC6/1031/19.

53   P.R.O. C76/86 m.2; *Cal. Plea and Memo. Rolls of London*, III, 194–7; Exeter City Library, loc. cust. accts, 28–29 Hen. VI.

54   Burwash, *English Merchant Shipping*, pp. 112–13, 115–16. Cargoes unloaded are only a crude pointer to a vessel's size as not all goods may be unloaded.

55   Burwash, *op. cit*, pp. 103–4, 106–8; P.R.O C76/123 mm.6, 20; 138 m.32.

56   See for instance P.R.O. E122/114/4, 7a, 9, 10, 11.

57   Exeter City Library, loc. cust. accts, 2–3 Ed. IV; P.R.O. E122/40/10, 36, 114/3, 28/9; C1/27/409.

58   Unger, 'Carvel building in Northern Europe before 1450', *Mariners Mirror*, LVII (1971), pp. 331–3.

59   Bernard, 'Les types de navires ibériques', *loc. cit.*, p. 212: the first reference he found to a carvel at Bordeaux was 1467 and to the first building there 1483.

60   On measures in general see Lane, 'Tonnages, medieval and modern', *Ec.H.R.*, 2nd ser., XVII (1964) which is still the best introduction to the whole debate; on Spanish measures in particular see also H. and P. Chaunu, *Seville et l'Atlantique*, I, 133; Guiard, *La industria naval Vizcaína*, p. 31 and note. Freightage from Andalusia in 1470 was charged at five butts to three *toneles* instead of two butts to the tun English—thus the *tonel* would be about five-sixths of a *tonelada* in the fifteenth as in the sixteenth century; *C.C.R.* 1468–76, No. 709.

61   P.R.O. C76/84–169. I have taken the ton as a constant measure although in fact there is no indication of whether the Chancery clerk used information just as it was given him, which might be in Castilian, Biscayan or English measures, or converted them to a standard.

62   Heers, 'Le commerce des Basques', *loc. cit.*, pp. 305–6; Carrère, 'Le droit d'ancrage', *loc. cit.*, pp. 103–4 (notes 191–5), 122, 132, 136.

63   M. Heers converts *cantares* to the metric *tonne*.

64   Two butts may be taken as a little under one ton.

65   For the numbers of safe-conducts granted see Table 3.

66   Gilliodts van Severen, *Inventaire*, VI, 1221.

67   Scammell, 'English merchant shipping . . . some east coast evidence', *Ec.H.R.*, 2nd ser., XIII (1961).

68   Braudel, *The Mediterranean and the Mediterranean World*, I, 299–312.

69   P.R.O. C76/137 m.1; 142–6 *passim*; 148 m.3; 149 m.21.

70   Printed in Carus-Wilson, *Overseas Trade of Bristol*, misc. records 182, 202.

71   Ms. S.P.B. 1459–60 Lib. Comm. (unfol.), 3 Dec.; P.R.O. E122/142/1; C76/142 mm.15, 18, 145 m.35; 146 m.21.

72   P.R.O. E159/208 Recorda Easter mm.10, 10d, 12d, Trin. mm.7, 8, 10.

73   See Table 2.

74   C.P.R. 1452–61, pp. 435–41; Richmond, 'English naval power', *loc. cit.*, p. 8.

75   R.L.C. 1224–7, p. 203b; P.R.O. C1/64/638; A.G.S. R.G.S. 1480, fo. 431.

76   P.R.O. E28/63 (20 Apr. 18 Hen. VI), *ibid.*, 64 (24 Oct. 19 Hen. VI), *ibid.*, 70 (28 June 20 Hen. VI).

77 C.P.R. *1476–85*, pp. 271, 330; A.G.S. R.G.S. 1475, fo. 445, 1478, fo. 136, 1480, fos. 107, 249; P.R.O. E356/22 mm.10d, 38d, 46d, 47.

78 C.P.R. *1452–61*, p. 76.

79 C.C.R. *1396–9*, pp. 327–31.

80 See C.S.P. *Spanish, 1558–67*, pp. 569–70.

81 Scammell, 'Shipowning in England *c.* 1450–1550', *T.R.H.S.*, 5th ser., XII (1962).

82 C.P.R. *1354–8*, p. 281; P.R.O. SC8/5504, 5863.

83 P.R.O. C76/92 m.5, 94 m.1, 95 mm.4, 13.

84 Scammell, 'Shipowning', *loc. cit.*, pp. 112, 116, 119–20.

85 Konetzke, 'Entrepreneurial activities of Spanish and Portuguese noblemen in medieval times', *Explorations in Entrepreneurial History*, vol. 6, No. 2 (1953–4).

86 C.P.R. *1401–5*, p. 361; C.C.R. *1402–5*, p. 203; P.R.O. SC8/9011; López was one of the guardians of Juan II in 1406.

87 P.R.O. C 76/92 mm.5, 8.

88 *Ibid.*, m.5.

89 C.P.R. *1452–61*, p. 439; P.R.O. SC8/15733.

90 P.R.O. C76/147 m.14.

91 *Ibid.*, 138 m.11.

92 P.R.O. C76/95 m.16.

93 P.R.O. C1/46/444; C.C.R. *1468–72*, No. 709.

94 P.R.O. C1/7/321; C76/137 m.19; C.P.R. *1441–6*, p. 370.

95 See Appendix.

96 Spelly: C.C.R. *1364–8*, p. 255; *ibid.*, *1377–81*, p. 24; C.P.R. *1391–6*, p. 594. Sampson and Spaynell (whose ships were often commanded by his son, Richard): Wadley, *Wills*, pp. 17, 30. Rowley family: P.R.O. C76/162 m.8; C1/47/62.

97 Carus-Wilson, *Overseas Trade of Bristol*, misc. recs. 182, 202.

98 C.P.R. *1429–36*, pp. 512, 540; *ibid.*, *1436–41*, pp. 166, 349, 481; C.C.R. *1435–41*, p. 33; P.R.O. C76/119 m.5, 123 m.18, 129 m.3.

99 Watkin, *Dartmouth*, pp. 365, 367, 375; *Cal. Plea and Memo. Rolls of London*, III, 194–7.

100 Heers, 'Le commerce des Basques', *loc. cit.*, p. 304.

101 See Appendix.

102 C.P.R. *1452–61*, p. 439; P.R.O. C76/137 m.19, 140 m.6; E101/128/37 fo. 3v.

103 P.R.O. C76/166 m.19; and see E28/90 14 Nov. 12 Ed. IV, where John Forster applied for a first voyage customs and subsidy free, apparently to offset the cost of building. A carvel of 120 tons without gear was sworn to be new and worth £180 in 1470; *Foedera*, V, ii, 180.

104 P.R.O. E159/166 Recorda Mich. (Somerset).

105 Heers, 'Le commerce des Basques', *loc. cit.*, p. 305; *Colección de Documentos Históricos*, Boletín de la Academia Gallega, I, 42.

106 P.R.O. E122/16/19, 17/10, 19/10.

107 C.P.R. *1334–8*, p. 520; *Colección de Documentos Históricas* (Gallegas), I, 42; P.R.O. C76/108 m.4, 109 m.5, 110 m.9, 111 m.3, 137 m.23; E159/207 Recorda Trin. m.8d.

108 Heers, 'Le commerce des Basques', *loc. cit.*, p. 304; A.G.S. R.G.S. 1480, fo. 431; see also Scammell, 'Shipowning in England', *loc. cit.*, p. 118.

109 Bernard, 'Les expedients du commerce anglo-gascon après la conquête francaise: ventes réelles et fictives de navires', *Annales du Midi*, 78 (1966).

110 Scammell, 'Manning the English merchant service in the sixteenth century', *Mariners Mirror*, 56 (1970).

111   P.R.O. C76/87 m.23.

112   *Ibid.*, 108 m.7.

113   *C.C.R. 1392–6*, pp. 49, 366.

114   Heers, 'Le commerce des Basques', *loc. cit.*, p. 303.

115   *C.C.R. 1389–92*, p. 250.

116   *C.P.R. 1361–4*, p. 536.

117   P.R.O. E122/15/8, 16/2, 5, 138/3.

118   *Ibid.*, 16/5.

119   P.R.O. E175 roll 28.

120   Wadley, *Wills*, p. 30; P.R.O. E122/16/19, 20 printed in Carus-Wilson, *Overseas Trade of Bristol*; for Ochoa see Appendix.

121   P.R.O. E122/71/16.

122   *Ibid.*, 194/12.

123   See Appendix.

124   See for example Geldo, Sans de Venesse, in Appendix.

125   For example: P.R.O. E122/40/10, 36, 71/13, 16, 142/3, 8.

126   P.R.O. SC6/896/3.

127   P.R.O. E122/40/10, 41/6.

128   See pp. 185–90 for partnership and agencies.

129   Dollinger, *The German Hansa*, pp. 153–4.

130   Professor Parry has pointed out that it was not unknown in the sixteenth century for heavily armed shipping to carry a man for every two tons, in *The Age of Reconnaisance*, p. 85.

131   *C.M.I.*, II, 1819.

132   *C.C.R. 1377–81*, p. 24.

133   *Ibid.*, *1369–74*, p. 508.

134   For example P.R.O. E122/76/34, 77/3, 194/11.

135   P.R.O. C47/32/24.

136   Ms. S.P.B. 1459–60, Lib. Comm. (unfol.), 20 Jan., 27 Feb.

137   P.R.O. C1/24/211–17, printed by Carus–Wilson, *Overseas Trade of Bristol*, misc. records 120.

138   Reddaway and Ruddock, 'The accounts of John Balsall', *Camden Miscellany XXIII*.

139   *Cal. Plea and Memo. Rolls of London*, III, 194–7. This corresponds to practice on the Anglo-Gascon wine route, James, *Wine Trade*, p. 136.

140   *C.P.R. 1361–4*, p. 151.

141   Gilliodts van Severen, *Consulat*, p. 73.

142   *C.P.R. 1327–30*, p. 168.

143   P.R.O. E122/26/10, 128/15, 194/23; Ms. S.P.B. 1459–60 Lib. Comm. (unfol.), 20 Jan.; *C.C.R. 1313–18*, p. 301.

144   P.R.O. E28/93(44).

145   P.R.O. E122/76/34, 128/15, 194/24; Ms. S.P.B. 1450–1, Lib. Al., fo. 106v; *ibid.*, 1455–6, Lib. Al., fo. 45; *ibid.*, 1459–60, Lib. Al. (unfol.), 11 Feb.

146   As note 141.

147   Finot, *Les Relations commerciales entre la France et l'Espagne*, pp. 204–8.

148   García de Cortázar, *Vizcaya*, p. 210.

149   A.G.S. R.G.S. 1480, fo. 81.

150   Blake, *European Beginnings in West Africa*, pp. 60–2; Quinn, 'Edward IV and exploration', pp. 278–80; Pérez Embid, *Los Descubrimientos en el Atlantico*.

151   Bagrow, *History of Cartography*, pp. 65, 107, 114.

152   The earliest surviving English rutter which gives details for a voyage from

Gibraltar to the north sailing direct across the Bay of Biscay was published in 1889, *Sailing directions for the Circumnavigation of England and for a Voyage to the Straits of Gibraltar*, ed. Gairdner, Hakluyt Society (1889). For an even more detailed rutter of Spanish interest see *Das Seebuch*, ed. Koppmann.

153   *Cal. Plea and Memo. Rolls of London*, III, 194–7.

154   P.R.O. C1/24/211–17 printed in Carus-Wilson, *Overseas Trade of Bristol*, misc. records 120.

155   C.M.I., II, 1679.

156   P.R.O. C1/48/114.

157   Connell-Smith, *Forerunners of Drake*, pp. 11-12.

158   Wey, *Itineraries*, p. 153; Mallett, *Florentine Galleys*, p. 89 and n. 4; Guiard, *Historia del Consulado de Bilbao*, p. xxxv.

159   Watson, 'The structure of the Florentine galley trade with Flanders and England in the fifteenth century', *R.B.P.H.*, XXXIX (1961), p. 1082.

160   *C.C.R. 1468–76*, No. 709.

161   The accounts do not give precise entry and exit dates but rather days when loading and unloading began, but they give a rough indication of stay in port.

162   P.R.O. C1/66/430–1.

163   P.R.O. E101/128/31: this also shows charges of £1 and 18s 4d from Rochelle.

164   P.R.O. C1/43/174–5, 46/334.

165   *Ibid.*, 44/160.

166   *C.P.R. 1452–61*, p. 76.

167   James, *Wine Trade*, pp. 141–6 and appendix 18; *Cal. Plea and Memo. Rolls of London*, III, 194–7.

168   P.R.O. SC6/1031/19.

169   P.R.O. E122/124/30.

170   P.R.O. E122/17/10.

171   P.R.O. E122/19/13, 14. Nearly all accounts furnish similar examples.

172   Nicolas, *Royal Navy*, II, 105; C.M.I., IV, 88.

173   James, *Wine Trade*, pp. 126–33; Carus-Wilson, *Medieval Merchant Venturers*, p. 35.

174   Haebler, 'Der Hansisch–Spanische Konflikt von 1419 und die aelteren Spanischen Bestaende', *H.G.B.*, VIII (1894), pp. 49-51, 54-5; Dollinger, *The German Hansa*, pp. 147, 303; Postan, 'England and the Hanse', *Studies in English Trade*, ed. Power and Postan, p. 127.

175   *Cortes*, III, 263-5.

176   C.M.I., IV, 88; a Genoese carrack and a Spanish ship were cut out by the English in 1378.

177   Grouping could be deceptive; three unloading the same day at Bristol in 1475 had in fact come from Seville, northern Spain and Bordeaux; P.R.O. E122/19/11.

178   P.R.O. C1/66/126.

CHAPTER 6

Mercantile organisation   *I*
Techniques and practices

The merchants who dealt in these goods did not rely for the prosecution of their business and the protection of their interests on stable, permanent structures like those of the Italian business houses or the privileged colonies or 'nations' in Bruges. Such a chartered organisation was perhaps on its way for the Spaniards in England in the early fourteenth century but it was stifled by the Hundred Years War. Instead these merchants found their trade much more dependent on the wealth, influence and reputation of individuals.

This dependence on the individual was basic in a tramping trade in which goods were shipped with no certain buyers in view, and often no particular destination envisaged, but with the accompanying merchant or agent doing the best he could wherever the ship called, offering his goods from the ship or from temporary warehouses. There was, of course, the grave risk, particularly with perishable goods, of not being able to sell profitably and quickly, and Spaniards and Englishmen were at times forced to buy licences to re-export Spanish goods for which they could not find suitable buyers,[1] but rarely after the fourteenth century.

Although some of the characteristics of this trade lasted into the later period, and Philip Wawton of London offered his cloth for sale from the *Mary Asshe* at Sanlúcar, and John Balsall, purser of the *Trinity of Bristol* and factor for seven Bristol merchants, offered some from temporary warehouses at Huelva,[2] the 'travelling bazaar' was not long adequate for the scale of Anglo-Castilian trade, and while crew members and small-time traders might still like coastal trade the prosperous man dealing in large amounts needed something safer, and found it in a variety of developments and more or less sophisticated usages.

One of his earliest aids was the concentration of trade in a few well-known, busy centres where a consignment could with near certainty find both a buyer and a return cargo. Although Spaniards visited the great English fairs,[3] already by the late thirteenth century much of their trade was at the main southern ports and they more rarely travelled inland.

London was throughout the most important centre for Spanish trade. It offered a safe harbour, was close to the great Flemish markets and to the main routes from them to the west and Mediterranean, was the centre of a network of roads and waterways for the collection and distribution of goods, as well as being in itself one of the best markets in England for both luxury goods and essentials with its large population which included wealthy merchants and nobility, and the artisans needing raw materials for its growing industry.

Sandwich was the only one of the Cinque Ports to retain importance. It and Winchelsea had been very important in the thirteenth century but Winchelsea suffered from erosion and silting; Dover, Faversham and Queenborough saw occasional Spanish visitors but were never important; Sandwich retained some attraction because of its closeness to the Flemish route and because it could easily serve as an outport for London.

Southampton's neighbours, Chichester and Portsmouth, were sometimes used but were far overshadowed by Southampton itself. This port was blessed with its sheltered harbour, and the 'double tide' which eased unloading. It was a busy international port, well placed on the channel route with a rich and accessible hinterland for the collection and distribution of goods. It too served partly as an outport for London and the roads between the two were busy not only with Italian goods but Spanish ones too. The heyday of Spanish trade in Southampton was probably in the second half of the thirteenth century and after that it settled to a smaller, but fairly steady level.

Bristol was the main western port important in the trade, but although it was prominent in the early Gascon trade there was only limited activity on the Spanish route and by Spaniards until the mid fourteenth century. Thereafter the Spanish connection throve, with Bristol exporting many of the fine west country cloths, providing a prosperous local population and local industry demanding Spanish goods and with a wide hinterland easily accessible by waterways.

Other smaller centres of course played a role too. The Devon ports, especially Exeter, Dartmouth and Plymouth, were steadily used, being reasonably sheltered, good refuges in bad weather en route to Flanders or London, and suppliers of local cloth and fish. Bridgwater was easily called at on the way to Bristol and provided local cloth, and the Somerset beans and peas. Cornish ports were smaller, less sheltered, on a more dangerous coast, but again useful first and last refuges from the Bay of Biscay, and as they could offer a little poor cloth and fish a certain amount of Anglo-Castilian trade trickled through Fowey, Falmouth and Mousehole. On the east coast after the thirteenth century little Spanish activity was apparent until the expansion of the late fifteenth attracted a few ships to Hull, Great Yarmouth and Ipswich, although some Hull men had maintained Spanish contacts in the fourteenth and early fifteenth, probably through the pilgrim transport to Corunna. Spaniards also began to use Chester in the fifteenth-century expansion. None of these centres could ever rival the main four, however, where Spaniards could be sure of finding ready markets, good cloth to buy in return and a sizeable merchant community ready to help them because of its own close interest in the route.

The English merchants in Spain also concentrated their trade at certain centres. In Guipúzcoa the most frequently used ports were Fuenterrabía and San Sebastián with their good harbours and easily accessible hinterlands. In Biscay the centre first used by Englishmen would probably have been Bermeo but by the time English activity was noticeable this had given way to its fast-growing rival, Bilbao; by 1401 Bilbao was already indicated as one of the main centres for English trade[4] and by the late fifteenth century it was the port to which many English merchants sent their factors, attracted by its sheltered harbour and good connections by road and water to the iron fields and to Burgos and the interior. Castro Urdiales to the west had sent many ships and men to England in the early period but was already declining when the English became active themselves, so probably saw little of them. Nor was the rest of the northern coast much visited by the English except that their ships frequently ran into Corunna with pilgrims for Santiago de Compostella. The coast was rockier, the hinterland poorer, although not devoid of interest, and there was less chance of quick sales of the large cargoes of cloth the Englishmen sent, so that apart from the Portuguese ports the English had no main ports of call between Bilbao and Andalusia.

In Andalusia they dealt in several centres all backed by a rich hinterland where they could easily dispose of costly foreign cloths. Huelva was frequently sought, placed on a sheltered river estuary and with a hinterland which included the Lepe area well known in England for its wine. Cadiz, also well sheltered from all but the north, saw plenty of English activity too but remained partly a military port and did not come to rival Seville commercially until the coming of American trade. Seville and increasingly Sanlúcar as its outport were the main centres of English activity and document after document refers to English ships lading there, English merchants sending goods there, ordering goods from there, English agents temporarily resident there. It was already attractive to the English before the Trastamaran usurpation, and once the worst political interruptions were over the English were soon back composing something very like a permanent commercial colony long before the sixteenth century.

From these Andalusian ports English merchants could reach the Atlantic islands, and North and West Africa: some of the ships preparing there were clearly bent on joining the Andalusians in voyages of exploration and plunder, but others, such as the *Trinity of Bristol* in 1481, were more concerned to use Puerto de Santa María as a supply port before perfectly legitimate if hazardous trading to Oran.

Besides these centres Spaniards and Englishmen could meet and trade in Bruges, which, although sometimes forced to ally with France or England, was mainly a neutral area where regular contact could be maintained. No study of Anglo-Castilian trade could avoid emphasising the great importance of Bruges to it. The English and Flemish trades were mutually reinforcing, as the Spaniards, like the Italians and Portuguese, could find good trade in both places so close together. The English and Spaniards could find in Bruges a market which would absorb any kind of goods they could supply and they could buy most of their needs in return, dealing either directly with each other or through a third party, and finding friendly neutrals to colour their goods into either country if they wished.[5] Although M. van Houtte has warned against seeing Bruges simply as an international exchange mart[6] this is often just what it was for the English merchants and their goods arrested in Flanders in 1371, at a time when the direct trade with Spain had been interrupted, showed their owning iron, almonds, oil, cummin, soap, licorice, resin, beaverskins and kermes dye, some of which must have been from Spain, and none of which were indigenous Flemish products.[7] Their purchases might of course be through Bruges men, as were the purchases of 96,986 livres of Spanish iron (about 43 tons) and 120 cases of Spanish soap in 1422.[8] Law suits also illustrate the close contacts of the two in Bruges: Robert Aylward of Southampton sued a Spanish merchant before the échevins of Bruges for non-delivery of 12 *toneles* and 180 quintals of iron to Southamption;[9] John Pikering sued there to force Juan López to provide the 21 barrels of good-quality Seville oil he had promised instead of the unsaleable stuff he had in fact delivered;[10] Thomas Wattes on the other hand sued Juan Seboll in London as factor for Spanish merchants in Bruges who had failed to deliver white soap ordered from them.[11] The English wool traders at Calais also came into contact with the Spaniards; John de Lopys was one of the Cely's best customers and paid them by letters of exchange drawn on Pedro de Valladolid in London; Diego de Castro was paid by the Celys in Calais for some London transaction;[12] de Lopys also in 1487 advised them to put their money into madder instead of paying by exchange and assured them that Gómez de Sorio, one of the richest Spaniards in Bruges at that time, would undertake the marketing and shipping for them.[13]

Besides such references the customs accounts show goods typical of Spanish provenance coming into England from Flanders as, for example, the Spanish iron and the dates, raisins, oil and smigmate taken into Boston in Edward IV's reign by ships of Camfer and Sluys.[14]

The Spanish merchant visiting the English centres, like the Englishman in Spain, expected to sell his goods wholesale and was less interested in retail trade, from which indeed he was usually formally debarred in favour of the local citizenry. So the goods outside the ports were left to the retail trade and distribution of natives: thus the Englishman sold Spanish leathers to the small craftsmen in Middlesex,[15] he sent Spanish iron up the Severn to the Midlands,[16] carted it through Hampshire,[17] or shipped it up the coast to Newcastle where the men of Durham Abbey might buy it.[18] Likewise in Spain the Englishman lost sight of his cloth at the ports, and native distributors, some of whom were clearly Jewish,[19] were left to get it to the customer.

For these bulk sales in the ports the merchants could rely on help from a regular network of brokers, agents, hosts, friends and contacts.

Brokers usually dealt in one commodity and were appointed by the relevant craft, but in London during the first peak of Spanish activity Iberian trade was so important that special brokers were appointed to deal with all goods coming from Spain and Portugal, given as 'leather, bazan, goatskins, baldred, cummin etc.' in 1283 and 1289 and as 'cordwain, bazan, peltry and all other merchandise coming from Spain', in 1318.[20] Leathers and skins predominated, but the brokers would need contacts outside the skin trade.

Brokers were generally required to be denizens and citizens but there was abuse of this in practice. However, the brokers for Spanish goods were citizens in the thirteenth century and, even when Spaniards in the four- teenth, seem to be men domiciled in London: in 1318 the 'Ferand son of Domyngoun de Bytoria' may have been Ferand Manion who was certainly a citizen by 1324.[21] In 1338 one Pedro López, a Spanish merchant and citizen of London, was a broker there, dealing not apparently with just Spanish goods but with cloth too.[22] He would seem to be an ideal contact for the Spanish merchants with whom he worked—of Spanish family, long resident in England, holding commercial office and familiar with English customs and trade.

Spanish brokers disappeared during the second half of the fourteenth century when trade was in trouble, but Spaniards again held office in the late-fifteenth-century expansion, when Juan Seboll, a merchant of Burgos who also acted as factor for other merchant families and lived in England for a decade, held the position.[23]

Likewise the Englishmen in Spain used the local brokers to facilitate business, but their identities remain shadowed. No Englishman appar- ently held office in the fifteenth century and such references we have are like those in Balsall's account which simply note that he paid brokerage fees for the cloth he sold in Huelva.[24]

When trading was regular there developed a group of merchants who were such frequent and long-term visitors or shippers that they built up their own circle of habitual, trustworthy contacts; they would hardly need a broker, and could advise compatriots who were newcomers. The con- stant activity of Spaniards at Southampton where they leased their own houses[25] and their activity at Portsmouth, Winchelsea and London in the thirteenth century helped them to develop such links. The merchants in London dealt repeatedly with the same groups of cordwainers, and among those trading Apparicius and Matteo of Burgos were active for over twenty years,[26] and Andrés Pérez de Castrogeriz of Burgos traded for about forty-eight years until 1325.[27]

A small group even settled here: some probably did at Southampton,[28] others certainly did in London. Ferand Manion, possibly the broker of 1318, and possibly the son of a merchant of Vitoria, was a London citizen by 1324, had leased a brewhouse there since 1322 and was actively helping Spaniards until 1338 at least and still living in England in 1345.[29] Pedro López Manion, possibly a relative, was another London citizen and Spanish merchant who often helped his compatriots.[30] There was possibly a small family group here at that time—Ferand Manion, Pedro López Manion, 'Dominicus dictus manion', and James Manion of Spain the clerk, who was associated in 1327 with M. Peter de Galiciano,[31] in whose company both Ferand and Pedro had gone abroad on royal business. Another Spanish London citizen was Dominic Ferandi at whose house in London Pedro de Losa of Castro Urdiales was staying in 1357.[32] During this period too the Genoese merchants, Antonio, Eduard and Niccolo Citeroun, who became London citizens might well have provided valuable advice to Spaniards, especially southerners, as their Andalusian contacts were strong enough for them to be falsely described as Spaniards.[33]

Such men of long-established trade, or settlers in London, or Italians with Spanish interests, must have considerably aided the business of other visiting Spaniards, especially when the small populations of the ports meant it was easy for all to know each other. Indeed the Spaniards over the period were well-entrenched enough to obtain some group privileges or exemptions but the developments were brought to a halt by the abrupt Trastamaran usurpation. Although Spaniards were resident in England after that most composed the Spanish court in exile and offered little commercial help when trading was again possible. Others were seamen who settled in English ports, and while some, such as John Domynges, merchant and sailor of Bristol who was a servant of Robert Russel, may have been of some help to compatriots beginning to trade in England again,[34] others, such as John Perot, a poor sailor who settled and married in Romney,[35] can have had little to offer.

The recovery of trade from the third decade of the fifteenth century saw a gradual rebuilding of the number of regular traders again. Martín Ochoa de Yrive worked in Southampton, Sandwich and London from at least 1432 to 1464 and had close links with John Emory and Piers James in Southampton.[36] His son Pedro was associated with him and continued to trade at least until 1475. Sancho de Ordogne traded for a shorter time than Ochoa but at least once lived for a year in London—in Tower Ward[37]—where he would have easily discharged his own business and could have been found to help others. The John Fernamy of London who imported Gascon wines to Bristol in 1471 sounds as if he might be a Castilian resident in London but nothing else is known of him.[38] Juan Seboll, the Burgos merchant and broker, traded for a decade and spent several periods in London, possibly most of his time in fact, and would thus have been useful to compatriots even without the office of broker.

The hosting arrangements probably helped rather than hindered Spaniards and indeed most aliens while they were in small numbers, although the Italians and Hansards objected to the supervision of their trade by others. The Spaniards at Southampton had the right to hold their own houses for seven years from 1263[39] but some clearly preferred to stay with Nicholas Barbeflete in 1267.[40] An English host could be a positive advantage as he might go surety for his guests, as did Barbeflete for Spaniards wishing to export wool in 1271,[41] and as did Hugo Ryse of Sandwich in 1414 for Pedro López, after the latter attempted to smuggle bullion from England, fled on discovery, and drew arms against the pursuing English officials.[42]

The records surviving from the attempt to tighten up the hosting regulations in 1439 indicate how close were the contacts between the Spaniards and hosts. In Southampton they were usually assigned to John Emory just as the Italians usually lodged with John Bentham or Nicholas Belet.[43] John Emory was actively interested in Spanish and Mediterranean trading and imported goods on Spanish ships[44] and Martín Ochoa, who lodged with him in 1441, was factor for him and for Piers James, buying bastard and romney wines in Andalusia.[45] The Spaniards in London were hosted with John Chirche or Richard Riche:[46] Chirche, a mercer, also traded with Spain and Portugal,[47] but Riche dealt mostly with Flanders although he may there have had some contacts with the Spanish colonies.

Again there is less information about the English arrangements in Spain. Some men traded for years: Robert Aylward of Southampton from 1430 to 1448,[48] William Soper of Southampton from 1424 to 1432,[49] of the many Bristol merchants the Rowley family traded from at least 1461 until 1486 and probably 1490,[50] the Shipwards from probably 1455 until 1480,[51] Robert Straunge of London and Bristol from 1454 to about 1480.[52] These must have had regular contacts. Davy Savage went to northern Spain several times for Soper and Fetplace and probably built up a circle of acquaintances[53] and William Botyller, factor for William Haddon, was accused by Haddon's executors of having so many friends in Bilbao that they were helping him subvert the course of justice,[54] but until Thomas Batcock, factor for Thomas Howell of London, settled there there is no evidence for English residency.[55] There was far more of a long-staying English colony in Andalusia, which is understandable as communications were less easy with the south. The merchants there formed a permanent and close enough circle to recognise a false florin belonging to one of their number.[56] Thomas Wilson and Thomas Walker were based there for some time,[57] as were John Bownde[58] and Richard Whitington;[59] but again it is not yet possible to find any regarding themselves as permanent emigrants.

Apart from using the advice and information given by brokers, hosts, resident compatriots and regular contacts the merchant could of course decrease the risks of venturing by taking orders instead of relying on the open market. Thus Robert Aylward ordered iron from Ochoa Pérez de Gayncha and Juan Darturiaga,[60] and Thomas Wattes ordered white soap from Diego de Coverrubias and Juan de Vermeo in Bruges.[61] Associated merchants sent each other information and instruction about the goods selling well. The letter of Juan de Medina to Juan Seboll is one chance survival of what must have been a constant exchange of paper.[62] Medina wrote that he had sold Seboll's last cargo of cloth, and in a longer letter sent with the return cargo apparently told Seboll how much he owed him from that sale. He also told Seboll just which cloths to send next time if he wanted an easy sale. He sent Seboll a cargo of wines, the full cost of which appeared in another letter, but the precise amounts of which appear in this one in words and numbers: 'veyntetres tonels machos de bastardos XXIII ts b⁰'. He wrote that he was sending Alonso Escudero to oversee the cargo and to deliver letters to Seboll which the last should see sent on to Bruges. Escudero was to deliver £2 in cash, and eight shillings in exchange. Medina wrote that he assumed Seboll had insured the cargo from London.

Often the orders were a form of credit: merchants were to bring back specified amounts of goods in return for merchandise sent out, and no money changed hands unless the goods were unavailable and in that case a date was set for payment in cash. Thus in 1404 Henry Devenyssh delivered cloth to merchants of Bermeo who were to bring him in return 36 tons 3 cwt of iron.[63] Similarly Richard Yea of Plymouth sold twelve blankets and other cloth for a future cargo of 400 bowstaves of Spanish yew to Juan Marchaunt of Spain,[64] and Thomas Wattes of London sold cloth worth £147 16s to Francis Dyes in 1457 on condition that he sent oil within two years.[65] Such arrangements were quite different from those with factors, who were to sell and buy at the best prices they then found current.

The use of factors and agents made the ordering of a prosperous business much easier, and they were widely used in Anglo-Castilian trade throughout the period, but to an even greater degree in the fifteenth century. Not that the travelling merchant ever died out: merchants of the poorer ranks had to travel with their goods as they could not afford agent's fees; others preferred to travel, particularly in their earlier years, to learn at first hand the characteristics of their markets, to establish and maintain the important personal contacts; some, like Thomas Howell who spent twenty-six years in Spain on and off, probably enjoyed the life of Andalusia.[66]

Such travelling merchants covered the whole gamut of wealth and influence: some were shipping very small amounts; some were men of moderate means such as William Plummer of Bristol,[67] or Henry Gardygan of Bristol whose credit was good enough to contract debts of 685 crowns in Guipúzcoa,[68] or Humphrey Coke who ran up debts of £70 in Sanlúcar.[69]

More prosperous were men such as William Spaynell, ship-owner of Bristol, who made his will at Lepe in Andalusia in 1391.[70] Philip Wawton the London fishmonger, and John Bownde the London draper at Huelva, Seville, and Sanlúcar seem to have been well off, although they never aspired to high municipal office.[71] William Folkys, another London draper concerned with the Spanish run, had been personally at least as far as Lisbon in his youth.[72] George Bulstrode, another London draper who went to Spain, presumably to Andalusia to judge from the lists of gifts to the widow he courted, was wealthy enough to spend some £465 at her behest and on her gifts.[73] At Bristol the Rowley family, especially William the Elder, could have afforded factors yet both William the Younger and the Elder died abroad, and the Elder left bequests to a Spanish church and hospital of which he presumably had personal knowledge.[74]

Many of the travelling Spaniards in England seem to be of modest means on the evidence of the customs records, but some of these might have been men of some substance with their main business in France or Flanders. Some Castilians who visited England were certainly rich, however. Andrés Pérez of Castrogeriz, who travelled in the thirteenth century when this was still more usual, was possibly one of the wealthiest, but he also employed factors, leaving them to collect his debts as he moved on. Martín Ochoa seems to have acquired wealth by his middle years but carried on his strenuous seafaring life. Francis Dyes was wealthy and so were Juan Seboll and the other Burgos merchants at Bruges who came to England.[75]

Factors were however necessary not only if the merchant stayed at home because of age or comfort but also if his trade expanded even when he continued to travel himself, since it was impossible for him to accompany all his goods to their destinations when it was common practice to spread risks by sending consignments on several ships to several markets. He sent servants to watch his interests, buy and sell, collect debts, and sue at court for overdue debts, stolen goods, or breach of contract. The records are full of references to factors occupied in these ways, in Anglo-Castilian trade as in all others.

Some factors ran the whole venture. Juan Amerous of Spain sending wine to Brittany in 1355 had 'mys en la dite vasshel un homme pour estr' marchaunt et agardier les dites vynz et est apelle Johan doria', and to whom he had entrusted 1,500 écus d'or for the journey's expenses and to use 'al profet de moy et de mes compaignons'.[76] Nearly a century later similar words were used by Emory and James of Southampton about Martín Ochoa, who was to be 'factour attournie & have Reule & gov-ernaunce of the sayd goodys to sylle esploye & demene them in Spayn or in othyr placys to the most avayle or your sayd suppliant' (in this case Emory).[77] Nicholas Palmer was in much the same position for Moses Conterini, taking his wheat to Andalusia, selling it as factor and attorney, buying and loading figs and raisins as instructed with the proceeds.[78] The agreement of Alan Jepson of Southampton with John Payn was that Payn should accompany the goods to Spain, sell them to best advantage, bring back goods to the value of the sales and make a true account on his return.[79] Sometimes a ship's purser was used for this, as was John Balsall of the *Trinity* by seven Bristol men: he travelled with the goods, did his best in the ports where they stopped, exchanging some for wine and the rest for ready cash which he does not seem to have employed for a return cargo.[80] This may underline one of the disadvantages of using ships' personnel: they had less time than factors, who could stay awhile to seek good returns.

With regular trade it was less necessary to send a man with each consignment, particularly to and from Andalusia, and often a shipmaster simply undertook to supervise the goods en route and hand them to a factor at the destination. Thus Antonio Duldua, master of a ship of Fuenterrabía, delivered a consignment of cloth in Fuenterrabía to men ready to receive it on behalf of its Bristol owners;[81] William Harper and Richard Fissher, master and purser of the *Mary Ratclyffe*, were entrusted by Humphrey Coke of Bristol with the carriage and delivery of his goods from Sanlúcar to Bristol;[82] and Danyell Moaso, patron of the carrack *St Marie*, undertook to deliver Spanish wool and orchell loaded in Lisbon and Corunna for Southampton.[83]

At times, rather than charge the ship-operators, merchants used other merchants aboard just to supervise the journey. Thus Richard Underwode had charge of Richard Hilton's goods between Southampton and Seville where he handed them over to Hilton's factors;[84] and as seen above Juan de Medina put Alonso Escudero aboard to supervise his wines, which Seboll would take over on arrival in London.

The factors at the destinations who would work 'to the best avayle' of their employers were at this date of course usually temporary residents, there for months and even years, but not yet settling. However they stayed long enough to form a near-permanent colony, although individuals constantly changed. There would be several at a time at Bilbao—men such as Davy Savage, William Botyller or Launcelot Thirkyll of London—and probably a dozen or a score at a time in Andalusian ports—men such as Thomas Wilson and Thomas Walker, to whom Underwode was to deliver his goods, John Davell, who handled goods for Herry Denys of London and other merchants, Richard Whitington, factor not only for William Wodehouse but also for John Mote of Suffolk, and William Frensshe, servant and factor of Thomas Hay.[85]

The factors varied from young apprentices to self-employed merchants. Those styled 'servant', as was Whitington when working for Wodehouse, Frensshe when working for Hay and Savage when working for Soper, were probably wage-earners whose main task was the prosecution of their masters' business, even if they managed to do some trading of their own alongside.[86] Others took on the agency as a temporary sideline for one venture only, and it is more likely that these took commissions on the value of the sales, as did the Italians in England and elsewhere. These usually received 1–2 per cent,[87] which seems a modest share considering the many steps in unloading, weighing, customing, warehousing, selling, buying and so on which they undertook. The rate at which Thomas Howell provided for his agents in Spain in the sixteenth century was rather more generous at $2\frac{1}{2}$ per cent,[88] and some men managed to arrange for more, as did John Payn of Southampton who was to receive one shilling in the pound for Alan Jepson's cloth sold in Spain.[89] Yet others might in fact have been receiving a share of the profits in a partnership of some type.

Many factors were men of the same nationalities as their employers but there might be advantages in using a man of the country visited. Robert Russel of Bristol employed John Domynges, now resettled in Bristol, on his business in Spain and Brittany;[90] Emory and James of Southampton used Martín Ochoa;[91] Chirche of London employed a Genoan in Seville—Gianotti Salvago;[92] and others too made use of this practice, especially in Andalusian ports.[93] There are fewer instances to be found of Spaniards employing Englishmen in this way, although they were quite likely to use Englishmen as attorneys to prosecute their interests at law. However, it is likely that some such factorship was involved when Juan Marchaunt of Spain's goods were attached in Plymouth for his non-delivery of bow-staves to Richard Yea of Plymouth. His goods there were in the hands of two Englishmen, a merchant and a barber, who were probably acting as his agents and collecting or distributing goods for him.[94] Some Spaniards also used Italians as agents in England, as did Antonio Ferández who employed Cristoforo Cattaneo.[95]

Factors and attorneys, although necessary, brought their own problems, the main one being how to ensure that they worked to their master's best advantage and were honest, sober and upright. Most factors were trustworthy, or the trade would have collapsed, but some embezzled and gambled. William Hody of Colchester had been in Sanlúcar when John Davell, Herry Denys's factor, had lost most of his money by 'riotous means and misguiding of himself' and had then tried to regain some of it by a complicated fraud involving a broken counterfeit coin, well known to be his among the colony at Sanlúcar, and a charge of robbery against Hody. His plot failed, his accomplice confessed and he found Sanlúcar too hot for him and returned to England where he continued to accuse Hody of robbery in an attempt to assuage Denys' wrath.[96] Diego de Castro chose badly too, and his kinsman and servant, Bernard, lost £28 playing at dice with Gascons in a London tavern.[97] William Haddon's executors accused his factor of embezzlement as did Alan Jepson John Payn. But there was sharp practice on the side of masters too; Moses Conterin refused the return cargo of fruit brought by his factor as it was late and sued him for the cost of the original outward bound cargo of wheat.[98]

A study of the legal documents always leaves the impression that trade was just about to founder under widespread dishonesty, cheating, violence, stupidity and jealousy, but the cases where things went wrong were only a small fraction of the total number of deals and on the whole merchants could trust their agents, servants and contacts.

They might of course try to ensure a real identity of interest by bringing in members of their family or partners, and family firms and partnerships were probably as widespread in this branch of trade as in the others, although information is scarce in the absence of private papers.

Many worked with kinsmen. Andrés and Pedro Pérez were brothers who followed their fathers, and Luke Pérez was probably related.[99] Juan Pérez, a shipmaster carrying goods for Domingo Aynes of Ribadeo in 1346, had his son aboard the ship with him.[100] Antonio Ferández was working with his brother and son in 1427–30.[101] Martín Ochoa de Yrive worked from about 1431 to his death in about 1464 and was associated with his son from 1456.[102] The Covarrubias group was probably a family one and so was the Pardo.[103] In England the Bristol accounts especially show father and son working together—the Spaynells in the fourteenth century, the Shipwards and Somerwells and Rowleys in the fifteenth. The Rowleys are the clearest example of a family group: the brothers Thomas and William were heavily involved in Spanish trade by 1461 and Thomas's son William junior joined them by 1474. They then sustained a series of disasters and by the autumn of 1479 all three and William junior's wife were dead. His mother-in-law, who also died before Easter 1480, was left to look after his four daughters, all under age, who clearly could not continue the business. William the elder left three sons, two under age, who possibly later went into the trade, and the eldest, another William, of age, who continued the business until he died in 1490 again leaving daughters under age.[104]

The family groupings serve to confirm yet again that medieval merchant families were rarely active in trade beyond two or at most three generations. As Dr Thrupp pointed out for London, this is partly through lack of adult male heirs, but also because heirs took up other careers, often preferring to settle on country estates bought by their fathers and grandfathers.[105] Land was a more stable investment and aided social ambitions. There is no comparable study of a merchant class in Spain but it seems unlikely that the picture would be different: the Spaniard too faced high infant mortality and the attraction of land. Indeed Spanish historians affirm in general that Castilian families who rose on trading wealth lasted no more than three or four generations before being absorbed into the military classes.[106]

Partnerships were not uncommon in the trade but are recorded more rarely than expected, not only because of lack of the appropriate records such as account books, but also because, as Professor Postan pointed out,[107] the English common law had not taken cognisance of partnership agreements, as had the Italian law, so that Englishmen found legal redress against a defaulting partner through laws on debt, trusts, or master–servant relationships, a practice giving full satisfaction but obscuring the terms of the partnership for posterity. Some of the men described as factors may well have been sharing the profits of the venture in a *commenda*-type partnership, and possibly this was what Botyller was claiming when he refused to pay Haddon's executors more than half the money from the sale of Haddon's cloth in Spain.[108]

There are some clear statements of partnership, although the precise terms are unknown. John Payn of Bristol stated that John George had been his partner in the venture in which they lost cloth worth some 2,000 gold crowns;[109] John Hotot spoke of his 'compartiners';[110] John Brome of Bristol and Robert Ruston of London as 'merchants together' bought £84 worth of cloth from William Heryot but clearly did not mean to sell it together as each took his part to Spain for his own trade; but Brome then found himself, as a partner with unlimited liability, being sued for the full £84.[111] A clear form of partnership, very close to joint-stock arrangements as Professor Postan pointed out, was shipowning.[112] Joint buying from Spaniards was widespread in London's thirteenth-century leather industry, and at times is clearly stated as when seven cordwainers acknowledged 'each for the whole amount' a debt of £66 to Juan de la Founs of Spain.[113]

On the Spanish side, perhaps Juan de Medina and Juan Seboll were in some sort of partnership association as the language used in their letter does not imply master–servant relationships.

Partnerships are indicated too in the customs accounts when one amount of merchandise is accredited to more than one merchant. At Bristol in 1398 Robert and Richard Talbot took sixty-seven cloths, and in 1400 John Canynges and Thomas Colstan took to Spain together forty cloths.[114] In the next century Richard Straunge and William Spencer brought in the *Pedro of Bilbao* iron, oil, and rosin worth £108 13s 4d.[115] At Southampton Martín Ochoa brought 23½ tons of iron jointly with Sancho de Sánchez in 1459[116] and three merchants of Lepe brought 32 tuns of wine to Exeter in 1480.[117] Other accounts record the entry of goods to one man *et sociis suis*; John Furnys and John *socius suus* brought iron, thread, mercury, kermes dye and wax to Sandwich in 1304.[118] Sometimes a whole cargo is put down to the master *et sociis* and such an association might be with the merchants freighting the ship or with his crew.[119]

Many medieval partnerships were formed for one voyage or venture only, and although if it worked well it might be renewed this system would leave fewer traces than permanent partnerships as it demanded less paper work; it is no wonder that we have so little detail left to us.

Other techniques used by the English and Spanish merchants further emphasise the 'liner' rather than the 'tramping' characteristics of the trade and imply a high degree of trust in the maintenance of the regularity of the trade as well as the integrity of the individual merchants. Credit practices are the most obvious of these.

Credit was widely allowed in English medieval trade, and not least in the Castilian trade. Although it does imply a belief in the endurance of the trade it could also be a necessity, as bullion exports were usually forbidden by governments, large sums in silver were bulky to transport and a constant temptation to robbery, and it might be difficult for a heavily committed merchant to raise large sums in cash if a shipment were delayed or sales slow. Small sums were needed to oil the wheels of commerce—to pay customs duties, for lodgings, petty tolls, or earnest penny, and some men may have been cautious and preferred to deal for cash only; but for many credit was normal and could form a high proportion of their business.[120]

In thirteenth-century London credit was widespread in the Spanish trade: Spanish merchants sold on credit for up to two years, although one to four months were more usual. The credit period bears no relation to the sum owed or the number of debtors, but must have depended on the merchant's personal standing and expectations of raising the money. Some of the longest times were allowed for the smallest debts, as when £2 19s 6d was to be repaid by Geoffrey de Braye, a currier whose resources must have been low, in quarterly instalments of half a mark,[121] while some of the largest were to be paid in under a month as with the £50 which Walter de Waleys, a cordwainer, owed Pedro Custes of Spain and which was to be paid at the next fair of St Ives.[122] Here was a man whose immediate liquidity was low but who expected to make considerable sales at the fair when he would be able to reimburse Custes at the right time and place for him to buy a return cargo. Incidentally the debts in the *Letter Books* and recognisance rolls show that the fairs are still of moderate importance to the Spaniards and the fairs of St Ives and St Botolph are made places of payment. The collection of the debts was reasonably streamlined: the merchant or his factor might move on to another market and arrange for the debt to be collected on his next visit to London, or he might appoint an attorney to collect it for him in his absence. The attorney might be another merchant but was sometimes a man otherwise unknown as a trader who possibly belonged to a supporting group growing up to deal with the routine administrative work commerce created.

Credit transactions continued even when tough political situations made collection difficult and integrity harder to ascertain. Inevitably there were failures, and both Englishmen and Spaniards were sued by their creditors: Henry Gardygan of Bristol left Spain defaulting on five debts to men of Deva and Motrico amounting to 685 crowns;[123] Rodrigo de Samodio also sued for recovery of debts amounting to £19 and four marks from five Bridgwater men;[124] and one of the most spectacular cases of default involved Francis Dyes.[125] Complaints against him were started in

1458 when silk worth £1,000 aboard a Venetian carrack was attached on the demands of Galiot and Leonellus Centurioni of Genoa to whom Dyes owed £400 and by two London drapers, William Brogreve and Amoneus Bertet, to whom he owed £28 and £150 respectively.[126] Thomas Cooke, the wealthy London alderman and draper, also lost £200 to him and managed to prevail on Henry VI to write to the King of Castile on behalf of Dyes' creditors.[127] Nothing seems to have been recovered.

The investigations into Dyes' affairs revealed not only that he was allowed a great deal of credit but he was allowed more than the six months demanded by law for repayment. Henry VI's government had tried to stop credit for aliens altogether on the grounds that some failed to settle up, but after protests that this hampered English merchants in their own sale of cloth a period of six months was allowed.[128] Dyes' creditors, and probably many others were quite indifferent to this: Thomas Wattes allowed him thirteen months, Robert Colyn twenty-two months, and John Derby over three years. Cases against them dragged into Edward IV's reign when they either bought pardons or found their cases dropping into oblivion.[129]

The day-books of William Styfford and John Thorp, London scrivenors, which cover the years 1457 to 1459, show other cases of disregard for the credit laws to please Spanish customers.[130] Styfford records the Wattes transaction to Dyes, and shows Dyes' debts to Homobono Gritti and Giovanni de' Bardi for longer than six months. Juan Divarola, the Navarrese merchant working with Baldwin Makanam, late of Gascony, was allowed thirteen months by John Gille a London tailor, to pay off £126 13s. But when he worked with another Spaniard, Pedro de Vitoria (Victori), they were to pay off £15 within four months, and Martin Doyci of San Sebastián also arranged to pay off £2 17s in three and a half months. Probably it was the small size of the original debt rather than respect for the law which led to these shorter periods.

The payment of the debt could be in cash or kind, as the statute recognised, and as Wattes' arrangement with Dyes illustrates. Wattes sold Dyes twenty-four cloths for £147 16s to be repaid by the Nativity of St John the Baptist 1459 unless Dyes delivered oil beforehand in which case the obligation was void. The whole was a credit arrangement for a sale of cloth but in practical effect was little different from placing an order, thus limiting the risks of venture trading.[131]

The scrivenors' books also indicate how important it was to some merchants to be paid exactly when and where they needed it. Divarola, Victori and Thomas de Conties, a Gascon emigré, owed John Gaucem, also from Gascony, debts of £24 and £10 to be repaid in just under the month on the Feast of All Saints, unless they paid him or his attorney £12 in gold and £5 in sterling within eight days of the arrival abroad of the *Mary of Navarre*, which Divarola owned. It seems clear that the important point was the payment of the money abroad, where Gaucem wanted to trade, or possibly had other commitments.

These books too illustrate one means of having business transactions publicly recorded. They fulfilled part of the functions of the formal public notary who, abroad, was the official most used to record commercial contracts and agreements. In England he was rarely used, although in 1459 Philip Mede and Robert Richard of Bristol went to the local notary for a formal, public and solemn document in which credible witnesses swore that Mede and Richard had fully paid off Juan Divarola for certain transactions made five or six years earlier, to counteract the rumour being put about by Divarola and another that they had not yet paid him.[132]

Merchants had various other ways of safeguarding contracts. Those in London in the thirteenth century had their obligations enrolled at the Guildhall in the *Letter Books*, and Ferand Manion had several of his enrolled in Chancery on the dorse of the close roll. Such obligations would have been formal documents with private seals. English law also allowed a means of quick recovery in the recognisance laws: if recognisances were enrolled in due form before the appropriate officials the creditors could obtain immediate execution as debts fell due without having to sue and produce proof at common law. It certainly speeded up repayment of outstanding debts where the offenders had goods which could be attached locally, and the Spanish merchants in London made use of the method. In the first recognisance roll of some 235 entries some one hundred involved debts to alien merchants and of those forty-four were Spaniards. The later surviving rolls fall in the period of hostility in Sancho's reign, and the Spaniards dropped out until 1299; but the numbers of alien merchants as a whole using the rolls drop steadily.[133] Since not many of the Spanish merchants who used the *Letter Books* went on to use the recognisance rolls, and the aliens relied on them so little after the first few years, it seems that merchants with regular contacts were probably relying much more already on the informal and much more flexible bill of obligation which they might write themselves, and which Professor Postan found to have enjoyed popularity in the fifteenth century.[134] No references to this practice have been found for this early period but it was certainly current in the fifteenth century in Castilian trade as in other branches. Martín Ochoa in his petition in about 1432 against Henry Gardygan mentioned that he had 'certeyn bylles made and writen by the seid Henry witnessing the seid duytees',[135] And Richard Potnale of Southampton gave his 'simple obligacion' to Richard Dehy for the cloth he was going to sell in 1486.[136] Some merchants trusted their clients and clearly did not even demand that when expecting a fairly quick settlement: Rodrigo de Samodio, complaining of the non-payment for wines of Bridgwater men, stated that he had no remedy at common law 'bycause he hath no sp'ialteis concernyng the same money'.[137]

Payment was made frequently by letters of exchange in medieval trade, and again the Anglo-Spanish branch was probably no exception although the number of instances known is small and all are linked to the London–Bruges–Calais triangle: John de Lopys paid the Celys for their wool by letters of exchange drawn on Pedro de Valladolid in London, and Diego de Castro was paid by exchange on William Cely at Calais.[138] Exchange was clearly used by the Spaniards between Andalusia and London, as the letter from Medina to Seboll showed, but whether the letter was drawn on Spaniards, Englishmen or Italians is not stated. The links between the Italians and Andalusia probably made it particularly easy for their exchange and banking facilities to be used on that route. For although the English and Spanish merchants were fully conversant with Italian methods and might use them where appropriate, they did not copy the sophisticated Italian banking methods. Again, not because they were incapable of it, as the English bankers under Edward III had shown, but because it was inappropriate to their scale of business and when they needed such facilities they could use the Italians'.

Some Spaniards, it is true lent money for Henry III's and Edward I's Gascon wars,[139] but when Edward I wanted to raise a large loan to help Alfonso in 1284 he turned to the merchants of Lucca.[140] Andrés Pérez could contemplate raising £6,000 in Castile for Edward II, but he seems to have had no formal banking support but to have relied on some *ad hoc* arrangements.[141] Ferand Manion in England may have been concentrating more on moneylending than trade in his later years, but there is no evidence for advanced banking activity. The Spanish bankers in Lombard Street ('Anthony Corsy and Marcus Strossy'[142]) mentioned by the Celys a hundred and fifty years later were in fact Florentines (Antonio Corsi and Marco Strozzi) and simply illustrate the strong Italian connection with Andalusia which can lead to cases of mistaken identity. In Spain there was not the major attempt to raise large sums of money from native bankers as there was in England, and many of the loans from merchants were simply small advances of cash from their working reserves as merchants, and more complex financial affairs were left to the Italians. This did not go without criticism in Spain and in 1438 the Cortes stated that it thought the amount of gold reaching Rome from Castile could be cut down if Castilians would undertake exchanges in Italian and Aragonese towns and urged the king to ask merchants of Burgos or Seville or Toledo to undertake this.[143] Their complaint had little effect and, although some Spaniards might have been stimulated towards banking activity in the early obscure years of the fairs at Medina del Campo, until the sixteenth century the Italians remained dominant in exchange transactions from Castile.[144]

In the art of book-keeping too the English and Spanish merchants lagged behind the Italians: few ledgers survive, but those that do, like that of Gilbert Maghfeld for the late fourteenth century, show a simple list of debts with dates of maturity. This would be quite adequate for the size of most Anglo-Castilian businesses, as indeed it remained so for many businesses into the nineteenth century.[145] By the sixteenth century Englishmen and Spaniards were copying the technique, and the English adoption of Italian methods may have come through contact with the Italians in Andalusia or with Spaniards adopting their techniques, as to some western merchants it was known as reckoning the Spanish way.[146]

Insurance was used further to safeguard their goods and fortunes. Special arrangements were made with the ship owner or the seller of the goods to void payments for the goods or freightage if the ship failed to arrive. Thus William Founs of Bridgwater claimed that the risks for the nine tuns of wine he bought in Bilbao for transport to England were to be borne by the vendor, Juan de Vessy, whom he was not bound to pay if they were lost through any adventure except seizure by other Englishmen.[147] In 1471 Bartolomeo Caretto of Genoa claimed that he was not liable for freight charges on his goods coming from Seville in the ship of Juan Periz de la Raule of Bermeo, which had been stolen by English pirates, since Periz, as owner, had agreed to waive charges if the goods failed to arrive safely: Periz however denied both the agreement and that Caretto's goods had been lost.[148]

Premium insurance was developed by the Italians by the early fourteenth century[149] but evidence of Englishmen or Spaniards using Italian insurers or this method on this route is lacking until the second half of the fifteenth century. By then Spaniards were clearly taking premiums for insurance: two Spanish merchants at Bruges—Alvere de Vege and Juan Covarrubias (Corubeas)—and Boromeo Salvati had insured in 1459 a cargo for a merchant of La Rochelle, but they were no more willing to pay than some modern insurers and claimed that when the ship was wrecked it was not on the voyage to Flanders for which it was insured but simply standing off La Rochelle for greater safety in the storm before the voyage and this was not covered; they were ordered to pay.[150] Juan de Medina wrote from Lepe to Seboll in London that he was not insuring the cargo as he assumed Seboll would have done this from his end. There is no indication of whether this was premium insurance, or whether it was done through Englishmen, Spaniards or Italians.

The rates were probably at least as high as those in Italian agreements, which stood at 15–20 per cent,[151] since the Anglo-Castilian trade was dangerous not only climatically but also from piracy. At such prices it is not surprising that English and Spanish merchants preferred, as did many Italians and Spaniards even in the following century and beyond, to spread the risk over several ships rather than transfer the risk and pay such high premiums.[152]

There was one alternative against piracy or war-seizure in fictitious sales, but this, although M. Bernard found it common on the Anglo-Gascon run in the late fifteenth century, does not ever seem to have been used on this route.[153]

Clearly the organisation and business techniques of the English and Spanish merchants working in this branch of trade lagged behind the sophistication of the Italian commercial houses. Like other European nations they worked alongside Italians closely enough to know their methods and that they were slow to adopt them was due to lack of stimulus not to lack of knowledge or skill. The scale of their business was in general much smaller, their routes were shorter, their cargoes demanded less heavy investment, their ships were smaller and cheaper to build. There was not the need to command such large amounts of capital, to draw in so many partners, to control the many factors in various centres. They had less need of such international organisation but if they occasionally wanted it they could call on Italian help. It would have been hard to overthrow the the well-entrenched Italian firms, and in many eyes this would have been quite unnecessary until the changing circumstances of world trade in the sixteenth century brought new developments.

It was easier in this trade for a man of modest means to break in and prosper and these men had developed practices suitable for the scale of their activity. Regular routes, concentrated centres, brokers, agents, hosts, regular customers, and family groups, the use of credit, order and trust combined to make a high volume of business possible. In this Anglo-Spanish trade showed characteristics in common with the vast majority of European trade routes at the time.

NOTES TO CHAPTER 6

1   See for example *C.C.R. 1333–7*, p. 643; *ibid.*, *1374–7*, p. 11; *C.P.R. 1334–8*, p. 571; *ibid.*, *1358–61*, p. 28; P.R.O. SC8/1493. These were last resorts because of the cost, extra loading and freight charges and the bother of supplying certificates when required that it was sent to a friendly destination: such a certificate of arrival in Antwerp of re-exported goods of Spaniards in 1337–8 survives in P.R.O. C47/13/6(2).

2   P.R.O. C1/66/430; Reddaway and Ruddock, 'The accounts of John Balsall', *Camden Miscellany XXIII*.

3   R.L.C. *1204–24*, p. 620b; *C.P.R. 1272–81*, p. 284; *V.C.H. Hampshire*, v, 37; C.M.I., I, 94; C.L.R. *1267–72*, No. 1675; C.Ch.R.V. *1277–1326*, p. 3; *Letter Book 'A'*, p. 27; London Record Office, Recognisance Rolls, I.

4   C.M.I., vII, 196.

5   *C.P.R. 1436–41*, p. 84: Baptiste Flisco brought goods for Spaniards and Flemings, probably from Flanders, to Southampton in 1436.

6   Van Houtte, 'The rise and decline of the market of Bruges', *Ec.H.R.*, 2nd ser., xix (1966), pp. 36–7.

7   Gilliodts van Severen, *Inventaire*, II, 616.

8   *Ibid.*, IV, 421, 427.

9   *Idem.*, *Consulat*, pp. 32–3.

10   *Ibid.*, p. 87.

11   C.P.R. 1467–77, p. 307.
12   *Cely Letters*, ed. Hanham, Nos. 26, 31, 41, 157, 201–2, 204–13, 215, 217–18, 220–1, 225, 231, 234–5, 237–9, 241, 243. See also Hanham, ' "Make a careful examination": some fraudulent accounts in the Cely Papers', *Speculum*, XLVIII (1973).
13   *Cely Letters*, ed. Hanham, No. 237. In 1495 when a loan was raised from the Spaniards in Flanders Soria alone contributed 2,400 livres, while the whole Biscayan nation gave 4,800 and the Spanish nation 7,871, Finot, *op. cit.*, p. 223.
14   P.R.O. E122/10/8, 9, 11, 13, 20, 22.
15   *Letter Book 'A'*, passim.
16   P.R.O. C1/45/127, 64/1146.
17   *Brokage Book of Southampton*, ed. Coleman, passim.
18   *Account Rolls of Durham*, ed. Fowler, passim.
19   In Navarre and Andalusia: *A.G.N. Catálogo*, ed. Castro and Idoate, XXIV, 504; XXV, 713; XXVI, 179, 695, 749, 772; XXVII, 1410; XXVIII, 296, 730, 734, 1045, 1441; etc.; Reddaway and Ruddock, 'The accounts of John Balsall', *Camden Miscellany XXIII*, p. 21.
20   *Letter Book 'A'*, pp. 206–7; *Letter Book 'E'*, p. 97.
21   *Ibid.*, p. 191. See Appendix: Ferand Manion.
22   *Cal. Plea and Memo. Rolls of London*, I, 147. See Appendix: Pedro López Manion.
23   See Appendix: Juan Seboll.
24   Reddaway and Ruddock, 'The accounts of John Balsall', *Camden Miscellany XXIII*, p. 21.
25   See Chapter 1, note 19.
26   C.P.R. 1247–58, p. 457; *Letter Book 'A'*, pp. 17, 27–8, 69, 83.
27   See Appendix: Andrés Pérez.
28   Conditions there were good; see Chapter 1, note 30, and pp. 13–14.
29   See Appendix: Ferand Manion.
30   See Appendix: Pedro López Manion.
31   C.C.R. 1327–30, p. 103. Professor Ekwall identified the name Manion with the occupation *mangon*, a small trader, and as such it may indicate occupation rather than family name; on the other hand this is the only time that it is found in English records, and James certainly was not a trader of any kind; Ekwall, *Two Early London Subsidy Rolls*, p. 266 note.
32   C.C.R. 1354–60, p. 367.
33   P.R.O. E122/69/1; C.C.R. 1327–30, p. 35, 40, 359, 364, 365, 522, 562; Beardwood, *Alien Merchants*, pp. 62, n.3, 69, 71, 72 n.3, 186, 197, 200.
34   P.R.O. C76/94 mm. 19, 27. See also p. 165.
35   *The Register of Daniel Rough*, ed. Murray, pp. 203, xlviii.
36   See Appendix: Martín Ochoa.
37   P.R.O. E159/236 Recorda Mich. m.3.
38   P.R.O. E122/19/8.
39   C.P.R. 1258–66, p. 258.
40   C.P.R. 1266–72, p. 169.
41   *Ibid.*, p. 593.
42   P.R.O. E159/191 Recorda Mich. m.12.
43   P.R.O. E101/128/31, 35; E179/173/110.
44   P.R.O. E122/141/21; E159/208 Recorda Trin. m.7; C76/120 m.4; SC6/896/1; Ms. S.P.B. 1429–30, fo. 60; S.P.B. 1435–6, ed. Foster, p. 36.

45   P.R.O. C1/16/656. 17/235.

46   E101/128/30; E179/144/45, 56.

47   P.R.O. E122/77/1, 3, 161/1, 203/1; E159/208 Recorda Easter mm.10, 10d, 12d, Trin. m.10; C1/11/204; C76/112 m.8, 113 mm.8, 14, 119 m.5, 120 m.4, 123 m.18; Ms. S.P.B. 1429–30, fos. 62v, 59v; Nicolas, *Procs. and Ords. of the Privy Council*, v, 177.

48   Ms. S.P.B. 1429–30, fo. 62v; Gilliodts van Severen, *Consulat*, pp. 32–3.

49   P.R.O. C76/107 m.10; C1/9/403.

50   P.R.O. E122/19/1–20/7: there are no records between 1486 and William's death in 1490. Rowleys are again evident in the sixteenth century; *The Ledger of John Smythe*, ed. Vanes, *passim*.

51   P.R.O. C76/137 m.14; E122/19/14.

52   C.C.R. 1447–54, p. 502–3; P.R.O. E122/19/14.

53   P.R.O. C1/9/403; C76/107 m.10, 114 m.7.

54   P.R.O. C1/66/98.

55   Connell-Smith, 'The ledger of Thomas Howell', *Ec.H.R.* (1950–1).

56   P.R.O. C1/66/230.

57   *Ibid.*, 61/441.

58   P.R.O. C1/66/430–1.

59   P.R.O. C76/136 m.12, 138 m.29, 140 m.22, 142 m.22, 147 m.11; E122/128/4; C1/43/174–6, 44/253.

60   Gilliodts van Severen, *Consulat*, pp. 32–3.

61   C.P.R. 1467–77, p. 307.

62   C.C.R. 1468–76, No. 709.

63   P.R.O. E28/13 [19 Sep. 5 Hen. VI].

64   P.R.O. C1/22/195.

65   P.R.O. E101/128/36; E159/235 Recorda Trin. m.46.

66   Connell-Smith, 'The ledger of Thomas Howell', *loc. cit.*, pp. 365, 370.

67   P.R.O. C1/64/828: for his business see E122/19/10, 10a.

68   P.R.O. C1/12/51.

69   P.R.O. C1/59/124.

70   Wadley, *Wills*, p. 30.

71   P.R.O. C1/66/430–1.

72   P.R.O. C1/44/200, 57/49, 59/250, 60/5, 66/126.

73   Thrupp, *Merchant Class of London*, pp. 106–7.

74   *Great Red Book of Bristol*, ed. Veale, text II, pp. 159–60; Wadley, *Wills*, pp. 161–2. For their trade and ship-owning see also P.R.O. E122/19/1, 4, 8–11, 14, 20/1, 5, 7; C1/47/62; C76/162 m.8.

75   For all these see Appendix.

76   P.R.O. SC8/12301.

77   P.R.O. C1/16/656, 17/235.

78   *Ibid.*, 48/114.

79   *Ibid.*, 98/10.

80   Reddaway and Ruddock, 'The accounts of John Balsall', *Camden Miscellany* XXIII, pp. 19–24.

81   P.R.O. C1/29/368.

82   *Ibid.*, 59/124, printed in Carus-Wilson, *Overseas Trade of Bristol*, misc. records, No. 181.

83   P.R.O. C1/43/177.

84   *Ibid.*, 61/441.

85   P.R.O. C1/61/441, 66/230, 44/253.

86 Professor Postan has warned that in *commenda*-type relationships the master–servant terminology might still be used; 'Partnership in English medieval commerce', *Studi in onore di Armando Sapori*, pp. 530–1.

87 Ruddock, *Italian Merchants in Southampton*, p. 100; and see P.R.O. C1/16/731.

88 Connell-Smith, 'The ledger of Thomas Howell', *loc. cit.*, p. 368.

89 P.R.O. C1/98/10.

90 P.R.O. C76/94 m.19.

91 P.R.O. C1/16/656, 17/235.

92 *Ibid.*, 11/204.

93 *Ibid.*, 66/431, 43/175.

94 *Ibid.*, 22/195.

95 See Appendix: Antonio Ferández.

96 P.R.O. C1/66/230

97 *Cal. Proc. in Chanc.*, I, cii.

98 P.R.O. C1/48/114.

99 See Appendix.

100 P.R.O. SC8/10455; *C.C.R. 1346–9*, 11, 20, 22.

101 P.R.O. C76/109 m.3, 111 m.5, 113 m.6.

102 See Appendix.

103 See Appendix.

104 P.R.O. E122/19/1–20/5; Wadley, *Wills*, pp. 161–2; *Little Red Book of Bristol*, ed. Bickley, II, 197; *Great Red Book of Bristol*, ed. Veale, text II, pp. 159–60, text III, pp. 157–8.

105 Thrupp, *Merchant Class of London*, pp. 199–206, 224, 227, 263–5, 297ff; see also Williams, *Medieval London*, appendix A; Carus-Wilson, *Medieval Merchant Venturers*, pp. 79–81.

106 *Historia social y económica*, ed. Vicens Vives, II, 187.

107 Postan, 'Partnership', *loc. cit.*, pp. 528–9, 539.

108 P.R.O. C1/66/98: a claim of half by the active partner would be in line with the classical *societas maris* arrangements.

109 *C.P.R. 1476–85*, pp. 271, 330: with the crown at 4s sterling their losses were £400.

110 P.R.O. E28/78 (24 Mar. 27 Hen. VI).

111 P.R.O. C1/64/841.

112 Postan, 'Partnership', *loc cit.*, p. 547.

113 *Letter Book 'A'*, p. 8.

114 P.R.O. E122/16/34, 17/1.

115 *Ibid.*, 19/6; see also 19/8, 11.

116 Ms. S.P.B. 1459–60, Lib. Comm. (unfol.), 3 Dec. on the *James of Deva*.

117 P.R.O. E122/41/6.

118 *Ibid.*, 124/14.

119 See p. 166 for further examples. Such statements in customs accounts are not good guides unless they are isolated cases chosen by the collector for a particular case. Professor Carus-Wilson showed that the Bristol account for 1466 in which it occurred was due to merchants buying shares in a customs-free trade licence (*Medieval Merchant Venturers*, pp. 83–4). The account for 1403–4 is similar and seems to be due to the collectors' desire for a short form rather than to wholesale adoption of partnerships (E122/17/10, 18/13).

120 James, 'A London merchant of the fourteenth century', *Ec.H.R.*, 2nd ser., VIII (1955–6), pp. 368–9, shows its importance to Gilbert Maghfeld. It was also very

important to the Celys' business, *Cely Letters*, ed. Hanham, *passim*; Hanham, ' "Make a careful examination" ', *loc. cit., passim*.

121   *Letter Book 'A'*, p. 55.
122   *Ibid.*, p. 27.
123   P.R.O. C1/12/51.
124   *Ibid.*, 59/60.
125   See Appendix.
126   P.R.O. E159/235 Recorda Mich. m.54, Hil. m.11. The silk was later claimed to belong to Juan Rudriges *juratus et bancarius de Seville*, who was an enemy alien without safe-conduct and therefore the silk was claimed as forfeit to the Crown.
127   P.R.O. E28/86(42), 88 (2 Dec. 37 Hen. VI).
128   *Statutes of the Realm*, 8 Hen. VI c. 24; 9 Hen. VI c. 2.
129   P.R.O. E159/235 Recorda Trin. mm.33, 46, 53; 236 Recorda Mich. m.37.
130   P.R.O. E101/128/36, 37.
131   See p. 185.
132   *Great Red Book of Bristol*, ed. Veale, text II, pp. 130-2.
133   London Records Office, Recognisance Rolls, 1–12. The numbers of aliens to Englishmen in the rolls is as follows:

Roll 1 (1284–85):	100 : 135	Roll 7 (1310–11):	12 : 538
2 (1290–91):	39 : 248	8 (1313–14):	11 : 150
3 (1292–93):	38 : 178	9 (1315–16):	7 : 133
4 (1295–96):	5 : 140	10 (1325–26):	11 : 448
5 (1298–99):	23 : 156	11 (1339–40):	1 : 142
6 (1309–10):	27 : 855	12 (1377–92):	4 : 424

134   Postan, 'Private financial instruments in medieval England', *V.S.W.G.*, XXIII (1930), pp. 36–7.
135   P.R.O. C1/12/51.
136   *Ibid.*, 82/22.
137   *Ibid.*, 59/60.
138   *Cely Letters*, ed. Hanham, Nos. 204–9, 235.
139   *C.L.R. 1226–40*, p. 156; *ibid., 1240–45*, p. 155; *C.P.R. 1232–47*, pp. 318, 321; *ibid., 1292–1301*, pp. 222, 489; *Rôles Gascons*, ed. Michel, I, 213–14, 401; *ibid.* ed. Bémont, III, 4395, 4907, 4928, 4959, 4974, 4988; *Gascon Rolls*, ed. Renouard, No. 202; P.R.O. SC8/3997, 13228. Some of the debts may be for pre-empted goods but not all were.
140   *C.P.R. 1281–92*, pp. 113, 122.
141   *Ibid., 1324–7*, p. 93.
142   *Cely Letters*, ed. Hanham, Nos. 234, 235.
143   *Cortes*, III, pp. 340–1. Spaniards were involved in banking at Nantes before the end of the fifteenth century; Mathorez, 'Les rapports de Nantes avec l'Espagne', *Bulletin Hispanique*, vol. 14 (1912), pp. 383–4.
144   De Roover, *L'Évolution de la lettre de change*, pp. 50, 65–6. The Juan Rodriguez of Seville, *juratus et bancarius* claiming Dyes' silk in London may still be no more than a money-lender; *ibid.*, pp. 23–5.
145   James, 'A London merchant', *loc. cit.*, p. 366; Yamey, 'Scientific book-keeping and the rise of capitalism', *Ec.H.R.*, 2nd ser., I (1949).
146   *The Ledger of John Smythe*, ed. Vanes, pp. 16–22.
147   P.R.O. C1/28/473.
148   *Ibid.*, 43/174–5, 46/334; the Florentine practice as cited in a case of premium

insurance between Italians in London in 1426 was that if at any time the stolen goods were bought back by the owner then any insurance agreement was void. Caretto is clearly insisting that de la Raule specifically agreed to waive this normal condition. See *Cal. Plea and Memo. Rolls of London*, IV, pp. 208–10.

149   Edler de Roover, 'Early examples of marine insurance', *J.Ec.Hist.*, V, 2 (1945).

150   Gilliodts van Severen, *Etaple*, II, 1010.

151   Edler de Roover, 'Marine insurance', *loc. cit.*, p. 183.

152   Datini instructed his agents always to insure goods properly (Edler de Roover, *loc. cit.*, pp. 194–5); Andrea Barbarigo preferred to split his cargoes (Lane, *Andrea Barbarigo*, p. 116); the Spanish Ruíz family at Antwerp in the early sixteenth century also rarely insured cargoes (Vazquez de Prada, *Lettres marchands d'Anvers*, I, 50).

153   Bernard, 'Les expédients du commerce anglo-gascon', *Annales du Midi*, vol. 78 (1966).

CHAPTER 7

Mercantile organisation *II*
The men and their influence

To the merchants the most immediate concern was less the level of technique at their disposal than the worth of the men with whom they dealt; their capital reserves, their influence and contacts, their trustworthiness, the numbers in any port with a vested interest in the trade, or the extent to which the whole port relied on the trade for prosperity. This importance of the individual was particularly marked in trades such as the Anglo-Castilian where there was no formal organisation to concentrate common activities and offer mutual defence or protection.

The lack of a nation or similar formal organisation was certainly not due to inexperience of mercantile associations either at personal or national levels, nor to inefficiency at forming and maintaining such formal structures. Both nationalities at times formed co-operative bodies to obtain privileges and protect interests. The Englishmen for example had obtained group privileges for their wool trade in the Low Countries and when the wool interest had shifted to the Calais Staple the Englishmen remaining in the Low Countries hung on to their privileges, developing an increasing cohesion, until by the end of the fifteenth century they had become known as a group of Merchant Adventurers in the Low Countries, with the Mercers' Company of London providing the core organisation. Similarly, groups of merchant adventurers grew up in home ports, and the commercial gilds and livery companies offered similar organisations as exemplars. The merchants adventuring to Spain, however, although they were beginning to form a sizeable group by the late fifteenth century, did not yet develop at home or in Spain any comparable formal grouping, nor is there a trace of regular leadership by any individual merchant.

The Spanish merchants were likewise used to banding together to obtain advantages or protect their interests. A wide-ranging grouping was evident in the *Hermandad* of the northern coastal towns in 1296 which agreed among other things mutual action in breaking off trade with Bayonne, England and Flanders until the Anglo-French war was over. Similar but smaller associations of towns were made throughout the period to appoint proctors to negotiate with English and Gascon officials over the constant warfare in the Bay of Biscay; provinces combined to obtain safe-conducts or compensations, and merchants combined for truces as in 1351 and 1369.[1] There were no permanent associations here, but clearly the leading merchants in the leading ports were used to forming associations and committees with enough backing from the commercial community to uphold agreements made.

The Spaniards abroad also show themselves perfectly capable of maintaining elaborate self-governing mercantile communities. In Bruges they had obtained charters of privileges and clearly considered themselves a cohesive group there from the mid fourteenth century,[2] and in the fifteenth evolved a formal structure, receiving in 1414 the right to use the Chapel of the Holy Cross of the Friars Minor for their brotherhood meetings and forming by 1428 an official gild. The divergent interests and rivalry between the Basques and the merchants of Burgos led to an experimental separation into two nations between 1455 and 1469 but for the rest of the century they worked and quarrelled as one. Their organisations in French ports did not develop into such formal gilds, as the volume of trade was so much smaller, but they were cohesive and numerous enough to maintain group privileges at La Rochelle, in Brittany and in Normandy, particularly at Harfleur, in the first half of the fourteenth century. Their generally privileged position in France was undermined however as the Franco-Castilian alliance cooled, but the merchants were well enough established in the main ports then not to move for anything short of a cataclysm.

In England nothing on a similar scale developed, although it might have done at Southampton or London had all gone well. When the Castilians were collecting their privileges in Flanders and France, they were also collecting various temporary privileges in England—letters of group protection at Southampton and Portsmouth, leases for houses at Southampton, freedom from certain tolls at Southampton and London,[3] and there are signs of a small expatriate Spanish community settling in London in the early fourteenth century.[4] That nothing further developed was partly because the trade, although probably big enough in total to justify asking for privileges, was divided between Southampton and London instead of concentrated in one centre; partly because the English kings were less favourably inclined to offer special terms than the Continental dukes and counts; and partly because after the mid-century it was disrupted by war, and although trade persisted the scale was not enough to justify special charters, nor were the kings likely to grant such things to enemy aliens. In the later fifteenth century when peace was re-established and the trading scale larger, representatives could easily be sent from Bruges to London if necessary, and duplication in London was less likely since so many of the Spanish merchants trading there also traded in Bruges where they could get together to discuss problems.

Lacking such formal protection, the merchants naturally relied more on their individual contacts, so it becomes important to assess the local weight, and influence, and numbers of merchants engaged in Anglo-Castilian trade: if a Spaniard in England or an Englishman in Spain faced injustice or prejudice, could he rely on finding enough influential people well-disposed to the trade and wishing to keep it running smoothly, free from the disruptions of letters of marque, bitter reprisals and impounding of goods and ships, who would take up his cause, or, better still, would be strong enough to prevent injustice in the first place?

The Spanish merchants of the late fifteenth and early sixteenth centuries who pushed into the northern ports of England and took their iron up to Chester or Hull must have felt fairly isolated and without obvious support in ports so firmly given to trade with Ireland on one side, and the Baltic and Low Countries on the other, but those who did not stray far from the English Channel could expect considerable interest and support.

Of the minor areas the Devon ports were clearly interested in Spanish trade and their ships and merchants frequently sailed there in the four-teenth century, and in the fifteenth were known to be willing to release captured Spaniards without ransom,[5] and to send shipping to Spain even in wartime.[6]

In Bristol, from the second half of the fourteenth century the trade had many participators, and between 1376 and 1402 the particular customs accounts show a total of 834 indigenous shippers exporting cloth, and of these 286 (34 per cent) exported at some time to Spain, Portugal or both.[7] The high total figure of 834 in fact gives a rather distorted picture of the merchant community since nearly half of those exported a single shipment or in one year only. A few of these were clearly wealthy: Robert Hornjoie could afford to send a single consignment of eighty cloths to Spain in 1391, and Nicholas Achi could send a shipment of sixty-one cloths to Ireland in 1379,[8] but most of these shipments were very small at one to four cloths[9] and many were to Ireland, which was more nearly an internal than an international trade, and could be carried on with small-scale investment by crew members or poorer Irish merchants.

A truer picture of the scale of Spanish trade is obtained by an exami-nation of the well-known, busy and rich merchant families who dealt easily and widely in all Bristol's main markets. Some 222 merchants may be seen as composing this wealthy core of the mercantile community,[10] and of these 59 per cent exported to Iberia. If the field is further narrowed to the top layer who both appear in three accounts or more and exported an average of thirty cloths in each, then of those sixty-eight merchants, 80 per cent had an interest in Iberia. As one would expect in a port which sent between 12 and 40 per cent of its total exports to Iberia, the vested interest in the trade was widespread through the community and strong in the busiest group.

Regularity of trade is one measure of a merchant's interest and many of the merchants traded often: among the richest were William and John Canynges who are recorded trading with Iberia for at least eight and nine years respectively; the Somerwells, John and William, are recorded in four and five years respectively; John Barstaple is recorded for at least seven years, and Thomas Colstan for six. At the middling to lower end of the scale John Wodele traded for six years but his average total exports to all markets reached only seventeen cloths.

The sizes of the shipments sent also indicate the strength of interest. Normally between twenty and forty cloths was the annual commitment by the wealthier classes to Iberia, but occasionally very high amounts were sent: 208 by Richard Spicer in 1378–9, 125 by William Canynges in 1382–3, eighty by Hornjoie in 1391, 110 by Thomas Colstan, 100 by John Hert and seventy-five by John Leman in 1398–9. This argues complete confidence in the stability and worth of the trade.

The percentage of a man's total trade sent to Iberia is another gauge of his interest, and this varied enormously. Thomas Colstan sent 69 per cent of his exports there; William and John Canynges sent 32 and 28 per cent respectively; John and William Somerwell 10 and 24 per cent respectively; Richard Spicer sent 42 per cent, but his colleague Ellis Spelly, possibly shaken by his losses in Spain during the civil war, was now cautious and sent only 6.5 per cent of his cloth. Thomas Blount, whose average exports in the three accounts in which he appears were very high at 162 cloths, was also cautious and sent only 6.5 per cent. Many of the other leading and middling merchants sent 10 to 20 per cent.

The all-pervasiveness of the trade made a pressure group unnecessary, but if one had been needed the public careers of the men involved show that it would have been a strong and able one, as so many were in official positions.[11] William Canynges was a frequent office-holder, M.P., escheator, customs collector, often a commissioner of oyer and terminer, and six times mayor.[12] His son John had a similar career and was mayor and sheriff. Richard Spicer was mayor three times, and Bristol's representative in 1371 with three others in discussions with the Chancellor on the salvation of the realm.[13] William Somerwell was twice bailiff, once sheriff and mayor and his son John held the same offices. John Barstaple was bailiff, sheriff, and mayor three times; Thomas Colstan, John Leman and John Viel held the same offices. Not all the greater merchants were attracted to Iberia, and one notable exception was Walter Frompton, eight times Mayor of the Staple, four times mayor, a shipowner and major exporter until his death in 1388; perhaps his losses there before 1369 had made him even more cautious than Spelly.

There was rarely a year in which two or three at least of the five holders of the offices of Mayor of the Staple, mayor, sheriff, and bailiffs were not personally concerned with Iberian trade. In only five years between 1370 and 1410 was the mayor not an active Spanish trader, in only nine years was the sheriff not an active Iberian trader, and at least thirty of the forty-three men who held the bailiffs' offices also traded there.

Few Spaniards shipped goods at Bristol, although some provided shipping, so they had little opportunity to test Bristol's friendship for them; but since the smooth running of the trade depended also on the good faith and honesty of the Englishman trading abroad, it was important to the Iberians that the weight of Bristol's municipal government would encourage fair dealing on the route.

The general easing of political relations in the next century encouraged more merchants to try the Iberian trade and when the particular accounts survive again in large numbers the route is busier still. This situation was encouraged by the disruption of Gascon trade, and as Bristol looked naturally westward it is not surprising that Spain and Portugal should benefit.

The accounts for Edward IV's reign, although less complete than for the late fourteenth century, are sufficient to provide a fairly clear picture of who were the busiest and wealthiest merchants even if the absolute amount of their trade and their role in each market is distorted.[14] Over a thousand indigenous shippers are recorded, 43 per cent of whom traded apparently only with other British and Irish ports, 47 per cent in Spain, or Portugal or both, and 10 per cent elsewhere in Europe. Thus of the 573 merchants dealing in international markets 82 per cent dealt in Iberia: more precisely, of the 472 men dealing in Iberia, 26 per cent sent shipments to Spain only, 29 per cent to Spain and Portugal and 45 per cent to Portugal only; but the predominance of Portugal is more apparent than real since the same accounts show 41 per cent of Bristol's cloth exports sent to Spain and only 23 per cent to Portugal. The heavy trade was with Spain, although many men sent minor shipments to Portugal.

The accounts for 1485–6 and 1486–7, which cover full years, show a similar picture but with even heavier dealing in Iberia.[15] Of 226 indigenous exporters, 31 per cent traded only with other British and Irish ports, 63 per cent with Spain and Portugal, and only 6 per cent traded with Europe without ever sending a shipment to Iberia. Thus of the international trading merchants 91 per cent dealt in Iberia: more precisely, of the 148 merchants, fifty-five sent goods to Spain, forty-two to Portugal, and fifty-one to both. The thirty-four most prosperous Bristol merchants[16] all traded with Spain, twenty-six of them committing over half their export business there, and of these, fourteen committing over 75 per cent. The interest has grown considerably since the fourteenth century.

The accounts also allow assessments of import values, and not surprisingly twenty-nine of the thirty-four busiest exporters were also the busiest importers with the most valuable cargoes, and the first eight on each list were the same with some minor changes of position. Of the thirty-four wealthiest importers nineteen had Spain, ten still had Gascony, and only five had Portugal as their main supply area.

As before, the vast majority of the merchants were Bristol men again joined by a few men from inland, such as John Griffith of Ludlow. At least eight Londoners also sent goods through Bristol and one of these, Robert Straunge, finally settled permanently there. They were joined too by a few merchants of Gascon origin who settled in Bristol after 1453, such as Janicot de Barrero and Guillem de la Fount.

Table 25   Trade of Bristol's wealthiest merchants, 1485–87.[1]

Merchant	No. Cloths	% to Spain	Other goods (£)	Value (£)	% from Spain
		Exports		Imports	
Henry Vaughn	663	66	86	1,194	50
John Esterfield	328	74	116	1,155	47
John Pynke	309	68	20	581	32
George Monoux	275	54	18	653	22
John Stephens	248	37	19	373	32
Guillem de la Fount	230	52	23	448	50
Richard Vaughn	227	98	47	533	67
Nicholas Browne	190	76	39	1,305	61
Clement Wiltshire	179	53	–	230	29
Philip Ryngston	172	97	23	319	75
William Lane	158	27	24	176	20
Robert Forthey	142	85	34	364	87
William Estby	125	33	57	170	20
Robert Thorne	122	75	19	201	83
John Walshe	122	43	3	165	9
Thomas Ap Hoell	114	69	–	320	44
Richard Sherman	109	28	14	177	45
John Popeley	103	89	–	290	63
John Hemming	103	66	141	339	21
John Jay	102	94	15	301	43
William Rowley	102	88	3	90	7
John Druez	100	71	5	212	31
John Gage	100	77	4	220	89

[1] P.R.O. E122/20/5, 7. Values are to the nearest £. Wine is included in the imports at £4 the tun. The names are of those who could afford to export one hundred or more cloths in the two years 1485–86 and 1486–87.

Spanish merchants took part, as they had not in the earlier period, and between 1461 and 1485, 102 Spanish shippers appeared alongside the 260 Englishmen, and a further thirty-nine newcomers appeared between 1485 and 1487. Most of these were shipmasters and many sent single small consignments, but their trade was regular and frequent, and no doubt encouraged by the favourable conditions offered Castilians, and especially Guipúzcoans. Clearly Bristol was too far off the main European routes to attract many big Spanish merchants, but those engaged in the carrying trade for the Englishmen were stimulated to take part in the trade itself and communicated their enthusiasm to some of the merchants at home.[17]

The Bristol merchants interested ranged as before from the richest to some of the poorest. The great William Canynges, although making most money from shipowning, sometimes traded, and followed the pattern mapped out by his forebears, including Spain in his markets. The Shipwards, father and son, sent regular supplies of cloth to Seville and Biscay as well as Bordeaux, Portugal and Iceland; like many of their contemporaries they liked to spread their ventures wide. John the elder who died in 1475 had been sheriff and four times mayor. Robert Straunge of London served in Bristol as sheriff, and three times as mayor; he was often on local commissions of gaol delivery, and served with others in the office of admiral before his death in 1501. He was a very regular trader under Edward IV with Gascony, Portugal and Spain and probably half his trade was with Spain. He seems later to have concentrated on shipowning.[18] William Spencer, his associate in obtaining trading licences, was also prominent in public life as bailiff, sheriff and three times mayor between 1449 and 1478, and also sent over half his exports to Spain and acquired about two-thirds of his imports from there. Philip Mede is an example of a merchant whose family began to move towards land. He was bailiff, sheriff and three times mayor before 1469 and rich enough to have his daughter marry into the Berkeley family,[19] and he left land in Somerset as well as Bristol. The Rowley family has already been mentioned as one heavily engaged in Spanish trade, and whose knowledge of the area was from personal travelling. Of his family only Thomas senior reached public office as sheriff, probably because of the series of calamitous deaths coming too early in their careers.[20]

Several of the prominent men of Edward's reign had died or retired by 1485, but others were coming to their peak then. John Esterfield traded from 1471, was later bailiff, sheriff and twice mayor, was in 1485–7 the second largest exporter of cloth and the third largest importer. Of his exports 74 per cent went to Spain and 23 per cent to Portugal; of his imports 47 per cent came from Spain, 26 per cent from Portugal and 23 per cent from Bordeaux. Henry Vaughn also reached his peak at that time. He was the largest exporter of 1485–7 with the enormous number of 663 broadcloths shipped in his name, 66 per cent destined for Spain, 28 per cent for Portugal and 6 for Bordeaux. He was the second largest importer, with 50 per cent of imports coming from Spain, 40 per cent from Bordeaux, and 10 per cent from Portugal. Similarly he was bailiff, sheriff and mayor three times between 1469 and 1494. Richard Vaughn too was busy, with 98 per cent of his cloth going to Spain, and 67 per cent of his imports from there and the rest from Bordeaux. A comparative newcomer was Nicholas Browne who dealt in Seville in 1477–8 and 1479–80 and in 1485–7 was able to import goods worth £1,305, although exporting only 190 cloths.

Again Spanish involvement was high with 76 per cent of exports going there and 61 per cent of imports coming from there, with the rest divided evenly between Bordeaux and Portugal. By 1495 he was holding high office for the first time as sheriff.

The import patterns of these men is interesting as it indicates that while many merchants sent most of their cloth to Spain they might spend considerable parts of the profits in Portugal or Gascony on the way home, often shipping goods from Gascony on Spanish ships. Some of those in the higher business ranks, such as Guillem de la Fount, did not hold office, probably because they were not born and bred Bristol men; others such as John Hemming, a shipowner and steady merchant with over half his interest in Spain also failed to make high office; but as before most of the prosperous Spanish shippers, such as William Bird, Edmund Westcote, John Pynke, John Jay and Clement Wiltshire did so. Over the period 1461–85 only three mayors and four sheriffs seem to have had no connection with Spanish trade, and for the rest of the century all the mayors and all but five sheriffs traded there.

It was probably with great justification that the irritated Genoese merchant complained that the 'Mair with othir gret officers and merchauntz of the same towne owith the nacion of Spayn so gret love and affiance' that they were refusing to execute sentence he had obtained against the Spanish shipmaster Godfred de Sasiola who had taken his goods there instead of to Southampton or London as agreed.[21] Too much of Bristol's prosperity, and too many of her merchants' fortunes, were dependent on trust and peace between England and Castile for it to be otherwise.

The situation in Southampton was not so rosy, but still fairly good. The late thirteenth and early fourteenth century records show so many Spaniards favouring Southampton, that they must have found a solid bank of supporters, but the town's internal troubles in the mid fourteenth century and the poor international relations later led to the Spaniards' disappearance, and probably any English merchants developing an interest in the trade then cut it short, particularly as the Italians could still supply them with southern cargoes. In the fifteenth century Spaniards began again to call at Southampton and by Edward IV's reign the trade could be said to flourish in a modest way.

The Spaniards would find here less vested interest than at Bristol, particularly because, as Miss Coleman pointed out, much of Southampton's commercial wealth flowed through the port rather than into it.[22] However, as at Bristol, the Spaniards could count among those directly interested and likely to view them kindly several of those who dominated local government, and this was more important to them here where they were part of a minor branch of trade and a pleasant well-ordered visit might depend far more on regular contacts being in the right quarter.

The regularity of the trade is indicated in the local and national customs accounts where the same merchants appeared over several years, and in the report of John Emory, host to three Spaniards in 1441 whose sales of iron were made to twenty English merchants, four of whom, Robert Aylward, Walter Fetplace, John Payn and William Fleccher, took substantial amounts of their deliveries as settlement of previous transactions.[23] The first three, and Piers James and William Nicholl who also appear in that list, were frequently in contact with Spanish trade.

Aylward, Fetplace and Emory, along with Nicholas Holmege and Richard Gryme, dominated the office of mayor for much of the middle of the century,[24] and all dealt in Spain or Portugal. Aylward imported goods on Spanish and Italian ships and placed orders with Spaniards;[25] Emory was deeply involved in Spanish trade as well as trading with Italians, petitioning for safe-conducts for Spanish ships, hosting Spanish merchants, importing goods on ships of Bilbao, Motrico, and Deva and using Martín Ochoa as his factor in Spain.[26] Fetplace was associated with William Soper, clerk of Henry V's ships, and with Piers James in sending Davy Savage as factor to Bilbao; Soper and Fetplace obtained safe-conducts for Spaniards;[27] both James, who also was mayor, and Emory used Ochoa as factor in Spain;[28] Holmege, Estfeld and Gryme also used Spanish ships for imports.[29]

Their opposing group in local government, although ready to accuse the first group of too ready attachment to Italian trade, traded only a little less vigorously than them with the Spaniards, and apparently found that wholly acceptable. John Payn, his son John, Robert Bagworth, Walter Aylward and Andrew James transported their goods on Biscayan and Guipúzcoan ships.[30] However, most of the Spanish ships coming in were loaded by Spanish shippers and the number of Southampton men actively trading abroad was relatively small. None the less the Spaniards seem to have been in the happy position of being welcome visitors whichever local group was in power.

In London the position was different again. Here the Spaniards themselves did more business than in any other centre, and at times did more than at all the other centres combined, and yet their share of London's trade remained fairly small compared with that of the Hansards or Italians until the later part of Edward's reign. In London they could not rely on the majority of the commercial community being vitally interested in the trade, nor on the vested interests of a smaller group which dominated local office; rather they had to rely on a desire for all trade to go smoothly, on law courts if necessary and on a few regular contacts, some of whom were men of weight and reputation, and whose numbers were steadily growing.

Of the 190 or so names found of Londoners in contact with Spain or Spanish merchants between 1400 and 1485,[31] some sixty were actively concerned in overseas trading with Spain, visiting it, sending their factors there, having their goods shipped to and from Spain. A further thirty were petitioners on behalf of, or pledges for, Spaniards seeking safe-conducts for shipping, and some of the thirty, at least two-thirds of whom were active merchants, probably intended to use the ship or had just used it.[32] Four men used Spanish shipping to bring their goods from the Mediterranean, and their venturing so far might be a natural extension of trade already established in Andalusia. A further twenty can be shown to have had direct dealings of a greater or lesser extent with Spaniards in London and the real number of these must have been very much higher. Beyond this thirty men are found shipping on vessels unloading in London which seem to have come from Andalusia, or Portugal, and are therefore interested in Iberia even if not provenly in Spain; and some forty are found importing typical Spanish cargoes of iron, beaverskins and licorice on Gascon ships—proof of Spanish trading being absent but the presumption of it is strong.

Among the first group were at least nine drapers, six grocers, three mercers, two vintners, two fishmongers and the occasional stokfishmonger, haberdasher, ironmonger, dyer or tailor. Among the second group were at least three drapers, four vintners, two grocers, three skinners, two hosiers and the odd tailor, saddler, goldsmith, tallowchandler, fishmonger and brewer. Of those dealing with Spaniards in London at least seven were drapers, three tailors, two mercers, one an ironmonger and one a leatherseller.

Such a sample is too small and incomplete for firm conclusions but it seems clear enough that the drapers were the group most concerned with Spanish trade, although any company might deal in cloth and the variety of Spanish imports made them attractive to several companies. The mercers, who held such a dominant position in export of cloth to the Low Countries, seem by comparison almost uninterested. Perhaps the drapers with their greater emphasis on wool cloth and imports for the cloth industry, and the need to escape from the dominance of the mercers, found the market of Spain particularly attractive, while the mercers were too well entrenched in the Low Countries to want new markets, especially ones which could not serve so well their near-monopoly of imports of luxury fabrics.

The majority of those in contact with the Spanish trade were now connected with the companies which dealt most closely with cloth and victuals while the skinners and leathersellers had decreased drastically in importance since the thirteenth century, a natural consequence of the marked decline in imports of fine leathers and coney skins from Spain.

The nature of the evidence allows us to see the numbers of those trading with Spain or dealing in Spanish goods in London only in hundreds for the whole fifteenth century, when the total number of traders and dealers must have run into thousands. Clearly this is not a complete picture of the scale of Spanish interest but as clearly the direct interest in Spain was never likely to be as all-pervasive as in Bristol, and the individual status of those involved becomes more important. Unfortunately the evidence is also too scanty to suggest what proportion of the municipal office-holders favoured Spanish trade from personal connections, but clearly some of the officeholders were involved.

William Stokker, draper, alderman, knight, sheriff and mayor imported Spanish wines, and intended to use the *Miguel of Bilbao* to import Gascon wines and send goods back to Spain in 1475;[33] William Heryot, also a draper, alderman, knight, sheriff, mayor and M.P. who had clients who sold cloth in Spain, was himself more heavily committed to Mediterranean trade, but used Basque ships to carry it, and his interest there may well have been an extension of an interest in Andalusia;[34] his friend John Fenkyll, draper, alderman and knight, was certainly shipping goods from Seville at this time;[35] Thomas Bledlow, grocer, alderman and sheriff, imported oil from Spain direct to Bristol;[36] in an earlier period Stephen Forster, fishmonger, alderman, sheriff, mayor and M.P. shipped considerable amounts of iron from the Gascon direction and in 1428 had stood pledge for the good behaviour of master and crew of the *Julián of San Sebastián*.[37]

Somewhat below this aldermanic level some merchants were more heavily engaged in Spanish trade. John Chirche, a mercer, host to Spaniards in London, never reached aldermanic rank but held public office as a victualler for Calais in 1447.[38] He dealt in Portugal and Spain with English ships, and obtained safe-conducts with John Langley, another mercer, for at least four Basque ships; his imports were varied but included considerable quantities of iron from the north on Deva ships, and he dealt in Seville through at least one Italian factor. He was a multiple ship-owner, so must have found the Iberian route very profitable.[39] Another of this rank, William Wodehouse, also found Spain profitable and bought licences for his factor, Richard Whitington, to trade there from 1454 to 1460, and then for a new factor, John Newman, in 1460. In 1463 he was associated with Whitington, apparently on equal terms now, in the export of corn to Andalusia.[40] John Mott came originally from Suffolk, became a London fishmonger, and also used Whitington as his agent in Seville trade. Mott was associated too in some way with William Folkys, who claimed that Mott had sold 124 tons of Folkys' iron at Southampton in 1462 without accounting for it to him.[41] This iron was probably Spanish as Folkys seems to have been involved in Spanish trade: he had certainly travelled as far as Lisbon; he and John Skirwith detained 120 tons of oil belonging to Juan Seboll for a month at Southampton, taken off a ship of Bilbao; he sued Martín de Lucerra, the master of a Bilbao ship, in Admiralty; and probably the *Marie Folkys of London* which was seized off Spain by Basque pirates was his. The loss of the *Marie Folkys* might be the occasion for his actions against Spaniards in London and Southampton, although he should have obtained compensation for the loss as the *corregidor* of Biscay found in favour of the English owners of the *Marie Folkys*.[42] John Treguran, a vintner, was another of this rank: he imported Spanish iron, was accused of helping Francis Dyes export cloth illegally in 1459; petitioned for a safe-conduct for a ship of Guetaría in 1464 and was importing wines on a ship of Deva in 1466.[43]

All in all there were in London enough men eager for Spanish trade to join in colouring Spanish goods, or breaking the credit restrictions for Spaniards, and there must have been many more who wished the Spaniards well as their trade rose in Henry VII's reign, and would use their influence to help them.

That such influence was necessary at times is clear. One of the most open statements comes from Juan Despaigne, a Spanish merchant at Southampton who complained that there was a reckoning between him and William Nedeham the sheriff of Southampton, and the sheriff 'considering he is in office and of might' and that Despaigne was a stranger started various actions against the latter before himself, intending to do him great mischief.[44] Two Spaniards in London complained that a miller they were suing for robbery had begun counter-accusations of assault and by sinister means had empanelled a biased court of his special acquaintance who owed him inordinate affection and refused to admit evidence from the Spaniards.[45] Laurence de Ortiz of Spain complained in 1491 that the jury empanelled to hear a case between himself and Robert Chattock were all twelve Englishmen instead of the statutory half Englishmen and half Spaniards; he also complained that Chattock had won the support of one of the aldermen.[46] Besides such as these there were complaints of false attachment and false imprisonment, but behind most cases was little malice but rather the difficulty of tying down an alien long enough for a case to be heard in a common law or a municipal court. Both sides no doubt were relieved if the case could come before the Chancellor and a speedier judgement could be given.

It is far more difficult to hazard a guess at the local influence, status and numbers of the Spaniards involved in English trade. Spain, as much as or possibly even more than other European countries of the time, was a country which placed emphasis on land as the gauge of authority, and on warfare as the important function, but trading affairs were not ignored by government or aristocracy, whose fortunes often depended on large-scale sales in overseas markets of wool, oils and wines from their estates, and whose prestige was enhanced by ships. The commercial life of the ports and their inhabitants therefore throve. But as yet studies of individual ports are few and it is impossible to estimate for any the numbers involved in total trade or English trade.

From English sources it is possible to identify for the whole period 1250 to 1489 some 2,500 Spanish shippers—merchants and masters—who traded with England, and in the busy time of Edward IV's reign alone some 380 Spaniards were dealing in Bristol, London and Southampton, with a further hundred appearing in Sandwich, the west country, Hull and Chester. This indicates that the busiest Spanish ports must have had groups of several scores with vested interests in English trade but no details are known.

One point which can be quickly made is that, although much has been written on the importance of the Jewish community in Spanish economic and financial life, it was not concerned with overseas trade. None of the Castilian merchants bear obviously Jewish names, indicating overt and conscious adherence to the Jewish religion and life, although converts may well have been present under their adopted Christian names.[47] The nearest clear connection any Jewish families had with the English trade was as small-scale retailers of cloth.[48]

In Andalusia, where English trade centred in Seville, Sanlúcar and Cadiz, as well as Huelva and Puerto de Santa María, contacts must have been built up with the Italian settlers who also had links with London and Southampton. Certainly Englishmen transported goods on their ships, and sometimes used them as agents. Probably these Italian houses were of considerable help to some Englishmen and the connection deserves more examination than I have been able to give it.

In the south too they could rely in a general way on the encouragement and partial protection of the Dukes of Medina Sidonia.

Andalusian merchants probably welcomed English cloth and custom for oil and wine, which by Henry VII's reign was so valuable. But numbers are impossible to assess. Certainly few were active overseas, and for both the fourteenth and fifteenth centuries only twenty-four named merchants in England have been identified as coming from Seville, Sanlúcar, Lepe or elsewhere in the south. Some of these, such as Francis Dyes, appeared to have considerable resources. So too had Alfonso Dies de Gobralyon of Seville and Rodrigo de Jaén, whose activity covered a dozen years, who may be taken as fairly typical of the area's men, and whose local importance was probably fairly high;[49] but other merchants from the south, such as Antonio García and Felipe de Lepe[50] or Pedro Guillelmi of Seville, remain nothing but names.[51]

Most of the active Spanish merchants came, like the seamen, from the north: in almost any port Englishmen should have found someone familiar with their trade, but the concentration was in the Basque Provinces, and in the fifteenth century particularly at Fuenterrabía, Rentería, San Sebastián and Bilbao. Inland the biggest centre supplying merchants for English trade was Burgos with a few men from Vitoria and Valladolid. In most of these centres, and above all at Bilbao, Englishmen must have had strong support since the Biscayans and Guipúzcoans went to considerable trouble to protect their English trade in the fourteenth and fifteenth centuries with special truces and safe-conducts,[52] and the English iron trade seems to have been equal in importance to the Flemish.

Again numerical assessment is beyond the evidence, but some of the northerners involved in English trade were men of wealth. In the four-teenth century Andrés Pérez of Castrogeriz of Burgos was the outstanding example. The ship-owner Juan Divarola was also prosperous. Alvaro Gomell and Sancho de Ordogne seem similarly well-off and the principals for whom they worked must have been the same. Martín Ochoa de Yrive of Deva, Pedro Sans de Venesse, and other wealthy ship-owners and master-merchants must have carried weight in their localities.[53]

A group of merchants about whom a little more is known and who were clearly of weight and importance, were those in the structured group resident at Bruges. These were early used to co-operative action to safe-guard their English trade, and doubtless would help Englishmen in need. Edward III had addressed them as a whole, as the 'Merchants of The Staple of Spain in Bruges' in the crisis of 1351, and had used them to check up on a merchant originally of Rouen then claiming to be a Spaniard.[54] In 1364 a group there who had had goods stolen by Englishmen met and formally appointed attorneys to sue for them in England; Edward's favourable response, while not proving formal recognition of them by the English king, suggests that he was willing to listen to a group conscious of their common interest and acting co-operatively.[55] After Pedro's assassination envoys were sent to England by the 'commonalty of Spain at Bruges' to discuss the best ways of protecting the truce of 1351.[56] Already it was much more of an entity than the group of Spaniards who worked in London or Southampton, and it was moreover so close to London and Southampton that it could make easy and swift contact in need. In addition many of the merchants dealing in Bruges also dealt in England so that in the expanding Anglo-Castilian trade of the late fifteenth century it is not surprising to find the Spanish staple and consuls taking action in England on occasion.

Formal complaints were made for instance in the early months of Richard III's reign by the 'consuls of the nation and merchants of Spain residing in Bruges in Flanders' against Sir John Arundel's seizure of a Basque ship lying at anchor off Portsmouth on its way from Flanders to Spain,[57] and Pedro de Salamanca, one of the consuls, came over to live in London that winter to sue in English courts as attorney for several other Spaniards who had had goods aboard Breton ships unjustly seized.[58] Clearly the Spanish officials could be mobilised for action in England, but they were sparingly called on, and it is not clear that in those cases which they pursued the victims received any better treatment than if they had sued alone: English royal courts were generally fair in their treatment of alien complaints, and Edward and Richard bent over backwards to please Spanish merchants.

The Spaniards in Bruges were often to take advantage of the good customs terms offered by the treaty of 1467 in England, and many of the names prominent in Bruges affairs were to be found in London and Southampton too: the Covarrubias family, with Juan Seboll as factor or associate; the Castros who dealt in London, Sandwich and Southampton as well as Bruges, Gascony and Toulouse; Ferand, Juan and Martín de Salinas, well-established at Bruges, traded here, as did Gonsalis and Pedro de Salamanca, Juan Pardo and Martín Maluenda.[59] These merchants might export several hundred cloths in their own names in a year from London, although at times they might also be acting as agent for another of the group.

The division of the volume of the trade between English and Spanish merchants was very unbalanced in the early period; in fact the Spaniards held a near monopoly until the early fourteenth century, and the English, as with Gascon and Flemish trade, were late participators. The area was not unfamiliar to them, since the Crusaders' ships had gone that way; Santiago was a well-known pilgrimage shrine; diplomatic activity was constant; Gascon possessions were geographically close; but if they visited it they left no trace except for the English ship at Corunna in 1234 which seems to have arrived there by mischance.[60] Thereafter, except for the merchants sent for horses—which were usually ordered and not real proof of normal speculative commerce—for nearly seventy years the English were content to leave the trade in the hands and ships of the Spaniards.

After the application of Andrés Pérez's to use ships of the king's dominion in his Spanish trade[61] (which may still mean only Gascon vessels) there are a few references to English ships going there and after about 1350 the numbers seem to have increased steadily. By the late fourteenth century the Bristol merchants had surged forward and carried a great deal of Iberian trade into Bristol, and men of London, Southampton and the west country joined them. The English never dominated the trade, and even in Bristol the Spaniards began to move in and take trade from the English by the later fifteenth century. In Edward IV's reign they composed a numerically strong group of about a hundred there. There were by then some 260 Englishmen engaged in the trade so the Spaniards composed about 28 per cent of the total shippers in the trade, but their share was lower at about 22 per cent of cloth exports and 20 per cent of the value of imports.[62]

This proportion was no doubt peculiar to Bristol as other ports had a longer tradition of alien activity and some had a long association with Spanish trade, and were better placed to attract the Spaniards. In Southampton, in the same period, although only about forty Spaniards were active they probably held a much higher proportion of the trade, although they were joined by Italian and even some Portuguese participants. Sandwich saw them with probably a fairly high share of a declining trade, as seventy Spanish shippers appeared there, and the values of their exports were high, particularly in the short period when they exported large amounts of corn through that port and Dover.

London was the greatest centre of Spanish trade in absolute terms and it is particularly unfortunate that the customs accounts do not provide a full picture of the port movements. At least 260 Spanish shippers were recorded for Edward's and Richard's reigns, far more than for Bristol, and their exports were much heavier: some men took enormous amounts. For instance, of the ninety-nine Spanish shippers recorded there in 1472–3, eight took over twenty cloths, Seboll taking 205, Donato seventy-two, and Sancho de Bilbao sixty-two. The following year Diego de Covarrubias took 379, Ferando de Covarrubias 181, Juan de Covarrubias and Seboll together eighty-two, and Juan Urtice seventy-two. Their share of the trade was doubtless much higher than at Bristol since the Englishmen played a relatively smaller share in each trade there and, moreover, many were more likely to be deeply entrenched in eastern rather than western markets, but no estimate worth the name can be made of the respective shares.

Altogether it is clear that Spanish merchants dominated the trade until the mid fourteenth century, when they were joined by English shippers, who dominated Bristol's trade but left the Spaniards elsewhere as the most important group; later these also moved in to Bristol, first achieving a reasonable division of the routes with Spanish ships dominating the northern run and English ships dominating the Portuguese and Andalusian run, then by the beginning of Henry VII's reign beginning to compete with Bristol men there too.

The trade was in the hands of a very large number of merchants covering the whole gamut from the wealthy merchant and ship-owner with a busy public career in his city government or his nation abroad or even in royal service, to the small shipper, working master, seaman or apprentice. The investment in Anglo-Spanish trade and shipping was possibly as great as in Anglo-Italian trade in the later fifteenth century, but by being open to many instead of in a few hands it did not produce the advanced and wealthy organisations of the Italian trade. M. Braudel pointed out that the Mediterranean trade in general demanded much less outlay than, and offered much less spectacular gain than, the long-distance and luxury trades between the eastern Mediterranean and the north of Europe; it could be done on a large or small scale. Anglo-Spanish trade was similar: it offered some expensive goods which needed high investment, and some fairly long voyages, it also offered bulkier and cheaper goods and short voyages so that men could break into it at any level, and provided they did not meet with too many shipwrecks and robberies could expect to prosper.

Together, rich and poor, Spaniards and Englishmen, made the trade flourish and evolved techniques, practices, and an organisation perfectly adequate not only to sustain the trade in the fourteenth and fifteenth centuries but to provide the opportunity for rapid expansion in the later fifteenth and early sixteenth.

NOTES TO CHAPTER 7

1 See Chapter 1 for details.
2 See pp. 215–16.
3 See pp. 13–14, 21.
4 See p. 183.
5 *C.M.I.*, VII, 552.
6 P.R.O. E28/83 (29 Aug. 31 Hen. VI).
7 The accounts for 1376–91 are particularly useful, being well-preserved, covering full years and giving ships' destinations. The accounts for 1393–6 are damaged and usually without destinations so have not been used here. The form of the accounts makes it necessary to consider Iberia as a whole; see p. 85. P.R.O. E122/15/8, 16/2, 4, 5, 9, 11, 13, 15, 19, 20, 22, 34, 40/12, 17/1, 4–6.
8 These may be examples of men making money in shipping, or manufacturing, turning to direct commerce only to find it less profitable or more troublesome, and so returning to their earlier occupation.
9 Of the 834 shippers, 402, and of the 285 Iberian shippers 94 (48 and 33 per cent respectively) were active in one account only, and most sent a single shipment—of the 402 only 41 made more than one shipment in the year they appeared.
10 These are 142 who appear in three accounts or more and 80 who appeared less frequently but could afford to send shipments of over thirty cloths. They are rough and ready divisions, but indicate that a man has committed himself to commerce, or is of some substance, investing over £60 or with credit standing of that scale.
11 Office-holders taken from *The Maire of Bristowe is Kalendar*, ed. Toulmin Smith, pp. 35–7; *The Staple Court Books of Bristol*, ed. Rich, p. 60, n.l; *P.R.O. List and Indexes*, IX, p. 166.
12 See also *C.C.R. 1381–6*, p. 291; *C.P.R. 1385–9*, pp. 244, 319; *ibid.*, *1388–92*, pp. 246, 349; *C.F.R. 1383–91*, p. 344; Wadley, *Wills*, p. 48.
13 *C.C.R. 1369–74*, p. 151.
14 P.R.O. E122/19/1, 3–4, 6–8, 10–11, 13–14, 18/39; details as for Table 11.
15 P.R.O. E122/20/5, 7.
16 Again, those able to export at least thirty cloths each year.
17 Exceptions were Gabriel Pardo, Diego de Castro and Juan Seboll, whose main business was in Bruges, London and Southampton but who sent occasional shipments through Bristol.
18 William Worcester's attribution of a fleet of twelve ships to a Thomas Straunge is probably a slip for Robert, as no Thomas appears in Bristol records, and such a rich shipowner is unlikely to have left no trace at all in his city.
19 Carus-Wilson, *Overseas Trade of Bristol*, misc. records, 183 note.
20 See p. 189.
21 P.R.O. C1/64/459.
22 Coleman, 'Trade and prosperity in the fifteenth century: some aspects of the trade of Southampton', *Ec.H.R.*, 2nd ser., vol. XVI (1963).
23 P.R.O. E101/128/31.
24 Ruddock, *Italian Merchants in Southampton*, pp. 169–73, 176–83.
25 Ms. S.P.B. 1429–30, fo. 62v; *ibid.*, 1433–4, fo. 43; *S.P.B. 1435–6*, ed. Foster, p. 36; Ruddock, *op. cit.*, p. 169; Gilliodts van Severen, *Consulat*, pp. 32–3.
26 P.R.O. C76/120 m.4; E101/128/31, 35; E179/173/110; E159/208 Recorda Trin. m.7; SC6/896/1; C1/16/656; Ms. S.P.B. 1429–30, fo. 60; *S.P.B. 1435–6*, ed. Foster, p. 36.

27   P.R.O. C1/9/403; C76/107 m.10, 111 mm.3, 5, 112 m.10, 113 m.4, 114 m.7.
28   P.R.O. C1/17/235.
29   P.R.O. E122/142/1, 3.
30   P.R.O. E122/142/1, 3, 209/8; E159/208 Recorda Trin. m.10; C76/142 m.27, 145 m.33; *S.P.B. 1435–6*, ed. Foster, pp. 36, 52, 54; Ms. S.P.B. 1459–60, Lib. Comm. (unfol.), 3 Dec., 28 June, 5 Aug.
31   The customs particulars are unhelpful here, as destinations, last ports of call and home ports of shipping are usually omitted. Moreover the surviving accounts are mainly of petty custom not tunnage and poundage; and on the former, Englishmen and, after 1466, Castilians do not appear except as cloth exporters. They have been supplemented with names found in the Early Chancery Proceedings, Ancient Petitions, Treaty Rolls, K.R. Memoranda Rolls, Exchequer Accounts (various) in the P.R.O., and from printed calendars of other records.
32   See Chapter 2, note 76.
33   Beaven, *The Aldermen of the City of London*, II, 14; Thrupp, *Merchant Class of London*, app. A, p. 367; P.R.O. E122/128/15; C76/159 m.13.
34   Beaven, *op. cit.*, II, 14; Thrupp, *op. cit.*, p. 349; P.R.O. C1/64/841; C76/153 m.14; E159/258 Recorda Easter m.3; E122/194/24; E356/22 m.33; Ms. S.P.B. 1484–5 Lib. Comm. (unfol.), 15 Nov.; see also Ruddock, *op. cit.*, pp. 218, 222.
35   Thrupp, *op. cit.*, p. 340; C.C.R. 1468–76, No. 1039.
36   Beaven, *op. cit.*, II, 14; Thrupp, *op. cit.*, p. 324; P.R.O. E122/19/8.
37   Beaven, *op. cit.*, II, 9; Thrupp, *op. cit.*, p. 340; P.R.O. E122/77/1, 77/4, 203/3, 73/23, 127/18; C76/110 m.10.
38   P.R.O. C76/129 m.3.
39   P.R.O. C76/112 m.8, 113 mm.8, 14, 119 m.5, 120 m.4, 123 m.18; E122/161/1, 77/1, 3, 203/1; E179/144/45, 56; E159/208 Recorda Easter mm.10, 10d, 12d; Trin. m.10; C1/11/204; Ms. S.P.B. 1429–30 fo. 62v; Nicolas, *Procs. and Ords. of the Privy Council*, v, 177.
40   P.R.O. C76/136 m.12, 138 m.29, 140 m.22, 142 m.22, 147 m.11.
41   P.R.O. C1/44/253; E122/19/8; C1/59/250; C.C.R. 1468–76, No. 1039.
42   P.R.O. C1/44/200, 57/49, 59/250, 60/5, 66/126.
43   Thrupp, *op. cit.*, p. 205 and n. 21; P.R.O. E122/203/4; E159/235 Recorda Trin. mm. 26–26d; C76/148 m.23, 149 m.1; C.C.R. 1461–8, p. 347.
44   P.R.O. C1/31/428. Nedeham was sheriff in 1464–5.
45   *Ibid.*, 64/638. This took place in 1479 or 1484.
46   *Ibid.*, 104/15.
47   It has been asserted and denied that many Burgos merchants were Jewish: Vicens Vives, *Manual*, pp. 228–30. The names of the alleged Jews in Valmaseda in 1487 were almost totally devoid of Jewish roots: Rodriguez Herrero, *Valmaseda en el siglo XV y la aljama de los judíos*, pp. 5, 21–177.
48   See Chapter 6, note 19.
49   See Appendix for these three.
50   P.R.O. E122/41/6.
51   C.C.R. 1349–54, p. 537.
52   For details see Chapters 1 and 2.
53   For these see Appendix.
54   C.C.R. 1349–54, p. 470; P.R.O. C76/28 m.2, 29 m.15.
55   C.P.R. 1364–7, p. 63; P.R.O. C47/30/8(4).
56   C.C.R. 1369–74, pp. 112–13.
57   C.P.R. 1476–85, pp. 370–1.
58   *Ibid.*, p. 426.

59 For some of these see Appendix.
60 C.P.R. 1232–47, p. 68.
61 *Ibid.*, 1301–7, p. 7.
62 That is the value according to the customs records.

Epilogue

Anglo-Spanish trade comforms broadly to the pattern of European economic expansion in the thirteenth and early fourteenth centuries and contraction in the fifteenth, but it does not conform to a picture of hardship, melancholy, and gloom which some historians would have us believe resulted from the contraction. Indeed not only the persistence and fortunes of their mutual trade, but developments in other aspects of these two western economies accord better with the view of the fifteenth century as one witnessing considerable constructive optimism and change, albeit punctuated with short slumps, and as a century in which the contraction of output was offset by the decline in population so that those who survived had a greater share of the remaining wealth.

England's export figures have provided ammunition for both sides of the picture: there was certainly a contraction in the volume of wool exported and the volume of wool now exported as cloth did not make up for this, but the total volume exported as raw wool and cloth was not dropping faster than the population and the value of the exports was still high, sometimes equalling or exceeding the value of wool exports at their peak in 1350–60.[1] The figures also warn against too much emphasis on the fifteenth century as a whole, since there were slumps and times of expansion within it. They seem to confirm that exports were earning more wealth *per capita* in the fifteenth than in the thirteenth century. Many historians now interpret the movements of prices, wages, rents and leases as signs of greater prosperity for many classes below the greatest landlords, and the cloth industry brought more wealth to some areas of the countryside. Some towns declined, but others, and notably London, throve and grew at times, particularly if they could handle trade as could Bristol or Southampton, or were at the centre of a cloth industry as was Coventry. The great landlords were undoubtedly reaping less from their lands, but they still lived well, and with careful marriages, royal grants, new acquisitions of leases could even extend their holdings. They certainly found resources to buy the colourful luxuries and comforts of fifteenth-century life so often depicted in contemporary paintings and writings; and those below them had both the desire and means to copy them, a movement which sumptuary laws stood little chance of checking.

England's trade with Flanders undoubtedly contracted, and her wool merchants declined in numbers and riches, but her cloth merchants found that trade with the Hanseatic areas, Gascony, Iberia and the Mediterranean increased, whether under direct English aegis or not. Shipping was stimulated, and instead of leaving much carrying in the hands of aliens as in the thirteenth century, English shipowners came to dominate Gascon trade, and play a large part in Iberian and Flemish trade; they made determined attempts on the Baltic and Mediterranean trades, and joined the voyages to Africa and the West. These may be signs that new markets are needed as older ones contract, but may equally underline that a new commodity will anyway need new markets. The fifteenth-century cloth merchant in England seems more confident than desperate, and the grumbles which occur are as much those at rising expectations frustrated as those in the face of severe hardship.

In Spain, with less detailed work as yet available, and little hope of firm figures, there are pointers in a similar direction. Her trade with England and the North persisted in the late fourteenth and fifteenth centuries, and slumped only in the face of war; by the first quarter of the fifteenth century her colony in Flanders was clearly big enough to justify special accommodation and organisation. Her oil trade was at least steady and may have increased as English demand grew; her wine trade was growing, possibly boosted by Gascon contraction; her iron was in wide demand, probably stimulated by a century of war. Wool exports certainly rose, although the stages are unclear, and by 1477 the Mesta organisation coped with some two and a half million sheep, already five-sixths of the number at its peak in the sixteenth century. As in England, while some towns slumped—Bermeo and Castro Urdiales—others, like Bilbao, throve and grew. Spanish shipping was ubiquitous and Spanish seamen too sailed in the Atlantic and to West Africa.

As with England, trading history shows a picture more of light than shadow. Possibly at home too developments were on somewhat similar lines, allowing for the enormous differences in social structure: the Black Death did cause a decline in population; price, wage and sumptuary legislation was felt necessary; chronic grain shortage and the demand for wool meant that those who could produce such crops would prosper. The nobility were, however, probably in a richer position than in England, some had enormous estates and could squeeze even more lands and grants of revenue from weak kings. Certainly the traveller Pero Tafur in 1437 considered his country a very rich one and advised Niccolò de Conti to sell his drugs, jewels, and curios from the East in Spain: 'he would find the best market in Spain, chiefly on account of the great wealth of our King, but also because in all our wars we are always victorious, and have never been beaten. The people, I said, were very rich and valued such things more than anyone else'.[2]

It cannot be denied that there was an overall contraction of volume in trade, but the contraction is not out of line with the contraction of population, and the value of some trades fell much less sharply. It cannot be claimed that there was a growing economy in the sense of one constantly inventing new techniques in financial and industrial practices to cope with greater demands. It cannot be proved that the apparent increase in western activity made up for the flagging in older centres. But it also cannot be denied that there was growth in certain places and fields, that there were further important developments and refinements of existing techniques, and that the production and wealth per capita may have increased. The study of Anglo-Castilian trade offers no firm proofs, but suggests that here there should be more emphasis on the positive side of the economic changes: the slumps were comparatively short; the changes of direction and type in trade took place in an atmosphere more of optimism, prosperity and hope than of unalleviated restrictive gloom.

NOTES TO EPILOGUE

1   Taking the decade 1350–60 as the base 100 the following trends in the volume and value of the wool exports as both raw wool and cloth appear:

	Volume	Value		Volume	Value
1350–60	100	100	1430–40	55	103
1360–70	95	103	1440–50	66	122
1370–80	78	86	1450–60	50	85
1380–90	69	86	1460–70	49	80
1390–1400	70	91	1470–80	58	98
1400–10	64	94	1480–90	65	116
1410–20	63	92	1490–1500	62	114
1420–30	72	116	1500–10	84	170

Estimates of ten-yearly averages are based on the tables rather than graphs in Carus-Wilson and Coleman, England's Export Trade to avoid any possible over-exaggeration of exports. Estimates of value are based on T. H. Lloyd, The Movement of Wool Prices in Medieval England (Cambridge, 1973) (taken at about £4 10s the sack 1350–1450 and about £3 10s the sack 1450–1500) and on Professor Carus-Wilson's suggested value of £3 the cloth with about four cloths made from a sack of wool (Medieval Merchant Venturers, p. xxiv, n. 2). No allowance has been made for changes in the price of cloth as figures and research on this are sparse, but the period is one of general long-term stability in prices and such a lack of adjustment would not greatly affect the generalised figures above.

2   Pero Tafur, Travels and Adventures, p. 92.

APPENDIX

Biographies of selected Spanish merchants to illustrate the types of business of merchants and masters from the Basque Provinces, Andalusia, Burgos and Bruges.

DIEGO DE CASTRO

Castro was a merchant of Burgos family who first appears in English records in 1473 when he exported 27½ cloths of assize and four yards of kersey from Southampton. From then until late in the reign of Henry VII he often imported wine, iron, madder, soap, pitch, rosin, linen, Breton canvas, beaver furs, silk, saffron and occasional grain of paradise, and exported cloth and tin through Bristol, Sandwich, Southampton and London.[1] He also took part in the corn trade with a licence to export 1,000 quarters from Orwell and Hull in 1475.[2] His factor in London was his kinsman Bernard, who lost some of his money gambling,[3] and his and Pedro de Salamanca's standing there by 1486 was sufficient for them to stand guarantor with Thomas Randyll for a debt of £280 of Bernard de la Force, the envoy often used between England and Castile.[4] His shipments were usually substantial like the 40 tons of iron brought to Sandwich and the silk and beaver worth £89 6s 8d at Bristol. He was one of the ten Spaniards with business in Bruges who obtained grants of £250 and 400 marks from their customs in 1484 and 1485 and between themselves (and probably as agents for others) exported 1,720 cloths from London in the year.[5] In Bruges he was involved in the oil trade with Fernando de Salinas[6] and was also established in the French wine trade and the Toulouse woad trade.[7] He had some dealings too with the Celys and in 1487 they took up £60 from him in exchange, payable by William Cely in Calais.[8]

PEDRO DE CASTRO

Pedro was also a Burgos man[9] and possibly a kinsman of Diego although no clear indication is forthcoming from the English evidence. Possibly he is the same man who had wool, cloth and lambskins at Sandwich in 1457[10] and probably the man who was a consul for the Burgos merchants in Bruges in 1468 with Fernando de Salinas.[11] Most of his trade in England was in the following two decades and his main activity was the export of cloth through London, sometimes for transhipment in Southampton[12] and in 1474 his trade was valuable enough for him with three others to buy letters of protection.[13] His high level of exports in 1480–1—over 570 cloths—suggests he was acting as factor for other Spaniards and certainly he was attorney in England for Ferand de Castro de la Hosse at about that time.[14] His exports also included corn in 1481.[15] His imports were certainly from the south as he imported raisins in 1481,[16] and he may have handled iron from the north as he was involved at law with John Gloys, a London ironmonger.[17]

FERANDO DE COVARRUBIAS

Fernando and Juan and Diego were all three busy in Bruges and also in English trade, often with Juan Seboll as factor, and probably constitute a family group originating in the village of Covarrubias about thirty kilometres south-south-east of Burgos. Ferando may have been the merchant of that name who was one of the judges for the Castilian nation in Bruges in 1447.[18] His English trade was important enough for him to obtain a letter of protection for two years in 1470 with Diego, Juan de Castro, Luis López and Juan Seboll. He also obtained a shipping safe-conduct in 1471, and another three-year letter of protection with Juan and Diego de Covarrubias and three others with Juan Seboll as their factor in 1473.[19]

His cloth exports from London were moderate—between fifty and seventy cloths—on Spanish and Flemish ships.[20]

DIEGO DE COVARRUBIAS

Diego was often associated with Ferando in safe-conducts. His imports of raisins, almonds and woad went to Sandwich in 1469 and 1470 and his exports of cloth were through Sandwich and London.[21] He also supplied Londoners with oil from Bruges.[22] His consignments were larger than Ferando's—132 cloths were exported from Sandwich and ninety-eight bales of woad imported in 1470, and over 374 cloths were exported from London in 1473. Diego acted as factor for Vincent Gyles, a Lisbon merchant, in the delivery of Spanish wool and orchell to Flanders on an Italian carrack but unfortunately the goods were arrested at Southampton at the suit of Davy Colwell who accused Juan de Covarrubias's factor Peter de Overlet of stealing his wines. Juan Seboll was sent to sort matters out for the Covarrubias, but Colwell won his point.[23] Colwell also had Juan de Covarrubias and Juan de Castro imprisoned despite their safe-conduct when claiming a £20 debt from them.[24]

JUAN DE COVARRUBIAS

He worked in association with Ferando and Diego and Juan de Castro. He appears exporting cloth with Seboll from London but his exports were smaller than either Ferando's or Diego's, suggesting a junior partner's role.

ALFONSO DIES DE GOBRALYON

Alfonso came from Seville, apparently a migrant from Gibraleón, just north of Huelva.[25] His activity in England emphasises the importance of Italian shipping to southern merchants, and, because of his use of it, most of his trade was through Southampton and London.

He exported a small amount of miscellaneous goods on an Italian galley from London in 1438[26] but was probably already a more substantial merchant than that suggested as in 1441 he was able to pay for safe-conducts for two 300-ton ships of Spain, Portugal or Brittany to trade for three years.[27] In December 1443 he and Rodrigo de Jaén and Gonsalve de Gobralyon obtained a safe-conduct,[28] but he and Jaén were already in England in November, living with Richard Riche in London.[29] In January 1444 they travelled down to Southampton where they stayed with John Emory,[30] probably to meet the cargo of sweet wine brought for Alfonso in the carrack of Giulio de Fornari.[31] By March they were back in London with Riche selling wines[32] but not until October were they back with Emory although Alfonso exported cloth on a Spanish ship and two Italian vessels in the summer.[33] Possibly he was delayed in London by a suit for £10 by John Hop of Almain.[34] Alfonso and Rodrigo applied for a renewal of safe-conduct presumably in 1446 but no grant has been found.[35] Dies's business was in moderately large consignments of twenty-eight, thirty-five, thirty-nine tuns of wine and exports of forty-eight whole cloths a time.

FRANCISCO DYES

Dyes may have been trading from 1425[36] and this would help explain his apparently sudden acceptance as a man of substance and integrity in 1453. He was almost certainly an Andalusian and was well known to the Genoese, Venetians and Florentines in London, with whom and for whom he stood surety and to whom he was in debt.[37] He obtained a safe-conduct for himself and five servants in 1453 for five years,[38] indicating larger business plans than most Spaniards, who bought safe-conducts usually for one to three years and for one or no servants. He traded on Italian, Spanish, Basque and Hanseatic ships between 1455 and 1458[39] and had his son James with him when Thomas Wattes ordered oil from them in 1457.[40] His exports were large at 80 to 132 cloths and so were his individual purchases—twenty-four cloths from draper Wattes, straits and westrons worth £171 14s 10d from draper John Derby and cloths worth £130 4s from an Essex dyer.[41] Silk worth £1,000 was alleged (and denied) to be his in 1458.[42] In 1458 cases concerning £778 of debts were begun against him,[43] and he disappeared thenceforth from English trade. Enquiries consequent on the suits established that at least three merchants had broken credit limits and one customs regulations for him; all faced charges until pardoned at the accession of Edward IV.[44] That Dyes was an accomplished fraud and never had the resources to cover trade on such a grand scale seems unlikely, since the Italian community could have checked his credentials in the south, and hardheaded merchants were used to weighing up a man's worth: more probably he had stretched his resources to the limits and beyond and then some misfortune such as wreck or piracy had caused a crash.

ANTONIO FERANDEZ

Ferández was another man of substance from Andalusia. He and his brother Juan received a one-year safe-conduct in 1427 on the petition and security of three Londoners, which had to be prorogued until 1429 owing to the prohibition on English trade by the Castilian king. In 1428 they used it to unload from a Portuguese ship eighty-two tuns of wine and three carpets at Southampton and ninety tuns of wine with other goods at Sandwich; Antonio then went up to London to buy cloth which he sent back down to Sandwich for loading on the Portuguese ship. In 1429 he exported more cloth worth £311 6s 8d from Southampton on another Portuguese ship. The customs paid on all this came nearly to the £100 the safe-conduct stipulated and his guarantors were quit.[45] Further safe-conducts were given to him and his son Juan with three carpet-workers in 1429 and 1430, and again he was permitted to use Portuguese ships.[46] He imported goods on Italian carracks to Southampton, sending wine on up to London, and he exported cloth from Southampton on another carrack using Cristoforo Cattaneo as his agent.[47] He bought an exemption from payment of extra alien poundage in 1431.[48] Juan Ferández, possibly his son, was still exporting from Southampton in 1433.[49]

Antonio's centre appears to be Andalusia, but his use of Portuguese ships indicates a strong interest there and his association with a Catalan in the poundage exemption suggests an extension eastwards too.

MARTIN GELDO

Geldo is an example of the modest northern shipmaster and merchant who worked for long periods in and out of English ports, but the possibility of there being a son or nephew of the same name makes biographical notes uncertain in places. On others' ships he exported cloth from London in 1463 and imported iron to Bristol in 1473[50] but generally he worked as master. He was a possible master for the *Juan of Guipúzcoa* with a safe-conduct in 1465, and of the *Juan of Pasajes* (probably the same ship) in 1466,[51] and he commanded the second, as the *San Juan of Pasajes*, in and out of Bridgwater that year. In 1472 he was master of the *Magdalene of Rentería* at Bristol but the following year brought the *Juan of Pasajes* there, unloading a cargo worth nearly £600, of which £50 worth was his, before leaving for Lisbon.[52] At about this time he was sued by Moses Conterin and John Hondeslo of Bristol for a trespass done abroad: no details were given but he may have been the master of the *San Juan of Pasajes* on which Nicholas Palmer had brought a cargo of fruit for Conterin too late for him to sell profitably.[53] In the cases against Geldo however he was called the master of the *San Juan of Fuenterrabía*, but this may be an error as the two towns are very close together. Geldo (or he and a namesake) continued to trade in and out of London, Plymouth, Bridgwater and Bristol from 1478 to 1491, generally as the master of the *Magdalene of Rentería* in later years.[54]

ALVARO GOMELL

Gomell is an example of a northerner whose interests soon extended to the south: he dealt mainly in iron and wine to Southampton from 1456 to 1469 using ships of Guipúzcoa, particularly of San Sebastián, but also one of Laredo.[55] His associates were mainly northerners such as Juan de Segura and Martín Ochoa (q.v.) but included Galicians such as Ferando de la Crouna (Corunna probably) and southerners such as Gómez de Baesa, and his cargoes of cork, fruit, bastard, romney and dates aboard Italian vessels indicate his southern interests.[56]

RODRIGO DE JAÉN

Rodrigo first appeared in England with a safe-conduct obtained in 1440 with Tomás de Gobralyon.[57] He then worked in London and Southampton at the same time as Alfonso Dies de Gobralyon (q.v.) and was still active in 1450 when he obtained a three-year safe-conduct for himself and an unnamed companion and attorney.[58]

FERAND MANION

The first reference to Ferand Manion of Spain comes in 1322 when he leased a brewhouse in London, and by 1324 he had become a citizen there.[59] He must have been in London for some time before that and may be the Ferand son of Domyngoun de Bytoria who was made London broker for Spanish goods in 1318;[60] to be made broker he must by then have been well known in London and may be the son of 'Domyngus mercator equorum de Ispannia' and 'Dominicus dictus manioun mercator de Ispannia', there in 1311 and 1312.[61]

He was well enough established in 1325 to be used in some capacity on a foreign embassy with Peter de Galiciano. Andrés Pérez de Castrogeriz and Pedro López Manion.[62] He was an active trader although relatively little is known of his business:

he was associated with Juan de Sagassola of Vitoria, and described as a Spanish merchant, in 1331 when John Pecche owed them £60, and again associated with Sagassola and was described as citizen of London when owed 200 marks in 1332.[63] He was among the richer men in Vintry Ward at this time but still far from the wealthiest.[64] He exported hides to Middelburg with a Londoner in 1337[65] and was guarantor for Spanish merchants in London in 1338.[66] He married in England, where he held land and travelled on business with his servants to Warwickshire and Leicestershire.[67] These Midland connections may indicate interest in wool, or may be to do with landholding. It is possible that he was turning to money-lending too, as the sums he was owed—£60 from Pecche and his son, 200 marks from Camois, £100 by Thomas of Lodlowe, Lord of Totyng, and £50 and £500 from the prior of Andover[68]—are suspiciously round numbers for mercantile transactions. He was one of the few merchants to have his debts enrolled in Chancery, indicating close association with Chancery business and clerks, possibly with James Manion of Spain, a clerk associated with Galiciano in 1327.[69] He was sent abroad on royal business again in 1345.[70]

PEDRO LÓPEZ MANION

Pedro was another of the merchants who settled in London and served the king abroad, and may have been a kinsman of Ferand.

He is possibly the Peter Loptz who was guarantor for men of Castro Urdiales, Santander and Laredo in a suit of compensation after piracy,[71] and possibly the Peter Manioun living in Cordwainer street and assessed at half a mark in 1319.[72] In 1325 Peter le Piz Mauron (also called Peter de Loupes Manioun de Ispannia) was sent abroad with Ferand Manion and Galiciano and in 1326 as Peter Loupes he was sent to Spain for Galiciano.[73] In 1330 as Peter Lopice Mangoun citizen and merchant of London he was sent to Gascony on the king's business.[74] By 1339, like Ferand, he was living in Vintry Ward.[75]

Throughout the period there are references to his trading activity, although the fairly common name of Peter López makes positive identification difficult at times. The Pedro Lup' bringing wine to London in 1318 and 1323 is probably he, but the Pedro López active in Sandwich in 1328 is said to be from Bermeo at a time when Manion is already a London citizen.[76] He was a London broker in 1338,[77] acting as guarantor for Spanish merchants exporting wheat in 1346,[78] and himself still exporting cloth in 1348.[79]

MARTÍN OCHOA DE YRIVE OF DEVA

Ochoa is a good example of the Biscayan master–merchant of solid means, probably also a ship-owner, who specialised in iron and wine but also had strong contacts with the south. For over thirty years he worked through Southampton, Sandwich and London. One of his earliest jobs in England was to sue Henry Gardygan of Bristol for debts owed to himself and other merchants of Deva and Motrico.[80] His consignments were generally large[81]—of iron he imported 58 tons in 1434, 298½ tons in 1436, 171 tons with 20 tuns of Biscay wine and beaver- and kid-skins, licorice and cummin in 1441, and the biggest single shipment was of 213 tons in 1457. His wine trade was only slightly smaller and in 1441 he brought 165½ tuns to Sandwich. This trade took him also to Andalusia where he arranged to act as a factor for John Emory and Piers James of Southampton.[82] Probably it was this southern trade which brought him into contact with the Italians for whom he stood surety in London in 1459.[83]

He applied for safe-conducts for Deva ships from 1436, particularly two called the *Jamys* and *Jacob* of Deva from 1441, and for the *S Jaime of Motrico* from 1460.[84] He himself was named a possible master several times, indicating a probable interest as owner or part-owner, and is recorded as master in several customs accounts. He was closely associated from 1456 with his son Pedro. Possibly he should be identified with Martín Ochoa de Irrasabar or Martín Cebala, both of Deva, who managed and owned ships in the Mediterranean: certainly Cebala owned a ship called the *S Jaime* and was associated with one Pedro of Deva.[85]

JUAN PARDO

He was another member of a Burgos family also involved in Bruges. Possibly he, as a young man, was the Juan Pardo who received a safe-conduct to come to England in 1440,[86] but in the later period he usually appeared in English records as a representative of Spaniards suing in England.

In 1483 he and Gonsalis de Salamanca complained of piracy against their goods being sent to England on a ship of Fuenterrabía,[87] and in December he and Pedro de Salamanca had to complain that their woad bound for Flanders had been seized by the English. In January 1484 he and Salamanca were described as Spaniards residing in London but this was probably only a temporary residence to sort out compensation.[88] Possibly wool had been among the cargo, because at this time an Englishman was to deliver wool to Pardo and Salamanca.[89] In August 1484 Pardo, the two Salamancas and seven others received a grant of £250 from their own customs and subsidies due, and a similar group obtained a further grant of 400 marks in March 1485.[90] These were no doubt in recompense for the Spanish and Breton ships seized with their goods. In 1491 Pardo was again suing for himself and others for goods lost from a wreck off Cornwall.[91] M. Mollat indicated that the Pardo family composed a network covering Bruges, Rouen, Lisbon and Seville by the early sixteenth century, but they were probably established in Seville some time before that.[92]

ANDRÉS PÉREZ DE CASTROGERIZ OF BURGOS

He and his brother Pedro were sons of another Pedro who was probably the Pedro Pérez de Bures in London in 1278.[93] Their home town of Castrogeriz is close to Burgos, but certainly Andrés and probably the others had moved into Burgos. The Luke Pérez associated with Andrés in 1281–2 may have been a kinsman too.[94]

Andrés and Pedro traded in London from 1278 to 1285 in skins, leathers, yarn and Spanish wool;[95] their activity seems to decline in the crisis of Sancho's accession but they continued to work in Gascony and their first safe-conduct given in 1297 referred to their service to the king during his wars in Gascony.[96] Pedro's name disappeared soon after this but Andrés periodically bought safe-conducts until his death twenty-eight years later.[97] He still traded substantially in London[98] and may have been exporting cloth from Boston in 1303 and Sandwich in 1304–5.[99]

Probably his Gascon activity brought him to the notice of the king, and he was known as king's merchant (probably a household supplier) in 1315, 1323 and 1324.[100] He went to Spain on the king's business in 1315 when he was also asked to help two English pilgrims to Santiago as they went through Burgos.[101] In 1325 he was a 'special envoy' from the King of Castile to England[102] and at this time he agreed to raise a loan of £6,000 in Spain for Edward II[103] and was further entrusted with 1,000 marks to buy warhorses there for Edward but he died (probably in the autumn of 1325) before he could do so.[104]

PEDRO SANS DE VENESSE

Pedro and his son, Juan, came from Fuenterrabía and Pedro traded with England for some thirty years—another example of the prosperous northern master-merchant.

He first appears in records in 1455 as a possible master of the *María of San Sebastián* and was then seven times possible master for various Spanish ships between 1456 and 1463.[105] Probably he had shares in some.[106] He certainly brought the *Katerina of Guipúzcoa* to Southampton in 1459 and 1460 and the *María* to Bristol in 1466.[107] It was through a Bristol merchant—William Isgar—that he obtained a safe-conduct in 1460 agreeing to pay the fairly heavy reward of £12 for each voyage made to Isgar.[108] He bought a trading licence to export beans in 1466 and a letter of protection to collect his debts in 1470 and 1471.[109] He also acted as part of the chain of communication between John Tryklowe in London and the Biscayan officials for Tryklowe's papers left in Biscay.[110] He dealt too in Bordeaux and La Rochelle.[111] He was probably a man of standing in his province and may have been among the negotiators of the provincial safe-conduct in 1470 and 1471 following which he received an annuity of £20 from Edward IV.[112] He died before 3 July 1482 when his son obtained protection against any marque for his servants, possessions and lands, which suggests that he held leases in England.[113] A Juan Sans de Venesse who was a possible ship-master from 1462 was probably his son.[114]

JUAN SEBOLL OF BURGOS

Here is a good example of the resident merchant willing to act as agent for others. His name is not a well-known Burgos one[115] but he was frequently associated with the Covarrubias from that city. In 1470 he, Diego and Ferando de Covarrubias and others obtained a two-year letter of protection for trading; in 1471 he was described as Ferand's factor, and in 1473 as factor of Ferand and others, and Diego called on him to rescue the Covarrubias goods claimed at Southampton by Davy Colwell. He and Juan de Covarrubias exported cloth from London together in 1472 and as a Covarrubias factor he was sued for their non-delivery of white soap to Thomas Wattes of London.[116] He was noted both as a factor for others and as a merchant in his own right in 1476.[117] Certainly his own interest extended to Andalusia where he sent cloth to and received wines from Juan de Medina at Lepe.[118] His name appears often in customs accounts for London, Bristol, Southampton, Sandwich and Dover, dealing in considerable amounts of oil, smigmate, iron, wine, woad, corn and occasionally coral and Venetian gold, some of it probably on behalf of principals.[119] He also had business contacts in Dartmouth and Lynn,[120] and not surprisingly came into contact at least with the Lomellini in London.[121] He seems too to have bought cloth in association with Londoners.[122]

In 1476 he was to go on the king's service with the Victualler of Calais,[123] and was permanently enough established in London to be a broker in 1470.[124]

PEDRO VALLADOLID

Pedro seems to have been fairly prosperous, deeply involved in London's cloth export, and linked with Bruges. Possibly the Pedro de Valea Dolyte, attorney for Pedro del Prado trading to England in two Biscayan ships in 1442, was this man at the beginning of his career[125] but forty years later he was of more substance. In 1480 he exported over fifty-two cloths from London, in 1481 over 270 from London and some from Bristol, and in 1483 over 116 from London.[126] In 1484 and 1485 he was among the group of merchants with grants from Edward IV payable out of their own customs and subsidies.[127] He continued to trade in the next decade and in 1490–1 had a close association with Thomas Boterell the London draper.[128]

Juan de Lopys from Bruges used him (called Peter Bayle et Delyte) to pay the Celys by exchange in London for their wool and to help acquire more of their wool.[129]

He may have been related to the Juan de Villa Doleta who was at Southampton to receive orchell from Corunna in 1470–1.[130]

NOTES TO APPENDIX

1   P.R.O. E122/19/11, 20/7, 142/8, 10, 194/23; SC6/896/14; E356/22 mm.40d, 72d.
2   P.R.O. C76/159 m.25.
3   *Cal. Proc. in Chanc.*, I, cii.
4   P.R.O. C1/82/38.
5   P.R.O. E356/22 mm.40d, 72d, 23 m.36; C.P.R. 1476–85, p. 531.
6   Gilliodts van Severen, *Étaple*, II, 220.
7   C.P.R. 1485–94, p. 340; Caster, *Le Commerce du pastel*, pp. 104, 113–16.
8   *Cely Letters*, ed. Hanham, No. 235.
9   P.R.O. E159/257 Recorda Hil. m.8.
10 P.R.O. SC6/896/10.
11 Gilliodts van Severen, *Consulat*, p. 103.
12 P.R.O. E122/194/19, 23, 24, 25.
13 P.R.O. C76/157 m.6.
14 C.P.R. 1476–85, p. 254.
15 P.R.O. C76/165 m.14.
16 P.R.O. E159/257 Recorda Hil. m.8.
17 P.R.O. C1/60/24.
18 Gilliodts van Severen, *Consulat*, p. 29.
19 P.R.O. C76/153 m.12; 155 m.28; 156 m.7.
20 P.R.O. E122/194/19, 20.
21 P.R.O. E122/194/20, 128/10; SC6/896/13.
22 C.P.R. 1467–77, p. 307.
23 P.R.O. C1/43/177–81.
24 *Ibid.*, 45/153.
25 P.R.O. C76/123 m.7.
26 P.R.O. E122/77/3.
27 P.R.O. C76/123 m.7.
28 *Ibid.*, 126 m.15.
29 P.R.O. E179/144/56.
30 P.R.O. E101/128/35.
31 P.R.O. E122/140/62.
32 P.R.O. E101/128/30.
33 P.R.O. E122/140/62; E179/173/110.

34   *Cal. of Plea and Memo. Rolls of London*, v, 61.

35   P.R.O. SC8/9257. This could be the petition for the 1443 grant in which case the 'previous grant' referred to must be one of 1440 or 1441.

36   P.R.O. C76/108 m.9.

37   C.C.R. *1454–61*, p. 311; P.R.O. E101/128/36 m.3; E159/235 Recorda Mich. m.54, Hil. m.11.

38   P.R.O. C76/136 m.14; this was temporarily violated at Rochester; C1/22/119.

39   Ms. S.P.B. 1455–6, Lib. Al., fo. 42v; P.R.O. C76/139 mm.12, 23; E159/235 Recorda Trin. m.26d.

40   P.R.O. E101/128/36.

41   P.R.O. E159/235 Recorda Trin. mm.26d, 33, 46, 53, 54; 236 Recorda Mich. m.38.

42   P.R.O. E159/235 Recorda Mich. m.54, Hil. m.11.

43   P.R.O. E28/86 (42); *ibid.*, 88 (2 Dec. 37 Hen. VI); and as note 42 above.

44   As note 41 above.

45   P.R.O. C76/109 m.3; SC8/9064; E159/205 Recorda Mich. m.25: SC6/895/13. The second ship was said to be a carrack with patron Felipe de Grimaldi so was probably Italian rather than Portuguese.

46   P.R.O. C76/111 m.5; 113 m.6.

47   Ms. S.P.B. 1429–30, fos. 76–7.

48   C.P.R. *1429–36*, p. 185.

49   P.R.O. E122/141/21.

50   *Ibid.*, 19/10, 194/14.

51   P.R.O. C76/149 m.17; 150 m.19.

52   P.R.O. E122/26/6, 28/9, 19/9, 10.

53   P.R.O. C1/48/114, 164.

54   P.R.O. E122/20/5, 7, 9, 28/10, 114/10, 194/23, 24, 25.

55   Ms. S.P.B. 1455–6, fo. 29; Ms. S.P.B. 1459–60, Lib. Comm. (unfol.), 3 Oct, 3 Nov., 20 Jan., 19 Feb., 31 Mar.; C.P.R. *1452–61*, p. 441; P.R.O. C76/142 mm.10, 28.

56   Ms. S.P.B. 1459–60, Lib. Al. (unfol.), 5 and 26 Mar.; C.P.R. *1452–61*, p. 439; P.R.O. C76/140 m.17; SC8/15733.

57   P.R.O. C76/123 mm.32, 23.

58   *Ibid.*, 132 m.6.

59   *Letter Book 'E'*, pp. 175, 186, 191.

60   *Ibid.*, p. 97.

61   London Record Office, Recognisance Rolls, VII, mm. 6, 8.

62   C.P.R. *1324–7*, pp. 82, 181; C.C.R. *1323–7*, p. 515.

63   C.C.R. *1330–3*, pp. 309, 391, 559; *ibid.*, *1334–7*, p. 308 (Sagassola was trading from 1326 in peltry and Spanish wool: E122/136/29; C.P.R. *1327–30*, pp. 241, 418, 493).

64   P.R.O. E179/144/4.

65   C.F.R. *1337–47*, p. 5.

66   C.P.R. *1334–8*, p. 571.

67   *Letter Book 'E'*, pp. 175, 186, 302; C.P.R. *1338–41*, pp. 10, 23.

68   C.C.R. *1333–7*, p. 339; *ibid.*, *1337–9*, p. 539; *ibid.*, *1343–6*, p. 127.

69   *Ibid.*, *1327–30*, p. 103.

70   P.R.O. C76/21 m.10.

71   C.P.R. *1313–17*, p. 34.

72   Ekwal, *op. cit.*, pp. 48, 266.

73   C.P.R. *1324–7*, pp. 82, 181, 305; C.C.R. *1323–7*, p. 515.

74   C.P.R. *1330–4*, p. 87.

75 *Cal. Cor. Rolls*, p. 216.

76 P.R.O. E122/69/9, 147/14.

77 *Cal. Plea and Memo. Rolls of London*, I, 147.

78 C.P.R. *1345–8*, p. 198; C.C.R. *1346–9*, p. 117.

79 *Ibid.*, p. 56.

80 P.R.O. C1/12/51.

81 P.R.O. E159/208, Recorda Easter m.10d, Trin m.10d, SC6/896/1, 10; E122/142/1, 3, 209/8; E101/82/5, 7, 128/31; Ms. S.P.B. 1433–4, fo. 16; *ibid.*, 1457–8, Lib. Comm. (unfol.), 11 Oct., 7 Feb.; *ibid.*, 1459–60, Lib. Comm. (unfol.), 3 Dec., 30 Apr., 19 Feb., 28 Jun.; S.P.B. *1435–6*, ed. Foster, pp. 36, 52, 58, 60.

82 P.R.O. C1/16/656, 17/235.

83 C.C.R. *1454–61*, p. 332.

84 P.R.O. C76/122 m.15; 123 m.20; 124 m.22; 126 m.4; 128 m.5; 131 m.10; 138 m.20; 139 mm.12, 23, 24; 141 m.16; 142 mm.15, 18; 145 m.35; 147 mm.12, 20; 148 m.7; Nicolas, *Procs. and Ords. of the Privy Council*, IV, 177.

85 Heers, 'Le commerce des Basques', *loc. cit.*, p. 304.

86 P.R.O. C76/123 m.37. He held it with Pedro de Giberlion.

87 C.P.R. *1476–85*, pp. 347, 355.

88 C.P.R. *1476–85*, p. 426; the Pardos became an important family in the Toulouse woad trade—Caster, *Le Commerce du pastel*, 120–1.

89 C.C.R. *1476–85*, No. 1222.

90 See above, p. 57 and under Diego de Castro.

91 C.P.R. *1485–94*, p. 358.

92 Mollat, 'Le rôle international des marchands espagnols', *loc. cit.*, IV, 106–7; Pardo's association with Pedro de Giberlion (Gibraleón, near Huelva?) in 1440, and Gabriel Pardo's imports to Bristol from Seville in 1475 (E122/19/11), suggest this.

93 *Letter Book 'A'*, pp. 20, 22, 23, 26: Bures, Buros, Burgo or Burgh' and Castro Suris are the usual forms of the names, but that Burgos and Castrogeriz are meant seems clear, especially as the name Andrés Péres de Castroxerix appears in the Burgos records of that time (Arch. Munic. de Burgos, ser. histor., num. 652.)

94 *Letter Book 'A'*, pp. 38, 55. Luke was also active in Gascony; *Rôles Gascons*, ed. Bémont, III, 4959; *ibid.*, ed. Renouard, No. 202.

95 *Letter Book 'A'*, pp. 26, 34, 35, 37, 38, 45, 46, 55; London Record Office, Recognisance Rolls, I.

96 *Rôles Gascons*, ed. Bémont, III, 4395.

97 C.Ch.Warr., I, 151, 401; C.P.R. *1292–1301*, p. 450; *ibid.*, *1301–7*, pp. 7, 165; *ibid.*, *1307–13*, pp. 139, 451; *ibid.*, *1313–17*, pp. 116, 299; *ibid.*, *1317–21*, pp. 2, 559; *ibid.*, *1321–4*, p. 266.

98 *Letter Book 'B'*, pp. 121, 166; London Record Office, Recognisance Rolls, VI; C.C.R. *1323–7*, pp. 334, 339.

99 P.R.O. E122/5/7, 124/13.

100 C.Ch.Warr., I, 417, 558; C.C.R. *1313–18*, p. 310; C.P.R. *1321–4*, p. 266; *ibid.*, *1324–7*, p. 2.

101 C.Ch.Warr., I, 417; C.C.R. *1313–18*, p. 310.

102 C.C.R. *1323–7*, p. 346; C.P.R. *1324–7*, p. 84.

103 *Ibid.*, p. 93.

104 *Ibid.*, *1330–4*, p. 230, 364; P.R.O. E159/108 Recorda Mich.

105 P.R.O. C76/138 mm.8, 30; 139 m.9; 140 mm.6, 20, 24; 141 mm.22, 34; 142 m.25; 145 m.9; 146 m.14; 147 m.19.

106 The phrasing suggests he owned the *María* of Guipúzcoa in 1466; C76/150 mm.4, 20.

107   Ms. S.P.B. 1459–60, Lib. Comm. (unfol.), 3 Oct., 3 Nov., 20 Jan.; E122/19/4.
108   P.R.O. C1/29/390.
109   P.R.O. C76/150 m.5; C.P.R. *1467–77*, pp. 205, 281.
110   P.R.O. C1/59/170.
111   P.R.O. C76/141 m.22; 155 m.24; C.P.R. *1467–77*, p. 378.
112   Ibid., p. 273; P.R.O. E159/254 Recorda Mich. m.13d.
113   C.P.R. *1476–85*, p. 323.
114   Exeter City Library, loc. cust. accts., 1–2 Ed. IV; P.R.O. C76/145 m.19, 146 m.14.
115   P.R.O. C1/60/5 describes him as from Burgos.
116   See Covarrubias, above.
117   C.P.R. *1467–77*, p. 599.
118   C.C.R. *1468–76*, No. 709; P.R.O. C1/46/444.
119   P.R.O. E122/19/8, 128/14, 15, 194/19, 20; C1/60/5; *S.P.B. Ed IV*, ed. Quinn and Ruddock, I, 73, 78.
120   C.C.R. *1468–76*, No. 1104, P.R.O. C1/67/122.
121   *Cal. Plea and Memo. Rolls of London*, VI, 69.
122   P.R.O. C1/64/254, 1069.
123   P.R.O. C76/159 m.5.
124   P.R.O. C1/32/354; *Acts of Court of the Mercers' Company*, ed. Lyell, p. 111.
125   P.R.O. C76/125 m.18.
126   P.R.O. E122/194/24, 25, 26.
127   See Chapter 2, note 139, and under Diego de Castro.
128   C.P.R. *1485–1500*, Nos. 530, 661.
129   *Cely Letters*, ed. Hanham, Nos. 201–2, 204–9, 215, 217–18, 221.
130   P.R.O. C1/43/177.

BIBLIOGRAPHY

PRIMARY SOURCES

The most productive records have been those of the English government preserved at the Public Record Office, and the only hope of quantitative information lies in the enrolled and particular accounts of petty custom and tunnage and poundage payments. These are supplemented by the local accounts for Sandwich, whose bailiff was a royal official, the accounts of the Keeper of the Ports for Cornwall, and the accounts of the King's Butlers and the Constables of Bordeaux.

Information on the organisation of the trade, in the absence of merchants' papers and notarial documents, which have done so much to clarify Italian trade of the time, has had to be drawn from more indirect sources. Privileges, licences, safe-conducts and legal suits can be found on the patent, close, liberate, fine and treaty rolls, among miscellaneous inquisitions and in petitions to king, council or chancellor, although all too often the defendant's reply, the evidence and the judgement are missing. Commercial cases brought before the Exchequer, subsidy rolls and the section on alien merchants in the Exchequer various accounts also provide valuable material.

Local archive material, much of it printed, has also proved particularly useful for London, Southampton, Exeter and Bristol, but local customs accounts, because of the numerous exemptions from local dues, cannot provide as reliable quantitative information as the national customs accounts.

The Spanish documentary evidence is more disappointing. In Castile a lack of any tradition of care in the keeping of royal records until the union of Aragon and Castile in the marriage of Ferdinand and Isabella (Archivo General de Simancas. Guía del investigador, ed. A. de la Plaza Bores, Dirección General de Archivos y Bibliotecas (1962), p. xxviii) means that there are not potentially rich economic sources surviving as in England: many of the documents at Simancas, Valladolid and other central depositories are post-medieval, and many of the medieval documents which do survive prove to be those of most concern to historians of Spain's internal history and politics rather than of overseas trade.

Local archives have also proved disappointing, and the municipal archives and Diputaciónes of Burgos, Bilbao, San Sebastián and Santander, the centres of the northern provinces most concerned with English trade, produced almost nothing. Many records have been lost and those best preserved are those of most value to the towns—their charters of rights and privileges. No records of the corregidors, before whom Englishmen sued, and few notarial documents survive for before the sixteenth century, but a number of single documents of local interest, and some of more general interest have been printed in local histories.

Most of the information about Spanish overseas trade prior to the sixteenth century has so far been found in overseas archives, and most modern Spanish works on economic history still find themselves forced to rely on such sources.

Printed sources have been listed under the name of author or editor except for well-known calendars and collections which are cited under their titles in the usual way.

A   *Manuscript sources*

Public Record Office
  Chancery:
    C1   Early Chancery Proceedings
    C47   Chancery Miscellanea
    C49   Parliamentary and Council Proceedings
    C61   Gascon Rolls
    C76   Treaty Rolls
  Exchequer:
    E28   T.R. Council and Privy Seal Records
    E30   T.R. Diplomatic Documents
    E101   K.R. Accounts, Various
    E122   K.R. Customs Accounts
    E159   K.R. Memoranda Rolls
    E163   K.R. Miscellanea
    E175   K.R. Parliamentary and Council Proceedings
    E179   K.R. Subsidy Rolls
    E356   L.T.R. Enrolled Customs Accounts
    E358   L.T.R. Memoranda Rolls
  Special collections:
    SC1   Ancient Correspondence
    SC6   Ministers' and Receivers' Accounts
    SC8   Ancient Petitions
British Library
  Additional Ms. 15524—account of the Constable of Bordeaux 1444–5
  Cotton Ms. Vespasian C xii—documents concerning negotiations between the
    Basque Provinces and Edward IV
Corporation of the City of London
  Records Office:
    Recognisance Rolls
  Guildhall Library Muniment Room:
    Registers of Wills proved in the Commissary Court of London
    Registers of Wills proved in the Archdeaconry Court of London
Exeter City Library
  Local customs accounts Edward I—Henry VII
Southampton Civic Centre
  Local customs accounts (Port Books) (these were read by means of the mic-
    rofilm deposited in the library of the London School of Economics)
Archivo General de Simancas
  Registro General de Sello
Archivo Municipal de Bilbao
  Cajón 4 Registro 2
Archivo Municipal de Burgos
  Serie histórica

B   *Printed sources*

*Archivo Histórico Español. Colección de documentos inéditos para la Historia de
España y de sus Indias*, 6 vols. Academia de Estudios Histórico-sociales de
Valladolid (Madrid, 1928–34).

Archivo General de Navarra. Catálogo de la Sección de Comptos: documentos, ed. J. Castro y F. Idoate, 46 vols. (Pamplona, 1952ff).

Baildon, W. P. (ed.), *Select Cases in the Court of Chancery (1364–1471)*. Seldon Society pubns., vol. 10 (1896).

Baldwin, J. F., see Leadam, I. S.

Balducci Pegalotti, F., *La Pratica della mercatura*, ed. A. Evans. Medieval Academy of America, pub. No. 24 (Cambridge, Mass., 1936).

Bémont, C., see *Rôles Gascons*

Bickley, F. B. (ed.), *The Little Red Book of Bristol*, 2 vols. (Bristol, 1900).

Borghetty, H., see Rosetti, G.

Boyd, P. (ed.), *Roll of the Drapers' Company of London; collected from the Company's Records and other Sources* (Croydon, 1934).

Brutails, J. A. (ed.), *Documents des Archives de la Chambre des Comptes de Navarre*. Bibliotèque de l'École des Hautes Études, No. 84 (Paris, 1890).

Calendar of the Black and White Books of the Cinque Ports, 1432–1955. Historical Manuscripts Commission (1966).

Calendar of Chancery Rolls, Various, 1277–1326 (London, 1912).

Calendar of Chancery Warrants, Privy Seals, 1244–1326 (London, 1927).

Calendar of Close Rolls, 1272–1500, 47 vols. (London, 1892–1956).

Calendar of Fine Rolls, 1272–1509, 22 vols. (London, 1911–63).

Calendar of Liberate Rolls, 1226–1272, 6 vols. London, 1917–64).

Calendar of miscellaneous Inquisitions, Henry III – Henry V, 7 vols. (London, 1916–68).

Calendar of Patent Rolls, 1232–1509, 52 vols. (London, 1891–1916).

Calendar of Coroners' Rolls preserved among the Archives of the Corporation of the City of London, 1300–1378, ed. R. R. Sharpe (London, 1913).

Calendar of Early Mayors' Court Rolls preserved among the Archives of the Corporation of the City of London, 1298–1307, ed. A. H. Thomas (London, 1924).

Calendar of Letter Books preserved among the Archives of the Corporation of the City of London, 1275–1498, Books 'A'—'L', 11 vols., ed R. R. Sharpe (London, 1899–1912).

Calendar of Letters from the Mayor, Aldermen and Commonalty of the City of London preserved among the Archives of the Corporation of the City of London, 1350–1370, ed. R. R. Sharpe (London, 1885).

Calendar of Plea and Memoranda Rolls preserved among the Archives of the Corporation of the City of London, 1323–1482, 6 vols. ed. A. H. Thomas (vols. 1–4) and P. E. Jones (vols. 5–6) (Cambridge, 1926–61).

Calendar of State Papers, Spanish, see *Letters, Dispatches* . . .

Calendar of Wills proved and enrolled in the Court of Husting, London, 1258–1688, preserved among the Archives of the Corporation of the City of London, 2 vols. ed. R. R. Sharpe (London, 1889–90).

Capmany i Montpalau, A. de, *Memorias históricas sobre la marina, comercio y artes de la antigue ciudad de Barcelona*, 2 vols. in 3 (reprinted Barcelona, 1961–3).

Carte, T., see *Catalogue des rolles gascons*.

Carus-Wilson, E. M. (ed.), *The Overseas Trade of Bristol in the Later Middle Ages*. Bristol Record Society pubns., VII (Bristol, 1937).

Castro, A., 'Unos aranceles de aduanas del siglo XIII', *Revista de Filología Española*, vol. 8 (1921).

Castro, J., see *Archivo General de Navarra*.

Catalogue des rolles gascons, normans et francois conservés dans les archives de la Tour de Londres, 2 vols., ed. T. Carte (London, 1743).

Cely Letters, see Hanham, A.
Chaucer, G., The Works of Geoffrey Chaucer, ed. F. N. Robinson, 2nd ed. (London, 1957).
Close Rolls 1227–1272, 16 vols. (London, 1902–38).
Cobb, H. S. (ed.), The Local Port Book of Southampton for 1439–40. Southampton Record Series, v (Southampton, 1961).
Cole, C. A. (ed.), Memorials of Henry the Fifth, King of England. Rolls Series, xi (London, 1858).
Colección de cédulas, cartas patentes, provisiónes, reales ordenes, y otros documentos concernientes a las provincias vascongadas, 4 vols., ed T. Gonzáles (Madrid, 1829–33).
Colección de documentos históricos. Boletín de la Academia Gallega, 3 vols. (Corunna, 1915–50).
Colección de documentos históricos del archivo municipal de la muy noble y muy leal ciudad de San Sebastián, 1200–1895, ed. B. Anabitarte (San Sebastián, 1895).
Colección de documentos inéditos para la historia de Guipúzcoa. Publicada por la exelentisima Diputación de Guipúzcoa, 3 vols. (San Sebastián, 1958).
Colección de documentos inéditos para la historia de España, 112 vols. (Madrid, 1842–95)
Coleman, O. (ed.), The Brokage Book of Southampton, 1443–4, 2 vols. Southampton Record Series, iv, vi (Southampton, 1960–1).
Colvin, H. M. (ed.), Building Accounts of King Henry III (Oxford, 1971).
Cortes de los antiguos reinos de León y de Castilla. Publica das por la Real Academia de la Historia, 5 vols. (Madrid, 1883–1903).
Curia Regis Rolls, Richard I–17 Henry III, 14 vols. (London, 1923–61).
Devon, F. (ed.), Issues of the Exchequer; being a Collection of Payments made out of His Majesty's Revenue, from King Henry III to King Henry VI inclusive (London, 1837).
Diez de Games, G., El Victorial. Crónica de don Pero Niño, conde de Buelna, por su alférez, ed. J. de Mata Carriazo. Colección de crónicas españolas, vol. i (Madrid, 1940).
Diplomatic Documents, 1101–1272, ed P. Chaplais (London, 1964).
Documentos reales de la edad media referentes a Galicia, ed. L. Sánchez Belda (Madrid, 1953).
Doehaerd, R. Les Relations commerciales entre Génes, la Belgique, et l'Outremont d'après les archives notariales génoises aux XIIIe et XIVe siècles, 3 vols. (Brussels, 1941).
Doehaerd, R., and Kerremans, C., Les Relations commerciales entre Génes, la Belgique, et l'Outremont d'après les archives notariales génoises 1400–1440 (Brussels, 1952).
Du Bus, G., Le Roman de Fauvel, ed. A. Långfors. Société des Anciens Textes Francais, No. 63 (Paris, 1914–19).
Edelstein, S., see Rosetti, G.
Ekwall, E. (ed.), Two Early London Subsidy Rolls. Skrifter utgivna av Kungl. Humanistiska Vetenskapssamfundet i Lund, XLVIII (Lund, 1951).
Ercker, L., Treatise on Ores and Assaying, trans. A. Sisco and C. S. Smith (Chicago, 1951).
Evans, A. (ed), see Balducci Pegalotti.
Evans, J. (ed.), The Unconquered Knight. A Chronicle of D. Pero Niño, Count of Buelna (London, 1928).
Fermoy, B., see Jenkinson, Sir H.

Flenley, R. (ed.), Six Town Chronicles of England (Oxford, 1911).

Foedera, see Rymer, T.

Fortescue, Sir J., The Commodyties of England, ed. Rev. T. O. Payne (1863).

Foster, B. (ed.), The Local Port Book of Southampton for 1435–6. Southampton Record Series, VII (Southampton, 1963).

Fowler, J. (ed.), Extracts from the Account Rolls of the Abbey of Durham, 3 vols. Surtees Society pubns., vols. 99, 100, 103 (1898–1901).

Gascon Rolls preserved in the Public Record Office, 1307–1317, ed. Y. Renouard under supervision of R. Fawtier (London, 1962).

Gidden, H. W. (ed.), The Stewards' Books of Southampton from 1428, 2 vols. Southampton Record Society (Southampton, 1935, 1939).

Gilliodts van Severen, L. (ed.), Cartulaire de l'ancien Consulat d'Espagne à Bruges. Recueil de documents concernants le commerce maritime et intérieur, le droit des gens public et privé et l'histoire économique de la Flandre. Première partie, 1280–1550 (Bruges, 1901–2).

——— Cartulaire de l'ancienne Étaple de Bruges. Recueil de documents concernants le commerce intérieur et maritime, les relations internationales et l'histoire économique de cette ville, 2 vols. (Bruges, 1903–6).

——— Inventaire des archives de la ville de Bruges. Section première. Inventaire des chartes. Première série. Treizième au seizième siècles, 9 vols. (Bruges, 1871–85).

Gras, N. S. B., The Early English Customs System. Harvard Economic Studies, vol. 18 (Cambridge, Mass., 1918).

Gross, C. (ed.), Select Cases concerning the Law Merchant, vol. 1. Seldon Society pubns., vol. 23 (1908).

Hall, H. (ed.), Select Cases concerning the Law Merchant, vols. 2–3. Seldon Society pubns., vols. 46, 49 (1929, 1932).

Hall, H. and Nichols, F. J. (eds.), 'Select tracts and table books relating to English weights and measures, 1100–1742', Camden Miscellany XV. Camden Society pubns., 3rd ser., vol XLI, R.H.S. (1929).

Hamilton Thomas, A. (ed.), Northumberland Pleas from the Curia Regis and Assize Rolls, 1198–1272. Newcastle-upon-Tyne Records Committee pubns., vol. II (1922).

Hanham, A. (ed.), The Cely Letters 1472–1488, E.E.T.S., No. 273 (1975).

Hawthorn, J. G. (ed.), see Theophilus.

Hemmant, M. (ed.), Select Cases in the Exchequer Chamber, 2 vols. Seldon Society pubns., vols. 51, 64 (1933, 1945).

Hingeston, F. C. (ed.), Royal and Historical Letters during the Reign of Henry the Fourth, King of England, 2 vols. Rolls series (London, 1860, 1965).

Jenkinson, Sir H., and Fermoy, B. (eds.), Select Cases in the Exchequer of Pleas. Seldon Society pubns., vol. 48 (1931).

Jones, P. E. (ed.), see Calendar of Plea and Memoranda Rolls.

Koppman, K. (ed.), Das Seebuch. Verein für niederdeutsche Sprachforschung, Niederdeutsche Denkmaler, vol. I (Bremen, 1876).

Lamond, E. (ed.), A Discourse of the Common Weal of this Realm of England (Cambridge, 1893).

Leadam, I. S. (ed.), Select Cases before the King's Council in the Star Chamber. Seldon Society pubns., vol. 16 (1902).

Leadam I. S. and Baldwin, J. F. (eds.), Select Cases before the King's Council (1245–1482). Seldon Society pubns., vol. 35 (1918).

Letts, M., see Tafur, P.

Liagre-de Sturler, L., Les Relations commerciales entre Génes, la Belgique et l'Outremont d'après les archives notariales génoises 1320–1400, 2 vols. (Brussels, 1969).

Libelle of Englyshe Polycye, see Warner, Sir G. (ed.).

Livre des Établissements. Archives Municipales de Bayonne, transcribed by E. Ducère and P. Yturbide (Bayonne, 1892).

Los codigos españoles concordados y anotados, 12 vols. (Madrid, 1847–51).

Lyell, L. (ed.), Acts of Court of the Mercers' Company, 1453–1527 (Cambridge, 1936).

Marsden, R. G. (ed.), Documents relating to the Law and Custom of the Sea, vol. I (A.D, 1205–1648). Navy Records Society, vol. XLIX (1915).

——Select Pleas in the Court of Admiralty (1390–1404; 1527–1545). Seldon Society pubns., vol. 6 (1892).

Mato Carriazo, J. de (ed.), see Diez de Games.

Memorial histórico español. Colección de documentos, opusculas y antigüedadas. Documentos de la epoca de D. Alfonso el Sabio. Real Academia de la Historia, 2 vols. (Madrid, 1851).

Mollat, M. (ed.), Comptabilité du port de Dieppe au XVe siècle. École Pratique des Hautes Études, VIe section, Centre de Recherches Historiques, Ports, Routes, Trafics, vol. IV (Paris, 1951).

Munimenta Gildhallae Londoniensis, see Riley, H. T.

Murray, K. M. E. (ed.), Register of Daniel Rough, common clerk of Romney, 1353–1380. Kent Archaeological Society Records Branch, vol. XVI (Ashford, 1945).

Nichols, F. J. see Hall, H.

Nicolas, Sir N. (ed.), Proceedings and Ordinances of the Privy Council of England, 10 Richard II—33 Henry VIII, 7 vols. (London, 1834–7).

Palgrave, Sir F. (ed.), Ancient Kalendars and Inventories of the Treasury of H.M. Exchequer, 3 vols. (London, 1836).

Patent Rolls, 1216–32, 2 vols. (London, 1901–3).

Payne, Rev. T. O. (ed.), see Fortescue, Sir J.

Power, E. (ed.), see Tawney, R. H.

Proceedings in Chancery in the Reign of Queen Elizabeth I, with examples of proceedings from Richard II. Calendars, ed. J. Caley and J. Bayley, 3 vols. (London, 1827–32).

Pyne, H. (ed.), England and France in the Fifteenth Century. The contemporary French tract entitled 'The Debate between the Heralds of France and England', presumed to have been written by Charles, Duke of Orleans (London, 1870).

Quinn, D. B., and Ruddock, A. A. (eds.), The Port Books or Local Customs Accounts of Southampton in the Reign of Edward IV, 2 vols. Southampton Record Society pubns., vols. 37–8 (Southampton, 1937–8).

Reddaway, T. F., and Ruddock, A. A. (eds.), 'The accounts of John Balsall, purser of the Trinity of Bristol 1480–1', Camden Miscellany XXIII. Camden Society pubns., 4th ser., vol. 7, R.H.S. (1969).

'Registre de la Comptablie de Bordeaux 1482–3', transcrit par M. G. Ducaunnes-Duval, Archives historiques du département de la Gironde, vol. L (1915).

Renouard, Y. (ed.), see Gascon Rolls.

Ricart, R., The Maire of Bristowe is Kalendar, ed. L. Toulmin Smith. Camden Society pubns, new ser., vol. V, R.H.S. (1872).

Riley, H. T. (ed.), Munimenta Gildhallae Londoniensis, 2 vols. Rolls Series, XII (London, 1859–60).

Robinson, F. N. (ed.), see Chaucer, G.

Rodriguez Herrero, A., *Valmaseda en el siglo XV y la aljama de los judíos* (Bilbao, 1947).

Rôles Gascons, transcrits et publiés par C. Bémont, 3 vols. Collection de documents inédits sur l'histoire de France, sér. I (Paris, 1896–1906).

Rosetti, G., *Plictho. Instructions in the Art of the Dyers which teaches the Dyeing of Woolen Cloths, Linen, Cottons, Silk by the Great Art as well as by the Common*, trans. of the 1st ed. (1548) by S. M. Edelstein and H. C. Borghetty (Cambridge, Mass., 1969).

Rotuli Litterarum Clausarum in Turri Londoniensi asservati, 1204–1227, 2 vols., ed. T. D. Hardy (London, 1833–44).

Rotuli Litterarum Patentium in Turri Londoniensi asservati, 1201–16, ed. T. D. Hardy (London, 1835).

Rotuli Parliamentorum, Edward I—Henry VII, 6 vols. and index (London, 1783, 1832).

Ruddock, A. A. (ed.), *see* Quinn, D. B., Reddaway, T. F.

Rymer, T. (ed.), *Foedera, Conventiones, Litterae, et Cuiuscumque Generis Acta Publica inter Reges Angliae et Alios quosvis Imperatores, Reges, Pontifices, vel Comunitates, ab Ineunte Saeculo Duodecimo, vix Anno 1101 ad nostra usque Tempora, Habita aut Tractata, 1066–1383 A.D.*, 4 vols. Record Commission (London, 1816–69), 1383 A.D. ff., 3rd ed. 10 vols. (The Hague, 1739–45).

Sayles, G. O. (ed.), *Select Cases in the Court of King's Bench under Edward I, II, and III*, 5 vols. Seldon Society pubns, vols 55, 57, 58, 74, 76 (1936–57).

Sharpe, R. R., *see Calendars of Coroners' Rolls, Letter Books, Letters from the Mayors, and Wills.*

Sisco, A. (ed.), *see* Ercker, L.

Smith, C. S. (ed.), *see* Ercker, L., Theophilus.

Smythe, John, *see* Vanes, J. (ed.).

Statutes of the Realm, ed. A. Luders, Sir. T. E. Tomlins. J. F. France, W. E. Taunton, J. Raithby, J. Caley, and W. Elliot, 11 vols. (London, 1810–28).

Stevenson, J. (ed.), *Wars of the English in France during the reign of Henry VI, King of England, Letters and Papers*, 2 vols. (London, 1861–4).

Studer, P. (ed.), *The Oak Book of Southampton*, 3 vols. Southampton Record Society pubns. (Southampton, 1910–11).

—— *The Port Books of Southampton, 1427–30*. Southampton Record Society pubns. (Southampton, 1913).

Tafur, Pero, *Travels and Adventures*, ed. M. Letts (London, 1926).

Tawney, R. H., and Power, E. (eds.), *Tudor Economic Documents*, 3 vols. (London, 1924).

Theophilus, *On Divers Arts*, ed. and trans. J. G. Hawthorne and C. S. Smith (Chicago, 1963).

Thomas, A. H. (ed.)., *see Calendars of Early Mayors' Court Rolls, and Plea and Memoranda Rolls.*

Torre, A. and E. A. de la (eds.), *Cuentas de Gonzalo de Baeza, tesorero de Isabel la Católica, 1477–1504*, 2 vols. Consejo Superior de Investigaciónes Cientificas, Patronato M. Menendez Pelayo, Biblioteca 'Reyes Católicos' Documentos y Textos, núms. V y VI (Madrid, 1955–6).

'Treatise concerninge the Staple and the commodities of this Realme', *Tudor Economic Documents*, vol. III, ed. R. H. Tawney and E. Power (London, 1924).

Treaty Rolls, 1234–1325, ed. P. Chaplais (London, 1955).

Twiss, Sir T. (ed.), *Black Book of the Admiralty*, 4 vols. Rolls Series, LV (London, 1871–6).

Vanes, J. (ed.), *The Ledger of John Smythe 1538–1550*. Bristol Record Society pubns., vol. XXVIII, and joint pubn. No. 19 of the Historical Manuscripts Commission (H.M.S.O., 1975).

Veale, E. W. W. (ed.), *The Great Red Book of Bristol*, 5 vols. Bristol Record Society pubns., vols. II, IV, VIII, XVI, XVIII (Bristol, 1931–53).

Wadley, T. P. (ed.), *Notes or Abstracts of the Wills contained in the volume entitled The Great Orphan Book and Book of Wills*. Bristol and Gloucestershire Archaeological Society (Bristol, 1886).

Warner, Sir G. (ed.), *The Libelle of Englyshe Polycye* (Oxford, 1926).

Watkin, H. R. (ed.), *Dartmouth*, vol. I, Pre-Reformation.Devonshire Association for the Advancement of Science, Literature and Art, Parochial Histories of Devon, No. 5 (1935).

Wey, W., *The Itineraries of William Wey, fellow of Eton College, to Jerusalem A.D. 1458 and A.D. 1462 and to St James of Compostella A.D. 1456*. Roxburghe Club (London, 1857, 1867).

Wilson, K. P. (ed.), *Chester Customs Accounts 1301–1566*. The Record Society of Lancashire and Cheshire, vol. CXI (1969).

SECONDARY SOURCES

This select bibliography includes all books and articles cited in the notes, and those uncited which none the less were found most useful in the general construction of the economic and political background to Anglo-Castilian trade.

My indebtedness to the many scholars whose work is not cited here as being not directly relevant to Anglo-Castilian trade is none the less enormous.

Aguado Bleye, P., *Manual de historia de España*, 3 vols., 6th ed. (Madrid, 1947–57).

Altamira, R., 'Spain, 1252–1410', and 'Spain, 1412–1516', *The Cambridge Medieval History*, vols. VII, VIII, ed. J. R. Tanner, C. W. Previté-Orton, and Z. N. Brooke (Cambridge, 1932, 1936).

Anderson. R. and R. C., *The Sailing Ship. Six Thousand Years of History* (London, 1926).

Arocena, I., 'Bermeo medieval', *Boletín de la Real Sociedad Vascongada de los Amigos del País*, cuaderno 4 año XX (1964).

Artiñano y de Guldacano, G. de. *La arquitectura naval española (en madera)* (Madrid, 1920).

Assas, M. de, *Crónica de la Provincia de Santander* (Santander, 1867).

Bagrow, L., *History of Cartography*, revised and enlarged by R. A. Skelton (London, 1964).

Ballesteros y Beretta, A., *Alfonso X el Sabio* (Barcelona, 1963).

—— *Sevilla en el siglo XIII* (Madrid, 1913).

Balpardo y las Herrerías, G. de, *Historia crítica de Vizcaya y de sus Fueros*, 3 vols. (Madrid, 1924–45).

Barbadillo Delgado, P., *Historia de la ciudad de Sanlúcar de Barrameda* (Cádiz, 1942).

Bautier, R.-H., 'Notes sur le commerce de fer en Europe occidentale du XIIIe au XVIe siècle', *Revue d'Histoire de la Sidérurgie*, vol. I, pt. 4 (1960), vol. IV, pt. 1 (1963).

Baylen, J. O., 'John Maunsel and the Castilian treaty of 1254: a study of the clerical diplomat', *Traditio*, vol. XVII (1961).

Beardwood, A., 'Alien merchants and the English crown in the later fourteenth century', *Ec.H.R.*, vol. 2 (1929–30).

—— *Alien Merchants in England, 1350–1377. Their legal and economic position.* Monographs of the Medieval Academy of America, No. 3 (Cambridge, Mass., 1931).

—— *The Merchant Roll of Coventry 1392–1416.* Dugdale Society pubns, vol. XVII (1939).

Beaven, A. D. *The Aldermen of the City of London,* 2 vols. (London, 1908–13).

Beck, S. W., *The Drapers' Dictionary. A Manual of Textile Fabrics, their History and Applications* (London, 1882).

Benavides, A., *Memorias de Don Fernando IV de Castilla,* 2 vols. (Madrid, 1860).

Bernard, J., 'Les constructions navales à Bordeaux d'après les archives notariales du XVIe siècle', *Le Navire et l'économie maritime du XVe au XVIIIe siècles.* Travaux du Colloque d'Histoire Maritime, 1956 (Paris, 1957).

—— 'Les types de navires ibériques et leur influence sur le construction navale dans les ports du sud-ouest de la France (XVe–XVIe siècles)', *Les Aspects internationaux de la découverte océanique, XVe–XVIe siècles.* Actes du 5e Colloque International d'Histoire Maritime, Lisbonne, 1960 (Paris, 1966).

—— *Navires et gens de mer à Bordeaux vers 1400–vers 1550,* 2 vols. (Paris, 1968).

Bertholet, C. L., *Elements of the Art of Dyeing,* trans. W. Hamilton (London, 1791).

Blake, J. W., *European Beginnings in West Africa, 1454–1578* (London, 1937).

Boissonade, P., *Histoire de la réunion de la Navarre à la Castille. Essai sur les relations des Princes de Foix-Albret avec la France et l'Espagne (1479–1521)* (Paris, 1893).

Boiteux, L. A., *La Fortune de mer, le besoin de securité et les débuts de l'assurance maritime.* École Pratique des Hautes Études, VIe section, Centre de Recherches Historiques, Ports-Routes-Trafics, XXIV (Paris, 1968).

Boutruche, R., 'Anglais et gascons en Aquitaine du XIIe au XVe siècle. Problèmes d'histoire sociales', *Mélanges d'histoire du moyen âge dediés à la mémoire de Louis Halphen* (Paris, 1951).

—— *La Crise d'une societé. Seigneurs et paysans du Bordelais pendant la guerre de cent ans* (Paris, 1947).

Bowden, P. J., *The Wool Trade in Tudor and Stuart England* (London, 1962).

Braudel, F., *The Mediterranean and the Mediterranean World in the Age of Philip II,* 2 vols., English ed. trans. from the 2nd ed. (London, 1972–3).

Braunstein, P., 'Le fer et la production de fer en Europe de 500 à 1500', *Annales,* vol. 27 (i) (1972).

Bridbury, A. K., *England and the Salt Trade in the Later Middle Ages* (Oxford, 1955).

—— *Economic Growth: England in the later Middle Ages* (London, 1962).

Burwash, D., *English Merchant Shipping, 1460–1540* (Toronto, 1947).

Cabrillana, N., 'La crisis del siglo XIV en Castilla: la peste negra en el obispado de Palencia', *Hispania,* vol. 28 (1968).

Cambridge Economic History of Europe, vols. I–III ed. M. M. Postan (1966), M. M. Postan and E. E. Rich (1952), M. M. Postan, E. E. Rich, and E. Miller (1963).

Camino y Orella, J. A. de, *Historia de la ciudad de San Sebastián,* reprinted with introduction and notes by F. Arocena (San Sebastián, 1963).

Carande, R., 'Sevilla, forteleza y mercado. Algunas institutiónes de la ciudad principalmente estudiades en sus privilegios, ordenamientos y cuentas', *Anuario de Historia del Derecho Español,* tom. 11 (1925).

Carmen Carlé, M. del, 'Mercaderes en Castilla, 1252–1512', *Cuadernos de Historia de España,* tom. XXI–XXII (1954).

Caro Baroja, J., *Los Vascos* (San Sebastián, 1949).

Carpenter Turner, W. J., 'The building of the Holy Ghost of the Tower, 1414–1416, and her subsequent history', Mariners Mirror, vol. 40 (1954).

Carrère, C., Barcelone: centre économique à l'époque des difficultés, 1380–1462, 2 vols. (Paris, 1967).

—— 'Le droit d'ancrage et le mouvement du port de Barcelone au milieu du XVe siècle', Estudios de Historia Moderna, tom. III (1953).

Carter, H. B., His Majesty's Spanish Flock (London, 1964).

Carus-Wilson, E. M., 'Études faites depuis 1945 sur les "customs accounts" anglais du moyen âge', Sources de l'histoire maritime en Europe du moyen âge au XVIIIe siècle. Actes du Colloque International d'Histoire Maritime, Paris, 1959 (Paris, 1962).

—— 'La guède francais en Angleterre: un grand commerce du moyen âge', Revue du Nord, vol. 35 (1953).

—— Medieval Merchant Venturers (Oxford, 1954).

—— The Expansion of Exeter. Harte Memorial Lecture in Local History, 1961 (Exeter, 1963).

—— 'The Iceland Trade', Studies in English Trade in the Fifteenth Century, ed. E. Power and M. M. Postan (London, 1933).

—— 'The medieval trade of the ports of the Wash', Medieval Archaeology, vol. 6–7 (1962–3).

—— The Merchant Adventurers of Bristol in the Fifteenth Century. Historical Association pubns., Bristol Branch, No. 4 (1962).

—— 'The overseas trade of Bristol', Studies in English Trade in the Fifteenth Century, ed. E. Power and M. M. Postan (London, 1933).

Carus-Wilson, E. M. and Coleman, O., England's Export Trade, 1275–1547 (Oxford, 1963).

Caster, G., Le Commerce du pastel et de l'épicerie à Toulouse 1450 environ à 1561 (Toulouse, 1962).

Castro, A., 'Unos aranceles de aduanas del siglo XIII', Revista de Filología Española, vols. 8–10 (1921–3).

Castro, A. de, Historia de Cádiz y su Provincia desde los remotos tiempos hasta 1814 (Cádiz, 1858).

Chapman, A. B., see Shillington, V. M.

Chaunu, H. and P., Seville et l'Atlantique (1504–1650), 8 vols. École Pratique des Hautes Études, VIe section, Centre de Recherches Historiques, Ports-Routes-Trafics, vol. VI (Paris, 1955–6).

Churruca, A. de, Minería, industría y comercio del País Vasco. Monografías vascongadas, núm. 6 (San Sebastián, 1951).

Ciriquian-Gaiztarro. M., La pesca en el Mar Vasco (Madrid, 1952).

—— Monografía histórica de la Noble Villa y Puerto de Portugalete (Bilbao, 1942).

—— Puertos maritímos vascongados (San Sebastián, 1951).

Cobb, H. S., 'Local port customs', Journal of the Society of Archivists, No. 8 (1958).

Coleman, O. 'Trade and prosperity in the fifteenth century; some aspects of the trade of Southampton', Ec.H.R., 2nd ser., vol. XVI (1963).

—— and Carus-Wilson, E. M.

Colmeiro, M., Historia de la económica política en España, 2 vols., 4th ed. (Madrid, 1965).

Connell-Smith, G., Forerunners of Drake: a Study of English Trade with the Spanish in the Early Tudor Period (London, 1954).

—— 'The ledger of Thomas Howell', Ec.H.R., 2nd ser., vol. III (1950–1).

Craeybeckx, J., Un Grand Commerce d'importation: les vins de France aux anciens

Pays-Bas, XIIIe-XVIe siècle. École Pratique des Hautes Études, VIe section, Centre de Recherches Historiques, Ports-Routes-Trafics, vol. IX (Paris, 1958).

Darby, H. C., *Historical Geography of England before 1800* (Cambridge, 1951).

Daumet, G., *Étude sur l'alliance de la France et de la Castille au XIVe et au XVe siècles*. Bibliotèque de l'École des Hautes Études, fasc. 118 (Paris, 1898).

—— 'Note sur quelques documents castillans des archives notariales', *Bulletin Hispanique*, vol XVII (1915).

Delafosse, M., 'Trafic rochelais aux XV–XVIe siècles. Marchands poitevins et laines d'Espagne', *Annales*, No. 1 (1952).

—— *and see* Trocmé, E.

Delameau, J., *L'Alun de Rome, XVe–XIXe siècles*. École Pratique des Hautes Études, VI section, Centre de Recherches Historiques, Ports-Routes-Trafics, vol. XIII (Paris, 1962).

Doehaerd, R., 'Les galères gênoises dans la Manche et la Mer du Nord à la fin du XIIIe siècle et au début du XIVe siècle', *Bulletin de l'Institut Historique Belge de Rome*, vol. 19 (1938).

Dollinger, P., *The German Hansa*, English ed. (London, 1970).

Echegaray, C. de, *Investigaciónes históricas referentes a Guipúzcoa* (San Sebastián, 1893).

Edler de Roover, F., 'Early examples of marine insurance', *Journal of Economic History*, vol. V (1945); reprinted 1959.

Elliot, J. H., *Imperial Spain, 1469–1716* (London, 1963).

Elliot-Binns, L. E., *Medieval Cornwall* (London, 1955).

Enciclopedia ilustrada universel Europeo-Americana, 70 vols and appendices, and annual supplements from 1934 (Madrid, 1908ff).

Espejo, C., *see* Paz, J.

Fayle, C. E., *A Short History of the World's Shipping Industry* (London, 1933).

Fernández Duro, C., *La marina de Castilla desde su origen y pugna con la de Inglaterra hasta la refundición de la Armada Española* (Madrid, 1893).

Finot, J., *Étude historique sur les relations commerciales entre la Flandre et l'Espagne au moyen âge* (Paris, 1899).

Flenley, R., 'London and foreign merchants in the reign of Henry VI', *E.H.R.*, vol. XXV (1910).

Fryde, E. B., 'Edward III's wool monopoly of 1337; a fourteenth century royal trading venture', *History*, new ser., vol. 37 (1952).

—— *The Wool Accounts of William de la Pole, a Study of some aspects of the English Wool Trade at the start of the 100 Years War*. St Anthony's Hall Pubns., No. 25 (York, 1964).

—— 'The English farmers of the customs, 1343–51', *T.R.H.S.*, 5th ser., vol. 9 (1959).

—— 'The last trials of Sir William de la Pole', *Ec.H.R.*, 2nd ser., vol. XV (1962).

Gaibrois Riaño de Ballesteros, M., *Historia del reinado de Sancho IV*, 3 vols. (Madrid, 1922–8).

García de Cortázar, J. A., *Vizcaya en el siglo-XV. Aspectos económicos y sociales* (Bilbao, 1966).

Gayángos, P. de, 'Mossen Diego de Valera', *Antología Española*, ed. C. de Ochoa (Paris, 1862).

Gil Farrés, O., *Historia de la moneda española* (Madrid, 1959).

Gill, C., *Plymouth: a New History* (Newton Abbot, 1966).

Gille, P., 'Jauge et tonnage des navires', *Le Navire et l'économie maritime de XVe–XVIIIe siècles*. Travaux du Colloque d'Histoire Maritime, 1956 (Paris, 1957

—— 'Navires lourds et rapides avant et après les caravelles', *Les Aspects internationaux de la découverte océanique*, Actes du 5e Colloque International d'Histoire Maritime, Lisbonne 1960 (Paris, 1966).

Girard, A., *La Rivalité commerciale et maritime entre Seville et Cadiz jusqu'à la fin du XVIIIe siècle*. Bibliotèque de l'École des Hautes Études Hispaniques, vol. 18 (Paris, 1932).

Gonsalez, J., *El reino de Castilla en la epoca de Alfonso VIII*, 3 vols. C.S.I.C. Escuela de Estudios Medievales. Textos, vols. 25–7 (Madrid, 1960).

Goris, J. A., *Étude sur les colonies marchandes méridionales (portugais, espanols, italiens) à Anvers de 1488–1567* (Louvain, 1925).

Gorosabal, P. de, *Memoria sobre las guerras y tratados de Guipúzcoa con Inglaterra en los siglos XIV y XV* (Tolosa, 1865).

—— *Noticia de las cosas memorables de Guipúzcoa*, 5 vols. (Tolosa, 1899).

Gras, N. S. B., *The Evolution of the English Corn Market from the Twelfth to the Eighteenth Century*. Harvard Economic Studies, vol. 13 (Cambridge, Mass., 1915).

Gray, H. L. 'English foreign trade from 1446–1482', *Studies in English Trade in the Fifteenth Century*, ed. E. Power and M. M. Postan (London, 1933).

—— 'The production and exportation of English woollens in the fourteenth century', *E.H.R.*, vol. XXXIX (1924).

Gross, C., *The Gild Merchant*, 2 vols. (Oxford, 1890).

Gual Camarena, M., 'El comercio de telas en el siglo XIII hispano', *Anuario de Historia Económica y Social*, vol. I (1968).

Guiard y Larrauri, T., *Historia de la Noble Villa de Bilbao* (Bilbao, 1905).

—— *Historia del Consulado y Casa de Contratación de Bilbao y del comercio de la villa*, 2 vols. (Bilbao, 1913).

—— *La industría naval vizcaína, anotaciónes históricas y estadisticas* (Bilbao, 1917).

Giuseppi, M. S., 'Alien merchants in England in the fifteenth century', *T.R.H.S.*, new ser., vol. IX (1895).

Haebler, K., 'Der Hansisch–Spanische Konflikt von 1419 und die aelteren spanischen Bestaende', *Hansische Geschichtsblaetter*, vol. 8 (1894).

Haepke, R., *Brügges Entwicklung zum Mittelalterlichen Weltmarkt*. Abhandlung zur Verkehrs- und Seegeschichte, vol. I (Berlin, 1908).

Halphen, L., *Mélanges d'histoire du moyen âge dediés à la mémoire de Louis Halphen* (Paris, 1951).

Hamilton, E. J., *Money, Prices and Wages in Valencia, Aragon and Navarre 1351–1500*. Harvard Economic Studies, vol. 51 (Cambridge, Mass., 1936).

Hanham, A., ' "Make a careful examination": some fraudulent accounts in the Cely Papers', *Speculum*, vol. XLVIII (1973).

Heers, J., *Gênes au XV siècle. Activité économique et problèmes sociaux*. École Pratique des Hautes Études, VIe section, Centre de Recherches Historiques, Affaires et Gens d'Affaires, vol. XXIV (Paris, 1961).

—— 'La mode et les marchés des draps de laine: Gênes et la Montagne à la fin du moyen âge', *Annales*, vol. 26 (1971).

—— 'Le commerce des Basques en Méditerranée au XVe siècle', *Bulletin Hispanique*, vol. LVII (1955).

—— *L'Occident aux XIVe et XVe siècles. Aspects économiques et sociaux* (Paris, 1963).

—— 'Types de navires et specialisation des trafics en Méditerranée à la fin du moyen âge', *Le Navire et l'économie maritime du moyen âge au XVIIIe siècle principalement en Méditerranée.* Travaux du 2e Colloque International d'Histoire Maritime, 1957 (Paris, 1958).

Hewitt, H. J. *Cheshire under the Three Edwards, A History of Cheshire,* vol. 5 (Chester, 1967).

Highfield, J. R. L. 'The Catholic kings and the titled nobility of Castile', in *Europe in the Later Middle Ages,* ed. J. R. L. Highfield, J. R. Hale, and B. Smalley (London, 1965).

Highfield, J. R. L. (ed.), *Spain in the Fifteenth Century 1369–1516, Essays and Extracts by Historians of Spain* (London, 1972).

Holmes, G. A., 'The "Libelle of Englyshe Polycye" ', *E.H.R.,* vol. LXXVI (1961).

Honoré Duverge, S., 'Notes sur la politique économique de Charles le mauvais en Navarre', *Actas del I Congreso Internacional de Estudios Pirenaicos, San Sebastián 1950,* 7 vols. (Zaragoza, 1952).

Hoskins, W. G., *Two Thousand Years in Exeter* (Exeter, 1960).

Huetz de Lemps, A., 'Apogeo y decadencia de un viñedo de calidad: el de Ribadavia', *Anuario de Historia Económica y Social,* vol. I (1968).

—— *Vignobles et vins du nord-ouest de l'Espagne,* 2 vols. Bibliotèque de l'École des Hautes Études Hispaniques, fasc. XXXVIII (Bordeaux, 1967).

Hurry, J. B., *The Woadplant and its Dye* (London, 1930).

Imamuddin, S. M., *Some Aspects of the Socio-Economic and Cultural History of Muslim Spain, 711–1492 A.D.* Medieval Iberian Peninsula Texts and Studies, vol. 11 (Leiden, 1965).

Imray, J. M., ' "Les bones gentes de la mercerye de Londres": a study of the membership of the medieval Mercers Company', in *Studies in London History,* ed. A. E. Hollaender, and W. Kellaway (London, 1969).

Iturriza y Zabala, J. R., *Historia general de Vizcaya* (Barcelona, 1884), reprinted and ed. by A. Rodriguez Herrero (Bilbao, 1937).

James, M., 'A London Merchant of the fourteenth century', *Ec.H.R.* 2nd ser., vol. VIII (1955–6).

—— 'Les activités commerciales des negoçiants en vins gascons en Angleterre à la fin du moyen âge', *Annales du Midi,* vol. 65 (1953).

—— *Studies in the Medieval Wine Trade,* ed. E. M. Veale (Oxford, 1971).

—— 'The fluctuations of the Anglo-Cascon wine trade during the fourteenth century', *Ec.H.R.,* 2nd ser., vol. IV (1951–2).

—— 'The non-sweet wine trade of England during the fourteenth and fifteenth centuries' (unpublished D. Phil. dissertation, Oxford University, 1952).

Kerling, N. J. M., *Commercial Relations of Holland and Zeeland with England from the late Thirteenth Century to the close of the Middle Ages* (Leiden, 1954).

Kingsford, C. L., *Prejudice and Promise in XV Century England.* Ford Lectures, 1923–4 (Oxford, 1925).

Klein, J., 'Medieval Spanish gilds', in *Facts and Factors in Economic History,* articles by former students of E. F. Gay (Cambridge, Mass., 1932).

—— *The Mesta. A Study in Spanish Economic History 1272–1836.* Harvard Economic Studies, vol. 21 (Cambridge, Mass., 1920).

Konetzke, R., 'Entrepreneurial activities of Spanish and Portuguese noblemen in medieval times', *Explorations in Entrepreneurial History,* vol. 6 (1953–4).

Kretschmer, K., *Die Italienischen Portolane des Mittelalters.* Veroffentlichungen des Instituts für Meereskunde und des Geographischen Instituts, Heft 13 (Berlin, 1909).

Krüger, H. C., 'Early Genoese trade with Atlantic Morocco', *Medievalia et Humanistica,* fasc. 3 (1945).

—— 'Genoese trade with north-west Africa in the twelfth century', *Speculum*, vol. 8 (1933).

Labayru y Goicoechea, E. J. de, *Historia general del Señorio de Biscaya*, 6 vols. (Bilbao and Madrid, 1895–1903).

Laborde, M., 'Apuntes históricos sobre la industría metalúrgica en Tolosa', *Libro homenaje a Tolosa* (Tolosa, 1956).

Lacarra, J. M., see Vázquez de Parga.

Ladero Quesada, M. A., *La Hacienda Real Castillana entre 1480 y 1492*. Estudios y Documentos núm. 26, Departimiento de Historia Medieval, Universidad de Valladolid (Valladolid, 1967).

Lambert, E., 'Les routes des Pyrenées atlantiques', *Actas del I Congreso Internacional de Estudios Pyrenaicos, San Sebastián 1950*, 7 vols. (Zaragoza, 1952), vol. 6.

Lane, F. C., *Andrea Barbarigo, Merchant of Venice (1418–1449)*. Johns Hopkins University Studies in Historical and Political Science, ser. LXII, No. 1 (Baltimore, 1944).

—— 'Tonnages, medieval and modern', *Ec.H.R.*, 2nd ser., vol. XVII (1964).

Lapeyre, H., 'Le mouvement du port de San Sebastián', *Actas del I Congreso Internacional de Estudios Pirenaicos San Sebastián, 1950*, 7 vols. (Zaragoza, 1952) vol. 6.

—— *Une Famille de marchands: les Ruiz*. École Pratique des Hautes Etudes, VIe section, Centre de Recherches Historiques, Affaires et Gens d'Affaires (Paris, 1955).

Laurent, H., *Un Grand Commerce d'exportation au moyen âge. La draperie des Pays-Bas en France et dans les pays méditerranéens (XIIe–XVe siècles)* (Paris, 1935).

Lewis, E. A., 'A contribution to the commercial history of medieval Wales', *Y Cymmrodor. The magazine of the honourable society of Cymmrodorian*, vol. XXIV (1913).

—— 'The development of industry and commerce in Wales during the middle ages', *T.R.H.S.*, new ser., vol XVII (1903).

Lewis, G., *The Stannaries: a Study of the English Tin Miner*. Harvard Economic Studies, No. 3 (Cambridge, Mass., 1906).

Liagre-de Sturler, L., 'Le commerce de l'alun en Flandre au moyen âge', *Le Moyen Age*, vol. LXI (1955).

Lipson, E., *A History of the Woollen and Worsted Industries* (London, 1921).

—— *A Short History of Wool and its Manufacture (mainly in England)* (London, 1953).

Littleton, A. C., and Yamey, B. S. (eds.), *Studies in the History of Accounting* (London, 1956).

Lloyd, T. H., *The English Wool Trade in the Middle Ages* (Cambridge, 1977).

Lopez, R. S. 'The origin of the Merino sheep', *The Joshua Starr Memorial Volume*. Jewish Social Studies pubns., No. 5, Conference on Jewish Relations (New York, 1953).

Lourie, E., 'A society organised for war: medieval Spain', *Past and Present*, No. 35 (1966).

Lucas, H. S. 'The great European famine of 1315, 1316, and 1317', *Speculum*, vol. V (1930).

McKay, A., 'Popular movements and pogroms in fifteenth-century Castile', *Past and Present*, No. 55 (1972).

Madurell y Marimon, J. M., 'Antiguas construcciónes de naves (1316–1740). Repertorio histórico documental', *Hispania*, vol. 28 (1968).

Mallett, M. E., 'Anglo-Florentine commercial relations 1465–1491', *Ec.H.R.*, 2nd ser., vol. xv (1962).

—— *The Florentine Galleys in the Fifteenth Century; with the Diary of Luca di Maso degli Albizzi, Captain of Galleys, 1429–30* (Oxford, 1967).

Maréschal, J., 'La colonie espagnole de Bruges du 14e siècle au 16e siècle', *Revue du Nord*, vol. 35 (1953).

Mathorez, J., 'Notes sur les rapports de Nantes avec l'Espagne', *Bulletin Hispanique*, vol. 14 (1912).

Maza Solano, T., 'Manifestaciónes de la económia montañesa desde el siglo IV al XVIII', *Aportación al estudio de la historia económica de la Montaña*. Centro de Estudios Montañeses (Santander, 1957).

Michel, F., *Histoire du commerce et de la navigation à Bordeaux principalement sous l'administration anglaise*, 2 vols. (Bordeaux, 1867–70).

Miller, E., 'The English economy in the thirteenth century: implications of recent research', *Past and Present*, No. 28 (1964).

—— 'The fortunes of the English textile industry in the thirteenth century', *Ec.H.R.*, 2nd ser., vol. xviii (1965).

Mollat, M., 'Anglo-Norman trade in the fifteenth century', *Ec.H.R.*, vol. xvii (1947).

—— 'Deux études relatives aux constructions navales à Barcelone at à Palma de Majorque au XIVe siècle', in *Homenaje a Jaime Vicens Vives*, 2 vols. (Barcelona, 1965), vol. i.

—— *Le Commerce maritime normand à la fin du moyen âge* (Paris, 1952).

—— 'Le rôle international des marchands espagnols dans les ports occidentaux à l'époque des rois catholiques', *V Congreso de Historia de la Corona de Aragon*, 5 vols. (Zaragoza, 1954–61), vol. 4.

—— 'Notes sur la vie maritime en Galice au XIIe siècle d'après l' "Historia Compostellana" ', *Anuario Estudios Medievales*, vol. i (1964).

Morison, S. E., *Admiral of the Ocean Sea. A life of Christopher Columbus*, 2 vols. (Boston, Mass., 1942).

Mugica, S., *Curiosidades históricas de San Sebastián*, 2 vols. (Bilbao, 1900).

Munro, J. H. A., *Wool, Cloth and Gold. The Struggle for Bullion in Anglo-Burgundian Trade, 1340–1478* (Brussels and Toronto, 1972).

Murray, K. M. E., *The Constitutional History of the Cinque Ports*, University of Manchester pubns., ccxxxv, Historical Series lxviii (Manchester, 1935).

Nicolas, Sir N. Harris, *A History of the Royal Navy*, 2 vols. (London, 1847).

Nordenskiold, A. E., *Periplus – an Essay on the Early History of Charts and Sailing Directions*, ed. F. A. Bather (Stockholm, 1897).

Parry, J., *The Age of Reconnaissance* (New York, 1964).

Pattison, G., 'Observations on the history of the bill of lading', *Mariners Mirror*, vol. 50 (1964).

Paz, J., and Espejo, C., *Las antiguas ferias de Medina del Campo* (Valladolid, 1908).

Perez, J., *La Revolution des 'Comunidades' de Castille (1520–1521)* (Bordeaux, 1970).

Pérez Embid, F., *Los descubrimientos en el Atlantico y la rivalidad castillano-portuguesa hasta el tratado de Tordesillas* (Seville, 1948).

—— 'Navigation et commerce dans le port de Seville au bas moyen âge', *Le Moyen Age*, vol. 24 (1969).

Perroy, E., *The Hundred Years War*, trans, W. B. Wells (London, 1951) from *La Guerre de cent ans* (Paris, 1945).

Pike, R., *Enterprise and Adventure. The Genoese in Seville and the Opening of the New World* (Cornell, 1966).

—— 'The Genoese in Seville and the opening of the New World', *J. Ec. Hist.*, vol. XXII (1962).

—— 'The Sevillian nobility and trade with the New World in the sixteenth century', *Business History Review*, vol. XXXIX (1965).

Postan, M. M., 'Credit in medieval trade', *Ec.H.R.*, vol. I (1928).

—— 'Études anglaises sur les "customs accounts" ', *Les Sources de l'histoire maritime en Europe du moyen âge au XVIIIe siècle*. Actes du 4e Colloque International d'Histoire Maritime, 1959 (Paris, 1962).

—— 'Partnership in English medieval commerce', *Studi in onore di Armando Sapori* (Milan, 1957).

—— 'Private financial instruments in medieval England', *V.S.W.G.*, vol. XXIII (1930).

—— 'The economic and political relations of England and the Hanse from 1400 to 1475', in *Studies in English Trade in the Fifteenth Century*, ed. E. Power and M. M. Postan (London, 1933).

Power, E., *The Wool Trade in English Medieval History*. Ford Lectures in 1939 (Oxford, 1941).

Power, E., and Postan, M. M. (eds.), *Studies in English Trade in the Fifteenth Century* (London, 1933).

Quinn, D. B., 'Edward IV and exploration', *Mariners Mirror*, vol. XXI (1935).

Ramsay, G. D., *England's Overseas Trade during the Centuries of Emergence* (London, 1957).

—— *The Wiltshire Woollen Industry in the Sixteenth and Seventeenth Centuries* (London, 1943).

Renouard, Y., *Études d'histoire médiévale* (collected articles), 2 vols. Bibliotèque Generale de l'École Pratique des Hautes Études, VIe section (Paris, 1968).

—— (ed.), *Bordeaux sous les Rois d'Angleterre* (Bordeaux, 1965).

Richmond, C. F., 'English naval power in the fifteenth century', *History*, vol. LII (1967).

—— 'The keeping of the seas during the Hundred Years War: 1422–1440', *History*, vol. XLIX (1964).

Rodriguez Herrero, A., *Ordenanzas de Bilbao de los siglos XV y XVI* (Bilbao, 1948).

—— (ed.), see Iturriza y Zabala.

Rogers, J. E. Thorold, *A History of Agriculture and Prices in England*, 4 vols. (Oxford, 1866–82).

Roover, R. de, 'Cambium ad Venetias: contribution to the history of foreign exchange', in *Studi in onore di Armando Sapori* (Milan, 1957).

—— *L'Évolution de la lettre de change XIVe–XVIIIe siècles*. École Pratique des Hautes Études, VIe section, Centre de Recherches Historiques, Affaires et Gens d'Affaires, vol. IV (Paris, 1953).

—— *Money, Banking and Credit in Medieval Bruges*. Medieval Academy of America pubns., No. 51 (Cambridge, Mass., 1948).

—— 'The development of accounting prior to Luca Pacioli according to the account books of medieval merchants', in *Studies in the History of Accounting*, ed. A. C. Littleton, and B. S. Yamey (London, 1956).

Ruddock, A. A., 'Alien hosting in Southampton in the fifteenth century', *Ec.H.R.* vol. XVI (1946).

—— 'Alien merchants in Southampton in the later middle ages', *E.H.R.*, vol LXI (1946).

—— *Italian Merchants and Shipping in Southampton, 1270–1600* (Southampton, 1951).

—— 'Italian trading fleets in medieval England', *History*, new ser., vol. XXIX (1944).

—— 'The Flanders galleys', *History*, new ser., vol. XXIV (1939–40).

—— 'The method of handling the cargoes of medieval merchant galleys', *B.I.H.R.*, vol. XIX (1941–3).

Russell, P. E. L., *The English Intervention in Spain and Portugal in the time of Edward III and Richard II* (Oxford, 1955).

—— 'Una alianza frustrada. Las bodas de Pedro I de Castilla y Juana Plantagenat', *Anuario de Estudios Medievales*, vol. II (1965).

Ryder, M. L., 'The history of sheep breeds in England', *Agricultural History Review*, vol. XII (1964).

Salzman, L. F., *Building in England down to 1540* (Oxford, 1952).

—— *English Industries of the Middle Ages* (Oxford, 1923).

Sapori, A., *Studi in onore di Armando Sapori* (Milan, 1957).

Sarasola, Fr. M., *Vizcaya y los Reyes Católicos* (Madrid, 1950).

Sayous, A. E., 'Partnerships in the trade between Spain and America and also in the Spanish colonies in the sixteenth century', *Journal of Economic and Business History*, vol. I (1928–9).

Scammell, G. V. 'English merchant shipping at the end of the middle ages: some east coast evidence', *Ec.H.R.*, 2nd ser., vol XIII (1961).

—— 'Manning in the English merchant service in the sixteenth century', *Mariners Mirror*, vol. 56 (1970).

—— 'Shipowning in England c. 1450–1550', *T.R.H.S.*, 5th ser., vol. 12 (1962).

—— 'Shipowning in the economy and politics of early modern England', *The Historical Journal*, vol. XV (1972).

Schanz, G., *Englische Handelspolitik gegen Ende des Mittelalters*, 2 vols. (Leipzig, 1881).

Schaube, A., 'Die Wollausfuhr Englands vom Jahre 1273', *V.S.W.G.*, vol. VI (1908).

Schubert, H. R., *History of the British Iron and Steel Industry from c. 450 B.C. to A.D. 1775* (London, 1957).

Schulten, A., *Iberische Landeskunde. Geographie des Antiken Spanien*, 2 vols. (Strasbourg, 1955–7).

Scofield, C. L., *The Life and Reign of Edward IV*, 2 vols. (London, 1923).

Sherborne, J. W., 'The battle of La Rochelle and the war at sea 1372–5', *B.I.H.R.*, vol. XLII (1969).

—— 'The English navy: shipping and manpower 1369–1389', *Past and Present*, No. 37 (1967).

—— *The Port of Bristol in the Middle Ages*. Port of Bristol Series, Historical Association, Bristol Branch (Bristol, 1965).

Shillington, V. M., and Chapman, A. B., *The Commercial Relations of England and Portugal*, *T.R.H.S.*, 3rd ser., vol. I (1907).

Simon, A., *The History of the Wine Trade in England*, 3 vols. (London, 1907–9).

Smith, R. S., *The Spanish Guild Merchant. A History of the Consulado, 1250–1700* (Durham, N.C., 1940).

Soraluce y Zubizarreta, N. de, *Historia general de Guipúzcoa*, 2 vols. (Vitoria, 1870).

Sprandel, R., *Das Eisengewerbe im Mittelalter* (Stuttgart, 1968).

—— 'La production du fer au moyen âge', *Annales*, vol. 24 (1969).

Storrs, C. M., 'Jacobean pilgrims from England from the early twelfth to the late fifteenth century' (unpublished M.A. thesis, University of London, 1964).

Sturler, J. de, *Les Relations politiques et les échanges commerciaux entre le Duché de Brabant et l'Angleterre au moyen âge* (Paris, 1936).

Suárez Fernández, L., *Intervención de Castilla en la guerra de los Cien Años* (Valladolid, 1950).

—— *Navegación y comercio en el Golfo de Vizcaya* (Madrid, 1959).

—— *Nobleza y monarquía. Puntos de vista sobre la historia castellana del siglo XV. Estudios y documentos num. 15*, Cuadernos de Historia Medieval, Universidad de Valladolid (Valladolid, 1959).

—— 'Política internacional de Enrique II', *Hispania*, vol. 16 (1956).

Thrupp, S. L., 'Aliens in and around London in the fifteenth century', *Studies in London History*, ed. A. E. J. Hollaender and W. Kellaway (London, 1969).

—— 'A survey of the alien population in England in 1440', *Speculum*, vol. 32 (1957).

—— *The Merchant Class of Medieval London (1300–1500)* (Ann Arbor, Mich. 1948).

Torre, A. de la, 'Los Castillanos en Guinea y Mina del Oro después del tratado de 1470', *Congreso Internacional de Historia dos Descobrimentos*. 6 vols. (Lisbon, 1961), vol. 5.

—— 'Telas extranjeros en la corte de los Reyes Católicos', *VI Congreso de Historia de la Corona de Aragon, 1957* (Madrid, 1959).

Touchard, H., *Le Commerce maritime breton à la fin du moyen âge*. Annales Littéraires de l'Université de Nantes, fasc. i (Paris, 1967).

Trocmé, E., and Delafosse, M., *Le Commerce rochelais de la fin du XVe siècle au début du XVIIe*. École Pratique des Hautes Études, VIe section, Centre de Recherches Historiques, Ports-routes-trafics, vol. v (Paris, 1952).

Unger, R. W., 'Carvel building in northern Europe before 1450', *Mariners Mirror*, vol. 57 (1971).

Unwin, G. (ed.), *Finance and Trade under Edward III* (Manchester, 1918).

Uría Ríu, J., see Vázquez de Parga.

Usher, A. P., 'Spanish ships and shipping in the sixteenth and seventeenth centuries', in *Facts and Factors in Economic History*, articles by former students of E. F. Gay (Cambridge, Mass., 1932).

—— *The Early History of Deposit Banking in Medieval Europe*. Harvard Economic Studies, No. 75 (1943).

Valdeavellano y Arcimis, L. G. de, *Sobre los burgos y burgueses de la España medieval. (Notas para la historia de los origenes de la burguesía)* (Madrid, 1960).

Valdeón Baruque, J., 'Aspectos de la crisis castellana en la primera mitad del siglo XIV', *Hispania*, vol. 29 (1969).

Van der Wee, H., *The Growth of the Antwerp Market and the European Economy (Fourteenth to Sixteenth Centuries)*, 2 vols. Université de Louvain, Recueil de Travaux d'Histoire et de Philologie, sér. 4, fascs. 28–9 (Louvain, 1963).

Van Houtte, J., 'Anvers aux XVe et XVIe siècles', *Annales*, vol. 16 (1961).

——'Bruges et Anvers, marchés "nationaux" ou "internationaux" du XIVe au XVIe siècle', *Revue du Nord*, vol. 34 (1952).

—— 'Les foires dans la Belgique ancienne', *Recueil de la Societé Jean Bodin*, vol. v, La Foire (Brussels, 1953).

—— 'The rise and decline of the market of Bruges', *Ec.H.R.*, 2nd ser., vol. xix (1966).

Van Werweke, H., 'Industrial growth in the middle ages. The cloth industry in Flanders', *Ec.H.R.*, 2nd ser., vol. vi (1954).

—— 'Note sur le commerce du plomb au moyen âge', *Mélanges d'histoire offerts à H. Pirenne* (Brussels, 1926).

Vázquez de Parga, L., Lacarra, J. M., and Uría Ríu, J., *Las peregrinaciónes a Santiago de Compostella*, 3 vols. (Madrid, 1948–9).

Vázquez de Prada, V., *Lettres marchands d'Anvers*, 4 vols. École Pratique des Hautes Études, VIe section, Centre de Recherches Historiques, Affaires et Gens d'Affaires, vol. XVIII (Paris, 1960).

Veale, E. M., *The English Fur Trade in the Later Middle Ages* (Oxford, 1966).

—— (ed.), *see* James, M. K.

Verlinden, C., 'Draps des Pays-Bas et du Nord de la France en Espagne au XIVe siècle', *Le Moyen Age*, sér. 3, vol. VII (1937).

—— 'Contribution à l'histoire de l'expansion commerciales de la draperie flamande dans la péninsule ibérique au XIIIe siècle', *Revue du Nord*, vol. 22 (1936).

—— 'La grande peste de 1348 en Espagne. Contribution à l'étude de ses consequences économiques et sociales', *R.B.P.H.* vol. XVII (1938).

—— 'La place de Catalogne dans l'histoire commerciale du monde méditerranéen médiéval', 2 parts, *Revue des Cours et Conferences*, sér. I, année 39 (1937–8).

—— 'The rise of Spanish trade in the middle ages', *Ec.H.R.*, vol. 10 (1940).

—— 'Le trafic et la consommation des vins francais', *Les Sources de l'histoire maritime en Europe du moyen âge au XVIIIe siècle*, Actes du 4e Colloque International d'Histoire Maritime, 1959 (Paris, 1962).

Vicens Vives, J., *Approaches to the History of Spain*, trans. J. Connelly Ullman (Berkeley and Los Angeles, 1967) from the 2nd ed. of *Aproximación a la historia de España* (3rd ed., Barcelona, 1962).

—— (ed.), *Historia social y económica de España y America*, 5 vols. (Barcelona, 1957).

—— with collaboration of Nadal Oller, J., *Manual de historia económica de España*, 3rd ed. (Barcelona, 1964).

—— *Homenaje a Jaime Vicens Vives*, 2 vols. (Barcelona, 1965–7).

Victoria County Histories: Cornwall, Dorset, Essex, Hampshire, Kent, Somerset, Sussex.

Viñas y Mey, C., 'De la edad media a la moderna. El Cantabrico y el Estrecho de Gibraltar en la historia politica española', *Hispania*, vol. I (1940–1).

Watson, W., 'Catalans in the markets of northern Europe during the fifteenth century', *Homenaje a Jaime Vicens Vives* (Barcelona, 1967), vol. 2.

—— 'The structure of the Florentine galley trade with Flanders and England in the fifteenth century', *R.B.P.H.*, vols. XXXIX, XL (1961–2).

Williams, G. A., *Medieval London: from Commune to Capital*. University of London Historical Studies, vol. XI (London, 1963).

Williamson J. A., 'The geographical history of the Cinque Ports', *History*, new ser., vol. XI (1926–7).

Wilson, K. P., 'The port of Chester in the fifteenth century', *Trans. of the Historic Society of Lancashire and Cheshire*, vol. 117 (1965).

Wolff, P., *Commerce et marchands de Toulouse vers 1350-vers 1450* (Paris, 1954).

—— 'English cloth in Toulouse (1380–1450)', *Ec.H.R.*, 2nd ser., vol. II (1950).

Yamey, B. S., 'Notes on the origin of double entry bookkeeping', *Accounting Review*, vol. XXII (1947).

—— 'Scientific bookkeeping and the rise of capitalism', *Ec.H.R.*, 2nd ser., vol. I (1949).

—— (ed.), *see* Littleton, A. C.

INDEX